The King of Karelia

The King of Karelia

Col P. J. Woods and the British Intervention in North Russia 1918–1919

A History and Memoir

Nick Baron

First published by Francis Boutle Publishers
272 Alexandra Park Road
London N22 7BG
Tel/Fax: (020) 8889 7744
Email: info@francisboutle.co.uk
www.francisboutle.co.uk

ISBN 978 1 903427 32 3

Printed by Biddles Ltd

Contents

Part Two
Karelian Diary

List of illustrations and maps

Preface

As an academic historian of twentieth century Eastern Europe, for a long time the focus of my studies was the Russian region of Karelia, a wild and remote territory of pine forests and glacial lakes abutting the north-western state border with Finland. My particular interest was the development of Russian Karelia during the early Soviet period – its formation as a separate unified region under Lenin and its evolution, through years of hope, hardship, hunger and terror, under Stalin. While conducting research on this topic in the Department of Documents of the Imperial War Museum in London, I happened across the two-volume typescript of Philip Woods' memoir, 'Karelian Diary'.

I recognised immediately that the 'Karelian Diary' offered valuable new information on the Allied intervention in North Russia of 1918-19 and the Russian Civil War, as well as on the history of Karelia and the Karelian people. As such, it was an important new source for military and political historians, specialists in international relations, scholars of nationalism and everyone interested in the peoples and cultures of northern and eastern Europe.

But as I read through the memoir I was transported back to boyhood readings of Ballantyne, Buchan, Haggard and Henty. Remarkably for a work languishing almost unknown for decades in a cardboard box in a dry (though not dusty) historical archive, Woods' memoir of his Karelian adventures was also a colourful and ripping yarn, told with elegance, vigour and wit. Before I was half-way through I decided that it had to be rescued from the archive and published not only for the edification of scholars, but for the entertainment of readers.

Having reached this decision, and found a willing and eager publisher for the memoir, I began to enquire into the biography of its author. The more deeply I investigated, the more intrigued and enthralled I became. What began as a brief introduction to the memoir text grew into a broader study of Philip Woods' life and times, which forms Part One of this book.

My fascination with Woods lies in both his own unique character and career, and the ways in which his story – in all its disorderliness and indeterminacy – was also the story of a generation of men. He was born in a working class district of Belfast in 1880 and died in a quiet English village in 1961. For much of his life he was a soldier. He fought in South Africa with Baden-Powell; in France and Flanders with the 36th (Ulster) Division; and in North Russia with the British intervention force. He was also, by training and profession, a designer of textile patterns, whose linenware adorned the tables and beds of the *Titanic* on its fatal maiden voyage. He was also an irrepressible, if inept, political player – a member before the Great War of the Ulster Volunteer Force, which armed itself with smuggled German rifles to resist Irish independence; between 1923 and 1929 one of the very few independent members of the new Northern Irish parliament; and during the 1930s the proprietor and director of the Institute of Political Secretaries in London, a venture that aspired to train a new generation of statesmen and *sahibs* for the salvation of Britain's empire.

Woods' career as an artist, adventurer, businessman, politician and soldier intersected with the lives of many prominent, often controversial figures in early twentieth-century history – revolutionaries and reactionaries, nationalists and imperialists, prime ministers and spies, Bolshevik commissars and British Nazis. Yet when I began to piece together the existing biographical information on Woods, it became evident that from a historian's perspective he led an elusive life. He appears only sporadically in the record, always on the margin and leaving few traces. Any attempt to construct an account of his life involves a great deal of detective-work.

A series of *Who's Who* articles, from his first entry in 1918 to the final draft version of 1961, give us the basic chronology of his career. But in using these sources it must be borne in mind that Woods himself wrote them. This raises questions of omission and distortion. Other contemporary publications, such as city directories and newspapers, yield meagre details which usually corroborate but add little of substance to his own account. Philip Woods is also to be glimpsed occasionally in the memoirs of his contemporaries and in the work of historians. But these writers mention him only in passing, and errors made in earlier sources are frequently reproduced in later ones. Brief allusions to his role in separate historical events rarely make any connections between different episodes in his life and invariably raise more questions than they answer. In particular, as we shall see, Frank Percy Crozier's memoirs make some enigmatic references to Woods' action on the Somme, the failure of his subsequent battalion command and the reason why he was offered the 'hush-hush' mission that would take him to North Russia. The memoir of a Finnish socialist politician describes Woods as an advocate of Irish independence, yet before the Great War he was a member of the Ulster Volunteer Force prepared to take up arms to preserve the union with Great Britain. Woods' claim in his memoir, published here, that he played no active role in the ill-fated Karelian nationalist movement is also controversial – many, at the time and later, believed that he was also engaging in dangerous political games. Private letters from a leading British fascist and wartime traitor open up further intriguing lines of enquiry about Woods' later career and political commitments. Using Philip Woods' personal papers, the public archives and oral history interviews, I try to shed some light on these mysteries.

Ultimately, the oblique and fragmentary evidence does not allow us to construct a detailed and systematic biography. This has not been my aim. Instead, in Part One of this book, I endeavour to evoke a sense of Philip Woods' 'life-world', of the drama – and the tragedy – of the decades of human destruction, social dislocation and political conflict, of decaying empires and new nationalisms, of broken hopes and discarded ideals, of dreams and disenchantments, which formed and shaped him. It is the history of a lost generation.

★ ★ ★ ★

Part One, then, is a study of Philip Woods' life and times. Chapter One uses Woods' private papers as well as the military archive to describe his part in the battle of the Somme, July 1916, the cataclysmic event that shattered so many of the lingering illusions of the nineteenth century and heralded the new delusions of the twentieth. Chapter Two backtracks to trace Woods' Ulster background and upbringing, while

Chapter Three outlines his first experience of imperial adventure with Baden-Powell in South Africa. Chapter Four discusses Woods' engagement in pre-1914 Ulster business and politics. Chapter Five traces the highs and lows of his military career during the Great War.

Chapters Six and Seven then offer a detailed analytical narrative of the British intervention in North Russia, based on previously published histories and memoirs in English, Finnish and Russian, as well as on my own archival research. These chapters will acquaint the reader with all the people and events that Woods mentions in his memoir and set them in their broader historical context. Chapter Six first discusses the historical evolution of Karelia, torn between predatory powers both east and west, and then describes the context and course of the British North Russian intervention during 1918, focusing particularly on Woods' first campaign with the Karelian Regiment against the Germans and White Finns. Chapter Seven carries the story forward to the evacuation of Allied forces in autumn 1919, and assesses Woods' controversial role in the rise and fall of the Karelian nationalist movement during the sixteen months of the intervention.

Chapter Eight follows Woods on a second Baltic mission, this time to Lithuania, and Chapter Nine assesses his Northern Irish parliamentary career during the 1920s. The final chapter discusses Woods' activities in England in the 1930s, engaging with the difficult and troubling question of whether during this period he was drawn towards far-right politics.

★ ★ ★ ★

Part Two of the book presents the edited text of the 'Karelian Diary' by Philip Woods, most probably written in late 1938 and 1939 (for dating the memoir, see Chapter Ten, n. 13, p. 331). This is divided into the author's original sixteen chapters. These include vivid descriptions of the Karelians' military exploits on behalf of the Allied intervention forces; his impressions of the region's wondrous sub-Arctic landscape, natural history and cultural traditions; and dark tales of the murderous political intrigues swirling around the Karelian Regiment, particularly during the long winter months.

Woods first chapter deals with his recruitment to the mission and the voyage to North Russia. Chapter Two sketches his arrival in the town of Kem and first encounters with the Karelians. Chapters Three, Four and Five describe the Karelian Regiment's autumn campaign against the

Germans and White Finns. Chapter Six returns to events in Kem, as well as including an account of his visit to the Solovetskii monastery and his description of its magnificent treasures.

In Chapter Seven, Woods returns to the complex political intrigues unfolding at Kem, while in Chapters Eight and Nine he describes the Karelian winter, with its joyful festivities and shattering frosts, its Christmas solemnities and New Year snowstorms, and its continuing conspiracies. Chapter Ten outlines Woods' role in Karelian nationalist activities, the visit of a former Finnish prime minister, and White Russian plotting against the British officers and their Karelian associates. Chapters Eleven and Twelve continue to discuss Karelian political intrigues, and the perceptions of the British command and other parties. In Chapter Thirteen, Woods tells the story of the Karelians' request to King George V for the status of a British protectorate, and the Allied response. Chapter Fourteen traces developments in the Karelian Regiment during the spring and summer of 1919. Chapter Fifteen recounts Woods' leadership of partisan operations at Sumskii Posad during the summer, and Chapter Sixteen the conclusion of Allied military action, the evacuation of forces, and the author's evaluation of the course and consequences of intervention.

Following the 'Karelian Diary', there is a detailed chronology of events to help the reader inter-relate the historical analysis of Part One with the memoir's account of Karelian military and political events in Part Two; and then an appendix of documents sourced in Woods' private papers relevant to understanding his role in these events.

★ ★ ★ ★

In compiling and publishing this work, my first debt of gratitude goes to Mr Mike Turney, the nephew of Philip Woods (by a second marriage) and holder of copyright on the memoir, who kindly permitted me to offer the typescript to publishers, as well as giving me access to additional private papers that shed light on Woods' fascinating and challenging life. I should also like to offer special thanks to the staff of the Department of Documents of the Imperial War Museum for facilitating my access to and use of the Woods' papers, and carrying out bibliographical and archival searches on my behalf.

In Ireland, Mr Edwin Woods (great-grandson of Philip Woods' uncle Jeremiah) was generous and enthusiastic in providing me with information on his family history, and Angela Clifford kindly provided some information on F. P. Crozier and made enquiries on my behalf regarding Belfast local history. In Long Crendon, Buckinghamshire, local historian Mr Eric Sewell gave unstintingly of his time to carry out oral history interviews for me regarding Woods' residence in the village in the 1930s. Historians of British fascism Julie Gottlieb and Richard Thurston (both of the University of Sheffield) and Peter Martland (Cambridge) kindly responded to my enquiries concerning the movement's membership and about William Joyce (Lord Haw-Haw), with whom Woods was associated for a time.

In addition, I should like to thank Jacky Hodgson, Head of Special Collections of the University of Sheffield Library, for access to the Joyce papers; the staff of the National Archives and British Library newspaper reading-room; Chris Wrigley (Nottingham) for guidance on early twentieth century English and Northern Irish social and political history; Richard Gaunt (Nottingham) for advice on using *Burke's Peerage* (not a reference work I usually consult for Soviet history); my many friends and colleagues in Karelia and Finland for supporting and encouraging me in my work over almost a decade, in particular (with regard to the present project), Elena Dubrovskaia (Russian Academy of Sciences, Karelian Branch, Petrozavodsk); and Peter Gatrell (Manchester) and my colleagues in the School of History, University of Nottingham, for indulging my sudden obsession with Irish history, the Somme, British fascism and a number of other subjects far removed from my usual historical stomping ground. Maiju Lehto helped untangle Finnish syntax for me. Linda Dawes drew the maps with great patience and professionalism. Many thanks, finally, to my publisher Clive Boutle for his enthusiasm for the project, his editorial professionalism and his patience.

The book is dedicated with love to my mother Delores Baron.

Note on text and Russian spellings

In Part One, Russian spellings have been transliterated using the Library of Congress system, except in a few instances where more familiar forms exist (e.g. Trotsky instead of Trotskii; Yermolov instead of Ermolov; Archangel instead of Arkhangelsk; Peter instead of Petr). Russian diacritics have been omitted. Names of Karelian places are given in their Russian rather than Finnish forms. References to Russian publications in the endnotes adhere strictly to transliteration conventions, including diacritics.

The text of Part Two is based on the original two-volume typescript of Philip Woods' memoir, entitled 'Karelian Diary', which is in the possession of Mr M. Turney (there is also a copy in the Department of Documents, Imperial War Museum), and with whose kind permission it is reproduced here. Only minor changes have been made to the text to ensure clarity and consistency of punctuation and presentation. Throughout the text, Woods' spelling 'Korelia' has been changed to 'Karelia'. Otherwise, his original phonetic rendering of Russian and Finnish names has been retained. Where the difference between his spelling of a Russian name and that in Part I might give rise to confusion, the standard Library of Congress transliteration has been inserted in square brackets after Woods' first use, for example: Ouchta [Ukhta]; Gregori Leziff [Grigorii Lezhev]; Nicoli [Nikolai]; Skobolcene [Skobeltsin]; Zveginsiff [Zvegintsev], Solievetski [Solovetskii], Nuchta

[Nukhta], Saroka [Soroka], etc. The maps also use conventional modern spellings, and discrepancies in Woods' text are noted. Square brackets have also been used for occasional editorial comments and clarifications.

Readers should note that the town of Kem is pronounced K-ye-m. The old Russian unit of distance, the *versta* (pl. *vërsty,* versts), which Woods uses in his text, is approximately two-thirds of a mile (1.067 km).

Part One

The Life and Times of P. J. Woods

Chapter 1

The Royal Irish Rifles
Thiepval Wood, July 1916

In the early morning of 2 July 1916, Major P. J. Woods, second-in-command of the 9th (West Belfast) Battalion, Royal Irish Rifles, received an unexpected order. In the place of Lieutenant-Colonel F. P. Crozier, his battalion commander, Woods was assigned to take charge of a force assembled from the exhausted men of the four Belfast battalions of the 107th Brigade who had survived the previous day's action. In the early afternoon, he was to lead them in a renewed attack from their position in Thiepval Wood, just south of the river Ancre in northern France, on the supposedly impregnable German stronghold known as the Schwaben Redoubt.[1]

This was the Battle of the Somme, day two. A week earlier, the Allies had launched a massive artillery bombardment of the German trenches. At 7.30 a.m. on 1 July, the first British infantry divisions had scrambled across no-man's land, to be met with devastating fire from the enemy. A few minutes earlier, Lieutenant-Colonel Crozier and Major Woods had been standing together in Thiepval sector. Among the soldiers lined up at the edge of the wood there was total silence. Crozier later recalled this moment:

> [...] a colonel approaches. I know him. His face is as white as death. 'Look at his face,' I say to Woods, 'what's wrong with him?' I ask. 'He fears

> death,' says the dry Ulsterman; 'but not as much as I do!' he adds, with a laugh. I blow my whistle. We're off across the causeways of the Ancre.[2]

The unnamed colonel was correct to fear the worst. Total British losses on that first day of the assault amounted to 57,470 men, including nearly twenty thousand dead. The 36th (Ulster) Division, of which the 107th (Belfast) Brigade with its constituent battalions was a part, suffered particularly devastating casualties in its two-pronged push north and south of the river Ancre towards the village of Beaucourt. Nevertheless, to the south of the river they succeeded in gaining a precarious foothold in German lines on the escarpment of the Schwaben Redoubt. Lt-Col Crozier had led seven hundred West Belfast men into battle on 1 July. Of these, only seventy returned at the end of the day.

The date on which this slaughter was unleashed had a particular significance for the Northern Irishmen of the thirteen service battalions raised in autumn 1914 from the loyalist organisation, the Ulster Volunteer Force, and attached to the three brigades of the 36th Division. By the modern calendar, the first day of July was the anniversary of the Battle of the Boyne, the victory of the Protestant William of Orange over the Catholic James II. According to loyalist folklore, this event had secured Protestant ascendancy and British sovereignty in Ireland. Reportedly, some Ulstermen of the 36th Division went into battle wearing the orange sashes or lilies customarily worn for the annual commemoration of the Boyne.[3]

On the night of 1 July, the divisional commander Major-General O. Nugent requested that Brigadier-General W. M. Withycombe of the 107th Brigade reinforce the scattered troops who had been left holding sections of the enemy lines after the conclusion of the first day's fighting. Withycombe collected together all the surviving men of his four Belfast battalions and placed this makeshift force, with two machine-guns units, under Woods' command. Crozier was not selected because in leading the attack on the first day of the offensive, he had disobeyed a general order issued by Allied headquarters that senior officers were not to participate in the fighting.[4] Major G. Gaffikin, the third officer of the battalion, had gone into battle on 1 July, waving an orange handkerchief, and had been killed. The choice therefore fell on Woods to assume the first position of command in his career.

At two o'clock on the afternoon of 2 July, Woods led 360 infantrymen (sixty of the 10th Battalion, whose commanding officer Col H. C.

Bernard had also ignored instructions on the previous day and been killed; together with one hundred soldiers from each of the other three volunteer units), out of the British position known as 'Gordon Castle' on the edge of Thiepval Wood into a maelstrom of German machine-gun fire, high explosives, shrapnel and glass bombs.[5] An hour later, the Allied signal post on Mesnil Ridge received a message from a beleaguered Lt Hogg of the 15th Battalion: 'I am hit and about done. O'Connor hit badly [...] only about 20 left of my party. Am doing my best tell Col Crozier.' At 3.15 p.m. Woods wired that he was 'working hard on consolidation' but had already lost about forty men from each of the four battalions. 'Send me signallers,' he added, 'I cannot find mine.'

Sometime in the afternoon, Crozier sent him a battle message: 'Dear Woods, I hear you are trying to get an officer over in a stretcher, don't by day, he must wait till dark very sorry. Come along over soon for God's sake!! You have done splendidly.'[6] At 6.00 p.m. Woods reported that he had reached and re-occupied the German 'A' line at Grandcourt, but at considerable cost: half the 15th Battalion alone had been killed. He requested supplies of grenades, red flares and water. Having established a command post in a German dug-out, Woods sent out parties of soldiers to secure other sections of the line and started to evacuate his wounded.

The Ulstermen fought through the night to hold the line against counter-attack. At 11 p.m. only one of two promised relief companies arrived, so Woods was able to send just half his men back. He himself remained in the captured enemy line. Only at 10.40 the next morning was Woods finally able to return to the relative shelter of Thiepval Wood from the front line, leading one hundred and sixty tattered, shattered survivors and a handful of German prisoners. According to some testimonies, of the seven hundred West Belfast volunteers of the 9th Battalion who had entered battle on the morning of 1 July, only sixteen were still alive by the third day of the Somme.[7]

Heroic the Ulstermen certainly were, but they were also human. Some soldiers had straggled during the first day's attack, or had turned back under fire. By the afternoon of 3 July, the few survivors were reportedly 'all roaring drunk'.[8] Brigade-Major Maurice Day of the 107th wrote soon afterwards to congratulate Woods on his leadership of the second day's action, adding laconically that 'the Brigade-General [Withycombe] greatly regrets the large number of casualties.'[9]

Out of a total strength of about fifteen thousand men the 36th

(Ulster) Division lost 5,500 soldiers, including over two thousand killed, on the edge of Thiepval Wood during the first three days of the Somme. Fleetingly, it had achieved one of the few successes of the initial thrust, capturing the Schwaben Redoubt – but within a day of Woods' evacuation of his men from enemy lines the division, with no support from other units, had to relinquish the hillside stronghold.

Back home, the Thiepval battle was rapidly assimilated into folklore, as tightly-knit, strongly self-conscious local communities struggled to make sense of the devastating losses they had suffered, and politicians sought to transform sacrifice into political capital. On 19 July, the *Belfast News-Letter* published a verse entitled 'The Charge of the Ulster Division at Thiepval':

> Was ever a Charge in the World like this?
> Shall ever a son of Ulster miss
>   A fame that is wholly and solely his –
> A fame of sublimest splendour?
> The lads who laughed in the face of Death!
> Above the roar of the cannon's breath
> Singing their sacred shibboleth
>   Of 'The Boyne!' and 'No Surrender!'[10]

The Somme still plays a major role in Ulster's collective memory and sense of identity. The colourful murals adorning buildings along the Shankill Road and in other Protestant areas of the city of Belfast that celebrate the Ulster volunteers and the events of 1–3 July 1916 are powerful testimonies to the enduring significance of the past for present-day communities.[11]

In January 1917, Major P. J. Woods received the DSO (Distinguished Service Order) for his part in the action. He was also promoted to the rank of Lieutenant-Colonel and assumed command of the 9th Battalion, Royal Irish Rifles. The future 'King of Karelia' was thirty-six years old.

Chapter 2

The Lad from Sandy Row
Family and Childhood

Philip Woods was an imperialist. But empire for him was not the absolute universal right of great and rich nations. It was specifically the British imperial ideal, that portrayed itself as a moral duty higher than sordid economic gain or brute power politics, to which he remained true even while, as we shall see, he disparaged the politicians and bureaucrats who administered its territories and populations. In the mud of France and Flanders, the snows of North Russia and the side-streets of Belfast, he grew increasingly bitter about the perceived betrayal of common people by the political and social elites, the 'old gang', of which he himself never felt a part, and whose self-interested cliquishness provoked in him a consistent, outspoken and reciprocated hostility. To grasp what empire meant to Woods, and to understand his amalgam of conservative anti-establishment instincts, we need to delve earlier into history to form a picture of his Ulster background and upbringing.

In the late sixteenth century, Protestant Queen Elizabeth I of England initiated the subjugation and settlement of north-eastern Ireland. Her purpose was both to exploit the territory's land and to secure it against her continental enemies. One historian has described the Ulster Plantation, established during the next fifty years, as a 'colonising enterprise matching in scale and character the contemporary English migrations to the New World'.[1]

Like American colonisation, the English conquest of Ireland framed itself in moral and spiritual terms, as a mission to accomplish, in the words of Elizabeth's successor James I, 'the Reformation and civilizinge of those rude partes of the countrie'.[2] Naturally, where the sturdy settlers could not convert the natives to 'dutiful behaviour' and a 'civill orderly life' by example, they would subdue them by sword and flame. The ambivalence of empire was already evident in its earliest years.

When the Woods family arrived to make their home on the Plantation some time in the 1660s, they settled near the townland of Taughblane, County Down (just south-west of Hillsborough). This site, on the fringe of Kilwarlin Wood, had been the scene of a massacre of the indigenous population by Major-General Robert Munro and an invading Scottish army some twenty years earlier. During the 1650s, Oliver Cromwell's campaign of mass executions, deportations and confiscations had cleared further land for the settlement of a new wave of colonisers, soldiers and adventurers.[3]

Most of the new colonists held their property under lease from the great estate-owning gentry of the region. The Woods' landlords were the Hill family, which fifty years earlier had been granted extensive demesnes across Down and Antrim by the English crown in reward for their military service. Across the Plantation the settlers cultivated potatoes, oats and barley. They also wove linen out of the fibres of the locally-grown flax plant, providing a subsidiary income between harvests.

Throughout Ulster, linen production grew to play an important role in domestic economies. In 1698, the Irish Parliament sponsored a Huguenot master-weaver to establish a community of skilled artisans in Lisburn, barely four miles from Taughblane. The Woods were doubtless among many of the Ulster farming population to learn during the eighteenth century from the technology and expertise of these specialists. They benefited also from the preferential terms of trade granted by England and from grants and subsidies offered by the Irish Linen Board.[4]

As Ulster's linen exports grew so the Woods family prospered. A lease of 1774 lists a Jeremiah Woods as a 'linen manufacturer', with property amounting to 'nine acres, three roods and four perches' (i.e. amounting to just under ten acres).[5] Censuses of 1815 and 1824 show that Jeremiah's household was paying forty shillings annual rent – the standard value of freehold land in this part of the country – to its landlords, the Hill family (whose eldest sons now bore the title Marquess of

Downshire, and proclaimed their colonialist inheritance with the motto 'I have won my possessions by God and the sword'). A neighbouring plot is registered to Henry Woods, presumably a relative.

The Woods family were typical of the medium-scale farming tenants of County Down, renting their land on long leases, engaging in commercial crop cultivation and linen weaving, and sub-letting a small acreage to cottiers. As devoted members of the local Church of Ireland parish of St John's, Kilwarlin (where their family gravestones can still be seen), and patrons of the village poor, the Woods family would have enjoyed social respectability and privileged standing in their small community. Middling gentry farmers like them were for centuries the backbone of rural Ulster society. A census-taker of 1802 characterised this social stratum as 'respectable ... sharp and clever'.[6] A modern historian describes them as 'obstinate, hardy, self-reliant and direct'.[7]

James Woods, the son of Jeremiah, had eleven children in the early nineteenth century, of whom at least four died in infancy or childhood. In the 1848 Kilwarlin Estate Rental Book, he is listed as holding two parcels of land, together amounting to nearly twenty-two acres. James' eldest surviving son, also Jeremiah (born 1827), inherited the family home and most of the land. The 1860 Griffith Valuation indicates that Jeremiah owned nearly twenty acres worth £21, with the house worth £8, and three other smaller properties with gardens which he sub-let.

He also by now employed several local people as labourers and linen-workers, most likely village hand-spinners or weavers who had lost their independent livelihoods as a result of the introduction of powered wet-spinning and mechanised weaving earlier in the century. Ulster's industrialisation and the impoverishment of its rural population, aggravated by famine, forced not only the most destitute to face the choice of emigrating overseas or moving to the rapidly expanding cities of Dublin and Belfast. The Woods household was large, and their land-holding and small-scale linen business insufficient to support all the siblings and their own families. Towards the middle of the nineteenth century, while Jeremiah remained at Church Farm, Kilwarlin (his descendents still live there), at least two of his younger brothers joined the migration to the cities.

Both brothers met with moderate success. William Woods entered the clergy and from the early 1850s ran a private day school in Rutland (now Parnell) Square in central Dublin. From 1859 to 1863, a sickly, impressionable boy named Abraham Stoker attended this establishment where, although achieving only mediocre grades, he developed a deep love of literature. One biographer of the future author of *Dracula* characterises the Reverend Woods as 'a man of broad scholarship and fearless eloquence' who had 'a kindly disposition and almost limitless patience'.[8]

The next brother, Hugh Woods (born 1833), moved instead to Belfast, where the new industrial linen manufacturers – and, later, the shipbuilding yards – offered plentiful opportunities for work. Hugh was one of over 85,000 rural immigrants who settled in the city between 1851 and 1871. Such rapid expansion – Belfast almost doubled in size during these years – brought with it all the social ills one would expect, as well as sectarian tensions arising from the close proximity of mutually antagonistic Protestant and Catholic working populations.[9]

Hugh Woods settled in Sandy Row, a poor and ardently Protestant linen-workers' district just south-west of the city centre, and the site of rioting in 1857 and 1864. The British Parliamentary report into the first outbreak of violence characterised the inhabitants of Sandy Row as 'people of the humbler order – none of the superior classes. Tradesmen, operatives and people connected with the mills'.[10] (By the 1880s, the centre of sectarian hostilities had gravitated a few miles north-west to the newer Shankill Road area, where the better-paid shipyard workers were concentrated.)[11] Hugh found employment as a clerk in a local business, and with his wife Emily Catherine had a daughter (who was born in 1864, the year of riots, and died only five years later; she was buried in the graveyard of St John's, Kilwarlin), and two sons, first Robert James and then, on 23 September 1880, Philip James, the subject of the present work.[12]

Though the family was by no means well-off, the two boys seem to have enjoyed a genteel upbringing as befitted close relatives of the gentlemen farmers of Kilwarlin, Hillsborough. Moreover, as Philip Woods later made a point of noting in his *Who's Who* entry, his mother came from noble stock, being the granddaughter of Sir John Puleston of Flintshire, Wales, who could trace his lineage back to the Norman Conquest. Sir Roger de Puleston had been appointed first sheriff of Anglesey by Edward I after the conquest of Wales in the late thirteenth century, and had been lynched by natives during an early revolt against English taxation. Established at Emral Hall (near Wrexham) on the northern Anglo-Welsh borderlands, this family of colonial settlers had subsequently been drawn into local life, acting as the patrons of many prominent Welsh poets. They had even initially sided with Owain Glyn

Dwr during the Welsh rebellion against the English throne in the early 15th century.[13]

John Henry Puleston (1830–1908), a notorious late nineteenth-century scion of the same family, was a distant cousin of Philip Woods' mother. Having made a fortune in the United States during the civil war, Puleston had returned to Britain where he made and lost another fortune in the City of London, served as Conservative MP for Devonport between 1874–92 and was knighted in 1887.[14] The young Philip Woods could not have been unaware of his kinship with this distinguished, if somewhat rakish, character, nor of his mother's ancestry, however strange this must have seemed to a boy born in a small terraced house on Norwood Street, Sandy Row.

By 1892, Hugh Woods was a better-paid clerk of works, and the family had moved to Lavinia Street, a respectable road inhabited by traders, teachers and white-collar employees, a mile or so south-east of Sandy Row near the Ormeau Road.[15] In 1894, they moved to Duncairn Avenue, north of the city centre, and the following year back to University Street, a yet more genteel road near the Queen's College, populated by merchants, church ministers and middle managers. Number 19 was occupied by 'the Misses Seymour, ladies' school'.[16] During these years, according to his own account, Philip was educated at the nearby Royal Belfast Academical Institution, one of the city's most prestigious schools.[17] In view of the family's modest circumstances, it is possible that their second son received a scholarship for some years of his studies.

The Royal Belfast Academical Institution had been founded in 1810 by a group of Presbyterian reformers who aspired to overcome the country's religious divide by promoting non-denominational education. One of its first patrons was William Drennan, a prominent Irish radical who in the early 1780s had been active in the Ulster Volunteers, and had later campaigned against the 'unification' of Great Britain and Ireland (promulgated by the Act of Union, 1801).

At the Institution's inauguration ceremony in February 1814, an older and more stately Drennan declared that the school's role was 'to diffuse useful knowledge, particularly among the middling orders of society, as a necessity, not a luxury of life'. Yet his commitment to the new establishment encompassed more than the social need for practical schooling, envisaging that:

> pupils of all religious denominations should communicate, by frequent and friendly intercourse, in the common business of education, by which means a new turn might be given to the national character and habits, and all the children of Ireland should know and love each other.[18]

The school thrived, though it failed to realise its founders' vision of religious integration and national reconciliation. By the time Philip Woods attended 'Inst' (as the school was known), the school principally educated the sons of Belfast's liberal Protestant professional classes. It already counted among its alumni the pioneering physicist William Thomson, 1st Baron Kelvin (whose father had taught at 'Inst' in its earliest days), and William James Pirrie, one of the owners of the gigantic Harland and Wolff shipyards in Belfast, who in 1896 was elected Lord Mayor and was later created Viscount Pirrie of the City of Belfast. Woods' fellow pupils and near-contemporaries included many who would later become prominent politicians, scholars, businessmen, engineers, churchmen, soldiers and journalists.

Alongside its academic curriculum, the school encouraged its boys to engage in team sports (especially rugby, at which the school excelled) and arduous outdoor activities, a favourite activity of pupils being to take small rowing boats out into Belfast Lough.[19] They also employed a sergeant-major from the Victoria barracks to take the boys through military drill. In accordance with contemporary educational beliefs, 'Inst' was as concerned with developing physical prowess and building 'character' as it was with educating young minds. It aspired to imbue its boys with what the foremost nineteenth century English ideologue of individualism and self-reliance had commended as 'that constitutional energy and vigour [...] so indispensable [to] a robust manhood'.[20] A photograph of Philip Woods at about the age of twelve shows a bright, alert, strong boy of medium height, smartly dressed in a short-trousered suit of a coarse material, with waistcoat and tie, a mature calmness in his demeanour, and a direct, slightly questioning gaze, good-humoured rather than impertinent, altogether in keeping with the contemporary ideal of youthful masculinity and proper character.

If 'Inst' instilled in Woods the basic Victorian values of loyalty to crown, country and empire, as well as a robust self-reliance and adventurous spirit, the school's founding ethos perhaps gave him the open, inclusive sense of national and religious identity that distinguished him later from many of his Protestant peers. A descendent on his father's

Philip Woods, aged twelve (1892)

side of Protestant settlers who had colonised and pacified the Ulster Plantation and, on his mother's, of English tax-collectors and sheriffs of the Welsh marches, Philip Woods remained throughout his life a dedicated Irish unionist and British patriot. But he was never given to chauvinistic jingoism or sectarian intolerance, and in his political career he vigorously defended the interests of both Protestant and Catholic ex-servicemen. Perhaps the example of the Pulestons' patronage of Welsh culture also inspired in him a respect for different traditions.

With roots both in the Irish and Welsh rural gentry and in Belfast's white-collar working-class, Woods grew up innately conservative yet deeply sympathetic towards the neglected and downtrodden, which later manifested itself in a paternalistic commitment to social justice and a defiant antagonism towards governing elites. Perhaps the lad from Sandy Row never felt fully accepted by the patrician class – many of whom had been his schoolmates – and it was a bruised social pride that bred his assertive independence and resentment of the narrow-minded coteries that dominated both the officers' mess and public life.

Philip Woods' individualism was perhaps also related to an artistic sensibility and aptitude that emerged during his school-days, and that prompted him, at about the age of sixteen, to enter the Belfast School of Art. His decision to study and then pursue a career in textile design, however, while doubtless arising from his own talents and inclinations, was also pragmatically linked to his family's fortunes.

The 1898 edition of the Belfast city directory (printed in October 1897) no longer lists Hugh Woods. This might mean that the boys' father had died during the preceding year. We do know that Hugh's elder brother Jeremiah died in 1900, leaving Church Farm to his own eldest son James (already listed independently in the provincial directory twenty years earlier under Hillsborough's 'Nobility and Gentry', an indication of the social standing of the rural branch of the family). Perhaps Robert and Philip Woods also benefited from their uncle's estate, or even from the patronage of Sir John Henry Puleston, their mother's wayward millionaire relative, who died in 1908. In any case, by the turn of the century, Philip's elder brother Robert had set himself up independently as a linen designer and manufacturer and within a decade had become a successful businessman, married to a renowned society beauty and resident in a grand house named Princetown Lodge in Bangor.[21] In 1908, Robert sent his son Cecil Philip Woods to study at 'Inst'.[22]

We have no specific information about Robert's business, but it must have expanded rapidly since within a few years it was supplying textiles to the White Star shipping company, whose ocean liners were constructed and outfitted at the Harland and Wolff shipyards in Belfast.[23] Among the ships supplied with Woods' linenware was the ill-fated super-luxury liner SS *Titanic* (built in 1909–1911 by Thomas Andrews, a nephew of William Pirrie, and another Old Instonian who may well have known

Robert or Philip at school). It is likely, then, that family expectations, as much as a sense of personal vocation, led Philip Woods to study applied art and, after a year, to start work as a textile designer in a firm of Belfast linen manufacturers.

The linen business, however, must have seemed a dull prospect to the energetic and robust seventeen-year-old boy, who evidently yearned for adventure. Four years later, British imperial mishap provided Philip Woods with an opportunity to pursue his dreams.[24]

Philip Woods in South Africa

Chapter 3

In Defence of Empire
South Africa with Baden-Powell, 1901–1903

In October 1899, Britain's South African colonies were invaded by forces from the neighbouring Boer republics. At first, the war went badly for the British army – by the end of the year, most of its troops were either besieged at Ladysmith, Mafeking or Kimberley, or pinned down on the *veldt* by the highly-mobile Boer commandos. In particular, the British needed more cavalry to match the Dutch settlers' agility. The army called for volunteers from the domestic Yeomanry, a part-time militia organised into English and Irish county regiments under the command of local gentry. These recruits would form a new mounted infantry force, to be called the Imperial Yeomanry, to fight alongside the regular army.

According to Woods' own account, as soon as the South African conflict started, he volunteered for service with the Imperial Yeomanry, but was rejected on account of his age.[1] Refusing to be discouraged, he applied to join the South African Constabulary (SAC) under Major-General Robert Baden-Powell, and was accepted. We do not know if he sent his application directly to Baden-Powell in Transvaal, or was signed up by one of the recruiting officers who were combing the empire to raise men for service in the colony. In any case, Woods quit his employment as a textile designer in early 1901, and landed in South Africa in July of that year. He immediately found himself involved not in constabulary work, but in the thick of fighting.

The background to the SAC's formation needs briefly to be explained. By the late summer of 1900, the British had captured the Boer capitals of Bloemfontein and Pretoria, relieved their own besieged forces, and occupied Johannesburg, and it seemed to imperial politicians and administrators that the conflict was drawing to a close. Therefore they decided to establish a paramilitary mounted police force to quell residual unrest and maintain peace in the countryside. In August 1900, Baden-Powell (the 'hero of Mafeking') was appointed to raise and command for this purpose a new force of ten thousand men, which was formally inaugurated on 22 October of that year. British Colonial Secretary Joseph Chamberlain, however, had acceded to the army's insistence that the constabulary should also discharge military duties so long as war continued.[2] Sir Alfred Milner, High Commissioner for South Africa, who strongly opposed the army's indiscriminate destruction of Boer farms, grudgingly agreed to permit this, but stressed that the police should be deployed differently to regular army units, substituting a 'policy of protection for that of reprisal' with the objective 'to slowly and gradually subjugate and hold one district after another'.[3]

As it turned out, the war was far from over, as the Boers pursued guerrilla operations against the British army for nearly another two years. In early 1901, a few months before Woods' arrival, Lord Kitchener, Commander-in-Chief of British troops in the colony, had therefore taken over command of SAC units. In accordance with Milner's conditions for the constabulary's military deployment, Kitchener agreed to use the police for securing specific areas – for example by building and holding lines of blockhouses to hinder the enemy's mobility – rather than for wide-sweeping offensive operations or punitive expeditions.[4] Only after the war came to a negotiated end on 31 May 1902 was the SAC returned fully to civilian jurisdiction, though it continued military operations against those whom Milner termed 'the more turbulent spirits' for several years.[5]

Woods spent eleven months in the SAC during the war, and remained with it for a year afterwards. On arrival, he would have undergone intensive training at Modderfontein, situated between Johannesburg and Pretoria, in riding, rifle-shooting, drill and field tactics, as well as in the construction of blockhouses and trenches with

Woods' photograph of Baden-Powell in South Africa

barbed wire entanglements.[6] Baden-Powell organised the force on a principle of 'decentralised responsibility' and sought to inculcate in his men discipline 'bred from within instead of being imposed from without'. His aim was to develop 'intelligent young fellows who could use their wits and who had not been drilled into being soulless machines only able to act under direct orders'. This approach doubtless suited Woods' own independent character. A photograph of Woods at the time (reproduced on p. 28) conveys also a quality of soulfulness: the young man stands solitarily on the *veldt*, his posture straight but reposeful, his hands resting on the muzzle of a 'Long' Lee-Enfield rifle (issued in 1900 to the Imperial Yeomanry and other volunteer units, but which soon proved defective in service), a cartridge belt wrapped around his left shoulder, his delicate sun-burned features cast thoughtfully down – a Byronic hero captured in a moment of melancholy meditation.

The South African conflict entailed gritty labour as well as romantic posturing. It introduced Woods to guerrilla warfare, as well to dealing in a conciliatory, constructive manner with antagonistic or suspicious civilian populations – experiences that would later serve him well in North Russia and the Baltic. His comrades were as irregular as the Boer commandos opposing them: the four SAC divisions comprised, in Baden-

Powell's own words, a motley collection of 'stock-riders from Australia, farmers from New Zealand, North-West constables and cowboys from Canada, planters from India and Ceylon, Royal Irish constables from Ireland, and Yeomen from England.' The force included nearly two thousand public school boys, the same number of indigenous Zulus and six hundred friendly Boers. After the war ended, the SAC undertook wide and varied duties beyond its security and policing functions, including resettling refugees, organising a census and registering voters, operating a postal service and customs, suppressing land-grabbing, cattle thieving, illicit liquor dealing and arms smuggling, destroying locust swarms and regulating a gold rush. It also took brutal measures to seize back weapons from local black communities whom the British had earlier armed to fight on their behalf against the Boers during the war.

Baden-Powell was immensely proud of his men, boasting of their fortitude in a letter to the military high command:

> Our horses are in good fettle, hospital and transport organised and working well. Our men are in rags and doing a lot of real hard work in night raids and ambushes. They have had no rest for eleven months, but they are full of go and keenness for work in the field.

Joseph Chamberlain told the House of Commons in 1902 that as well as recognising the SAC's military prowess, he also attached 'the utmost importance to [it] as a great civilising and uniting influence'. Others were not so impressed: 'Where on earth was such a low, rough, almost criminal-looking crew raked together?' asked Emily Hobhouse, who was trying to organise relief for women and children who had suffered as a result of the war, 'Poor South Africa! Will no nice English people ever come out here?'[7] Once again, the representation and reality of imperialism diverged.

Philip Woods' experience in South Africa with these rag-tag irregulars doubtless served as a valuable apprenticeship, preparing him well for the particular nature of operations which his assignment to Karelia fifteen years later would entail – raising and commanding his 'most excellent bandits' against a hit-and-run enemy, rallying the local population to ensure friendly support, and, in the process, bringing the beacon of English civilisation and culture to the dark northern forests.

Woods left South Africa in June 1903, four months after Baden-Powell relinquished command of the SAC. Baden-Powell established the Boy Scouts soon after his return, giving them both the motto and a modified version of the constabulary's uniform. It is worth quoting here a passage from John Buchan's 1910 novel of South African adventure *Prester John*, as it encapsulates the romance, mythology and mystique of empire, as well as the assumptions and attitudes concerning race, morality, masculinity, duty, discipline and degeneracy, which informed and shaped Britain's imperial project at the turn of the twentieth century. (Buchan, five years older than Woods, also spent 1901–1903 in South Africa, in the official capacity of Lord Milner's private political secretary).

This excerpt also offers an insight into the values that doubtless inspired the young Philip Woods to seek adventure in South Africa, echoes of which are still discernable – though with none of the raw racialism of this novel, and refracted through the disillusion and doubt bred of later experience – in both the style and subject of his Karelian memoir. Buchan's hero, having performed fantastical derring-do (and, not incidentally, vastly enriching himself in the process), undertakes the arduous, selfless task of resettling the conquered native armies and organising the logistics of their transport, food supply and security – work not unlike that of the SAC – and finds in this operation, and the labour it entailed, both personal fulfilment and a better understanding of Britain's imperial mission:

> Yet it was an experience for which I shall ever be grateful, for it turned me from a rash boy into a serious man. I knew then the meaning of the white man's duty. He has to take all risks, recking nothing of his life or his fortunes, and well content to find his reward in the fulfilment of his task. That is the difference between white and black, the gift of responsibility, the power of being in a little way a king; and so long as we know this and practise it, we will rule not in Africa alone but wherever there are dark men who live only for the day and their own bellies. Moreover, the work made me pitiful and kindly. I learned much of the untold grievances of the natives, and saw something of their strange, twisted reasoning. Before we had got Laputa's army back to their kraals, with food enough to tide them over the spring sowing, Aitken and I had got sounder policy in our heads than you will find in the towns, where men sit in offices and see the world through a mist of papers.[8]

Chapter 4

No Surrender!

Linen, Gun-Running and the Ulster Volunteer Force, 1904–1914

For a while after his return from South Africa, Philip Woods seemed to be settling down and prospering – no longer the 'rash boy' but a 'serious man'. He resumed his career as a Belfast textile designer, probably in his elder brother's firm, working at a studio at No 4 Howard Street in the very centre of Belfast and living at No 225, The Elms, Belmont Road, in the leafy eastern suburbs near Stormont castle and estate. As already mentioned, the business prospered, developing not only in Ireland, but in Scotland and on continental Europe.[1] Perhaps to enhance his artistic credentials, Woods also temporarily seems to have adopted a new, more courtly sounding second name – the 1907 Belfast directory lists him as 'Philip Villiers Woods, designer'.[2]

On 7 August of the same year he took another step towards a gentility, marrying Florence Edith Blacker Quin. The ceremony took place at the Methodist Church in Bundoran, a popular seaside resort on the Atlantic Coast in County Donegal, known because of its aristocratic patrons in the early nineteenth century as the 'Irish Brighton'.[3] Florence was the eldest daughter of Stewart Blacker Quin, owner and director of a Belfast firm of chartered accountants which principally served local linen manufacturers. In time, Blacker Quin became chair of the Linen

Trade Associations, one of the most prominent roles in Belfast business circles. He was also an active philanthropist, whose charitable work included being honorary auditor of the Belfast Hospital for Sick Children, and was by repute a 'genial, kindly, loveable man [with] a magnetic manner which endeared him to all'.[4] Both his sons, Herbert and Stewart, were pupils at 'Inst' at the time of their sister's marriage.[5]

Stewart Blacker Quin was also a founder member of the Ulster Unionist Council. This organisation had been established just two years earlier to reinvigorate loyalist organisation in the province, and to co-ordinate opposition to the Irish nationalists' lobbying of the British government to revise or abrogate the 1801 Act of Union.[6] But for over twenty years Ulster businessmen had been at the forefront of resistance to Irish home rule.[7] Their stance was motivated both by sentiment and by sturdy self-interest.

For one thing, Ulster's entrepreneurs and professionals understood that Irish independence would mean an end to the imperial subsidies which they received from London. In August 1886, William Pirrie, the Old Instonian chairman of shipbuilders Harland and Wolff, declared to a party of Belfast businessmen that if home rule were ever to become law, he would move his firm's operations to Glasgow. A journalist later recalled Pirrie's guests agreeing that 'under an Irish Parliament and Government there would be no security for life nor property, no fair play to the Loyalists in the North of Ireland, and that utter want of commercial confidence without which Belfast could not continue to prosper.'[8] Ulster's smaller commercial interests, including the huge number of companies engaged in linen manufacture and trading, shared these concerns, as did most Protestant artisans and skilled workers.

More generally, Northern Ireland's Protestants mistrusted their Catholic neighbours, believing them to be seditious and resentful, only waiting for the opportunity that independence would yield to rise up against the settlers' descendents, to murder and dispossess them. As already mentioned, these antagonisms sporadically erupted into sectarian violence, often associated with loyalist celebrations of 'the Twelfth', the anniversary of the Battle of the Boyne.[9] Sometimes the Ulster Unionists exploited these popular energies; at other times they considered their interests better served by restraint.

By the start of the twentieth century, a Conservative-Unionist political alliance had already twice defeated attempts by Liberal prime minister W. E. Gladstone to legislate Irish home rule, in 1886 and 1893.[10] In the early years of the new century, however, Unionist fears grew that divisions within the English governing classes over tariffs and imperial preference might leave the Irish nationalists holding the balance of power after the next election, enabling them finally to achieve home rule. With this in mind, the Ulster Unionist Council was formed in March 1905 to unify Ulster's loyalist interests: its members of parliament, its local political associations and the Orange Lodges.

The Orange Lodges were the local branches of the Orange Order, which had been founded as a Protestant 'self-defence' organisation in the 1790s. One of its precursors had been the Ulster Volunteers, with which William Drennan had been involved in his youth before committing himself to the republican cause and religious reconciliation. The Orange Order, however, was far from non-sectarian. Banned for much of the nineteenth century for fomenting violence, by the start of the twentieth it had grown into a powerful provincial network, in the words of a modern writer, 'part social, part political and wholly bigoted'.[11] (The Catholics had an equivalent organisation, the Order of Hibernians, led by Grand Master Joseph Devlin, MP for West Belfast – the constituency for which Woods would stand in 1929.)

In the event, the General Election of 1906 returned the Liberals to power with such a large majority that they did not need to rely on the Irish vote in parliament. For the time being, the new government could overlook the nationalists' calls to re-open the issue of self-rule.

We have no information about Philip Woods' political views at this time, although we do know that, faithful to his school's founding principle, he was not a member of the Orange Order. When in 1912, however, Irish home rule once more returned to the political agenda and Unionist politics began to hot up again, Woods (in the sparse and vague words of his own *Who's Who* entry) became 'interested in the Ulster Volunteer Force and took a prominent part in the ensuing gun-running, etc...'

That Woods participated in these events is unsurprising in view of his father-in-law's commitment to the loyalist cause, and his own taste for soldiering and adventure. Even if he could have suspected that it would lead him to the murderous trenches of northern France, to the no less savage little civil wars of revolutionary, post-imperial eastern Europe and then into the fierce populist politics of a new parliamentary order, he would in all likelihood have taken the same decision. Woods had lived out his twenties in the warm haze of the 'Indian summer' of Edwardian

Britain, developing a career and embarking on marital domesticity. Now, with the storm clouds gathering, he was restless for excitement and engagement with the wider world, tired of seeing it merely 'through a mist of papers'. It was to be several decades before the tumult of history receded from his life.

★ ★ ★ ★

On the morning of Monday, 27 April 1914, *The Times* carried the following report:

> A remarkable scheme of wholesale gun-running was successfully carried out by the Ulster Volunteer Force between 9 o'clock on Friday night and 6 o'clock yesterday morning. It is estimated that between 35,000 and 40,000 rifles and about a million rounds of ammunition were landed at Larne, Bangor, Donaghadee, and other places on the coasts of Antrim and County Down. The whole operation was conducted in a manner unparalleled in the history of the United Kingdom, and the daring and audacity, as well as the completeness of the scheme, have astonished even those in Belfast who were fully aware of the efficiency of the Volunteer Force as a mobile organisation.

This was 'Operation Lion', carried out to provide the recently-formed Ulster Volunteer Force (UVF) with weapons in case the crisis that was developing around the Third Home Rule Bill exploded, as seemed increasingly likely, into civil conflict.

Much of British public opinion shared *The Times*' correspondent's excited admiration for this operation. There was, in any case, great sympathy throughout Britain for the Unionist cause. In August 1911, the Irish Nationalist Party had supported Liberal Prime Minister Herbert Asquith in pushing through the Parliament Act, which curtailed the Lords' power of veto over legislation. In return, Asquith introduced a Third Home Rule Bill in April 1912 which included far-reaching provisions for Irish self-government. Not only Conservative politicians, with whom the Unionist Party was formally in alliance, but numerous eminent public figures (including Sir Alfred Milner), perceived this as a dangerous and perfidious deed, and spoke out vocally in support of the Irish loyalists.[12]

To these observers it seemed, as one historian has written, that

Ulster's 'only crime was loyalty to the Crown. To thrust Ulster out of the British empire against her will was to attack the idea of "empire" at its very heart.'[13] The writer and poet Rudyard Kipling, who was an impassioned advocate both of Irish unionism and British imperialism (and who partially bankrolled the Larne gun-running), articulated in verse the intensity of the loyalists' sense of betrayal and rebellious ardour:

> The dark eleventh hour
> draws on and sees us sold
> To every evil power
> We fought against of old.
> Rebellion, rapine, hate,
> Oppression, wrong and greed
> Are loosed to rule our fate,
> By England's act and deed.
>
> [....]
> What answer from the North?
> One Law, one Land, one Throne.
> If England drive us forth
> We shall not fall alone.[14]

In 1910, Sir Edward Carson, a prominent politician and barrister, took over leadership of the Unionist Parliamentary Party.[15] Although of southern Irish origin, Carson soon won the confidence of the Ulster loyalists, led by Captain James Craig, a wealthy Belfast man who had served with the Royal Irish Rifles and the Imperial Yeomanry in South Africa and then, like Woods, restless and unsettled on his return, had been drawn into political activity by family ties. In 1906, Craig had been elected to Westminster as MP for East Down.[16]

In September 1911, to demonstrate Ulster's stalwart opposition to Irish home rule, Craig organised a march of fifty thousand men from the centre of Belfast to his own residence on the city's outskirts. There Carson addressed the assembled crowds with a rousing speech in which he promised to resist home rule even if it meant establishing Ulster's own government and defending it by force. In the course of 1912, Unionists began to form local volunteer militias and on 28 September nearly half a million loyalists signed a 'Solemn League and Covenant' at ceremonies across the province, pledging them to defend their equal British citizenship and the 'unity of Empire'. Philip Woods put his name to the Covenant at the Orange Hall at Ballylumford near Larne in East Antrim, about eighteen miles north of Belfast.[17]

In January 1913, the Ulster Unionist Council resolved to unite loyalist militias into the 100,000-strong UVF, organised into county divisions, regiments, battalions, companies and sections. The Belfast Division comprised four regiments, one for each of the city's parliamentary constituencies. It is likely that Philip Woods joined the force, since a membership badge, depicting the Red Hand of Ulster and inscribed with the motto 'For God and Ulster', is preserved among his private papers, though we do not know to which unit he was attached or what rank he held.

As the Liberal's Home Rule Bill progressed through its consecutive readings, tensions mounted in Ulster. The UVF established a Special Service Force to act as the organisation's shock troops in the city. The 300-strong West Belfast Special Service Section, recruited mainly along the ardently Unionist Shankill Road, was placed under the command of Captain Frank Percy Crozier. A stocky, stubborn and fiercely outspoken character, Crozier was later Philip Woods' commanding officer in France and Lithuania, and (according to his memoirs) was also responsible for Woods being invited to participate in the British mission to North Russia, which is the focus of the present work.

Crozier was a year older than Philip Woods. He was not an Ulsterman by birth, but had been born and raised near Dublin by a long-established Anglo-Irish landowning and military family, and then educated at an English public school. He had tried to join the regular army at the age of eighteen but to his lasting chagrin had been rejected because of his small stature and physical weakness. Like Woods, he had then sought adventure in South Africa on his own initiative. In 1900, Crozier travelled to Durban in Natal province, where he joined a mounted infantry regiment. At the end of the war, he transferred to the West African Frontier Force.

During his period of colonial service, he recalled in a 1930 volume of his memoirs (in language strongly echoing that of Buchan's hero in *Prester John*), 'I had gained great Imperial experience and had had my eyes opened to the greatness of England. I had seen Zulus, Basutos, Cape Boys, Hottentots and Swazis obeying the white man and respecting the flag, and I had seen that this had only been achieved by fair dealings.'[18] However, while keenly aware of 'Imperial responsibilities and obligations in regard to the "uplift" of humanity,' Crozier, like Woods and other men we shall encounter in this narrative, was already losing faith in what he later sardonically termed the 'civilised product' of the 'white man's burden'.[19]

On his return from the tropics to Britain in 1908, Crozier was physically debilitated and an alcoholic. A resulting scandal over unpaid debts forced him to resign his army commission the following year and depart to Canada to start a fresh, vigorous life of farming, trapping and scouting in the northern territories.[20] In 1912, Crozier returned to Britain, re-energised and teetotal, and was invited by Carson and Craig to join the UVF.[21] Under Crozier's leadership, the 'Shankill Boys' of the West Belfast Special Service Section rapidly gained the reputation of being the UVF's elite unit. In April 1914 they were given responsibility for Carson's personal protection when rumours circulated of his impending arrest.

Meanwhile, the UVF had grown rapidly into a powerful movement, with a Military Council under the command of Lieutenant-General Sir George Richardson, and committees responsible for personnel, finance, intelligence, railways, supplies and medical aid. The Military Council established a special unit led by Major Frederick Crawford, a colourful character who combined a career as a soldier, businessman, adventurer and radical unionist, to furnish the citizen army with weapons. Crawford immediately set about arranging for consignments of rifles and ammunition to be smuggled into Northern Ireland. Having had several shipments seized by police and customs during the summer, Crawford began to recruit a network of conspirators among Ulster businessmen with connections in England and continental Europe and access to storage and transport facilities.

It is most likely that Woods became involved at this stage. 'The game,' as one historian has written, 'provided a spice of adventure to many a young Ulsterman who felt stifled in the dreary routine of an office.'[22] Early in 1914, concerned by the possibility of a pre-emptive move by the British government to disband the UVF, its leadership agreed to permit Crawford to smuggle into Ulster a huge shipment of arms acquired in Germany. Woods, who, as mentioned, had signed the Ulster Covenant at Ballylumford, a small town on the shore of Larne Lough not far from the port, doubtless played a role in this clandestine enterprise. Whether he was involved in unloading the cargo or coordinating the arrival and departure of the five hundred cars mobilised to transport the shipment inland, or in the cutting of communications between Larne and Belfast, is not known (as already cited, his own account merely states that he 'played a prominent part in the gun-running'). Whatever role he fulfilled, his South African experience of guerrilla tactics, policing and logistics would have stood him in good stead.

After it had successfully armed itself, the UVF faced the prospect of resisting home rule with renewed determination, even as the bill progressed through its third reading on 14 July. The Catholics now mobilised their own paramilitary movement, the Irish Volunteers (spanning the northern and southern counties), and civil conflict seemed inevitable. British army officers in Ireland declared they would not raise arms against their loyalist comrades. Only Britain's declaration of war against Germany on 4 August 1914 halted the UVF's preparations for a unionist coup-d'état.

By the time home rule passed into law on 18 September (with a provision deferring a decision on the precise form of its implementation until after the end of the European war), the UVF was dissolving as a cohesive force. Most of its officers had been recalled to their regiments and the majority of the rank-and-file rushed to enlist in Lord Kitchener's 'New Army'. Now was an opportunity to demonstrate their dedication to King and Country not by rebellion but by serving the patriotic cause. As the bard of a local newspaper proclaimed:

> And wherever the fight is hottest,
> And the sorest task is set,
> ULSTER WILL STRIKE FOR ENGLAND
> AND ENGLAND WILL NOT FORGET.[23]

Chapter 5

The Shankill Boys
France, 1915–1918

Among the UVF recruits to Kitchener's army was Philip Woods, who signed up alongside the West Belfast Volunteers, Crozier's 'Shankill Boys', to form the 9th Service Battalion of the Royal Irish Rifles which, as we have already seen, became a unit of the 107th (Belfast) Brigade and of the 36th (Ulster) Division on the latter's formation at the end of October. The other three Belfast UVF units made up the 8th (East Belfast), 10th (South Belfast) and 15th (North Belfast) Service Battalions.

Woods immediately received his commission as Lieutenant, thanks principally to his service experience in South Africa.[1] It may also indicate that he had already served as a UVF officer, although we have no information to confirm this.[2] Crozier ignored orders to report to the Royal Irish Fusiliers to remain with his West Belfast men and (his earlier record of drunkenness, debt and dishonour having been mistakenly overlooked) was given the rank of major.[3]

The men of the 36th Division, the West Belfast volunteers and Woods among them, spent an impatient, frustrating year in training camps in Ireland, before being transferred in July 1915 to Seaford on the English south coast. During this period, Crozier and Lieut-Col G. S. Ormerod, in command of the battalion, concentrated (in Crozier's words) on 'knocking the beer and politics out of all ranks and building up an esprit-de-corps in its place' while, at the same time, aiming 'to foster, inculcate, teach and build up the blood lust for the discomfiture of the enemy'.[4] Crozier's approach to training and leading his men did not endear him to all his subordinates, some of whom came to think of him as 'a callous and overbearing martinet'.[5]

Crozier and Ormerod also tried in these months to address what the former called delicately the 'officer problem'. First, the officers having been recruited from the same district, they 'all knew too much about each other's business and there was a tendency to bring the petty rivalries of civilian life into the mess'. Secondly, these 'middle-class men' with the same accent and all-too public 'private histories' were not all able to exercise proper authority over the rank-and-file, drawn from the same neighbourhoods.[6] Ormerod therefore applied for a transfer of non-local personnel into the unit; he received nine new officers. During this time, Woods evidently impressed his superiors, as he was promoted twice – first, to captain in November 1914, then to the rank of major in September 1915. Early the following month, the division embarked for France.

Crozier's training of his men had not been altogether successful. Nor, as we shall see later, had the 'officer problem' been fully resolved. The 36th Division as a whole had a poor disciplinary record, and the 9th RIR were no exception (though they were not the worst among the service battalions). In November 1915, General Nugent lambasted Crozier personally for his 'undisciplined mob'.[7] The principal cause of their disruptive, insubordinate behaviour was heavy drinking, among both enlisted men and officers. During their first year in France, thirty-one West Belfast men were tried by court martial for various offences, and one received the death penalty for alleged desertion (this was eighteen-year-old James Crozier, whom F. P. Crozier testified to the court martial was a 'shirker' and 'of no value' as a soldier). Several officers were dismissed or disciplined.[8] To knock the 107th Brigade into shape, Nugent despatched it to the trenches for three months, on attachment to another division, soon after its arrival in France.[9] In January 1916, Crozier was promoted to lieutenant-colonel and given command of his battalion.[10] Woods was now his second-in-command. In early March 1916, the 36th Division (which the 107th Brigade had now rejoined) was deployed to Thiepval Wood, in anticipation of the 'big push' in midsummer. During June, Woods used his skills as a draughtsman to draw a large cloth wall-map for Crozier's lecture to the battalion on the

Woods' photograph of a trench in northern France

impending battle.[11] If Nugent had had earlier concerns about the Ulstermen's fighting-fitness, their valiant and tragic sacrifice on 1–3 July, described in the first chapter, proved him wrong.

In the days after the slaughter of the Somme, the 36th Division was moved north to rest and regroup. For several months, the lines they occupied in the Messines area were relatively quiet. In mid-October, Crozier sent Woods back to Britain to enrol in a senior officers' training course at Aldershot, evidently preparing him for further promotion.[12] During Woods' absence from France, he found time to give thought to other matters. On 27 October 1916, *The Times* newspaper published a 'Remarkable Appeal to the Cabinet by 1,000 Representatives of the Brain-Power of the Nation', calling for the prohibition of alcohol consumption during wartime and measures to halt the increase in infant mortality.[13] It considered 'the peril of the child-life of the State' to result from the spread of venereal disease, itself aggravated by uncontrolled drinking. Many of the leading military men, industrialists, writers, politicians and other public figures of the day put their name to this petition.

Near the bottom of the list of military signatories we find the name 'Major P. J. Woods, The Trenches'. In Ulster both hard drinking and zealous temperance were established traditions – in the 9th RIR alone, both Crozier and the late Gaffikin were reformed alcoholics who refused the rum ration before battle – but Woods himself had neither any particular predilection for drink nor any strong aversion to it (there are frequent references to alcohol in the Karelian memoir, often in the context of humorous anecdotes, and, as we shall see, his political career was partly sponsored by publicans' and brewers' interests). Most likely, Woods was prompted to put his name to this document after witnessing the uninhibited consumption of spirits in the trenches which had caused so many disciplinary problems in his division. Possibly family connections also played a part, since we also find his father-in-law's firm 'Stewart, Blacker, Quinn & Co, Belfast' [*sic*] listed among those from 'Finance and Industry' who have put their name to the document.

At the end of November 1916, Crozier was rewarded for his gallant though insubordinate action on the Somme with the rank of brigadier-general and command of the 119th Infantry Brigade (not an Irish unit). At this point, Nugent asked him who should take over command of the 9th RIR, and it became clear that the 'officer problem' had persisted. According to Crozier's memoirs, published in 1930, his immediate recommendation was Major Horace Haslett, whom he described as 'a very sound Belfast businessman and a son of a former Lord Mayor of Belfast.' Haslett had lost an eye at the Somme, but was recovering rapidly. In the absence of both Woods and Haslett, the 9th Battalion's third major, William Montgomery, a Belfast surveyor and auctioneer (and Haslett's brother-in-law and close friend), took over its acting command. Crozier later explained his recommendation as follows:

> I pointed out that my second in command, Woods, was at the Senior Officers' School at Aldershot. I had sent him there to qualify for a battalion. He had quite a good military mind, but there were difficulties of which I was aware. He could never command any battalion in the Belfast

Philip Woods, 8 August 1917

> Brigade, or, I really believe, in the Ulster Division, because the fellows have their peculiarities, prejudices, petty jealousies and favourites. I always meant him to command a battalion in another Division, where he would be free from petty jealousies, and unable to indulge in reprisals. I was now getting a brigade, and was willing to fill my first vacancy by asking for Woods.[14]

Crozier gives us no hint as to the nature or source of the antagonism towards Woods amongst his fellow officers. As Crozier evidently had confidence in Woods' military aptitudes, the 'difficulties' were more likely of a personal nature; and as Crozier considered him fit for a command outside the 36th Division, the 'petty jealousies' must have been related specifically to his Ulster background.

Perhaps Woods' colleagues refused to accept him socially. Most of them were upper middle-class Belfast businessmen and professionals or former officers of the regular army. Many were also prominent civic officials and most were members of the Orange Order. They came from families that were inter-related and of long standing in the city. Many had been to the Royal Academical Institution so knew of Woods' background (Haslett had started in 1894, so was probably one of Woods' contemporaries). To such types, Woods might have seemed an upstart and outsider of uncertain class credentials and suspiciously democratic opinions. He was not even an Orangeman! Perhaps, on the other hand, the rank-and-file resented what they perceived as the pretensions to gentility of a lad from Sandy Row, at a stage in the war when the majority of officers were still 'gentlemen' by social origin.

Judging by Woods' belligerency towards to Ulster's social cliques and political coteries during his later political career, he himself would have done nothing to mollify the hostility of his fellow officers, and might well have actively incited or exacerbated it – as implied by Crozier's allusion to 'reprisals'.

Crozier's 1930 memoir alludes to one further detail which might, or might not, be relevant to this story. During one of Woods' election campaigns in the 1920s, a political opponent implied that he 'had sheltered in a dug-out, when he should have been elsewhere, during the first battle of the Somme.' Crozier was 'forced to intervene by telegram and letter in order to keep the good name of [his] old battalion ... free from mud-slinging.' He, after all, had recommended Woods for the DSO and was therefore 'the best person to judge the happenings of those three strenuous days.' Crozier then vindicated Woods, albeit with ostensibly greater concern for the honour of the battalion than that of the maligned individual:

> Of course, only bad soldiers and fools neglect to take cover when the best interests of the State are thereby served, but to make an imputation that the second in command showed cowardice in the presence of the enemy, and then received a DSO, struck me as being the height of political knavery, which reflected on the battalion.

It is hard to know what to make of this allegation. It presumably refers to the night of 2–3 July when Woods occupied a German trench on the slope of the Schwaben Redoubt and sent out parties of men to secure deeper enemy lines (the action for which he was mentioned in despatches and awarded a commendation). There is nothing in the official Battalion War Diary to indicate that Woods' establishment of an overnight command position in the German dug-out was motivated by 'the better part of valour' rather than by genuine tactical considerations. During the 1920s, several of the 9th Battalion's surviving officers spoke out against Woods' political ambitions, but none of them was reported as casting any aspersions on his war record. Crozier's battle message to Woods on 2 July (which he reproduced in the second volume of his memoirs – one wonders if Woods had interceded after reading the first) is further evidence that the latter's conduct involved nothing untoward. It is therefore likely that either an unprincipled opponent fabricated this allegation for cheap expediency during one of the election campaigns (Woods was, after all, standing as the 'Fighting Colonel', the friend of the ex-serviceman), or that, if it originated in rumours already circulating among Woods' comrades-in-arms during the war, then the gossip was motivated by prior malice towards him rather than being the cause of ill-feeling.

Regardless of Crozier's warning, Nugent promoted Woods to the temporary rank of lieutenant-colonel and appointed him to lead the 9th RIR (evidence that Woods enjoyed high standing among the senior command, if not among his peers).[15] While Woods was in England, his rival Horace Haslett assumed temporary command. On 6 January, Haslett himself departed for the senior officers' course at Aldershot, and two days later Woods returned to France and took up his command. Woods' entries in the Battalion War Diary reveal that the next two months were spent training and relaxing, with cross-country competitions and field cinema shows. Woods left for another three-week course in late March (Montgomery taking over during his absence), but returned to lead his men into battle on 7 June at Messines Ridge, south-east of Ypres, in the Flanders province of Belgium.

In the early morning, the Allies detonated nearly 450,000 kilogrammes of explosive buried in nineteen vast mines under the German front line. The blast was heard in the south-east of England, and an estimated ten thousand German soldiers were killed instantly, together with some men of the 36th Division who were caught by a slight delay in the explosion of the Spanbroekmolen mine. Despite this setback, the Ulstermen – including the 9th RIR under Woods – continued their advance, capturing an entire German Battalion Headquarters before linking up with the 16th (Irish) Division, their religious and political differences forgotten in the heat of war.[16]

Following this successful engagement, Woods took brief leave but returned by the end of June. Throughout the previous seven months, however, Woods' subordinates had reportedly been writing 'SOS's' to Crozier regarding their new battalion commander. 'Finally,' Crozier wrote in his memoir, 'intrigue, jealousies, the removal of eyes from victory to the "main chance", all told their tale, which eventually led to the disruption of the unit and the unwarranted removal of Colonel Woods from command.'[17] Again, he does not indicate precisely what form this 'disruption' took, nor who had allowed personal ambition to take precedence over military duty – though the description of Woods' removal as 'unwarranted' suggests that Crozier did not hold him primarily responsible for the trouble his leadership had caused. The Battalion War Diary simply indicates that on 2 August Woods 'vacated the command' and handed over to Lieut-Col H. C. Elwes, formerly of the Scots Guards. Haslett remained as the battalion's second-in-command.

On 30 August, the 8th and 9th Battalions of the RIR were amalgamated, and in October the combined unit participated in the battle of Passchendaele, where it was (in Crozier's words) 'slaughtered in its trenches before it got going.' Haslett was again wounded, and this time invalided out of the war.[18] The survivors of the 8th/9th RIR then fought at Cambrai until mid-December when they were finally relieved and withdrawn from the front line. In February 1918, the battalion was disbanded.

Immediately after relinquishing command of the 9th RIR, Woods returned to Belfast. He was doubtless dispirited at the turn of events. A hint of cold, sad anger can be read in his face in the portrait photograph taken a few days later (reproduced on p. 46). Around this time, Woods submitted his first *Who's Who* entry, from which we learn that Florence and he had one daughter, and that his recreations included football, tennis, yachting and riding. In January 1918, Woods was given command of the 19th (Reserve) Battalion, RIR, based in Ireland. In April, the battalion moved to England and was absorbed into another unit. In June, therefore, Woods found himself in London, a seasoned soldier with experience of leadership but no troops to lead. It was at this moment that he was summoned to an empty house in Waterloo Place off Pall Mall in central London. There, in a small back room in the company of two other senior officers, he was asked: 'Will you volunteer for service out of uniform, and in any part of the globe to which you may be sent?'

This is how Woods' Karelian memoir starts (see p.149 of this book), with no explanation of why he was summoned or how it happened that he was available at this time for special duties. For this, we need to turn again to Crozier's memoir.

> [...] I eventually met General Nugent [Crozier wrote] and discussed the matter after Colonel Woods had gone home. I was genuinely sorry for Colonel Woods, as I knew what did happen would happen, so took the first opportunity of going to the War Office about him, which resulted in his sailing for North Russia with the original 'Hush, Hush' expedition.

The War Office evidently agreed with Crozier this time that Woods was a talented but awkward individual who was best deployed at a distance. Can we trust Crozier's account of these events? Rather, we might ask what motives he might have had in 1930 for not telling the truth. As there seems to be little in this story which might serve to aggrandise or exculpate its author (the main reasons why memoir writers choose to put pen to paper), there seems no particular reason – in the absence of other evidence – to dismiss it.[19] Whether the trouble which caused Woods to lose his command was rooted in schoolboy feuds, personal rivalries or political differences remains hidden. It is unlikely the truth will ever be known.

Chapter 6

King of Karelia (1)
Intervention in North Russia, 1918

Some time towards the end of the first millennium of the modern era, a Finno-Ugric tribe named the Karelians migrated north-west from the central Eurasian plain to settle in the territory between the White Sea and the Gulf of Finland, a sub-Arctic landscape of lakes, marshes and dense coniferous forest. Sporadically over the succeeding centuries, two historically hostile civilisations, Sweden-Finland in the west and Muscovy-Russia in the east, struggled over this remote frontier.

The Karelian land was divided in the early fourteenth century, and populations east and west of the ill-defined and shifting border developed with distinct dialects, cultures and religions. Karelian history since has been characterised and shaped by extended phases of differentiation alternating with campaigns launched from both west and east to effect rapprochement or re-unification – with each power seeking to impose its own political, administrative, cultural or religious terms on the other, and neither paying heed to the interests of the Karelians themselves.[1]

Since the middle ages, the population of eastern (Russian) Karelia has been at least nominally Orthodox Christian, although many pagan rites survived into the early twentieth century. The inhabitants of the southern part of this territory, roughly between lake Ladoga and lake Onega, which became known as Olonets Karelia, lived in close proximity to Russian populations. This strongly influenced their linguistic and cul-

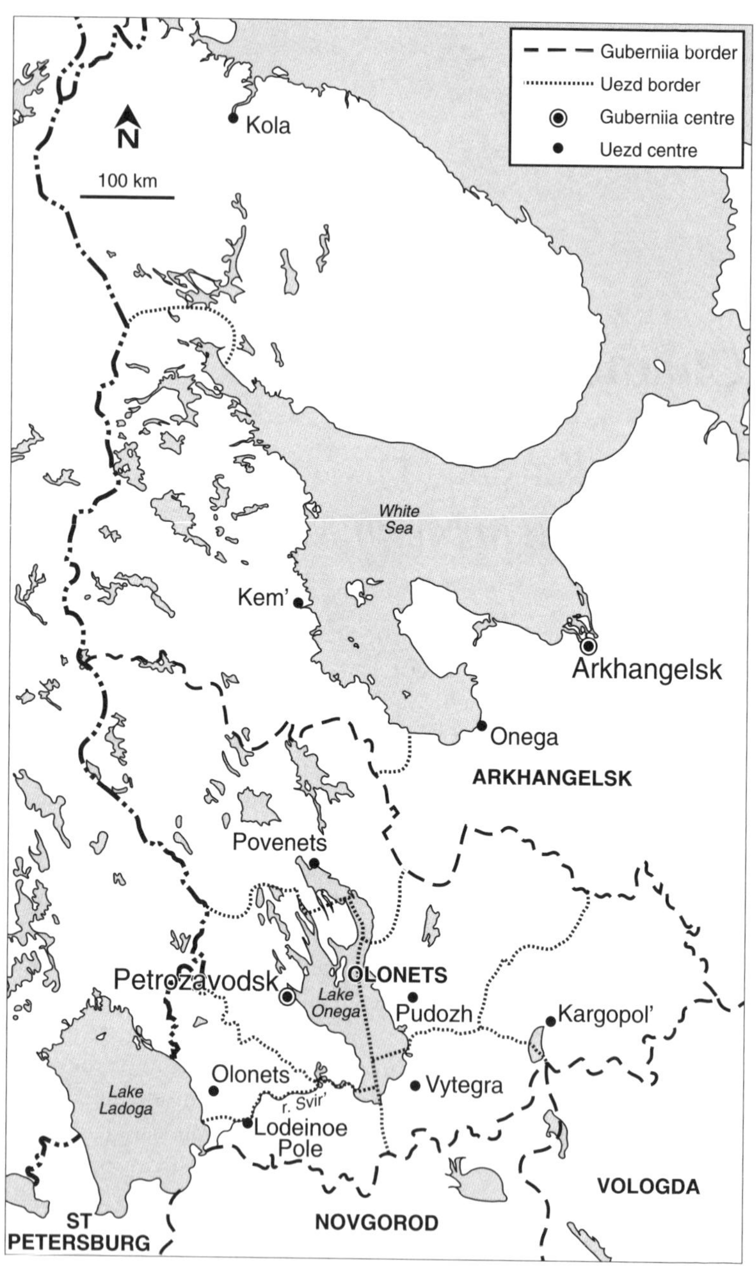

Map 1. Eastern Karelia within the Russian Empire (19th century)

tural development. At the start of the eighteenth century, Peter the Great's construction of his new capital St Petersburg on the Gulf of Finland transformed south-eastern Karelia, with its expansive forests and peat-bogs, ore and mineral deposits, into the hinterland of the imperial metropolis, supplying ships' timbers, fuel and building materials, as well as munitions and metalwork manufactured in the Petrovskii works on Lake Onega's western shore.

The Petrovskii foundry grew into the town of Petrozavodsk, which by 1788 had fifty thousand inhabitants (of whom eighty-three per cent were serfs, owned by the state) and was the administrative capital of Olonets province (*guberniia*).[2] During the nineteenth century, up to twenty thousand peasants from the region, approximately ten per cent of the total provincial population, travelled every year to the factories of St Petersburg or Riga to find employment.[3] Nearly sixty per cent of the Olonets population was Russian, with Karelians accounting for only fifteen to twenty per cent (by 1897, equivalent to about sixty thousand people), concentrated in the north-western part of Povonets county (*uezd*), the north-eastern part of Petrozavodsk county and Olonets county (see Map 1 opposite).[4]

The northern part of Russian Karelia, between the Finnish border and the White Sea, a harsher, rockier landscape than in the south, was never penetrated by tsarist economic, political and cultural influence to the same extent. The spoken tongue of the population of this region, White Sea Karelia, remained 'purer' than that of their southern compatriots (neither had a written language). The only bastion of Russian power in this area was the mighty fortified monastery on the Solovetskii islands, approximately thirty miles east of Kem, in the south-western corner of the White Sea. From the fifteenth century, the monks developed timber, salt and fishing resources along the shores of the White Sea, employing conscripted local Karelian peasants and Russian settlers, and amassing great wealth.[5]

During the sixteenth century English explorers sailed into the White Sea. They were followed by enterprising merchants who established fur trading posts. From the new port of Archangel [Arkhangel'sk], on the south-eastern shore of the White Sea, English ambassadors travelled southwards to Moscow to visit the court of Ivan the Terrible, bearing back to Elizabeth I of England the tsar's proposal of marriage – which she declined.[6] While a major trading route developed between Archangel and Moscow (the road is still a major highway, lined with monasteries and churches, reaching right to the heart of the capital city), the remoteness of White Sea Karelia made it a place of refuge from central rule.

In the seventeenth century, the Solovetskii monastery became a focus of resistance to the Romanov tsars' centralising and modernising reforms (it also housed a prison for noble exiles; during the nineteenth century it became a centre of pilgrimage and tourism, bringing it yet more wondrous wealth, as Woods witnessed on his visit to the monastery's treasury). In the same period, religious opponents to church reform, the so-called 'Old Believers' (Woods refers to them as adherents of the 'Old Religion') fled into the dense forests and sacred groves of central and northern Karelia to establish communities which exist to this day.[7]

The town of Kem, a few miles inland from the coast, grew to be the hub of the Solovetskii monastery's mainland activities (the Kem river flowed into the sea at Popov, one of the main ports of embarkation to the islands). In the early eighteenth century the town's rapidly growing population built a magnificent wooden cathedral. In the later eighteenth and nineteenth centuries, Kem county was a destination for those political exiles from St Petersburg whose misdemeanours did not warrant lengthy banishment or harsher punishment – because of this, the region became known as the 'suburban Siberia' [*podstolichnaia Siberiia*]. At the start of the twentieth century, the town of Kem, prospering thanks to its proximity to the Solovetskii monastery, built a new stone Cathedral of the Annunciation, in which Woods (disguised and fearing assassination) celebrated Christmas Day, 1918 (see pp. 223–24).

By the time of the first Russian imperial census of 1897, the population of Kem district, which was part of Archangel province (see Map 1), was just over thirty-five thousand. By 1907, it had grown to over forty-two thousand. About half of this population, living exclusively along the coast, was Russian; the other half, living mainly inland, was Karelian.[8] The White Sea Karelians subsisted largely from hunting and fishing, although by the later nineteenth century Karelian pedlars were conducting an active cross-border trade with Finland in furs and handicrafts. This brought wealth to a few of them, and the possibility of an education (in Finland) for their children. Long into the twentieth century, however, the majority of Karelians in this region existed in abject poverty, living in vermin-infested wooden huts (which could only be cleansed by an annual freeze-out), isolated for much of the year by dense forest, snow, bog or river rapids from the outside world, and with only the sparsest scattering of village teachers and field-doctors, as a result of which congenital syphilis and other infectious diseases were rife, as Woods describes in his memoir (pp. 169, 284) with vivid horror.

During the mid-nineteenth century, Finnish researchers began exploring White Sea Karelia, visiting villages like Ukhta (in Woods' phonetic spelling, Ouchta; in the 1930s, the village was renamed Kalevala), Rugozero and Panozero, and noting down the language, customs and oral traditions of the inhabitants.[9] Because of the relative absence of Swedish or Russian influence in this region, the northern Karelian people and landscape came to be seen as the source and essence of 'Finnishness'. The first professor of Finnish at Helsinki University, Matthias Alexander Castrén (himself of Swedish origin) travelled to White Sea Karelia in 1839, to be entranced by what he perceived to be 'a wholly new world' resonant with the hitherto 'lost' mythology of the Finnish nation.

At about the same time, Elias Lönnrot was collating folklore from village singers in the region as the basis for the epic Finnish poem, the *Kalevala* (the first edition of which he published in 1835).[10] Nationalist scholars such as Castrén and Lönnrot, creating and codifying a written Standard Finnish language derived from an assembly of closely interrelated Finno-Ugric vernaculars, drew eagerly on the 'pure' spoken language of the White Sea Karelians. Consequently the Finns came to perceive it as a dialect of their newly-created language rather than as a distinct tongue. White Sea Karelian is more or less comprehensible to modern Finnish speakers, whereas the Olonets Karelian 'dialects', with their heavily russified vocabulary, are nearly as unintelligible to Finns as they are to Russians.

In the late nineteenth century, Finland's new middle classes embraced the vision of Karelia as fount and repository of ancient national lore. The landscape and its people became a core motif of nationalist culture, exemplified by Jean Sibelius' music (not least, his *Karelia Suite* and symphonic poems based on *Kalevala* legends) and the graphic art of Akseli Gallen-Kallela.[11] The 'alienation' of eastern Karelia under Russia became a rallying cry of political nationalism. More radical patriots called for a sovereign 'Greater Finland', embracing not only Russian Karelia within its borders but extending as far east as the Ural mountains.[12]

The Finnish 'rediscovery' of Karelia prompted irredentist enthusiasts in the first decade of the twentieth century (often financed by Finnish lumber traders) to undertake cultural and religious propaganda and Lutheran missionary work across the eastern border.[13] On 21 October 1905, immediately after Tsar Nicholas II, as a result of the revolutionary upheavals of that year, conceded limited constitutional rights to his imperial subjects, three hundred White Sea Karelians, mainly wealthy traders and intellectuals living in Finland, assembled in the large village of Ukhta (see Map 2, p.144; in Woods' spelling Ouchta) to discuss the region's closer integration with Finland. A further two-week congress in January 1906 resulted in the establishment in August of the 'Union of White Sea Karelians', led by Karelian merchant Paavo Ahava, with the aim of promoting his homeland's cultural, economic and spiritual development under the benevolent auspices of its western neighbour.[14]

At the same time, the Russian Orthodox Church launched a forceful reaction against these Finnish-Karelian activities, organising religious schools with Russian-language tuition, missions and reading rooms.[15] Two extreme right-wing 'Black Hundred' organisations were founded in Karelia to conduct anti-Finnish propaganda. One pamphlet preached that the Finns were striving to 'separate our Karelian periphery from Orthodox Russia' by the 'fennicisation' (*ofineniia*) of Karelians (especially by converting them to the Lutheran heresy) and the promotion of 'jewifying' (*evreistvuiushchikh'*) political parties that supported autonomy for the border nationalities.[16] Another Black Hundred brochure published on the eve of war claimed that without intervention 'the border of inimical Finnish culture would have moved further to the east, threatening with its insidious influence the already successful russification of the neighbouring Karelians of Olonets province.'[17]

A cynical observer, especially one viewing reality from a Marxist perspective, might have suggested that Karelia's abundant forest resources represented more of a motive for these territorial claims and counterclaims than the immortal souls or cultural identity of the region's inhabitants. Western European powers had not failed to notice the region's economic potential, even if it had remained underexploited by domestic interests. The predominance of British capital in the North Russian lumber industry prompted Vladimir Lenin to quip in 1914 that Archangel served 'as an external market for England, not an internal market for Russia.'[18]

When the British-led expeditionary force landed in Murmansk in June 1918, driven at least partially by a concern for protecting national commercial interests, Karelia and the wider northern region had been cast loose from the Russian centre of power, itself convulsed by revolutionary chaos and incipient civil war. The territory, its resources and the allegiance of its population were all for the taking. During the next year, a group of Karelians based at Kem sought to assert, for the first time in their history, an identity and destiny separate from both Russia and Finland.

According to most accounts, that they did so was in large part owing to the 'exuberant' espousal of their cause by an 'enterprising' Irish officer who was appointed to recruit and train them for the Allied army. We next consider the context and course of British intervention in North Russia, before turning to Woods' controversial role in the unfolding of these dramatic, ultimately tragic, events.

★ ★ ★ ★

The primary objective of the Allied intervention in Russia following the Bolsheviks' take-over of power in October 1917 is still a contentious issue among historians.[19] Soviet and some left-wing studies have portrayed the three-pronged invasion, from Siberia in the east, Ukraine in the south and Murmansk and Archangel in the north, as a crude effort by the western imperialist powers to overthrow the new revolutionary Russian government, reinstate the tsarist regime and re-assert their own semi-colonial dominion over its territory and natural riches.

Other scholars have depicted it as developing from a reasonable and successful strategy by the Entente states to sustain an Eastern Front against the Germans after Lenin's conclusion of peace with the Kaiser by the Treaty of Brest-Litovsk in March 1918. These accounts propose that the Armistice of November 1918 left the expeditionary forces floundering for some months without direction or purpose. During this period certain particularly fervent anti-Bolshevik individuals, notably Winston Churchill (who was appointed as the British Minister of War on 10 January 1919) and some of the British commanders in Russia, committed their forces more heavily than ever planned in support of the 'White' Russians (those political and social groups opposed to the revolution), in the hope of dislodging the 'Reds' from power before the British and other Allied governments ordered their own withdrawal. In this view, the Allies never intended to launch a war against the Bolsheviks.

In fact, Allied objectives were from the start ill-defined, obscure and subject to continuous dispute both within and among the various national governments which participated in the intervention, in particular Britain, the United States, France and Japan. Furthermore, once these powers, with greater or lesser alacrity and enthusiasm, had landed their military forces in Russia in mid-1918, they found themselves drawn into a confused and many-sided conflict on the ground which permitted individual leaders to pursue semi-independent agendas dictated by their own prejudices, preoccupations and personal inclinations. As General Sir Charles Maynard, chief of the Allied forces in Murmansk, and Woods' commanding officer, wrote in 1928 of the North Russian intervention: 'those responsible for its conduct [...] found themselves enmeshed by a skein of political intrigue so complex and tangled that many of its threads [remain] yet unravelled.'[20] Only now, with the first publication of Woods' Karelian memoir, set alongside already published materials and new archival evidence, can we undertake to form a full picture of the complex, cross-cutting and often contradictory political manoeuvres that dictated the course of the intervention.

As early as 23 December 1917, the Allied Supreme War Council agreed to support anti-Bolshevik Russian forces assembling to oppose the new revolutionary regime. Lenin was considered to be controlled by the Germans, who had delivered him back to Russia in a sealed train in April to foment internal revolt with the slogan 'Peace, Bread and Land'. The Allies were most concerned by Lenin's promises of peace to the Russian people. On 15 December, the Bolsheviks agreed an armistice and opened peace talks with the Germans. The Kaiser immediately took the opportunity to commence the re-deployment of troops to the Western Front. Lenin also looked likely to cede to Germany many of the Russian empire's western borderlands, with their rich soils and coal seams, as the price of peace. These resources, and the populations of these territories, would reinvigorate the German war effort, and nullify the effects of the Allied sea blockade. The Allies' worst fears were seemingly being realised.

The Entente governments were also deeply troubled by Lenin's promises to the people of 'bread' and 'land', entailing the expropriation and socialisation of private property. The capitalist nations feared that the virus of revolution, if left to fester and propagate, would ultimately infect their own populations. From the start, then, there were influential Allied voices calling for intervention in Russia also to be directed at containing and cauterising the revolutionary ferment in the few cities and hinterland regions where it had taken root.

One of those lobbying hardest for action against the Bolsheviks was General Alfred Knox, an Ulsterman (born in County Down in 1870), who had joined the Royal Irish Rifles in 1891, and served as military attaché in St Petersburg from 1911 until October 1917.[21] In early 1918, after his return to London, he submitted a memorandum demanding immediate intervention on three fronts to bring about the internal collapse of the new regime before it could 'complete the robbery of the propertied classes in Russia' or incite 'general communist revolution in the world'.[22]

In the winter of 1918, it looked for a while as if Lenin's desire to export revolution had achieved its first victory, as pro-Bolshevik Finns took over the government of their country, which only a few weeks earlier – thanks to Lenin's nationalities policy – had obtained its sovereign independence from Russia.[23] After a brief but brutal civil war, the 'Red' Finns were defeated by anti-revolutionary 'White' forces. By March, the Whites had reinstated a parliamentary system under their own government. Some of the Red Finnish leaders fled to Stockholm, some to Petrograd (and thence to Moscow), while a few thousand hardcore fighters crossed the border to seek refuge in northern Karelia. Among this last group was Iivo Ahava, the radical twenty-two year old son of émigré Karelian merchant Paavo Ahava (founder of the 'Union of White Sea Karelians').[24] In the meantime, Germany had responded to a White Finnish call for assistance by landing about fifty-thousand troops in Helsinki under the command of General von der Goltz, who from early April proceeded northwards and eastwards, with his own forces and an equal number of White Finns, sweeping the country clean of revolutionary partisans.[25]

The German presence in Finland, however, ignited new anxieties among the British military planners, who believed that von der Goltz's progress might signify an intention to move into North Russia. There the Germans could seize the new railway built in 1916 between Petrograd and the Arctic coast to handle Allied deliveries of war supplies. They could also establish submarine bases at Murmansk (the newly-built port town at the northern terminus of the railway) or Petsamo on the Arctic coast, or at Kem and Kandalaksha on the White Sea, from where they could launch attacks against the Allies' crucial Atlantic supply convoys.[26] The German presence also endangered the vast quantities of raw materials and munitions which the Allies had landed in North Russia in recent years for equipping the Russian army and which were still in store at Archangel. The British wished to keep these supplies, as well as their own North Russian timber concerns, out of the hands of both the Germans and the Bolsheviks.[27]

In early March, the British landed a small contingent of 130 marines in Murmansk. These were reinforced by another 370 troops at the end of May under the command of Major-General F. C. Poole, a professional artillery officer with nearly thirty years service in the colonies, France and North Russia. In fact, the Bolshevik government itself, fearing Germany's predatory intentions before the conclusion of peace negotiations, had initially invited the Allies to defend Murmansk. Although Lenin and his Commissar for War Leon Trotsky withdrew their request when the Peace Treaty with Germany was finally signed in mid-March, the local Murmansk soviet (council) independently acquiesced to the Allied landings, for which Lenin first reprimanded them, and then declared them to be counter-revolutionaries. Henceforth, the Murmansk leadership had nothing to lose and all to gain by strengthening their relationship with the Allies. Through the mediation of Major-General Nikolai Ivanovich Zveginstev (in Woods' spelling, Zveginsiff), a former officer of the Tsarskoe Selo Hussar Regiment of Guards, whom the Bolsheviks had appointed to command land forces in the region, and Lieutenant-Commander Georgii Mikhailovich Veselago, the local navy commander, they pledged to lend Russian support to any Allied venture.[28]

Poole, a talented soldier but lacking in political subtlety and tact, addressed his Russian allies with the good-natured condescension of the British imperial officer conversing with friendly natives. As Maynard recalled in his memoir, Poole called Zvegintsev and Veselago 'Sviggens' and 'Vessels' respectively, and

> … treated them rather as a house-master might treat a couple of his prefects; giving them to understand that they must realise their responsibilities, and act for the good of the house, yet determined none the less that no action taken by them should run contrary to his own preconcerted plans.[29]

As Ullman has noted, this observation 'said as much about Maynard as it did about Poole.'[30] The Russians, as we shall see, did not take kindly to such an attitude, which did nothing to advance the cause of Anglo-Russian friendship or cooperation.

When the Allies agreed on 3 June to send a more substantial force to Murmansk, they hoped not only for the full cooperation of local Russian leaders but also to be able to mobilise local populations against the advancing German and White Finnish force (and, if needed, also against the Bolsheviks). At the least, the landing was intended to prevent von der Goltz's troops from taking the Murmansk railway and reaching the Arctic coast and, by pinning them down, to preclude their redeployment to the west. At best, there were hopes – fuelled by Knox's optimism in particular – that the North Russian force might link up with other anti-Bolshevik units, in particular the Czech Legion in central Russia and White Russian and Allied armies in Siberia, and raise substantial new armies from local populations, with a view to re-forming the Eastern Front.[31] To this end, a large part of the Murmansk expeditionary force was to transfer to Archangel, not only to guard the Allied stores there, but to clear the area in preparation for the arrival of reinforcements from the south and east whom they would then train and equip. Knox himself departed for the Russian Far East to set up a training mission and liaise with White Russian forces grouping in that region before advancing west towards central Russia.

The Murmansk force was code-named 'Syren' and came under the command of Major-General Charles Maynard, a forty-eight-year-old veteran of Burma, South Africa and France, who in typical English fashion was recruited to this mission over lunch at his London club. It was to the Archangel force, code-named 'Elope' and commanded by Poole (who also retained overall direction of the North Russian operation), that Woods was initially enlisted.

Officially, then, the intervention was motivated by 'purely military' considerations. 'The political destiny of Russia,' stated a War Office report of February 1919, 'was no immediate concern of the Allies except in so far as it might, in the event of an inconclusive peace, assist in the continuity and enhancement of German military power.'[32] Since the Allies considered the Bolsheviks to be lackeys of the Germans, however, Lenin's overthrow was of course an immediate concern, even if the post-Bolshevik destiny of Russia was to be left to the Russians to decide. Clearly, the purpose and priorities of the intervention were impossibly entangled from its inception, which did not augur well for its success. In retrospect, Maynard assessed the enterprise as having been 'somewhat in the nature of a gamble.'[33]

On 18 June, the Murmansk 'Syren' force, comprising around six hundred British infantry of the lowest category of physical fitness, with some machine-gunners and engineers, and approximately 560 members of the 'Elope' training mission, left the northern English port of Newcastle on board the *City of Marseilles* bound – though they were still ignorant of their destination – for North Russia. As Woods recounts (p. 150), the passengers included some Russians returning home to fight the revolutionaries. One of these mysterious characters was Maria Botchkareva, formerly commander of the 1st Women's Battalion of the Russian army, known as the 'Women of Death', who had been stationed in the Winter Palace in St Petersburg on the night of the Bolshevik take-over of power eight months earlier (they had been disarmed by Red Guards without a fight). The War Office was sending her with the 'Elope' mission to Archangel.[34]

The sea journey lasted five days, during which time the already debilitated men were weakened further by an outbreak of the vicious Spanish influenza, raging to pandemic proportions across much of the world at this time. Particularly hard-hit were the Indian stokers of the ship, although some observers (including Woods, who refers to them as Lascars, p. 152) attributed their deaths to self-starvation.[35] The Muslim holy month of Ramadan, which entails abstinence from food during daylight hours, fell that year in midsummer, when in high northern latitudes there was no darkness at all. (This had also presented a problem in 1916 during the building of the Murmansk railway, to which large numbers of Russian imperial subjects from Muslim regions of Central Asia had been conscripted.)[36] A combination of prolonged fasting and the 'flu would indeed have been deadly. Another consequence of the epidemic was that Woods volunteered while on the ship to transfer to Maynard's depleted 'Syren' force. It was this decision that would take him to Karelia.

* * * *

Murmansk, when Woods arrived, was a small, drab port settlement, mainly of wooden huts, recently built to handle Allied stores loaned during the war.[37] Another British officer described it as having appearance of 'a temporary town, erected by a cinematograph company for some Wild West drama complete with its cowboys and Indians'.[38]

Having established his headquarters in the town, General Maynard began to plan his course of action.

In addition to the marines already stationed at Murmansk, and those whom Poole had sent south down the railway to Kandalaksha and Kem, Maynard had at his disposal a Serbian battalion (which had fought its way north from Odessa), an 'armoured train' operated by a French military mission (which had arrived from the Rumanian front) and the Red Finns. Already in May two of the exiled Finnish socialists then in Moscow, Oskari Tokoi (a respected trade union activist and Prime Minister of the short-lived Finnish revolutionary government at the start of the year) and Otto Kuusinen had agreed to cooperate with the Allies against the Germans and White Finns.[39] Poole had then formed a Red Finnish Legion, which he placed under the command of a Canadian officer, Major R. B. Burton, and stationed at Kandalaksha.[40] Maynard understood, however, that the Red Finns would not fight against Bolsheviks troops, which were now advancing north from Petrograd up the railway. The Red Guards' forward units, under Commissar Ivan Dmitrievich Spiridonov, a former factory worker, had in fact already reached Kandalaksha.

As a priority, Maynard decided to reinforce Allied troops along the railway to prevent further Bolshevik progress and defend the vital strategic route against possible German incursions.[41] He also resolved immediately to mobilise and arm the local population of the region. On his first trip south, Maynard captured and expelled southwards a trainload of Spiridonov's troops at Kandalaksha, and then arrested Bolshevik officials in Kem.[42] On learning that the Reds had regrouped at Soroka (in Woods' spelling, Saroka) and were returning up the line, Maynard ordered the British officer commanding the Kem detachment, Captain L. A. Drake-Brockman, to prevent their northwards progress, and sent him a small number of reinforcements.[43]

On 3 July, at five o'clock in the morning, Woods and two fellow officers entrained with these reinforcements at Murmansk and headed south.[44] After an arduous trip, Woods arrived in Kem, where he witnessed Drake-Brockman's disarming of the Bolshevik garrison, and later took charge himself of an elaborate bluff to repel a renewed advance by Spiridonov, as described in the memoir (pp. 158–60).

At around the same time, in Woods' own words, he received 'a deputation of bearded brigands' who turned out to be Karelians asking for Allied aid against the Bolsheviks (p. 157). The Karelians also petitioned

Maynard for assistance to defend themselves against the Germans and White Finns.[45] Returning to Kem a short while later, Maynard acceded to the Karelians' request, which accorded with his own plans to raise local troops, and gave Woods the task of recruiting, training and leading a new Karelian Regiment (another officer, Col J. Jocelyn of the Suffolk Regiment, was charged with raising a Slavo-Britannic Legion from the local Russian population).[46]

Under an agreement signed on 6 July between the Murmansk soviet and General Poole, the Allies had undertaken to supply the region south as far as Kem with food, textiles, tools and military equipment. Woods was given responsibility for seeing these terms carried out with regard to the Karelian population. Significantly, though, Poole also formally stated in this document that Allied aims were limited to defending Murmansk against the German coalition and that 'the sole reason of concluding this agreement is to save the Murmansk region in its integrity [i.e. including Karelia] for a great Undivided Russia.'[47] Even as the Allies were arming the Karelians, they were denying them any possibility to assert their separate territorial identity or to pursue political self-determination.

On 9 August, Maynard returned again to Kem, where he interviewed Drake-Brockman and Woods, and reviewed the latter's five hundred or so Karelian recruits, newly-equipped, newly-drilled and newly-shaven.[48] By now Woods had also designed regimental badges (as he describes in 'Karelian Diary', pp. 164–65) in the form of shamrocks cut from the green baize of a damaged billiard table found in his headquarters building. That Woods, a Protestant Ulsterman, chose an Irish nationalist symbol to designate his men is significant. It certainly underlines that he bore no sectarian prejudice. It also perhaps suggests that he sympathetically acknowledged affinities between the Karelians and the indigenous Irish of his homeland – two poor peasant societies dominated by outside powers and denied the chance of self-determination.

Woods' sense that the Karelians had been treated badly by history coexisted with his assumption of British cultural superiority, and a belief – that had apparently survived his experience of the Western Front – that the 'enlightened standards of Europe' were inapplicable to 'a people so far behind in social development' (see 'Karelian Diary', pp. 176–77). In this scheme of cultural evolution, the Karelians, like the Irish, had matured from mindless infants into proud and wilful children. 'The Karelians,' Woods wrote in his memoir (p. 245), 'resembled the Irish in one respect – that they could be led, but never driven.'

His was the ideology of empire in its most contradictory form. On the one hand, it strove to bring enlightenment to the natives (even against their will) so that eventually they might discover and assert their own cultural life and identity. (Finns and Russians, of course, believed in this notion of progress as well, except that they believed that their benign tutelage would transform the backward Karelians into Finns or Russians respectively, rather than into modern Karelians.) At the same time, Woods' imperialist outlook, as articulated in his memoir, was inflected by a twilight *angst* that admired in these 'noble savages' a simple, natural code of morality, pure in both its kindness and its cruelty, that 'civilisation', for all its cultural and technological vainglory, had sacrificed.

In the second week of August, Maynard received intelligence of German-led Finnish troops massing along the Finnish frontier, seemingly intent on a move towards Kem and Kandalaksha (this information was gleaned from intercepts of Berlin-Moscow wire communications by British master spy Sidney Reilly, at this time operating in Moscow).[49] Maynard decided to despatch mobile columns of the Karelian Regiment and the Red Finns towards the frontier. At the same time, British and Serbian troops under Brig-Gen F. G. Marsh, commanding officer of the British 237th Infantry Brigade (to which all Kem district forces, including the Karelians, were now subordinated) would move against the Bolsheviks in Soroka in central Karelia to protect the railway and create a false impress of the Allies' overall strength. A small British seaplane carrier in the White Sea, HMS *Nairana*, would provide these forces with minimal air cover.

As Burton led the Red Finns westwards into the dense, rocky northern Karelian forests from Kandalaksha, further south Woods set off up the Kem river into the interior. Departing on 15 August, Woods had three columns under his direct command, by now comprising over one thousand men. Drake-Brockman, meanwhile, moved southwards into Olonets Karelia with a handful of British officers, the French mission with their armoured train, and about five hundred British and Russian soldiers, to raise volunteers in that area for a separate Karelian battalion.[50]

Woods' detailed and colourful account in his memoir of the Karelian Regiment's successful campaign against the German-led White Finns is corroborated by documents and communications in his own papers and the public archives. By 28 August, one Karelian column had engaged

White Finnish forces at Uskozero and re-occupied the village (see Map 2, p. 144). On 30 August, Woods confidently wired to Marsh from Panozero: 'heavy fighting in progress, will finish them tomorrow.' His scouts were reporting, however, that over two thousand White Finns were counter-attacking from the south-west. In the face of such strength, Woods wryly communicated his position and prospects to his commanding officer: 'Tomorrow will be within 96 hours from Kem IF not a casualty.'[51]

Despite being outnumbered, the Karelians pushed the White Finns back eastwards towards Ukhta, where the latter reportedly embarked on unbridled murder, looting and destruction.[52] A week later, Woods wrote from Uskozero to Marsh: 'I will commence my advance on Ouchta tomorrow or Tuesday. I am writing to the 'Nairana' to drop a bomb or two on that place on Thursday if they would like to – I don't mind if they don't, but they know the WF [White Finn] HQ and it would help.'[53] The Karelians engaged the White Finns at Ukhta on 11 September, and two days later Woods reported: 'The enemy suffered a severe defeat ending in a complete and disorderly rout.'[54]

Within a week, Woods had established a garrison at Ukhta, organised a system of intelligence along the frontier, and set off with four hundred of his force to sweep the remaining enemy troops out of the region.[55] Meanwhile, local Karelian men were flocking to the shamrock, so that by early October the Karelian Regiment numbered over 1,560 men, despite being hit hard by the influenza.[56] On 22 September, the Karelians surrounded those White Finns who had escaped from Ukhta, together with two hundred newly-arrived reinforcements, on an island near Voknavolok (at the south-western tip of the lake on which Ukhta is located, see Map 2).[57] Two weeks later, the White Finns attempted to break the siege. Most of them were slaughtered. On 13 October, Woods reported: 'There are no White Finns now in Karelia in the area under my command.'[58] Mopping-up operations against Bolsheviks and bandits, mainly in the southern area of White Sea Karelia, were taken keenly in hand by Captain Krugliakov's detachment of wild and ruthless Russian partisans.[59]

Already on 19 September, General Maynard had sent a despatch to Poole (who had transferred with 'Elope' to Archangel at the end of July) reporting the rout at Ukhta and noting: 'This success has been due mainly to the able leadership of Lieut-Col P. J. Woods, DSO, Royal Irish Rifles, coupled with the bravery and determination of the Karelian

Troops under his command, who are fighting to free their own homes of the invader.'[60] Ten years later, Maynard wrote in his memoir of the Karelian operations:

> Compared with even the smallest offensive in France or Flanders, they could be regarded as nothing more than a prolonged military picnic – a mere series of skirmishes, fought by half-trained local levies in a waste of forest, lake, and bog. But the results they achieved were, nonetheless, outstanding.

Their victory, he continued, 'speaks volumes for the grit and determination of the [Red] Finns and Karelians alike, and for the fine fighting qualities of British officers and NCOs who led them.'[61] Maynard recommended Woods for the CMG (Companion of the Order of St Michael and St George, conferred for service by British subjects abroad), which was duly awarded. In October, Woods was also promoted to the local rank of full Colonel.

The success of Woods' 'Royal Irish Karelians' (so named, of course, because of their regimental insignia) had a significantly positive effect on the morale of all Allied forces in North Russia, and also increased the rate of recruitment. By the end of the year, the Karelian Regiment numbered nearly four thousand men.

With winter drawing on, it was now time to think of other things. In early October, a new medical officer, Captain Muir, arrived in Kem (taking over from Captain Harrison), and established a regimental hospital, which served both military and local civilian patients.[62] There was also the question of how to maintain morale during the long months of northern darkness. Towards the end of the month, Marsh sent Woods a telegram from his Kandalaksha HQ: 'It is proposed to form scratch bands. What instrument players have you that will require instruments?' Woods' reply on the same day testifies to his high spirits at this time:

> … from enquiries already made upon this subject, information is as follows: 12 balalaika performers minus instruments – 4 melodian players minus melodians – 1 bugler no bugle – 2 church organists no organs – a paper and comb band of 9 exists but is not proficient. 1 Russian officer has a cornet but I have forbidden him to play within 1 mile of human habitation under DORA [Defence of the Realm Act]. McKilligan is a bagpipe performer but has no bags. The SNO [Senior Naval Officer] Kem Port

> reports that the consul performs on his flute. There are said to be several old fiddles in Kem, but I do not know this from personal knowledge ...[63]

While celebrating Woods' autumn successes, General Maynard was also preoccupied with the question of how to dispose his forces during the oncoming winter. As the first snows fell, the roads were becoming increasingly impassable. By late November, the White Sea would be iced over and the general would no longer be able to supply his Karelian bases from Murmansk or Archangel. He had already summoned the explorer Ernest Shackleton to advise on special winter preparations.[64] In his memoirs, Maynard represents himself struggling over the advantages and disadvantages of leaving his forces in the field as opposed to withdrawing north and cutting the railway line, before finally deciding that there should be no withdrawal.[65]

In fact, Woods' papers suggest that Maynard instructed him to take his troops north, and that the Karelians refused point-blank to abandon their homeland, since this would leave their families exposed to both White Finns and Bolsheviks. Woods, who had already developed a deep affection for his men, as is evident in his memoir, understood their refusal and also had no wish to abandon them. On 29 August, Maynard sent a long letter to Woods (reproduced in Appendix A in the present volume) explaining the 'broad military situation' and urging him to return first to Kem, and then north to Kandalaksha, with his forces. He reiterated that the Allies' chief opponent, and their reason for being in North Russia, were the Germans, not the White Finns or the Bolsheviks (who both of course presented a greater danger to the Karelians), and he warned Woods of the risk of remaining deep in the country during the winter, poorly equipped and with no hope of reinforcements or supply. 'You see,' he wrote, 'there are other things to think of besides the feelings of your Korelians [*sic*].'

Maynard conceded that if Woods could not persuade the Karelians to move north he could remain with them, though this was inadvisable 'unless you are prepared for an exceedingly rough winter as a sort of King of Karelia.' He continued:

> Do not think I don't sympathize with your position. I do most heartily but I have to take a broader outlook than you have to. If you can persuade your fellows to go to Kandalaksha, you will have done the best day's work of

> your life. Best of luck to you whatever course you are compelled to follow.'[66]

Woods evidently felt that Maynard's attitude was insensitive or condescending. He may have felt insulted at being asked to abandon his men, having (we may assume) made promises to them regarding the Allies' material and moral support. It would have been, for him, a matter of honour. It was what Buchan's hero in *Prester John* had called the 'white man's duty', that entailed 'recking nothing of his life or his fortunes', and in the fulfilment of which he exercised 'the gift of responsibility, the power of being in a little way a king'. (Woods was not the only British officer to assume the burden of royalty in this region. Lieutenant Peter Crawford of the Royal Scots was stationed with seven men in a Lapp village near Murmansk, where he was dubbed the 'King of Restikent'.)[67]

Maynard, however, was not a man to pull rank or be aggrieved by his subordinate's expression of injured pride or wilfulness. We do not have Woods' reply to Maynard, but we have the general's subsequent mollifying note:

> I can't believe you have really misunderstood the letter. In these times, which are somewhat troublous, and demand something out of the beaten line of routine, I feel that I'm entitled to a gentle leg-pull, even though I may be a GOC [General Officer Commanding]. Anyway, I try to be human and practical, and you may be quite certain that I should not have left you a free hand with your most excellent bandits had I thought you anything approaching a fool.[68]

This second note concluded by agreeing that Woods could remain in Kem district with his Karelians for the winter.

On the same day, Marsh issued a secret order confirming the commander-in-chief's forced decision not to withdraw the Karelian Regiment from Kem or to damage the railway. The order stipulated that this would leave Woods free 'to carry out his plan of clearing Southern Karelia' until the end of September, when he should return to Kem to take over command of the Kem garrison and district from Major Drake-Brockman (who was now commanding the recently recruited 4th Olonets Battalion of the Karelian Regiment in Soroka district, to the south), and to organise the evacuation northwards of the bulk of the non-Karelian Allied troops stationed in Kem (comprising most of the Serbian battalion, the Royal Marines, the French armoured train, some Polish soldiers, and half of Captain McKilligan's contingent of Royal Engineers).

Woods would remain for the winter at the Kem HQ of the Karelian Regiment, with Capt McKilligan and his remaining sappers, a unit of the Slavo-Britannic Legion, and some detachments of the new White Russian Murmansk Army also under his command.[69] The four thousand Karelian troops were distributed across their territory in four battalions, the largest being based in Uskozero and others at Voknavolok (charged with frontier defence), Siding No 44 (on the railway about halfway between Kem and Kandalaksha) and Soroka.[70]

Fluttering over the town hall at Ukhta, on the wireless mast at Uskozero, above the Kem barracks and (underneath the Union Jack) at Woods' Kem HQ was the Karelian Regiment's new flag – a green shamrock on an orange field, which Woods had designed himself (neatly combining the Irish unionist and republican colours), and had manufactured back in Bangor by his brother Robert (see 'Karelian Diary', pp. 186–87).

The White Russian officers of the Murmansk Army, newly arrived in Kem, clearly perceived Woods' sympathy for the Karelians, whom they considered with undisguised disdain, suspicion and hostility. Knowing that Woods was Irish, they also assumed that he was a nationalist firebrand intent on igniting separatist sedition among the men under his command. As we shall soon see, their reports to the White Russian military and political leadership in Archangel increasingly turned British generals and diplomats against the Karelian Regiment, and confirmed the suspicion of British HQ at Murmansk (already implicit in Maynard's gently admonishing communications of August and September) that Woods had 'gone native'. The scene was set for a winter of conspiracy, double-dealing and malicious rumour-mongering, colourfully described in Woods' memoir.

Chapter 7

King of Karelia (2)
Nationalist Dreams and Imperialist Realities, 1919

By the end of 1918 it was obvious to most observers and participants that the Allies' main enemy, so long as they remained in North Russia, was now the Bolshevik regime, even if no new policy had been formally announced. The Armistice of 11 November had removed the German threat. The White Finns' own persisting ambitions to annex Karelia had never been a concern. In early 1919 United States President Woodrow Wilson and British Prime Minister Lloyd George proposed to the Russian belligerents that they hold peace talks on the island of Principo in the Sea of Marmara. The Bolsheviks accepted the offer of discussions but the White Russians (with French backing) refused, destroying any hopes of a negotiated end to the civil war. Although the Americans continued to try to broker peace, the main question now facing the Allies was whether to stay in Russia in the hope of destroying the revolutionary state, or to disengage their troops (as many western governments, and most of their populations, desired) and lend the White Russians only moral and material support in their continuing struggle.

By this time, the Allies had already committed substantial forces to North Russia. The British and Canadians together had over thirteen thousand troops, many physically unfit, divided equally between

Murmansk and Archangel; the Americans had over five thousand soldiers at Archangel, fit but inexperienced and of low morale; the French had about 2,500 men scattered across both regions, including some very cold and angry African troops; and the Italians and Serbs each had about 1,200 soldiers along the Murmansk railway.[1] Drunkenness was rife among all these forces, and Bolshevik propaganda intensified their war-weariness and lack of purpose.

In addition, the Allies had recruited about 7,500 men from the local population, of whom the largest single contingent was the four-thousand strong Karelian Regiment. The White Russian 'Provisional Government of the Northern Region', which had been established at Archangel in August (and in October took control of the Murmansk region from the local soviet), had been unable to mobilise the far more numerous but apathetic Russian inhabitants of the region.[2] Many of the Russian peasants who were enlisted promptly mutinied or deserted. (After dissolving the Murmansk soviet, the White Russian administration placed Zvegintsev under investigation because of his earlier collaboration with the Bolsheviks. Woods suspected Zvegintsev both of dealings with the Reds and of staging several attempts to assassinate the British officers at Soroka, see 'Karelian Diary', pp. 205–08. Zvegintsev later escaped from Russia, and in 1928 was reportedly living in Paris.)[3] The White Russian Deputy-Governor of the Northern Region, Vasilii Vasilievich Yermolov (in Woods' spelling Yermoloff), who took over the administration of Murmansk and White Sea Karelia in October 1918, demonstrated particular ill-will towards Woods, in large part because of the Irishman's evident success in recruiting and training the Karelians.

Even if the Allies decided to evacuate their troops, they would need to establish a secure bridgehead to keep the Bolsheviks at bay during its implementation, and, ideally, to prevent them from immediately over-running the White Russian forces remaining after the withdrawal. This, paradoxically, could necessitate the despatch of reinforcements as a precursor to evacuation. In any case, the Allies were ice-bound until spring, so deferred taking any decision. They also needed time to prepare the handover of their own locally-raised forces – including the Karelians and the Slavo-Britannic Legion – to the White Russian army. The Russian commanders in the meantime sought to augment their own numbers by instituting conscription across a wider region.

The Allies also still hoped that Admiral Alexander Kolchak's White

Russian army in Siberia, to which Alfred Knox had enthusiastically attached himself, and which had made some advances, could press westwards far enough to join up with the White Russians in Archangel region, providing the strength first to safeguard an orderly Allied withdrawal and then, in conjunction with General Denikin's Volunteer Army in southern Russia, to defeat Bolshevik power. During the first half of 1919, therefore, Allied forces pushed south on the Archangel front (hindered more by mutinies of their own forces than by enemy resistance) and deeper into Olonets Karelia. By early summer, Maynard's troops in Karelia, with White Russian units, had reached the north-western shore of lake Onega (see Map 2, p. 144).[4]

In the meantime, there had been some changes in the structure of the British command. In October 1918, the tactless General Poole was replaced by Brigadier-General Edmund Ironside, who was only thirty-seven years old but already had a reputation as a brilliant infantry commander and deft political operator (even if he was inclined to make crudely disparaging remarks about all nationalities other than the English).[5] At the start of his career, Ironside had operated undercover in German South-West Africa (where he participated in a genocidal German campaign against native Herero tribesmen), and then served in South Africa, where he met John Buchan. The novelist was so impressed by the gigantic Englishman that Ironside became the model for Richard Hannay, dauntless hero of *The Thirty-Nine Steps* (1915).

After Ironside's arrival, Maynard's Murmansk HQ became independent of the Archangel command. In late September, Lieut-Col E. O. Lewin had taken over as Maynard's chief of staff.[6] This officer was close to the White Russian clique at Murmansk HQ, and hostile to Woods, whom he believed (according to 'Karelian Diary', p. 236) to suffer from 'a sense of superiority' which required him 'to be sat upon'. In December 1918, Marsh was invalided home. For four days, Woods assumed temporary command of the 237th Infantry Brigade (a very brief but creditable promotion that he does not mention in his memoir or *Who's Who* entry), until he was replaced first by Brig-Gen M. N. Turner of the 236th Infantry Brigade (which comprised Allied units operating north of Kandalaksha), and then Brig-Gen G. D. Price who arrived in mid-January (also with instructions from Lewin 'to sit upon Woods', p. 248) and held the brigade command until the evacuation.[7]

By summer 1919, the Bolsheviks had checked the westwards advance of Kolchak's Siberian army. In early June, Knox wired the War Office two variants for dealing with the new situation. Either the Allies should substantially reinforce Archangel and land fifty thousand troops in Estonia to advance on and take Petrograd and then to strike at Moscow, or they should demand that the Whites and Reds agree an armistice, then organise elections under external supervision for a Constituent Assembly to decide Russia's future political shape. This latter plan, Knox remarked, would be opposed both by the 'Jew Commissary' (i.e. Lenin's government, commonly – though incorrectly – believed to dominated by Jews) and by the 'useless bourgeois', but would be welcomed by ninety per cent of the population.[8]

The Allies, however, had already begun to formulate practical and more realistic plans to evacuate their restive North Russian forces later in the summer. To soften British public opinion towards the despatch of an eight thousand strong relief force to North Russia, Winston Churchill initiated a newspaper campaign boosting the operation's ease and success to date. On 3 April, *The Times*' Murmansk correspondent reported, for example, that 'there is no greater discomfort here than at Farnborough [in Hampshire, centre of military aviation construction and testing] – good food, entertainments and sport, with a spice of adventure in the form of a brush with the Bolsheviks.' On 8 April, he wired an article that was published under the heading 'Royal Irish Karelians. A Tale of Two River Amazons', which described, with several careless inaccuracies, the regiment's victory the previous year, its shamrock badge, and the award of the Military Cross to some Karelian women responsible for river transport (as Woods describes in his memoir, pp. 181–82).

Price's 237th Infantry Brigade was meanwhile pressing south to secure forward positions against the Bolsheviks in Povonets district of central Karelia (see Map 1). By early July, the White Russians in Murmansk and Karelia had still mobilised only about five thousand men (excluding the Karelians, whose separate history during this period will be recounted below). These Russian conscripts were placed under the command of General Vladimir Stepanovich Skobeltsin, who impressed Woods with his combination of clear-sighted fatalism and sense of duty (he is referred to as Victor Skobolcene, p. 209). Maynard shared this assessment: 'his quietness indeed was so marked,' the British general recalled of Skobeltsin in his memoir, 'as to lend an impression of habitual sadness – an impression, I think, not far removed from fact, for his country's sorrows were his own.'[9]

Although the White Russians were not yet up to strength, Maynard had already received definite orders for evacuation. The French troops left in early June, the Americans in mid-July. The evacuation of British and other Allied troops from Archangel was completed during September. At the same time, after a final push southwards towards Petrozavodsk, Maynard's Murmansk HQ transferred its own locally-raised forces to White Russian command and withdrew all remaining troops. The last British soldiers left Kem on 29 September, and Murmansk on 12 October.[10]

A month earlier, Churchill had announced in *The Times* that the Allies would evacuate all Russians who had helped them. Ironside expected around eighteen thousand applications in Archangel. In the event, the British took with them only about six thousand Russian refugees, the remainder opting to stay and fight.[11] Responsibility for the Russians who remained (most of whom fell victim to the victorious Bolsheviks early the following year), Churchill later wrote with undisguised bitterness, rested 'upon the mighty and resplendent nations who had won the war, but left their task unfinished.'[12]

In retrospect, Maynard considered the intervention to have largely succeeded in its aims. 'A mere handful of Britishers and Allies,' he wrote in his memoir, 'despatched to almost unknown Arctic wilds, had done more to assist in the overthrow of Germany than could have been accomplished by many times their number employed in any other theatre of war!'[13] The Chief of the Imperial General Staff (CIGS), Sir Henry Wilson, reviewing events in a memorandum to Churchill in December 1919, offered a soberer appraisal of the intervention (in which the British had sustained around one thousand casualties, including 41 officers and 286 other ranks killed). The main lesson to be learned, he concluded, was that, 'once a military force is involved in operations on land it is almost impossible to limit the magnitude of its commitments.' He added presciently: 'In the present state of world chaos it will surely be wise to bear this principle in mind …'[14]

★ ★ ★ ★

How did these events affect the Karelians and their national aspirations? The February 1917 revolution in Russia, which overthrew the tsarist regime and installed a Provisional Government pending nationwide elections to a Constituent Assembly (i.e. one that would decide Russia's future constitutional structure), opened new perspectives for many of the smaller border nationalities. For the first time, it seemed that the Karelians no longer faced an 'all-or-nothing' choice between Russian imperial domination or being swallowed up by irredentist Finland, itself intent on securing independent statehood. A liberal democratic Russia might offer the Karelians the chance to establish their own self-governing territory within its borders or even to secede (as, for example, demanded by the three Baltic states, each about a third to half the size of Karelia and barely more populous).

In July 1917, the newly-formed Ukhta district council drew up a draft constitution for a Karelian autonomous region within a Russian confederation, which it intended to submit in due course to the Constituent Assembly. The Ukhta council, which was neither pro-Finnish nor vigorously anti-Bolshevik, and understood the advantages of adopting a 'wait and see' policy, also proposed the distribution of state lands and forests to the people as a means of garnering popular support.[15]

After October, Lenin's new government dissolved the democratically-elected local councils. This seemed for the time being to foreclose any solution to the Karelians' aspirations based on territorial decentralisation. Such a turn of events might have pushed the Karelians back towards Finland, if White Finnish volunteers had not launched two armed raids in early 1918 into Olonets Karelia. The Karelians, who would not necessarily have refused Finnish backing for their own schemes of self-determination, regarded these incursions as blatant attempts at territorial conquest, and mobilised local forces to resist further encroachments.[16]

With the Allied landings in early summer, the Karelians hoped that they could attract sufficient material and political support to assert their right to autonomy or independence from both Russia and Finland. This ambition was wholly in accordance with the principle of national self-determination articulated in January 1918 by US President Woodrow Wilson in his fourteen-point programme drawn up as the basis of the peace conference which opened a year later in Paris.[17] The Karelians did not, of course, reckon with Poole's agreement of 7 July 1918 with the Murmansk authorities, concluded for the sake of pragmatism and without consideration of principle, by which he recognised the maintenance of regional territorial integrity and a 'great Undivided Russia' as the *sine qua non* of securing White Russian cooperation. Nor was this act of political realism the sort of argument that would deter Woods, pugnaciously principled as he was, in his desire to support those who had served him so well.

In late 1918, Maynard acknowledged that the Karelians' very success in military operations during the autumn was creating political difficulties. Having enlisted and fought for the Allies against the German-led White Finns, they now believed that the Allies owed them support, or at least an impartial hearing. The Allies believed that they owed the Karelians nothing, and continued to demand obedience, docility and service. They did not appreciate, as Woods did, that the Karelians 'could be led, but never driven'.

At the start of November, Maynard held a meeting in Kem with White Sea Karelian leaders (including Iivo Ahava, who had transferred from the Red Finnish Legion to Woods' regiment in early autumn). The British general afterwards reported to the Director of Military Intelligence in London that while the Karelians could be given responsibility for the 'maintenance and inviolability of the present frontier' (i.e. to resist further German or White Finnish incursions) he was not confident that they would fight on behalf of the White Russians against the Bolsheviks. He was possibly correct. Lenin's government, after all, had proclaimed a nationalities policy based on anti-imperialist principles, which offered the Karelians some hopes of winning concessions, whereas the White Russian leaders demonstrated nothing but arrogant intransigence towards the former empire's subject peoples.

Maynard cautioned that any attempt to bring about better relations between the White Russians and Karelians would most likely aggravate the latter's discontent. In other words, the Karelians were demanding terms for their continuing cooperation that he knew could not be met. Nevertheless, Maynard continued, 'if an allied withdrawal is decided upon the attempt must be made, as without Karelian assistance Russians on this side [are] not likely to be able to withstand [the] Bolsheviks.'[18]

The British commander-in-chief was correct that the White Russians and Karelians were irreconcilable. On the one hand, the Russians regarded any British dealings with the Karelians as 'treacherous' – the archival evidence demonstrates that Woods' tales of murderous duplicity on the part of the White Russian officers in Kem and Murmansk were not merely the product of an overactive imagination.[19]

On the other hand, the Karelians now embarked on pursuing their nationalist aims with yet greater vigour and resolution. In late January, a Karelian delegation gave Woods a handwritten letter addressed to 'His

Majesty the King of Great Britain' to be transmitted to the British High Command, then on to London (Woods reproduces the document in 'Karelian Diary', pp. 263–65, although he dates it to late February). It was signed by representatives of seven White Sea Karelian districts, by three Karelian officers of the regiment (Major Grigorii Lezhev – whom Woods refers to throughout his memoir as 'Gregori'; his adjutant Captain Petr Lezhev; and Captain S. Peterson), and by Iivo Ahava on behalf of the districts occupied by the Red Finnish Legion. It succinctly presented their dilemma, and proposed a solution:

> To live together with Russia, we cannot, and point blank refuse to do so. With Finnland [*sic*], which in a very low way attempted to govern our Home-land, after having robbed our villages, taking away our last penny, to be friends is an impossibility [...] We do beseech the British to take Karelia as a British Protectorate, as every Power is tearing Karelia to pieces.

Woods forwarded it to Price marked 'confidential' but without any commentary.[20]

A week later, on 7 February, Maynard arrived in Kem. (This visit and all subsequent events relating to the Karelians' political activities are described in Woods' memoir with an engaging immediacy, but a rather vague and confusing chronology). In the morning, the Allied commander-in-chief reviewed and issued decorations to the regiment (including to the two female rowers, mentioned above). Later he held a meeting with Price and Woods, during which he apprised them of the British government's outright rejection of the Karelian petition. Furthermore, rather than appeasing the Karelians, Maynard stipulated that Woods needed to prepare the regiment to be transferred to Russian command 'when the time for evacuation arrives'. To this end, Maynard proposed that Russian officers should gradually be introduced into the regiment. The first Russian to be appointed was Count Bennigsen, a former Imperial Guardsman, who joined Drake-Brockman's 4th (Olonets) Battalion during March, and whom both Maynard and Woods esteemed highly.[21]

The following night, Maynard, Price and Woods were joined for dinner in the officers' mess at Kem by a number of White Russian officers, including Yermolov, the Deputy-Governor of the Northern Region.[22] Six days later, on 14 February, Yermolov submitted a report on the Karelian Regiment to Governor-General E. K. Miller at Archangel. The

Karelians under Woods, he wrote, had a 'distinct Red Guard tinge [... that] evinced itself in acts of violence against Russian officials, the local and better off classes, and in a system of "terror" towards the bourgeoisie – the White [Finnish] Guards – the enemies of the Allies'.[23] He conceded that Woods and the other British officers had to some extent 'softened' the regiment's political radicalism. However, Woods and his men had allowed themselves to become 'unwittingly involved in the persecution of those [i.e. the White Russians] who are desirous of fighting with Red Guards and Bolsheviks.' Yermolov continued:

> Colonel Woods – a strong and energetic man – in his solicitude for his subordinates, has been carried away by his role. A new Karelian flag has appeared (orange colour with a shamrock – apparently Irish); with this same shamrock not only are the Karelian soldiers and officers decorated but also the British officers who lead the Karelians. The 'Karelian nation' for the first time in history has appeared on the scene, and the newly baked officers, among whom are two or three former teachers, are clumsily discussing questions which have been harped on for the last ten years by a gang of Pan-Finn agitators in Karelia. They have in their hand the authority of the British command, and are able to work upon solid reserves of food supplies.[24]

Yermolov described local Russians as 'openly perturbed' and admitted that they 'vent[ed] their dissatisfaction personally on Colonel Woods and his officers.' This in his view was unfortunate but understandable. Having become acquainted personally with Colonel Woods, he concluded, 'there can be no doubt as to his sincerity, and his mistakes are therefore all the more sad, as in them he evinces characteristic British persistency.'[25]

To remedy this situation, Yermolov proposed that recruitment to the Karelian Regiment should cease; that it should be prohibited from operating south of Kem district (he feared that otherwise it would spread its radicalism among the Olonets Karelians); and that in southern Karelia the 4th Battalion should be merged with Russian troops of the numerically weak Slavo-Britannic Legion in a new mixed regiment. In addition, the Karelian soldiers should no longer be granted the 'privileged' rations they had received as a unit of the Allied force: instead they would subsist on the same, smaller allowance as White Russian detachments.

At the same time, the new Kem council (*zemstvo*), elections to which the Russian authorities were in the process of organising, should ensure better provisioning of the northern Karelian population and undertake a programme of public works (road-building, hospitals, etc.). This approach would encourage Karelians to mix with Russians – presumably thereby weakening their false sense of national distinction – and give them a stake in the victory of the anti-revolutionary movement. Finally, the British officers of the Karelian Regiment should gradually be replaced by Russians, which would afford the Allied command 'a good way of extricating itself' from this irregular and awkward position.[26]

Yermolov had, according to a handwritten note at the foot of this document, obtained Maynard's agreement to all these points. This was confirmed in a meeting on 18 February between Yermolov and Col Lewin, Maynard's senior staff officer in Murmansk, a man already ill-disposed towards Woods and his Karelians. During March, Drake-Brockman's 4th Battalion of the Karelian Regiment was transferred out of Woods' command and attached to Slavo-Britannic Legion detachments operating in southern Karelia. The new mixed formation, named the Olonets Regiment, and comprising two battalions (one, confusingly, called the Karelian Battalion), was placed under Lieut-Col L. G. Moore, who reported directly to General Price.[27]

The Kem Karelians, meanwhile, were preoccupied seeking to advance not Bolshevism but their national cause. According to Woods' memoir, the delegation that had submitted their petition to him in late January had also asked his advice, 'as a private person and not in an official capacity', about their situation (p. 237). When Woods refrained from doing so, they had asked his permission to invite Oskari Tokoi, the former Finnish socialist premier who was now serving with Burton's Red Finnish Legion, to travel down the line from Kandalaksha and offer his expert opinion on how they should proceed. The Colonel agreed to this – a risky decision given that Maynard already had Tokoi, together with his fellow Red Finn Captain Verner Lehtimäki, in his sights as dangerous subversives (it is not clear whether Woods knew this before he acceded to the Karelian request; his memoir implies that he did not).[28]

The outcome of the Karelians' meeting with Tokoi – in Woods' attendance, according to his memoir – was a decision to hold an assembly of Karelian representatives later in the month. The meeting was convened by officers of the Karelian Regiment, Grigorii Lezhev and Iivo Ahava, and took place on 16 February in the regimental headquarters.[29] Ahava gave a rousing speech, reportedly written by Tokoi, demanding the right of self-determination, and international recognition and representation at the international peace conference which, at that very time, was gathering in Paris to discuss the new map of post-war European nationhood.

Maynard had been informed of the Kem meeting in advance, and had directed Brig-Gen Price to attend and read out a telegram from the commander-in-chief threatening to withdraw Allied assistance to the Karelian population should they pursue their separatist demands. Price did so, then delivered his own extended harangue. (Both texts are reproduced in Appendix B in the present volume). If the British generals addressed Russian leaders like school prefects, they treated the Karelians like miscreant pupils. The objective of the Allied intervention, Price stated, had been from the start 'the eradication and annihilation of the Bolsheviks' (this must have surprised some of his listeners) whose creed was 'anarchy and devastation'. The Karelians must participate in the anti-Bolshevik campaign, he continued, so as to win the favour of the White Russians, who after victory and the restoration of their empire might then be inclined to grant them some degree of autonomy. In the meantime, the delegates must return home and explain to their people that 'the peace, prosperity, and happiness of Karelia are only possible [...] through the restoration of a great, unified and free Russia.'

The Karelians were not swayed in their views either by Maynard's blackmail or Price's patronising arguments, which must have rung hollow given the open contempt and hostility demonstrated towards the local population by the White Russians. Instead, the Karelians voted in favour of Ahava's demands, and resolved to form a five-man National Committee – a provisional government – to prepare regional elections for a Karelian National Constituent Assembly which would decide on whether their country's destiny lay with Russia, Finland, or with neither. The National Committee was mandated to open negotiations with Karelia's 'neighbouring states' (i.e. Finland, the White Russian Provisional Government of the Northern Region, and Soviet Russia) to secure recognition of its independence, as well as to send two delegates to the Paris congress and to Principo island (should that conference take place) to obtain the commitment of the peace-making powers to its right to self-determination.[30] Major Grigorii Lezhev of the Karelian Regiment and his adjutant Captain Peter Lezhev (presumably brothers) were given a special mandate by the assembly to participate in the National Committee, and agreed to collaborate so as long as this entailed no conflict of interest with their military duties (this undertaking is significant in view of the accusations made later against the Karelian officers).[31]

To just about everyone except to Woods and the Karelians themselves, these demands seemed both ridiculous and dangerous. The White Russians professed to believe that the Karelian assembly heralded an imminent pro-Bolshevik uprising in the district, to be initiated and led by the regiment itself. Certainly it was in their interest to represent the Karelians' activities to the British in such a light. While Maynard remained unconvinced that the regiment was intent on revolt, and Woods strenuously and repeatedly denied this, other Allied commanders and officers were inclined to believe that it was the case.

On 5 March, Drake-Brockman wired Price at 237th Brigade HQ at Kem stating that 'Commdr Bataillard, the French Intelligence Officer, forwarded a report [probably Yermolov's, which was doing the rounds at this time] saying that the Karelian Regt was in his opinion not trustworthy and that measures should be taken to render harmless any rising which might take place.'[32] Murmansk HQ had evidently reached the same conclusion, and Price immediately summoned Woods to instruct him to disarm his regiment. The British military archives do not record what happened next. Woods' memoir, however, relates how he convinced his commanding officer that the story of the Karelians' planned revolt had been concocted by White Russians as a ruse to enable them to murder the British in Kem and then lay the blame on the Karelians. Price agreed that the Karelians, so long as they were seen to be disarming, could retain all their weapons except their Lewis guns (a light machine gun operated by two men, widely used by the British army). Woods devised a ploy to ensure the Karelians retained even these (the first time, Woods states in his memoir, p. 251, that he had 'deliberately disobeyed in spirit [...] a direct order from superior authority'), and then disposed his troops with their machine guns so as to prevent the Russians' planned attack.

The British government had already given its unequivocal answer to the Karelian petition through Maynard. At the start of March, the Foreign Office sent Francis Lindley, their North Russian chargé d'affaires, to Kem to reinforce the message. According to Woods' memoir (p. 266), Lindley greeted him briskly at the station with the words: 'Well, Colonel Woods, is this another Irish leg-pull?' The diplomat reiterated that the British government would not accept Karelia as a protectorate, before proceeding to a meeting with the Karelians which Woods did not attend, as he had 'no wish to witness [their] disappointment'. Lindley also advised Woods that the Karelian petition 'had occasioned much annoyance to some of our allies' and that Woods himself was held responsible as the instigator of 'the British plot to seize Karelia'.

While we know that part of this accusation was pure White Russian fantasy – Britain never entertained any 'plot' to seize territory in the region – it is not so clear what part Woods played in the Karelians' political activities in this period. Was he indeed their instigator, as some perceived, or merely a passive bystander? His memoir makes it evident that he was wholeheartedly in sympathy with the Karelian aspirations – he had become towards them 'pitiful and kindly [having] learned much of the untold grievances of the natives', to cite again the hero of Buchan's *Prester John*. He believed and hoped that their petition for the status of a British protectorate might succeed not least because of the land's timber, minerals and ores, which he understood might be enticing to the empire, p. 266).

According to Woods' account, however, he maintained a strict professional impartiality when acting as mediator, offering advice to the Karelians (for example, to organise an electoral system, form a National Savings bank and cooperative trading society, p. 271) only in a personal capacity. That his first loyalty was to the British command is not in question. When during the Ukhta campaign of August to October 1918, Woods learned that some Karelians had met in Panozero to discuss political demands, he advised them earnestly to be cautious in their aims and not let themselves be distracted by their longer-term ambitions from battling the White Finns and Germans. He understood that this was his immediate priority, and theirs.[33]

However, the fact that Woods did blatantly 'disobey in spirit' the order to disarm the Karelians in March the following year, and indulged in creatively reinterpreting instructions on several other occasions (for example, when told to arrest Tokoi at the time of the Finnish politician's visit to Kem, p. 239), suggests that perhaps he did not always maintain the distinction between his professional and personal roles. This also lends credence to other accounts which portray Woods as playing a more active and constructive part in the development of the Karelians' nationalist aims.

We have already encountered Yermolov's opinion that Woods had been 'carried away by his role' and that he was now demonstrating 'characteristic British persistency' in refusing to be budged from his misguided position. It is quite likely that Yermolov also believed, as Lindley intimated, that if Woods was encouraging the Karelians in their 'half-baked' nationalist ambitions, it could only be at the behest, or with the connivance, of the British government, even if the Deputy Governor had enough tact not to reveal these suspicions in the report he submitted to Miller, which was translated and circulated among British military and diplomatic officials, eventually reaching the Whitehall desk of British Foreign Secretary Lord Curzon.

Other White Russians were more forthright in their accusations. Vladimir Ivanovich Ignatiev, a left-wing anti-Bolshevik, and Minister of the Interior in the Russian Government at Archangel until August 1919, recalled a few years later in his memoirs (written in a Soviet prison, and then published in a Soviet journal):

> In Karelia, the English organised a wild adventure – an English colonel in command of regional military forces arranged a secret congress of Karelians and, playing on their national feeling, carried through a resolution on independence .... It was obvious to all that the English were carving out their first colonial bridgehead in our North. We protested and disrupted their plans.[34]

Ignatiev's memoir, of course, might be dismissed as a typical Soviet re-writing of history, as well as an exercise in self-exculpation, shifting the focus from his own role to the devious English imperialists (evidently successfully, as he was freed from prison in 1922 on grounds of having fully 'broken with his counter-revolutionary past').

However, General Vladimir Vladimirovich Marushevskii, former Russian Imperial Guardsman and commander-in-chief of the White Russian armies in Archangel and Murmansk from November 1918 to August 1919, had a very different political perspective and wrote his memoirs in the late twenties in emigration, yet offered a similar account.[35] Marushevskii (whom we shall meet again) denied the very existence of a distinct Karelian people among the Russian population of the region, considering 'Karelian nationality' to be a brazen British 'invention' and the population's desire for 'self-determination' to be a British initiative, based on the arrogant inability of the 'proud sons of Albion to imagine the Russians in any way other than as a small, savage tribe of Indians or Malays or the like'. The Russian general was evidently still smarting at the memory of how he had been treated:

> The English responded to any Russian views, even those pronounced by people of the highest rank in imperial Russia, with benevolent condescension, back-slapping and that typical English joviality that makes interlocutors wonder if they are dealing with a very clever and cunning person or with a complete simpleton. The outcome of this Russian-English exchange of opinions was always the same. The English always did everything in their own way, and always met with failure.

In just such a fashion, Marushevskii continued, the English dismissed Russian objections to the formation of a Karelian military unit. The British armed, clothed and fed the Karelians as if they were part of the British army, with the only difference that the newly enlisted peasants wore bronze shamrocks on their caps (he also noted that the new Karelian flag was a shamrock on an orange background). 'It is impossible to imagine,' he concluded, 'how much political intolerance, strife, conflict and embarrassment this formation brought to the region.'[36]

It is clear from the British military records that Price and Lewin considered Woods a thorn in their sides as far as maintaining a workable political relationship with the Russians was concerned (and during the long dark winter, there was little other than politics to occupy them). Maynard, as we have seen, had a soft spot for Woods, and seems generally to have given him the benefit of the doubt – his memoirs are silent on the extent or nature of Woods' political activities.

British diplomats were less sympathetic but, predictably, more euphemistic in their condemnations. A Foreign Office official passing through Murmansk and Kem in March 1919 reported back to London that Woods was an 'enterprising' officer who had 'done much to foster the national spirit' of the Karelians, not least by designing an emblem and flag for them.[37] In this context, 'enterprising' evidently connoted the quality of being energetic, creative and independent in a manner specifically designed to embarrass and irritate diplomatic sensitivities.

Lindley, forwarding Yermolov's report to Lord Curzon, commented that it 'ascribe[d] recrudescence of this old [pro-Bolshevik] agitation to influence of Col Woods and other British officers' (though in fact Yermolov had written that Woods and his subordinates had done something to 'soften' the regiment's political radicalism). He also noted that Yermolov held Woods responsible for preventing Russian officers from carrying out their duties in Karelia.[38]

Lindley had evidently formed his own opinion of Woods on the basis of discussions with the White Russians and Maynard, as well as his own visit to Kem at the start of March:

> Woods [he wrote to Lord Curzon] appears to have attained considerable influence over [the Karelians], and to have done much to foster national aspirations amongst a people who have up to now always considered themselves an integral part of Russia [...] The exuberance of Colonel Woods has caused some uneasiness amongst the Russians, but General Maynard assures me that he has issued strict instructions to him to cease his political activity, and to discourage separatist tendencies which at present appear to be confined to a small number of the inhabitants of the district.[39]

If Maynard indeed felt it necessary to order Woods to desist from 'political activity', this suggests that the commander-in-chief did feel that his officer had overstepped the bounds of professional military conduct. In the light of Lindley's testimony, the fact that Maynard did not mention this episode in his memoir also gives rise to a suspicion that he thought Woods' activities were not altogether appropriate, but wished to maintain a benevolent silence on this matter so as not to malign someone whom he held in high regard for his military competence. On the other hand, Maynard might, of course, have issued such instructions merely to appease his irate allies or to soothe Lindley's diplomatic sensibilities. It could finally be argued that the White Russians and British generals and diplomats all belonged to the same Murmansk 'clique' (as Woods called it, p. 248), and therefore their separate views cannot be taken as corroborative of each other.

The left-wing Finnish politician Oskari Tokoi, however, offered a similar interpretation of Woods' role in his memoirs, although he viewed events from an entirely different political perspective and formed his interpretation of events separately, having been Woods' guest for two days in Kem in early February (without the knowledge of Murmansk), and again briefly in April. He was also well aware that the British had no plot to seize Karelia, and that the Karelian nationalist movement had a prehistory of which most of the White Russians and British were wilfully ignorant, and so was a better informed and less biased observer. Tokoi's account (written in the 1950s) states: 'The [February] Assembly's proposals and Karelian independence were [both] backed by the commander of the Karelian Legion Wood [*sic*], who was an Irishman and an ardent supporter of Ireland's independence.'[40]

Tokoi's characterisation of Woods as an Irish nationalist is curious. The Finn was an astute and highly intelligent politician, and it is unlikely that he would have misinterpreted Woods' own political beliefs as represented to him at the time, although he might well have misremembered them when writing his memoirs over three decades later. It was presumably the Karelian shamrock, widely recalled in the 'folklore' of these events, which prompted Tokoi to associate Woods with Irish separatism. It must be assumed that the Ulsterman himself was well aware that this inference would be made when he designed the regimental cap badge and flag, and did not care.

While Woods' assertions in his memoir that he did no more than passively advise the Karelians are doubtless sincere, it is evident that his attitude and behaviour were interpreted differently by others, both at the time and later. If Woods actively inspired and promoted the Karelian cause, which any dispassionate observer, however noble and romantic they believed it to be, should have realised was also hopeless, then he shared responsibility for the consequences of its failure. Perhaps Woods' vocal indignation in subsequent years at what he perceived to be the arrogant, amoral, treacherous and hypocritical behaviour of the British ruling classes was fired by a nagging awareness of his own unwitting complicity in the small nation's downfall. Probably Woods felt that the imperial elites had also betrayed his own imperialist ideals.

★ ★ ★ ★

Woods' memoirs are especially foggy on the sequence of events over the next half-year until the evacuation, as he fought an increasingly bitter and ultimately unsuccessful rearguard action against subversion of his regiment, from without and within, until through a combination of conspiracy, circumstances and his own forthright stubbornness he finally, once again, lost his command.

The Karelians, doggedly unwilling to accept the official British rebuttal of their earlier petition, had sent the minutes of their February meeting to Maynard early the next month to demonstrate that their political activities were not mutinous. After meeting Yermolov on 11 March, Maynard replied to the Karelians with a letter rejecting their claim for self-determination as 'preposterous', refuting each of their demands and reiterating his belief that 'owing to its underdeveloped condition Karelia cannot exist as an independent state at the moment.'[41]

According to Maynard's memoir (which confuses the chronology), Yermolov had argued that the Karelian ringleaders should be arrested and punished immediately, but the British general had dissuaded him from any drastic action, believing that it would certainly prompt mutiny. He proposed that Yermolov restrict himself to giving the Karelian leaders a stern reprimand and warning instead.[42] Yermolov then headed to Kem, where he subjected the Karelian National Committee to a violent scolding, which (according to Woods' memoir, p. 271, also misdating this encounter) included telling them that they were 'mutinous swine, dogs of no pedigree and that the whole breed would be shot.'

Reconciliation was obviously still impossible. Later in March, the Karelian National Committee sent a long document to Maynard (again via Woods) pointing out quite justifiably that 'the contents of [the general's] letter hardly appear to be founded upon principles either of democracy or of the autonomy of individual races; although the Allied Governments have solemnly declared that these principles are the basis of their present policy' (see 'Karelian Diary', pp. 267–70).

The National Committee then addressed each of the points the commander-in-chief had made in his letter. They stated that the Committee's members had received the democratic mandate of the local population; that their requests for representation at Paris or Principo had been in accordance with the declared terms of reference of these meetings; that they had never had a say in the establishment of the White Russian Provisional Government of the Northern Region or appointment of the Deputy Governor (and, by implication, considered these authorities to be illegitimate); and that the White Russians were deliberately excluding the Karelian population from the upcoming elections to the new Kem regional council, and from the council itself, by decreeing that only the Russian language was to be used for notices and proceedings. The Karelians no longer desired anything from the Allies, they concluded, except to be left to pursue their objectives unhindered, and that the Allies should not support the White Russian imperialists.

Matters had reached stalemate. Maynard, however much he felt Yermolov to be 'too frankly unpropitiatory' on the Karelian question, could not afford to antagonise his White Russian colleagues, on whose continuing cooperation the success of the British withdrawal depended. The Karelian soldiers at Kem, meanwhile, were making clear their extreme unwillingness to be placed under the command of Russian officers. Further south, the Olonets Karelians, according to Drake-Brockman, were now 'bloody angry' with the Kem regiment, whom they no longer trusted to fight off the Red Guards advancing from Petrograd. The southern Karelians were now considering inviting the White Finns back into their country to help them repel the Bolsheviks.[43] The Red Finns at Kandalaksha, awaiting the outcome of negotiations between the British and Finnish governments about their repatriation, were becoming increasingly restive. In Murmansk, the White Russians continued to voice their intransigent opposition to all Finns, both Red and White, and to all Karelians, as well as squabbling amongst themselves. A difficult situation was getting rapidly worse.

In late March, Maynard received reports, doubtless originating in Yermolov's staff headquarters, that the Karelian Regiment at Kem was planning a pro-Bolshevik uprising on 10 April to coincide with a Red Finnish mutiny at Kandalaksha and an uprising in Murmansk.[44] He was also told that the Karelians (presumably those in the south) were intending to stage a revolt and to proclaim their separation from Russia and incorporation into Finland, backed up by Finnish forces which were known to be massing on the border.[45] Facing such a complex threat, Maynard reinforced potential trouble-spots with reliable troops; in the event, no uprisings occurred.[46]

Maynard also interviewed Tokoi and Lehtimäki, the Red Finnish leaders, who agreed to restrain their men from any irresponsible action. In return, the British general promised free passage for any Red Finn who wished to travel south to join the Bolsheviks (many, including the two leaders, took up this offer; Woods reports their transit through Kem in his memoir, p. 251). Most of the remaining Red Finnish soldiers returned to Finland in September.

How close the Finnish Legion and Karelians were to revolt on 10 April is open to question. In Archangel, British diplomat Lindley thought that Maynard's belief in an imminent uprising was alarmist and 'panicky', the general's perception distorted by his enfeebled mental and physical condition.[47] There is some evidence that the stridently pro-Bolshevik Lehtimäki had been planning some form of action, but was dissuaded by the more politically-minded and circumspect Tokoi. According to one Red Finnish memoir source, Lehtimäki had hoped to cooperate with the Karelians, and communicated with Captain Ahava regarding a possible coup, but had found his old comrade and the regiment determinedly faithful to the British.[48] This vindicates Woods' repeated insistence, at the time and in his memoirs, that the Karelians at no point plotted mutiny, and that any doubts as to their loyalty originated in the White Russians' campaign of black propaganda against him and his men.[49]

Even in the absence of any proof of disloyal intentions, the White Russians embarked on mass arrests of suspected Bolshevik agitators and sympathisers among the Finnish and Karelian soldiers and population. In what was plainly an act of provocation related to this campaign of repression, Lieutenant E. Bogdanov, a White Russian officer in Kem, complained to Woods on 12 April that Ahava had behaved towards him in an insubordinate and rude manner, and demanded punitive action be taken against the Karelian officer. Woods investigated, and decided that a 'difference of political opinion' underlay the conflict. To avoid escalating an already tense situation, he recommended that Ahava rejoin the Red Finns, and accompany them south. On 22 April, Captain Ahava was given civilian clothes and escorted to the train.[50] A few days later, a group of Serbian soldiers acting on White Russian orders, waylaid Ahava on his journey and killed him.[51] Whether Woods came to know of the murder at the time or later is not know – he does not mention this affair in his memoir at all.

Despite Woods' reiteration to Murmansk of the Karelians' loyalty, *The Times* published a report on 8 April implicating his regiment in a rumoured mutiny. By strange coincidence, the very next day the newspaper ran the laudatory tale of the 'Royal Irish Karelians' mentioned earlier, generated by Churchill's public relations campaign before the despatch of a relief force. As Woods describes in his memoir (p. 257), the Karelian Regiment protested to him about the first report, and he himself wired Maynard asking politely for an official retraction. When the commander-in-chief prevaricated, Woods sent him a much blunter cable: 'As the report published was official from the WO. I assume that the WO and public believe my command to be out of hand and disloyal' (p. 258). Thereupon, Maynard sent the War Office a statement affirming the Karelians' loyalty, although hedged with phrases indicating that he did not share Woods' absolute faith in the regiment:

> Undoubtedly there were many in this regiment who would have been ready to throw in their lot with Finns had [the] latter started a successful uprising, but as matters turned out they were denied an opportunity. To all

> outward appearances, Karelian Regiment as a whole stood by us, and they all affirm now that I have no soldiers more loyal than themselves. They state that having loyally stood by us at a critical time they now bitterly resent charge of attempted mutiny. This is also felt by all British officers of the regiment.[52]

On 29 April, *The Times*, doubtless to the further confusion of its readers, reprinted a War Office statement under the heading 'Staunch Karelian Allies'.

The White Russian campaign of disinformation and persecution took its toll on the Karelian Regiment. Despite their heartfelt loyalty to Woods, men began to desert in increasing numbers, especially as summer drew on and it became increasingly likely that the regiment would soon be transferred to Russian command. By summer, very few of Woods' original recruits, those who had participated in the previous year's successful campaign, remained in the regiment. During April and May, as mentioned earlier, Price's forces advanced south to secure a sound bridgehead against the Bolsheviks on the northern shores of lake Onega. The Olonets Regiment participated in this operation (during which two of Woods' former officers, Major Drake-Brockman and Lieutenant Muir, were killed).[53] Murmansk did not, however, trust the Karelian Regiment at the front.

On 3 May, Woods was given temporary command of the newly-created Kem Military District; this was made permanent on 11 May.[54] The appointment was evidently intended to soften the blow of what followed, for on 20 May Maynard issued Syren Order No 31, decreeing the 're-organisation' of the Karelian Regiment. The document, issued under the signature of Maynard's second staff officer Major P. J. Mackesy (who had conducted a tour of Karelian units in February, and unlike his senior colleague Lewin was well-disposed towards Woods), acknowledged that the Karelians had acquitted themselves well the previous year against the Germans and White Finns, but noted that 'the conditions which existed when the first volunteers [...] enlisted having now completely changed, the Regiment as a whole is not fulfilling any purpose which justifies the large expenditure entailed.'

The priority now was to ensure that Bolshevism was 'crushed', and the regiment was being re-formed in order

> to enable those Karelians who have the best interests of their country at

> heart to prove that they are ready to take their share of restoring law and order, and to enable them in years to come, when the reconstruction and remodelling of Russia is being carried out, to point with pride to their share in bringing about this desired end.[55]

In place of the regiment's existing three fighting battalions (the fourth, it will be recalled, having already been merged into the Olonets Regiment in March), only one Karelian Volunteer Battalion would be employed on active service, the other units being reformed as Pioneer and Garrison Guard companies, a Frontier Guard and an unarmed Labour Battalion. These would only be recruited in White Sea Karelia (all Karelians enlisted in the south being sent to the Olonets Regiment), and would receive Russian army rations. The order was to come into force on 30 June.

The truth, as Maynard conceded in his memoir, was that the Karelian Regiment was being 'disbanded' because it was no longer trusted.[56] The fact that Woods retained his command of the new regiment, and was gazetted full Colonel (i.e. his local promotion of the previous year was formalised by publication in the *London Gazette*), did nothing to console him, or to reassure the handful of new men he managed to enlist to replace the original volunteers. The posting to the regiment of new British officers, who had just arrived with Churchill's relief force and were ignorant of North Russian conditions, also did nothing to improve matters. Nor did an escalation of Bolshevik propaganda among the local population and the regiment.

In early June, a newly arrived Royal Air Force (RAF) officer assaulted a Karelian soldier, then tried to have him locked up. The Karelian troops protested, and further trouble was only avoided when Woods was summoned and he promised to investigate the matter. Even then, the Volunteer Battalion 'refused to obey the order to march back to barracks until Colonel Woods returned and explained to them through "Gregory" [Major Grigorii Lezhev] that orders as such had to be obeyed.' The Karelians evidently still placed a high degree of personal trust in their commander. He in turn was still confident that, given a little time, he could overcome the regiment's present difficulties.[57]

Woods undertook several measures to achieve this. First, he issued a confidential circular to all British officers in the district admonishing them to maintain their own discipline and decorum as an example to local troops. A British officer should not, for one thing, walk in public with his hands in his pockets; nor should he, when walking with a lady, 'be so much engrossed with his companion's looks and conversation that salutes of passing soldiers are ignored.' He should also endeavour to restrain himself and his companion from all physical displays of affection, since such behaviour 'merely excites ridicule and not the envy of onlookers.'[58]

Second, Woods took steps to counteract Bolshevik agitation among the Karelian volunteers. The source of this new disturbance was suspected to be US Navy Admiral Newton A. McCully's flagship, then moored at Popov island at the mouth of the Kem river.[59] On 19 June, Lieut-Col Meiklejohn, one of Maynard's intelligence officers, accompanied Woods and his Russian interpreter Lieutenant N. Mende to interview the Admiral, who gave them permission to cross-examine his crew. (Both Maynard and Ironside had intelligence services under their command. Col C. J. M. Thornhill, whom Woods mentions frequently in his memoir, was the Head of Allied Intelligence at Archangel.) Woods had brought along a Karelian soldier to point out those responsible for stirring up trouble. 'One man was strongly suspected,' records the General Staff War Diary, 'but no action was then possible as the Karelian, who seemed much frightened, refused to identify the man.' Nevertheless, the Admiral agreed to cooperate in investigating Russian-speaking Americans in the ships under his command.[60] This episode is also recounted in Woods' memoir (pp. 277–78).

Allied HQ planned to despatch the Karelian Volunteer Battalion to central Karelia in early July to prepare for action against the Bolsheviks. At the start of the month, however, Woods was still concerned about the indiscipline of his men. On 2 July, he sent Maynard a telegram attributing their continuing high rate of desertion to the agricultural season and Bolshevik propaganda, and requested that rations for his soldiers and their dependants should be increased and distribution improved.[61]

In private, Woods attributed the Karelians' dissatisfaction also to the attitude of the new commanding officer of the Karelian Volunteer Battalion, Lieut-Col H. S. Filsell. Woods describes the conflict in his memoir ('Major Filsell was in many respects an excellent officer [...] but ten years' service in the King's African Rifles [...] did not fit him to command these men of the Arctic', p. 276), but the bitterness of their feud and its consequences emerge more clearly in his private papers and the military records.

On 2 July, Woods sent Filsell a forthright letter (reproduced in

Appendix C in the present volume) disparaging the condescension shown by the new British officers towards the Karelians. 'I know what they can do,' Woods wrote with evident fury, 'and if treated as "White-Men" [they] will act as such, better than many other men who have had a better chance.' He especially singled out Captain Nikolai Rogiev (whom Woods mistakenly refers to his memoir as Nicoli Petroff), one of the veterans of the Ukhta campaign, for his experience of forest fighting, his 'extraordinary brilliancy' in military leadership and his 'letter perfect' knowledge of the Russian Drill Book. 'Therefore,' Woods ended sharply, 'if you persist in treating him as an ignorant native – why, you are wanting a little in brains yourself.'[62]

On 5 July, the Karelian Volunteer Battalion was assembled on the parade ground in Kem to be addressed by Generals Maynard and Marushevskii, the White Russian commander-in-chief. 'I cannot understand,' declared Marushevskii, 'how you as men have the impudence to believe that the Allies will find clothes and pay you, that they will fight in our country for you, while you, like cowards, will do nothing but loaf about.'[63] Maynard berated the Karelians no less harshly, calling them 'ignorant fools' and a 'laughing stock', and reminding them that deserters faced the death penalty (Maynard's speech is reproduced in Appendix D).

It must have been difficult for Woods to listen to the two senior officers lambasting his Karelians, even if the congregated men were largely new recruits, and no one was openly suggesting that their current discontent had anything to do with his own involvement in political schemes during the winter. Maynard was sensitive to Woods' feeling. He had resolved, he told the men, to give them one more chance, 'chiefly for the sake of Colonel Woods who has worked heart and soul on your behalf for a year, and who is bitterly disappointed at your conduct.' Those men who did not wish to remain under arms could surrender their weapons and go home. Those who left, however, would no longer receive either military or civilian food supplies and would immediately be liable for conscription into the White Russian army. As the prospect of transfer to Russian command was one of the main causes of unrest among the Karelian soldiers in the first place, this hardly represented a desirable alternative. The Karelians were once again caught in an impossible situation.

Maynard's appreciation of Woods' dismay is also evident in a gentle note he penned to his subordinate three days later, which is worth quoting in full for the insight it offers into the characters of both men:

> My dear Woods, I'm most awfully sorry to hear you are so seedy, and I do hope you'll be all fit again shortly. I know you are feeling this Karelian business a bit too, so that altogether you are looking at life with a jaundiced eye. However you must not take the affair of your fellows too much to heart. It's a disappointment to me of course, but more so to you, and I fully realize this. At the same time you could not have done more to make the show a success, and there is no blame attached to a partial failure if one has done one's best, as you most undoubtedly have. Besides we may yet make something more out of the Karelians than we imagine at present. Anyway, I hate to think that you are worrying about it. I've failed to do lots of things I wanted to do, but I know, like you, that I tried my level best, so failure does not worry me. Make haste and get well, and become your cheery self once more. Yours sincerely, C. M. Maynard.[64]

In his memoirs, too, Maynard offers a gracious conclusion to the troubled history of the Karelian Regiment. 'As my wild and undisciplined soldiers of Karelia pass finally from my tale,' he wrote, 'it is, I am glad to think, the remembrance of their one-time greatness that takes the foremost place in my mind.'[65]

On 11 July, the Karelian Volunteer Battalion, comprising thirteen British officers, and only 285 other ranks, detrained from Kem at Siding 11 (in central Karelia) and marched to Povonets on the northern shore of lake Onega to prepare for operations.[66] A week later, Woods' feud with Filsell became public. Woods telephoned a Major Grove of the 237th Brigade HQ staff to complain that Filsell 'persists in treating the Karelians as black men, an attitude that is keenly resented by both Officers and men.' Woods stated that he had sought a reconciliation of views but without success (hardly surprising given the tone of his 2 July letter). Filsell had now tendered his resignation, and Woods recommended that brigade headquarters should accept it. He proposed that Captain J. B. Noel, one of the company commanders, should be appointed in his place.[67]

In the meantime, the Karelians were continuing to desert in droves from the new formation, as the handover of command to the Russian army approached. According to Woods' memoir, the last two Karelian officers, his trusted and faithful comrades Grigorii Lezhev and Nikolai Rogiev, quit around this time (p. 277). On 5 August, the General Staff recorded: 'Karelian Pioneer Battalion has ceased to exist.'[68]

More and greater trouble was brewing further east, however. While General Skobeltsin and Brig-Gen Price pressed south – without the Karelians – along the western shore of lake Onega, the Archangel front was disrupted by a further series of mutinies. On 20 July, the 5th Russian Infantry Regiment under Col Andrews stationed in the town of Onega (situated, confusingly, on the southern shore of the White Sea, see Map 2, p. 144) went over en masse to the Bolsheviks. The loss of Onega and its surrounding territory drove a wedge between the Murmansk and Archangel forces, threatening communications and the successful co-ordination of offensive operations prior to the upcoming withdrawal. (Curiously, Woods reports in his memoir that Col Andrews, after release from Bolshevik prison, was killed in 1923 in a garage jointly owned with F. P. Crozier, p. 282.)

Maynard understood that Woods operated best independently, and commanding irregular troops whom he could deploy imaginatively. He also knew that Woods was deeply distracted and upset by the difficulties with the Karelian Regiment. The 237th Brigade HQ was investigating the dispute with Filsell, but Price was disinclined to trust Woods' recommendation (he already knew the Ulsterman to be an obstinate and awkward character), and it was in any case an inopportune time to replace an experienced officer just as he was preparing his men to be sent into battle.

Maynard therefore decided to put Woods in command of a small force and despatch him to Sumskii Posad, south-east of Soroka. There he was to raise additional partisan fighters and organise a line of defence protecting the Murmansk railway from any Bolshevik advance westwards, before pushing eastwards himself to re-open communications between the two fronts. Woods left Kem on 25 July.[69]

This was a vital yet dangerous mission. That Maynard entrusted it to Woods demonstrates the confidence that he retained in his subordinate's abilities of military leadership. It was also a clever means of getting him out of the way. Woods retained command of the Karelian Regiment (as well as of the Kem district), but, preoccupied with operational matters, would not be able to cause any further disruption or offence within the regiment's new structure. Woods had not formally been deprived of his command, but he had lost his regiment.

This left Price free to retain Filsell, who eventually led the Karelian Volunteer Battalion into battle in mid-September with notable success.

The Brigadier-General later informed Maynard that Filsell 'has had a difficult task seeing that his men were nearly all raw recruits. He has done extremely well under my command [...] This officer has the gift of training men, has power of command and is capable and energetic.'[70] No more pointed contradiction of Woods' views can be imagined.

Meanwhile, Maynard was equally pleased with Woods' operations at Sumskii Posad:

> He was just the man for the job [Maynard wrote in his memoirs], and in a very few days he had gathered together quite a respectable following. Who they were and how he got them were unknown to me; nor did I make indiscreet enquiries. Some of them perhaps were his old Karelian friends drawn to him by ties of the past, and others were probably Russians who had either avoided the mobilization order or were outside the limits of age for conscription.[71]

Maynard was correct. Woods did not manage to raise many local fighters (in his memoirs he writes that he only enlisted 'some really hefty women and one man whom [Capt] Luck said we had "rifled the graveyard to find",' p. 283), but among his clandestine companions was Grigorii Lezhev, who gathered together some other old Karelian volunteers who had earlier returned to their homes, refusing to serve with Filsell or to answer the Russian draft. Their loyalty to Woods is remarkable – these men were fighting the Red forces on behalf of the Allies, with nothing to gain themselves by this action, but if discovered by the Whites or detained by Price's British troops they would have been shot as deserters. Woods also later collected a group of Serbians.[72]

This motley partisan force took the village of Nukhta (in Woods' spelling, Nuchta), to the south-east of Sumskii Posad, and held it successfully against Bolshevik counter-attack, as described in the memoir, until the Red forces abandoned the town of Onega on 7 September and Ironside's troops from the Archangel force marched in, thus re-connecting the two fronts.

On 14 September, on the eve of the evacuation, Major Mackesy signed an order finally disbanding the Karelian Volunteer Battalion, rendering all its men liable for conscription into the White Russian army, and transferring the Karelian Labour and Garrison Guard companies intact to the Russians. On 19 September, Woods handed over his command of Soroka and Sumskii Posad districts to Russian officers, and returned to Kem to take over administrative arrangements for the evacuation.[73] When he finally embarked on 29 September at Kem port for transit to Murmansk, and thence on 3 October home to Britain, he was aware, as he wrote in his memoir, that despite his own recent military triumphs, it was 'a very unsatisfactory ending' to the intervention.

⋆ ⋆ ⋆ ⋆

The Allied intervention, and Woods' leadership and encouragement in particular, had given the Karelians hopes of being able to secure their right to self-determination in accordance with the principles upon which the post-war settlement of the rest of Europe was proceeding. If the Allies, having accomplished their primary stated purpose of blocking the German advance to the Arctic coast and preventing redeployment of these troops to the Western Front, had then maintained a strict neutrality in the Russian civil war or had pursued their peace initiatives with greater conviction and impartiality, the Karelians might at least have been able to bring their cause to the attention of the world powers before it was too late.

The intervention, however, had from the start been confused in its objectives – as we have seen, it was driven not only by strategic considerations with regard to the Germans, but also by a revulsion on the part of many Allied political and military leaders towards the Bolshevik regime, its values and worldview. The Allied alliance with the White Russians thus combined political principle and opportunism. It also obliged them to sideline and suppress the claims of the local Karelian population, even though the Karelian troops had been largely responsible for securing the Allies' supposedly central strategic objective of engaging and repelling the German forces. Woods keenly resented the ingratitude and lack of principle on the part of British imperial power demonstrated by this disregard for what he saw as the just claim of a oppressed, victimised yet valiant people, just as he sympathised with the Karelians' rejection of both Russian imperialism and Finnish rapaciousness.

Woods' conclusion to the memoir, which states that the Karelians 'made peace with the Soviet and obtained the Status of an "Autonomous Republic" ' (p. 296) is an understandable but inaccurate interpretation of the subsequent history of the region. In reality, Allied backing for the White Russians pushed the Karelian nationalists back towards Finland.

They were never able again to assert a truly independent line.

During the first half of 1919, pro-Finnish Karelian émigrés like Paavo Ahava, with an explicitly anti-Bolshevik (as well as anti-Russian) programme, backed the renewed White Finnish incursions into Olonets Karelia as campaigns of liberation, and decried the Kem-based Karelian National Committee's more independent stance.[74] By the summer of 1919, the pro-Finnish Karelians again dominated the national movement, as White Russian arrests, murders (like that of Paavo's son Iivo Ahava) and expulsions, facilitated if not abetted by the British command, weakened the numbers and morale of the activists concentrated in and around Woods' regiment.

A meeting of Karelians at Ukhta on 21 July ratified the February assembly's resolution and established a 'Provisional Government of White Sea Karelia' replacing the defunct National Committee (its five members being dead or dispersed). The new Provisional Government was strongly oriented towards Finland.[75] During the summer, the Allies cut back food supplies to the Karelians (as Maynard had threatened to do). Since the White Russians had no desire, capability or intention to assist them, the regional population became increasingly dependent on food shipments from Finland across the border. The provision of welfare assistance to White Sea Karelian villages served further to reinforce Finnish claims on the territory.

Following the Allied evacuation, the Karelian Provisional Government sought to organise resistance to the Bolsheviks advancing from the south, as well as distributing Finnish food aid to the population in the face of relentless White Russian hostility, interference and repression. Even when Governor-General Miller's White Russian administration was on the edge of collapse at the end of the year, it still refused to recognise the Provisional Karelian Government (though he now offered the Karelians limited autonomy within Russia in return for military support – it is possible that the Kem activists of Woods' regiment would have accepted had the White Russians not earlier conspired to destroy their influence). With the pro-Finnish Karelians refusing to be drawn into the White and Red Russians' internecine conflict, the Bolsheviks overran the last remaining White Russian forces at Murmansk on 23 February 1920.

In the absence of the White Russians, with Bolshevik control still weak in the region and Finnish troops still occupying some districts of Olonets Karelia, it looked for a short while as if the Karelian Provisional

Government based at Ukhta had a chance. In January 1920 it declared Karelia independent, and commenced arrangements for popular elections at the end of March to a Karelian Constituent Assembly, with a view to holding a plebiscite afterwards on becoming an autonomous region within Finland. On 19 March, however, the Red Army occupied Ukhta. Under the Bolsheviks' watchful eyes, 120 representatives from twelve Karelian districts met to discuss the future of their homeland. Despite promises by Lenin's government that Soviet Russia would offer the region autonomy, the Karelian congress resolved to separate from Russia pending a referendum on a constitution, and insisted that the Red Army withdraw. It did so temporarily, but returned on 18 May, forcing the Provisional Government to flee into exile in Finland. There its members remained, campaigning, conspiring and intermittently lobbying the League of Nations for the next twenty years.

Meanwhile, on 7 June, Red Finnish activists, backed by the Red Army and supported by Lenin, inaugurated a Karelian Labour Commune unifying White Sea and Olonets Karelia, which enjoyed extensive autonomy in its administration and economy, but in which the Karelians' 'petty' nationalist aspirations were subsumed in a grander Finnish 'revolutionary nationalist' vision to build a 'Greater Red Finland'.[76] The Red Finnish conception of Karelian identity was in fact little different from that of White Finnish nationalists. The programme of cultural development launched by the Karelian Labour Commune, which in 1923 was promoted to the status of an autonomous republic, was in Standard Finnish and was designed to accelerate the 'evolution' of the 'backward' Karelians into fully-fledged, modern Finns.

The Finnish government warily accepted this form of national autonomy, though suspicious of its political colouring, withdrew its troops and renounced its territorial claims for the sake of securing a peace treaty with Soviet Russia in October 1920. The Karelians peasants themselves revolted against Soviet power in the winter of 1921–1922, encouraged by White Finnish activists who then failed to deliver reinforcements or material assistance and left them to be bloodily repressed by the Red Army, which included substantial Red Finnish detachments.

Within the next two decades the Soviet government withdrew most of the powers of self-administration it had initially granted the 'Karelian' autonomous republic. Already by the end of the 1920s, a vast territory of central Karelia was occupied by a network of forced labour camps, which included a fearsome prison housed in the Solovetskii monastery.

The Karelian Gulag expanded further during the next decade.[77] The Kem building that had housed Woods during his sojourn in North Russia became the headquarters of a major transit point for forced labourers destined to toil, and many to die, in the region's forests. Industrialisation brought not only prisoners, but huge numbers of new Russian workers to Karelia, diluting the national population to a small minority in its own territory.[78]

In 1935, Josef Stalin removed the Red Finns from power in Karelia (most were shot during the next few years), and for a brief while sponsored 'Soviet Karelian' cultural development, which occasioned the precipitous creation of a Karelian written language that in most respects (including its use of the Cyrillic alphabet) bore an uncanny resemblance to Soviet-style Russian.[79] For a few years, the youngest Karelian schoolchildren were taught to read Pushkin and Stalin in Karelian. In January 1938, the Finnish language was banned in the autonomous republic.

This experiment only lasted two years. When the Soviet Union launched its 'Winter War' against Finland in December 1939 (in preparation for which it constructed extensive fortifications along the Karelian border, which Woods mentions at the end of his memoir), it reinstated Finnish communist control over Karelia – although apart from the sly survivor Otto Kuusinen, Stalin had problems finding Red Finns he had not executed to appoint to the republican leadership. Early in 1940, Karelia was promoted to the status of a union republic (i.e. on the same administrative level as Russia, Ukraine, etc.) and renamed the Karelian-Finnish Soviet Socialist Republic, in the hope that eastern Karelia plus a small stretch of land the Red Army had just conquered in its otherwise disastrous campaign (and which a small but vocal Karelian lobby in Finland has been demanding back from Russia ever since) might form the nucleus of a future socialist Finland.

In this vision, the Karelians were again to be relegated to a sub-category of a larger existing nation, their spoken tongue eliminated in favour of someone else's written language, and their territory subsumed into another state, as had been the case throughout their history. (In 1956, Soviet leader Nikolai Khrushchev demoted the region to its previous status of an autonomous republic within the Russian republic.) Only for a few months in 1918–1919, with Woods' prompting and support, had the Karelians, organising themselves under the green-and-orange shamrock flag, pursued a dream of a separate, self-determined destiny.

Chapter 8

Baltic Interlude
Lithuania, 1919–1920

Across Europe, massive numbers of demobilised men searching to find a place again in civilian life produced widespread social and political destabilisation. Economic crisis, unemployment and inflation compounded the problems of peace. In Britain, the traditional class system, underpinned by deference, had been disrupted. The rank-and-file returned home to promises of 'homes fit for heroes' – but found their ruling classes unable or unwilling to respond to their demands and needs. On leaving the officers' mess for the last time, a new caste of 'temporary gentlemen', working and lower middle class men who had earned officer rank during wartime, resented being relegated to their former social status.[1] Throughout Europe, the bitterness and sense of betrayal felt by millions of ex-servicemen generated a newly radicalised mass politics of both the far left and far right.

Philip Woods was hardly a 'temporary gentleman' – before the war he had a profession, and both his brother's family and his own in-laws were prominent and wealthy members of Ulster society. Nevertheless, on returning from North Russia to Belfast in October 1919, he too faced an uncertain future. In Ulster, as elsewhere, the linen trade was in crisis owing to the sudden cancellation of government contracts after the war and a shortage of raw materials, especially of flax. Northern Ireland entered a prolonged period of economic decline.[2] Although Robert

Woods' business survived, his younger brother faced the unhappy prospect of sitting idle as their orders dwindled. In any case, Philip Woods had no desire to return to an office job or to settle back into bourgeois domesticity. He was a soldier and leader of men. Within a few weeks of his return, Woods learned that his former commanding officer, F. P. Crozier, had just embarked for Lithuania. He had been contracted to organise the nascent army of this infant state, born in the chaotic collapse of the Russian empire, against those powers who wished to strangle its independence in the cradle. Woods (after gaining War Office release to do so) signed up to join the mission.

The history of the Baltic states in this period is so complex that it makes the Karelian conflict seem quite straightforward.[3] It will suffice here to say that the Lithuanians, who had a more substantive claim to historical nationhood and discrete ethnic identity than the Karelians, as well as a substantial North American diaspora financing their cause, were able to lobby for independence more persuasively. It was at the Paris peace conference in August 1919 that a delegation from the new, still unrecognised, Lithuanian national government encountered Crozier (who was in Paris to be awarded the French Croix de Guerre) and asked him to help organise their new army.[4]

Crozier had relinquished his British army commission at the end of July, after two 'distasteful' months in southern England overseeing demobilisation and quelling mutinies by soldiers impatient to return home.[5] He was on the Foreign Office list for a diplomatic posting in the Middle East, but eagerly accepted the Lithuanian job offer, on condition that he, and the officers whom he would recruit to accompany him, were paid British army rates.[6] Crozier recalled later that they had all 'looked forward to rendering useful service in difficult times, when it appeared that Bolshevik influence throughout the world could best be countered by the careful introduction of British influence.'[7] They were evidently unaware of the political, military and diplomatic intrigues in which they would immediately be embroiled.

Lithuania had recently expelled Soviet Russian troops from its borders, but was still struggling against other enemies on two fronts. On the one hand, it was engaged against marauding *Freikorps* battalions of German volunteers whom General von der Goltz had recruited after the Armistice left him stranded in Finland (many of the *Freikorps* men later became Hitler's street-fighters and shock troops). These irregular forces aspired to preserve Prussia's dominance over the eastern Baltic, as well

British officers in Lithuanian uniform, 1919. Crozier is seated third from left, Woods fourth from left.

Source: F.P. Crozier *Impressions and Recollections*

as to indulge their taste for unbridled violence acquired during the world war. On the other hand, Lithuania was also facing Polish forces, who had been occupying the city of Vilna (Vilnius) and its surrounding area since April.[8]

During the summer and autumn, the Polish delegation at Versailles had lodged further territorial claims against its new neighbour. The United States, France and Britain argued over the best policy to pursue in the Baltic, aiming variously to conciliate Poland, keep Soviet Russia and Germany apart and not antagonise the White Russian North-Western Government, which was poised to attack Soviet Petrograd, by over-hastily recognising Baltic independence. Finally, numerous political and military factions within Lithuania, some aligned with foreign states or forces, were vying for power. The population as a whole, and the army in particular, were restless, some elements looking for salvation in extreme nationalism, others in communism.

Crozier landed in Lithuania in September to take up his post of Inspector General in the Lithuanian Army and military consultant to the government. Woods arrived during November, and was appointed to the Lithuanian General Staff as Inspector of Forces, Kovno District. It seems that the Lithuanians originally intended to establish an English-speaking legion of up to thirty thousand volunteers, to be recruited mainly among Lithuanian émigrés in the United States with offers of high pay and eventual land settlements. This force would cooperate with General Silvestras Zukauskas' national army to undertake 'reconstruction and development work […] and help clear that country from all foreign forces.'[9] Presumably, Crozier and his subordinates would have had a leading role in forming and integrating the legion.

The Lithuanian government, although it raised one million dollars for this venture, decided to spend the money instead on reorganising, training and equipping its own regular army.[10] Crozier's contingent was directed to fulfil this task.[11] By mid-December, Lithuanian troops had repelled the German adventurers, and were holding back a renewed Bolshevik advance that had followed the defeat of White Russian General Nikolai Yudenich's attack on Petrograd a month earlier. Despite, or perhaps because of, these successes, Crozier and his staff provoked the antagonism of certain indigenous political and military interests, led by the Prime Minister Augustinas Voldemaras. These parties resented the privileged position, especially the high salaries, that the British officers – whose country had not yet formally recognised Lithuanian independence – were enjoying within their own national army, and resisted the reforms that the foreigners were trying to implement.[12] General Zukauskas, who supported Crozier and his men, resigned in frustration at his rivals' continuous scheming.

For much of December, Crozier was absent attending military conferences, and we can imagine that Colonel A. Muirhead, his chief of staff, and Woods were the main targets of conspiracy and propaganda. Woods' role as regional army inspector, which involved purchasing uniforms, arms and munitions, as well as securing food supplies, would have left him particularly vulnerable to plotting and rumour-mongering by corrupt Lithuanian officers and officials, resentful that he was obstructing their speculative schemes. In a British officers' group photograph in Lithuanian uniform, Woods sits rather limply, with an expression mingling mild dejection (see opposite), light bemusement and wearied stoicism, next to the puff-chested, proud but slightly pitiful-looking Crozier.

Crozier acknowledged the problem. 'On my return to Kovno,' he later recalled, 'I found the place in a ferment. Many more British officers had been sent out than I had use for, or the Lithuanians could afford to pay for. Some of those sent out were of the wrong type [... having their] eyes on the "main chance".'[13] He sought to negotiate a settlement that involved despatching home some of his newer subordinates of lesser quality or less noble motives, while reducing the pay of those who remained. This was only reasonable. Since his appointment, Crozier had received a monthly salary of fifty thousand Lithuanian marks, while the salary of a Lithuanian general of equivalent rank was only 1,800 marks.[14] In the meantime, Crozier ordered his staff to withhold their services until a resolution had been reached.

The inactivity of the British officers did little to appease their critics. By early February 1920, the Assistant British Commissioner for the Baltic Provinces reported to Lord Curzon that 'the situation with regard to these officers has at last come to a head after a long period of rather unpleasant negotiations and difficult suspense, during which time I am afraid that the prestige of the British officers has not improved.' As a result, Crozier dismissed all but two of his subordinates. We know that Woods was one of those to remain, indicating that he still retained the confidence and trust of his former commanding officer. The three remaining British officers, together with four new recruits, agreed to accept reduced pay.[15] Their patron General Zukauskas was reinstated as commander-in-chief. Back in London, *The Times* reported that 'Crozier still retains the complete confidence of the Government, despite the fact that active propaganda is being employed against him from many quarters.'[16]

Within a month, however, Crozier had resigned, convinced that his 'powers were a sham', and refusing any longer to be 'a passenger in the ship.'[17] He soon returned to Britain, accompanied by most of his officers. There is some evidence that Woods remained in Kovno for several months longer, either in an unofficial capacity or as an instructor paid by the British army.[18] Crozier, evidently not bearing any grudge against the Lithuanian nation because of the conduct of some of its politicians, continued to lobby on its behalf to the British government, parliament and press.[19]

On 11 April, the Lithuanian parliament, while acknowledging 'differences of opinion', passed a resolution conveying 'the thanks and indebtedness of the country to General Crozier and Colonel Muirhead for the work and efforts on behalf of the new State during the last seven months, during which time the assistance rendered by these officers against the Germans and Bolshevists, who had occupied the country by force, had been great.' It [illegible] thanked Crozier and Muirhead for their success in promoting mutual understanding among Lithuanians, Poles and Latvians.[20]

Woods, although equal-second in seniority among the British officers in Lithuania, and seated next to Crozier in the centre of their group photograph, is not mentioned in the official resolution, being for reasons unknown (or perhaps for no good reason) once again consigned to historical invisibility.

Chapter 9

Belfast's Fighting Colonel
Northern Irish Politics and Parliament, 1921–1929

When Woods returned from the Baltic to Belfast in the spring of 1920, he found the province in tumult. Not only in Eastern Europe had older political tensions, nationalist aspirations and territorial disputes erupted with renewed vigour and unprecedented levels of brutality, as men inured to violence at the front returned to resume killing at home. By July 1920, escalating sectarian violence in Northern Ireland prompted Carson to revive the UVF. Armed Unionist volunteers in the north now faced the well-organised forces of the Irish Republican Army (IRA), who had re-grouped in the south after the bloodily suppressed nationalist uprising of Easter 1916. A favoured tactic of both sides was arson.[1]

As Ulster burned, British mainland opinion watched the 'Orange glow in Belfast' with increasing dismay.[2] In an attempt to constrain and channel popular energies, the Prime Minister David Lloyd George resolved in late autumn of the same year to form an Ulster Special Constabulary, comprising full-time 'A Specials', part-time and unpaid (though uniformed) 'B Specials', and reservist 'C Specials'. Large numbers of UVF rank-and-file and officers joined the new force, which became in effect 'an officially sanctioned Protestant paramilitary force'.[3]

In the meantime, the Government of Ireland Bill, introduced on 25

February 1920 (on the basis of the 1914 Home Rule Act, the implementation of which, it will be recalled, was deferred until after the war), aimed to provide a political settlement to the crisis. This legislation, enacted on 23 December and due to come into force on 3 May the following year, provided for two Irish parliaments. Twenty-six southern counties were to enjoy dominion status within the British empire. The six counties of north-eastern Ulster would remain within the United Kingdom, with limited powers of self-administration devolved from Westminster.[4] In reality, the new Northern Ireland parliament was little more than a 'glorified county council' squeezed between obstreperous local authorities on the one hand and the sovereign imperial parliament at Westminster on the other.[5] Many Unionists remained dissatisfied with both the constitutional and territorial settlement.[6]

On 24 May 1921, Ulster held its first elections to the new Northern Ireland parliament. James Craig, who had recently succeeded Carson as leader of the Unionist Party, feared that the Belfast labour movement would split the loyalist camp, especially under the existing system of proportional representation. His fears proved unfounded: the popular vote returned forty Unionists and twelve Nationalist and Republican-Sinn Fein members. However, neither the elections nor the formal inauguration of the parliament at the Presbyterian College in Belfast on 22 June 1921 succeeded in quelling sectarian violence.

Partly this violence was an overspill of civil conflict in the south, which pitted the IRA's flying columns against the British army and volunteer troops recruited during 1920 to augment their forces. These irregular forces, the Black and Tans (so-called because of the colour of their uniforms) and the Auxiliary Division, were recruited from among recently demobilised soldiers, the former unit from the rank-and-file, the latter from officers. They attracted to their ranks the same type of listless adventurers as the free-booting German *Freikorps* that attained notoriety in the Baltic wars of the period.

In July 1920, the Irish Office invited F. P. Crozier to take command of the Auxiliary Division. Though callous and overbearing, Crozier was also a man of rigid principle who believed in discipline, order and sobriety. British government officials soon came to regret their nomination. For several months, Crozier strove to restrain his wild, often drunken, troops from marauding, torturing, pillaging and burning their way across southern Ireland. In February 1921, only six months after assuming command, Crozier handed in his resignation when the British government refused to take action against twenty-six officers he had arraigned for arson and looting.[7]

Subjected to mud-slinging from all directions, Woods' former commanding officer spent the next years fighting publicly both to clear his name of any association with the murderous activities of his troops, and to bring the extent of government complicity to the public eye.[8] In 1923, Crozier stood for election to the Westminster parliament 'in order to call attention to the defects of British bureaucracy'. He was angered that the 'rank and file of the British armies [had] been thoroughly let down after the war', and concerned to ensure that 'the drawing-room, boudoir and smoking-room electors of the "all's well" class were taught the lesson of their lives.' Crozier chose to stand as a Labour candidate, although he rejected class-based politics, in the belief that this party represented 'the very best elements of the late British armies which had secured us victory in the field.'

He did not win the seat, and in his 1930 memoir admitted that since he was simply 'for the underdog' and had no party allegiance, his venture into parliamentary politics had been a naive mistake.[9] Conventional self-interested politicians and political parties had a stranglehold on power but no desire to save loyal ex-servicemen from warmongering, unemployment, homelessness or the evils of the liquor trade, or to salvage the empire from disaster. 'These are times,' he wrote in 1930, 'when men are required.' The nation was in need of 'a leader [...] a "sahib" construed in terms of today [...] one man [...] who is capable of telling the people that this country [...] now requires deeds, not words, and is sick of shilly-shallying and party manoeuvres.' Where, he asked, was 'this superman' with the 'Mussolini touch' to be found?[10] As we shall see, Crozier was by no means alone in rejecting traditional partisan politics and calling for a new man – his explicit and repeated emphasis on this figure's masculinity implying the weak-willed, effeminate nature of old-style politicians – to initiate a new start.

Meanwhile, in July 1921, the IRA and British government had agreed a truce and launched negotiations on a settlement. These resulted in the Anglo-Irish Treaty in December, which superseded the Government of Ireland Act in the south, inaugurating an independent and sovereign Irish Free State. The effect of these events in Ulster was to intensify the violence, as southern IRA units disengaged, regrouped and moved north of the border, and Ulster Unionists mobilised to defend the six counties against these attacks, the perceived territorial ambitions of the new southern state and presumed subversion on the part of their own Catholic neighbours.

During late 1921 and the first half of 1922, the IRA expanded their campaign of violence in the north, and the Ulster police and 'B Specials' opposed them with equal brutality.[11] As always, innocent civilians suffered the most. The reciprocal terror practised by both sides reached a crescendo in May 1922 with over 606 violent incidents recorded, sixty-six civilian deaths (forty-four Catholics and twenty-two Protestants), widespread arson and wholesale evictions of people from their homes and workplaces. Between 20-22 May, there were no fewer than fourteen sectarian assassinations.

Among those killed was thirty-eight year old William John Twaddell, a draper, prominent freemason, temperance leader, Orangeman and Ulster Unionist member of the Northern Irish parliament for the West Belfast constituency.[12] In response to Twaddell's murder, Sir James Craig, now the Northern Irish Prime Minister, declared: 'if those who committed this dastardly outrage thought that it would for a moment weaken the functions of this Parliament or the steadfast courage of the people of Ulster they never made a greater error.'[13] Nevertheless it was decided to postpone the election of Twaddell's successor until civil order had been restored.

During the summer and autumn, the Northern Irish government re-organised the police into the Royal Ulster Constabulary (RUC), expanded the special constabulary and assumed special powers to restore civil order. As Ulster's security clamp-down took effect, IRA units in the north redirected their energies towards the Irish Free State, where civil war between pro- and anti-treaty factions was gathering force. By the end of the year, Ulster had achieved relative tranquility. In early 1923, the electoral authorities called the West Belfast by-election. On 1 March, to the surprise and dismay of almost everyone concerned, Colonel P. J. Woods declared his candidacy for this seat.

★ ★ ★ ★

We do not have much information on Philip Woods' activities during the three years following his return to Ulster in spring 1920. In this period, Ulster's post-war linen crisis was further exacerbated by a severe slump in international prices, causing widespread unemployment and intense suffering in the province, where in better times over half the population had been engaged in textile manufacturing.[14] Woods may well have found himself unable to pursue his former occupation as a linen designer. Or perhaps his extended experience of soldiering and command had left him reluctant to return to the civilian routine, restless and eager to put his expertise to work for the good of his homeland during its turbulent transition to self-rule.

Ulster's present status, after all, was not wholly dissimilar to that demanded by the Karelians, when they sought autonomy under the King's protection from their own rapacious neighbours. Perhaps Woods' dismay at Britain's betrayal of his faithful Karelian and Russian friends prompted him to volunteer his services, as Crozier would do later the same year, to help the underdogs at home and deliver a pointed lesson in loyalty to the 'all's well' class.

We know for certain that Woods did not follow Crozier to southern Ireland with the Auxiliaries in late 1920.[15] Woods retained his commission in the Royal Irish Rifles, and might have rejoined his regiment on his return from Lithuania, though he did not accompany them on active service in Mesopotamia, where they were deployed at this time to suppress rebellions by Iraqi tribesmen. In 1922, Woods was transferred to the reserve of his regiment (since Irish independence renamed the Royal Ulster Rifles). He then applied to be an inspector in the newly-formed RUC and, his application having been declined, for numerous positions in the new Northern Irish administration and in public organisations (including the Irish Temperance League), also without success.[16] We can only speculate that his repeated failure to gain a responsible post in public service had something to do with the local rivalries and resentments which had caused difficulties for him during the war.

Unemployment, we may also assume, did not cause him any material hardship. In late 1921, Woods' father-in-law Stewart Blacker Quin had died, leaving a substantial estate to his eldest son Herbert, himself now a prosperous businessman, and probably also a comfortable bequest to Woods' wife Florence. Philip's elder brother Robert, whose own linen business survived the crisis, could also provide support if necessary. Regardless, Woods' failure to obtain gainful work induced in him an intense moral dismay, if not desperation, and an even greater antagonism towards the locally entrenched elites who, as he saw it, could make or break a man. It also deepened his sense of solidarity with the demobilised soldiers who languished in unemployment. He became honorary treasurer of the Ulster Ex-Servicemen's Association, in which role he would have learned much about the overcrowded and dilapidated housing, appalling sanitary conditions and high mortality then endemic in the province.[17]

He also perceived that the Unionist government of Northern Ireland was utterly incapable of resolving these social and economic problems. In addition to the constitutional, and hence fiscal, weakness of the government's position, Unionist political culture was critically ill-suited to the tasks of administration. Loyalist leaders had built their organisation on the sole principle and with the sole objective of opposing home rule. As Buckland notes, they had failed to develop any 'constructive philosophy [to equip them] to govern a state they had neither expected nor wanted.'[18] Any hope for genuine reform and progress had therefore to entail a challenge to Unionist domination of parliament, and such a challenge could only come from outside the ranks of the party machine.

Sometime in late 1922 or early 1923, Woods was approached by a group of former soldiers who requested that he stand for parliament to represent their interests, which they felt poorly served by official Unionist politicians. At first, it seems that Woods nonetheless did seek formal Unionist backing for his nomination. In January 1923, he even joined the Orange Order, a move that was seen by his opponents, probably correctly, as being opportunistic and too long overdue for anyone who sincerely believed in the movement's creed of extreme loyalism.[19] In any case, it did not help him. The Unionist Association nominated as their candidate for West Belfast a wealthy local businessman, Sir Joseph Davison, a former High Sheriff of Belfast, and the Grand Master of the Orangemen of Belfast.[20]

Branded a traitor to the Unionist cause by Davison's supporters, Woods fought his campaign with characteristic obduracy and assertiveness. The 'Fighting Colonel' (as he proclaimed himself) had nothing to lose. In fact, Woods' candidacy did not create disunity within loyalist ranks as his opponents claimed, but merely exploited existing divisions. Although Northern Irish Labour politicians had been decisively beaten in the 1921 election, there were still many Ulster Protestants who, in the words of one historian, resented the 'unrepresentative nature of some local unionist associations, said to be dominated by aristocratic cliques,' and wished for more democratic and independent-minded representation.[21]

Woods appealed to this constituency. 'I am essentially a Democrat,' he declared to the West Belfast electorate, 'therefore your interests are mine.'[22] He called for a renewal of the Rent Restriction Act (which would ensure cheaper housing), and measures to improve and expand housing, education and employment. He denounced the 'old gang' who dominated provincial politics, proclaiming 'there was nothing but graft and corruption in that clique.' In contrast, he invoked his own solidarity and familiarity with the ordinary soldier built over long years of shared hardship in the 'brotherhood of the trenches'.[23] Ex-servicemen, he declared, were no longer 'going to be crushed by a huge machine. They had had enough of the "bang the big drum and follow me" representation.'[24] Woods likened the Ulster government to New York's notoriously corrupt city administration at Tammany Hall. Northern Irish voters, he stated, were not at present choosing representatives but rulers: 'they were simply electing another boss, and he in turn was bossed by another big boss, and the three little bosses at the top ran the whole show – three insignificant worms who never fought for their country except by word of mouth' and whose only visit to France was 'with a big escort to open the memorial at Thiepval.'[25]

Alongside Florence Woods, who made resounding appeals on her husband's behalf to female voters, his brother Robert was also a regular speaker at the hustings, launching scathing attacks on 'the tyrannical clique which ran that pocket edition of a so-called Parliament so that they could defy all opposition.' 'The whole thing,' Robert declared, 'could only be likened to a Gilbertian absurdity, a great rehearsal of a farce.'[26] By contrast, Philip Woods was 'a man who was a man, and not a member of the old clique [...] the independent man, the man who could not be bought.'[27] (The Northern Ireland Parliament debated the next day whether Robert Woods should or could be held in contempt for public calumny, or even sued for libel, but then decided not to condescend to any action, declaring him to be as harmless as he was contemptible.)

At first, Davison and his supporters concentrated on attacking Philip Woods' loyalist credentials ('if Colonel Woods was a true Orangeman he would retire in favour of the Grand Master'), and stressed the danger of splitting the Protestant vote in a constituency with a substantial Catholic population.[28] They also accused Woods of appealing to Nationalist voters (he had, they alleged, even issued pamphlets on green paper). If only they had known that five years earlier he had used the green shamrock as his regimental badge! Davison also enrolled the active support of a num-

West Belfast Election, 1923

(PARLIAMENT OF NORTHERN IRELAND).

P. J. Woods.

An Ex Serviceman – for ex service men, working men and their Dependants.

Printed and Published by W. & G. Baird, Ltd., Belfast.

Front cover of Woods' election pamphlet, April 1923

ber of former officers of the 9th Battalion, RIR. Among them were both Horace Haslett and William Montgomery, Woods' wartime rivals for the battalion's command. (Woods' campaign, on the other hand, recruited several of the 9th Battalion's more junior officers as well as several non-commissioned officers and lower ranks.)

At the same time, Davison realised the need for a more constructive approach, and strove to persuade voters that even as a businessmen he could champion working-class interests.[29] His own attempts at this were clumsy and patronising, and his supporters struggled to make a case for his populist credentials. Instead, they issued time-worn and lack-lustre calls for deference on the part of the working people. 'They had won the war,' one of Davison's supporters declared, 'because they had trusted and obeyed their leaders, and if the loyal electors of West Belfast would trust and obey their leaders in the same fashion West Belfast would also be won.'[30]

Such statements played straight into Woods' hands, of course, since his principal argument was precisely that ex-servicemen should not trust and obey those who had 'waxed rich upon the unfortunate misery and hardship of the wives, widows, and families of the men out in France', and then betrayed their own promises to provide decent housing and jobs for the homecoming heroes.[31] The 'Fighting Colonel' was, as green and white placards on the Catholic Falls Road proclaimed on 2 May, the day of the election: 'Friend of the ex-servicemen, enemy of the landlords and the man who is out to split up the clique!'[32]

The following day, shortly after noon, police struggled to restrain huge crowds from invading City Hall, where the votes were being counted. 'Conspicuous in the crowd,' reported the *Belfast News-Letter*, 'were a number of soldiers in hospital blue, whose sympathies were obviously with Colonel Woods.' The result of the election was a convincing win for Woods, who polled nearly eight thousand votes of forty-eight thousand cast.

After thanking the returning officer and his staff, Woods held out his hand to his defeated opponent. Davison refused to take it. Pandemonium erupted in the hall, and Woods struggled to make himself heard over the cheers, counter-cheers and booing, as he attempted to make a conciliatory speech. He evidently failed, as fighting broke out a few moments later, and the police intervened to restore order. Davison's supporters then began to carry their candidate out of the hall, booing the victor. At this, Woods cunningly launched into a loud rendition of 'God

Save the King', forcing Davison and his adherents to stop in their tracks and join the refrain.

After this, Woods returned to his headquarters, borne on the shoulders of his supporters, the crowd led by a 'one-legged soldier in hospital blue [...] waving one of his crutches'. That evening, the Colonel held a torchlight procession through the main streets of the Shankill Road district, with pipe and flute bands in train, 'acknowledging the vociferous welcome of the multitudes which thronged the streets.'[33]

The same day, the *Belfast News-Letter* editorial, barely disguising its disgust, attributed Woods' victory to the support of Nationalist-Sinn Fein and the Licensed Traders' interests (the temperance movement having declared for Davison on the eve of the poll, the anti-prohibitionists for Woods). Of course, the Colonel owed his success to more than the backing of publicans and republicans. He had captured the resentment and sense of betrayal among many voters, sick of old-style sectarian politics and looking towards a fresh start. It was doubtful, though, whether Woods alone could either realise his own vision or fulfil their expectations.

The Northern Irish parliament, which convened in Belfast City Hall from late 1921 until 1932, when it moved to far grander premises at Stormont Castle, was not an impressive political institution. The Unionist government's huge majority, the absence of any opposition (most Nationalist and all Republican members boycotted parliament for its first decade), and its circumscribed powers meant that the conduct of parliamentary business was long-winded, uncritical, ineffective and preoccupied with petty and parochial issues. As one historian has noted, the parliament 'was very much a part-time affair, usually meeting a few months each year and seeming to exist largely to endorse government policy'.[34]

At the time Woods took up his seat in the Northern Irish House of Commons on 16 May 1923, it comprised fifty-two members, of whom he was the only one without formal party affiliation. From the start, Woods was sharply aware of his position as 'the only Opposition' in the house, and used his gently fatalistic and self-deprecating wit to establish himself in this role.[35] 'I know that I am but a voice in the wilderness,' he declared a few months later during a debate on finance, 'I just want to register my opinion on this matter. I know that no notice will be taken of it, but I still have to say what the people outside are thinking.'[36]

In the official reports of these debates, Woods comes across as a man of honour, integrity and solid common sense who is determined to make himself heard, not only because that is his right and his duty, but also because he derives pleasure from needling the pompous, condescending, protocol-obsessed Unionist dignitaries and party-men who strive to taunt and intimidate him into silence. At times, Woods loses his way on matters of parliamentary etiquette, legislative detail or constitutional competence, and his opponents are swift to point out his errors, but he invariably salvages the situation with a good-natured, modest apology or humorous remark. He earns respect among some members for his stubborn, single-minded defence of ex-servicemen's interests. On occasion, the house accepts his proposed amendments (which invariably entail petty matters of principle), and ministers agree to look into individual cases which his indefatigable questioning brings to their attention.

On the other hand, Woods – never the canniest or subtlest political operator – frequently did not grasp the machinations or motives of the party machine he was up against. In particular, he consistently supported Sir James Craig's proposal to replace proportional representation with single-member constituency voting.[37] Woods reasoned correctly that a first-past-the-post system would greatly reduce the electioneering expenses of independent candidates. He failed to see that electoral reform would also serve to consolidate existing majorities and make it substantially harder for independents to win seats. This, of course, was the Unionist leadership's main objective in introducing this legislation.[38]

The honourable and gallant member for West Belfast might have been only an amateur politician, but he was a professional nuisance, and took evident delight in this role. His first sustained intervention, less than a week after taking his seat, was to denounce the Intoxicating Liquor Bill (which sought to ban the sale of alcohol on Sundays without an accompanying meal) as 'one of the most perfect documents if the policy of the Government is to create Bolshevism in Ulster'. Only the wealthy, he argued, could always afford a hearty repast alongside their tipple, and this would provoke envy and 'class hatred' among the majority of the population. The measure epitomised, in his view, the contempt shown by 'extremists' with 'narrow-minded views' for 'ordinary and reasonably sane citizens' who desired merely to be granted sufficient trust, independence and freedom to lead their lives.[39]

In the remaining eight weeks of the 1923 session, Woods spoke out no fewer than ninety-five times, paying closest attention to matters of employment, vocational training, housing, health care, pensions and insurance – the issues that most concerned his constituency of ex-servicemen. The following year he was no less vocal on these topics, as well as on motoring and road safety legislation, and irritated his fellow members no less. Woods' light-hearted but relentlessly insistent interventions provoked particular antipathy in Sam McGuffin, the earnest Ulster Unionist Labour Association representative for North Belfast, a denizen of the Shankill Road.

Outside parliament, however, Woods' stance won public sympathy and support. When Ulster held its second general election in April 1925 (still under proportional representation), the 'Fighting Colonel' was nominated to stand in two districts, both his current seat of West Belfast and South Belfast, where he now lived. Woods' campaigning, again steadfastly supported by his brother and wife, was as fierce as two years' earlier, and his opponents' attacks as vindictive. Thomas Moles, official Unionist and deputy speaker of the lower house in the first parliament, who stood against Woods in South Belfast, declared that 'during his career he had seen strange figures appear and disappear, but never had he seen anything to equal Colonel Woods.'[40] Another South Belfast Unionist candidate, Hugh McDowell Pollock, a former President of the Belfast Chamber of Commerce and Minister of Finance in the previous government, denounced Woods as an 'irrelevancy' and a time-waster.[41] The other two Unionist big-guns standing in the division, Sir Crawford McCullagh, a former (and future) Lord Mayor of Belfast, and Andrew Black, an eminent barrister, shared their colleagues' contempt for the impertinent interloper.

In return, Woods dismissed his Unionist rivals as 'four mouldy old men' (it was true that Pollock was seventy-three years old, but Moles was only nine years older than Woods himself).[42] In West Belfast, he promised to fight 'for truth and fair play [...] against the combined forces of the Ulster Press, the Political Manipulators and Dictators'.[43] He was, he asserted, a true Orangeman (and, he claimed, also a member of the 'higher' Royal Arch Purple and Royal Black brotherhoods) and resolute on the border question. However, he refused to toe the party line on crucial social and economic issues, demanding lower taxation, rent restriction, measures to increase employment and lower the cost of living, and the repeal of prohibitionist liquor laws. Robert Woods was more belligerent: 'The Colonel,' he promised, 'would go into that Parliament and drive the fat clique out at the point of the bayonet, just as the 9th Battalion drove out the corpulent Germans in Flanders.'[44]

In South Belfast, Woods topped the poll. In West Belfast he came second to Joe Devlin, Ulster's leading Nationalist politician (who refused again to take up his seat). Woods opted to continue to sit for his former constituency, while considering himself the 'moral representative' of the other division.[45] Overall, the Unionist government saw its previous majority cut by seven in this election. Independents won four seats in Belfast (including the two won by Woods), Labour secured three and a farmers' delegate was returned for a rural division.[46] In addition, the Nationalists won ten seats, and the Republicans two. The Nationalist *Irish News* welcomed the result as an 'electoral debacle' for the loyalists, and even Unionist newspapers acknowledged that it represented a decisive vote of no-confidence in the leadership.[47] It was Woods' surprise victory in 1923, as well as his stalwart, assertive performance in the first parliament, that had prepared the way for others to challenge the hegemony of official unionism.[48]

Woods was no more deferential in his second parliament than in his first, but he was less rough-edged and garrulous, and provoked less antagonism. Evidently he was growing accustomed to protocol and etiquette and more attuned to the niceties and subtleties of political debate. The increased number of independent and oppositionist members in the house (by 1927, all ten Nationalist representatives, including Devlin, had taken up their seats) also meant that he was no longer in such an isolated, anomalous and beleaguered position as earlier. Most of Woods' interventions addressed similar social and economic issues as before, especially matters which concerned the welfare of ex-servicemen. On these issues, he sometimes voted alongside the socialists against the government. He regularly railed against civil service and parliamentary expenditures, which he thought exorbitantly high, and against the employment of Englishmen in Northern Irish civil service and police posts which he thought should be filled by unemployed Ulstermen.[49]

He also became involved in parliamentary committee work, reviewing and redrafting the detail of legislative proposals. In 1926, he was particularly engaged with the Motor Vehicles (Traffic and Regulation) Bill. In 1927, he turned his attention to a new Intoxicating Liquor and Licensing Bill.[50] The same year, he introduced his own Employment of Disabled Ex-Servicemen's Bill. This was a worthy piece of legislation which included some radical and innovative provisions to create jobs for veterans. Its author, however, once again demonstrated that his principles were stronger than his sense of pragmatism. Instead of seeking Unionist backing, Woods asked a Labour colleague to second the bill. This automatically alienated the government majority, never enamoured of his maverick politics anyway. The bill was rejected.[51]

Woods also resolutely denounced any policy-making or practice tainted by sectarianism. 'If he is an ex-Service man,' Woods declared in 1926, 'he should be treated equally with others no matter what his convictions may be. The sooner these people [Roman Catholics] are treated in a proper and just spirit the better it will be for the honour of [...] the Government.'[52] His concern was not merely for Catholic ex-servicemen, but for the principle of equality. Three years later, during a debate on the government's long-delayed legislation introducing single-member constituencies, Woods decried the tendency to 'keep on talking about this Roman Catholic and Protestant business. Could we not cut that out? [...] Could we not all be Ulstermen and work for the good of the country? Is that not what we are here for?'[53]

Two months later, in June 1929, Craig dissolved parliament and called the first elections to be held under the new voting system. The West Belfast district was now split into four constituencies. Woods stood for the St Annes division, centred on his birthplace of Sandy Row. His opponents were Major J. H. McCormick, a Canadian ex-soldier and official Unionist, who attacked Woods with the customary allegations of political treachery, and Mrs Emily Moffat Clow, a temperance campaigner, who denounced the Colonel on the grounds that he was backed by the licensed trade. The Woods brothers retaliated with the usual denunciations of the 'old clique' which, they said, had established 'an intellectual reign of terror [when] a man dare not come out to speak his mind'.[54] The accusation was overstated. After three pugnacious campaigns, replete with street-corner hustings, torchlight processions and fife and drum bands, and six years of indomitable obstinacy in parliament, the 'Fighting Colonel' did not seem to have been intimidated into silence.

The day before the Northern Irish elections, Woods declared his candidacy for the impending Westminster general election, scheduled to take place only eight days later. We cannot know whether he now harboured serious political ambitions, and wished to set his sights higher than the frustratingly introverted and in-bred provincial assembly in which he had served his parliamentary apprenticeship. His stated reason for standing for Westminster was a desire to pursue the question of protection for the linen trade, a matter that he had already raised in Northern Ireland only to be told it was reserved for the imperial parliament.[55]

We do not know if he was being overconfident in entering this contest (he was the favourite to win the St Anne's division in the provincial election, which would be his third provincial victory), or, conversely, whether he was already anticipating defeat locally and realised he could give himself a second chance at the polls without having to incur more than a week's additional campaigning expenses. Or perhaps he had other reasons for wishing to move to London at this time. In any case, his decision does prove he was not merely a stooge of the Ulster publicans, who had partly funded his domestic electioneering, since they had no special interest in the imperial parliament.

In the Westminster constituency of West Belfast, Woods' old rival Sir Joseph Davison had proposed as Unionist candidate the twenty-eight year old, Eton-educated scion of one of Belfast's richest families, W. E. D. Allen. His opponent was a prominent Nationalist barrister. With the district divided between the lower Shankill area and the strongly Catholic Falls Road, it was clearly a two-horse race. Woods therefore chose to stand in South Belfast. There the Unionist candidate, his only opponent, was another prominent local millionaire, W. J. Stewart. The Stewart family firm happened at the time to have a £650,000 contract to construct a new, grandiose building for the Northern Irish parliament at Stormont castle.[56]

The Northern Irish elections took place on 22 May, and the results were announced the following day. The new electoral system had yielded the outcome desired by the government. The Unionists increased their majority from fourteen to twenty-two. In St Anne's, Woods was the runner-up by a relatively narrow margin, but as the new single member constituencies allowed for no transfer of second-choice votes this meant that he lost his seat. *The Times* newspaper called his defeat 'one of the surprises' of the election.[57]

Woods thereupon turned his energies to campaigning for Westminster. In the previous imperial parliament, Ulster's thirteen-strong representation had been exclusively Unionist. At this election, Unionists retained two seats uncontested, but had already ceded Fermanagh and Tyrone to Nationalists Joe Devlin and Thomas Harbison, and in the remaining nine seats faced ten challenges from Liberals, independents and temperance campaigners. In South Belfast,

Stewart challenged Woods to announce his party allegiance: 'Would he vote with the Conservatives, the Liberals or the Socialists?'[58] Woods' answer was that he would support Stanley Baldwin's Conservative Party, being loyal to all their policies except that on pensions for disabled men. He was interested in protecting linen, creating employment and housing, but, above all, he would continue to look out for the ex-serviceman.[59]

On two occasions, Woods stated that he had worked in the linen trade for over seventeen years; once he referred to his nineteen years in the business. Since he could not have been employed for more than fifteen years before the war, this might imply that he had supplemented his meagre parliamentary remuneration with part-time work as a textile designer during the last few years. In any case, he presented himself as a man of independent means motivated solely by the instinct of charity: 'he had nothing else to do,' he was reported as declaring piously, 'and nothing gave him greater pleasure than to work both in and out of parliament for the good of the people.'[60]

Woods' brief campaign was unsuccessful. For the Westminster poll, it was the backing of a party machine or big money that counted, and Woods had neither. In the event, Stewart polled over twenty-four thousand votes, Woods ten thousand fewer.[61] After the announcement of such a creditable defeat, Woods thanked his supporters 'who have not forgotten that patriotism, principle and loyalty still count.' He continued, 'I think I will leave it at that, but there is always a future.'[62]

Chapter 10

New Beginnings
London and Lord Haw-Haw, 1930–1939

Woods' own future must have seemed uncertain at this moment. Disappearing from public life, he almost disappears from the historian's view. In the mid-1920s, Woods had joined the Junior Naval and Military Club in Pall Mall, London (previously his only club membership had been of the Ulster Reform Club, a dignified liberal Unionist establishment in Belfast).[1] This might suggest that he was starting to travel to the capital more often. We know that on 16 February 1928, Woods attended a reception at the Lithuanian Legation at Palace Gate, London, held in celebration of the small state's tenth anniversary of independence.[2]

We also know that during 1930 Woods became romantically involved in the capital with an Englishwoman named Veronica 'Billie' Quested.[3] Then early the following year he left Belfast to settle in London, embarking on a new stage in both his personal and professional life. In December 1933, Philip Woods was divorced from Florence.[4] A few months later he and Veronica were married. Initially, the newly-weds lived in a flat in Woodstock House, James Street (just off Oxford Street, central London). A couple of years later, they moved to Well Cottage, a quaint Elizabethan black-beamed, thatch-roofed dwelling in Long

Crendon, an archetypally English village situated in Buckinghamshire in the shadow of the Chiltern Hills, halfway between Oxford and Aylesbury.[5]

Although only a thirty-five mile drive or short train journey from central London, Long Crendon must have seemed a world away from the bustle of the capital. This was the time of the Great Depression, when the industrialised world, and those countries which supplied industry's raw materials, were shaken by economic upheaval and mass unemployment, increasingly bitter political and social divisions and ever more sharply polarised debates on new radical solutions.[6] The great cities were both the focus and symbols of crisis and change. British politics too was in tumult. In Westminster, the older statesmen of the moderate centre faltered while on the streets radicalism of both left and right grew in stridency and popular appeal.

In May 1930 Oswald Mosley, then a Labour member of parliament and junior minister, withdrew from the minority government that veteran Labour leader Ramsay MacDonald had formed after the general election a year earlier. Mosley was one of a younger generation of public men (he was born in 1896) who had been radicalised by trench warfare and embittered by post-war politics. This generation spoke of 'the decay of democracy and parliamentarianism' and the need for a fresh start.[7] In response to this, Mosley's ambition, in the words of his biographer, was to create a 'new type of movement which combined the passion for social reform with the Übermensch psychology that could alone bring it about.'[8] He believed in populism and patriotism, imperial preference, economic planning and public works, in building a 'land fit for heroes' and in 'the union of the 'young minds' of whatever age against the 'old gangs'.[9]

In early 1931, Mosley left the Labour Party. His first venture was to establish the New Party with a group of like-minded parliamentary rebels. Their failure in the general election later that year, however, prompted a change of strategy. After a visit to Mussolini in 1932, Mosley founded the British Union of Fascists (BUF), which during the next few years grew into a huge and potentially powerful organisation. One of Mosley's earliest and keenest followers (and the only Conservative politician to defect to the New Party) was W. E. D. Allen, the young Ulster millionaire and West Belfast MP, who helped finance the fascist movement in its early days and became, for a while, one of its leading propagandists.[10]

For a while it must have seemed to Woods that many of his own resentments of the old order and prescriptions for renewal were, for better or worse, beginning to shape the mainstream of national political life. On moving to London, he set up the Institute of Political Secretaries (IPS), a correspondence school for people aspiring to a career in public affairs. It is likely that Woods' motives for this venture were both pragmatic and political. With high levels of unemployment among the educated classes and intense public interest in political life, the IPS must have seemed a viable and potentially lucrative business proposition. Woods' own experience of Ulster's amateurish parliamentary politics and inefficient bureaucracy had doubtless also prompted him to reflect on the need to cultivate a more professional breed of political operator and public servant. Additionally, it is easy to see how his long-standing antagonism towards the 'tyrannical clique' of 'mouldy old men' translated into a desire to train new blood, as wilful and independent as himself, to challenge entrenched interests and traditional elites. To these ends, the IPS offered training in public speaking and political writing, secretarial skills and foreign languages, as well as opportunities to study political, economic and social issues of contemporary concern. As we shall see below, the IPS's curriculum offered ample scope for individual tutors to shape their students' perceptions and beliefs.

Woods launched the IPS, headquartered at his new home address, with an advertisement in the 'Personal' column of *The Times* on 8 July 1931:

> Many successful men and women have commenced their careers as Political Secretaries. There are great opportunities both Home and Abroad in the Diplomatic and Consular Services – Write or 'phone the Secretary, The Institute of Political Secretaries, 5, Woodstock House, James-street, London, W.1. Tele., London 2183.[11]

These notices appeared almost weekly for a few months, then every two to four weeks for seven and a half years (with a break between September 1933 and July 1934, during which period Woods was presumably preoccupied with his domestic re-arrangements). In 1932 Woods altered the first part of the text to read: 'Politics to-day offer immense opportunities for trained Political Secretaries under the Imperial and Dominion Parliaments, The League of Nations, Private, &c.'[12] At the end of 1935, after the Woods had moved out to Long

Crendon, the IPS transferred a short distance to premises in Gilbert Street, Mayfair, heart of London's clubland and diplomatic district.

While principal of the IPS, Woods joined the Royal Empire Society, founded as the Colonial Society in 1868 to promote public knowledge of Britain's overseas territories (it was renamed the Royal Commonwealth Society in 1958 and is still in existence). Woods also became a member of the Publicity Club of London, a meeting-place for those involved in advertising, public relations and the media, presumably because he was interested in techniques of political communication. He remained a member of the Ulster Arts Club, a centre of provincial cultural life, to which he had been elected in 1931. He also joined the Royal Automobile Club in Pall Mall, through which he could pursue his long-standing enthusiasm for motoring.

Meanwhile the IPS's fortunes fluctuated. At one point, Woods was forced to borrow capital from the Quested family to keep the business solvent. At the end of 1938, the IPS ceased placing its regular advertisements. Only two much shorter notices appeared the following year ('excellent opportunities offering important positions; splendid prospects'), the second and final one appearing on 20 June 1939. The IPS probably ceased to operate soon afterwards. Woods had already started collecting material for his Karelian memoir in early 1938, and wrote the text during the following year when, presumably, he had an increasing amount of free time.[13]

At no time did the IPS have a large full-time staff, instead employing a roster of freelance tutors. In 1932–1933, the IPS's letterhead identified only Woods as principal and a certain Eric C. Lawford as secretary. Later in the decade, its stationery listed Woods plus eight tutors by name.[14] Among these were a Mr L. W. Desbrow, who was identified as a Barrister at Law, but was in fact a recent graduate of the London School of Economics and was concurrently lecturing in economics at his old university. After the Second World War, Desbrow became a major figure in the British advertising industry.[15] The list includes four others with English names who boasted qualifications in economics, chartered accountancy and secretaryship, and three with foreign names who were presumably language tutors. One of these was Alexander Gambs, the son of Ernest Gambs, who had been a Russian Vice-Consul in London before the revolution and was President of the Russian Refugees Association in England and a prominent member of Russian émigré circles during the 1930s. Since the early 1920s, Alex had been earning a meagre living by giving piano recitals, and tutoring in Russian, French and German.[16]

The sparse historical record enables us to identify one other person whom Woods employed as a tutor soon after he established his school. This was William Joyce, who within a couple of years would achieve notoriety as a fanatical fascist agitator, later garnering yet more opprobrium as the Nazi wartime broadcaster Lord Haw-Haw, and in January 1946 would be hanged for treason.

Joyce was born in 1906 in New York to an Irish father and English mother. Three years later the family resettled in Galway, southern Ireland. As Joyce told British interrogators in 1945, he 'was brought up as an extreme Conservative with strong Imperialist ideas.'[17] He claimed to have served, at the age of fourteen, as an irregular attached to the intelligence unit of the 2nd Battalion, Royal Ulster Rifles (Woods' regiment), during the Irish civil war and to have participated alongside the Black and Tans in operations against the IRA and their suspected sympathisers.[18]

After the Anglo-Irish Treaty, the strongly pro-British Joyce family fled to England. In 1927, William obtained a first-class degree in English at Birkbeck College, University of London, and then, having been turned down by the Foreign Office because of his 'extreme views' and advocacy of 'violence in political action', began teaching languages and history at the Victoria Tutorial College.[19] During the 1920s, Joyce became involved first with the British Fascisti movement and later the Conservative Party in Chelsea and the Junior Imperial League. The Tories were impressed by his enthusiasm, dedication and oratorical skills, but became increasingly concerned by his authoritarian tendencies, his 'aggressive nationalism' and vicious anti-Semitism, which he made no effort to hide.[20]

By 1931, Joyce had been forced to resign from the constituency organisation. Sometime in the second half of the year, he established contact with Woods and the IPS, and soon began offering tuition for them on a freelance basis, even though he was already working thirty-two hours a week at the Victoria Tutorial College.[21]

None of the numerous biographies of William Joyce mentions his association with the IPS, or the name of Philip Woods, and only sparse documentary evidence exists substantiating this link. In late 1931, Captain Charles Cecil Courtney Lewis, late of the Indian Army, was working in a lowly, dead-end diplomatic post in Jeddah on the Arabian

Peninsula. Wanting desperately to return to Britain with his wife and young child, and with vague ambitions for a political career but little idea of how to embark on one, he read the IPS's newspaper advertisement promising 'great opportunities' and enrolled for a correspondence course in political rhetoric. Woods assigned William Joyce to be Lewis' tutor.

For the next six months, Joyce had his student compose and send him every week (via the diplomatic bag) drafts of political speeches, mock newspaper articles and essays on current affairs. Joyce read these assignments thoroughly and returned them with dense annotations and extensive commentaries. The two young men also exchanged private letters, in which they discussed their political ambitions, Colonel Woods and the IPS. It is clear from these materials that Joyce saw Lewis less as a pupil than as a protégé, impressionable, tractable and reassuringly less talented than himself, and derived a sense of self-importance from cultivating their relationship. While fastidiously correcting Lewis's turgid and plodding prose and his frequent errors of spelling and grammar, Joyce praised his student's critical stance towards modern politics and urged him towards even more hostile perspectives. 'It is refreshing,' Joyce wrote in the margin of one of Lewis' practice speeches, 'to read your antiseptic philosophy in a poisonous age.' 'Your answer contains much good thought and much concentrated venom,' he wrote in another. 'Really,' he opined elsewhere, with a revealing parenthetical remark, 'I am beginning to think that the oratory of Hitler (absit omen) is in danger of losing its laurels.'[22]

When Lewis asked to which party he should attach himself, Joyce responded that the Labour Party was dead – its 'men of culture' were all without principle and its 'filthy proletarians' would sooner or later turn to fascism or communism. Then, demonstrating the same expediency he condemned in others, Joyce recommended that his student seek a Conservative nomination, and volunteered his own help (free of charge) in teaching Lewis 'a few dodges of the trade' based on his own experience. 'Despite my vile cynicism in a previous letter,' Joyce wrote, 'I tell you that you can get into Parliament if the getting there is your supreme motive.'[23]

Joyce also assured Lewis that the IPS undertook to place its successful students in appropriate jobs. 'I believe that Col Woods will leave no stone unturned to help a satisfactory pupil,' he commented, adding that it was after all in the school's interest to arrange employment for its graduates. He advised Lewis to 'cling with bulldog tenacity to the Institute' but not to spend more than he originally intended. 'The Colonel,' he warned, 'believes in the efficacity of longer courses, not realizing, possibly, that you conquered the law in a matter of months.' (Lewis had recently received a legal qualification, presumably also by correspondence.) Joyce promised to intervene with Woods – whom he called 'an old friend of mine' – on his student's behalf should it be necessary. 'I have occasionally been disappointed by the Colonel's fits of lassitude and philosophic detachment,' Joyce confided. 'He works best under high, ruthless, but noiseless pressure.'[24]

In another letter, Joyce states that Woods was 'under the same obligation' to find him a job as well.[25] Indeed, Joyce probably first contacted the IPS also after reading its advertisement, in the hope that it would help him to get his political career back on track, rather than for employment as a tutor. He was still cursing his own 'awful tactlessness and general recklessness' that had recently wrecked his chances of advancement via the Chelsea Conservative Association.[26] Woods had presumably assured Joyce that he would do his best to help him, perhaps thinking he glimpsed in the twenty-six year old Irishman's 'extreme' conservativism and 'strong' imperialism something of his own youthful ardour and audacity, and taking him on as a protégé or project, without perceiving the psychopathic dimensions of his character. In any case, after half a year or so Joyce was evidently becoming frustrated with the Colonel's apparent inability, or disinclination, to fulfil his undertaking.

As it happened, Woods did not need to find work for either of the young men. In May 1932, Joyce registered for a PhD in educational psychology at King's College, London. At first he threw himself headlong into his research. During 1933, however, he joined the BUF and towards the end of the year dedicated himself full-time to the movement, at the same time giving up his studies and most of his tutoring work. In early 1934, Mosley appointed Joyce to be the BUF's Director of Propaganda. In 1937, Joyce fell out with the fascist leader and was fired from the movement. Mosley was, he complained bitterly, 'not the man that he [Joyce] had thought he was.'[27] Joyce then founded the National Socialist League (NSL), earned some money from private tutoring – refusing to take Jewish or black students – and descended into ever deeper extremes of racist and anti-democratic frothing until his eventual defection to Germany on 26 August 1939, eight days before the outbreak of war.[28]

Captain Lewis, meanwhile, had returned to Britain in the summer of 1932. As well as contacting Woods and Joyce, he made Mosley's acquaintance, gave a few public lectures on Middle Eastern politics, and at the start of 1933 was appointed the founding editor of the BUF's first weekly newspaper, *The Blackshirt*.[29] In April, Lewis accompanied Mosley on the latter's second visit to Mussolini in Rome.[30] So when Woods contacted his former student in March 1933 to offer him the post of secretary of the IPS (Eric Lawford having resigned, on his wife's insistence, to become a local councillor in Eastbourne), with the remit of developing its 'Indian Branch' and a not inconsiderable salary of £400 a year, Lewis was already otherwise occupied.[31] He continued to edit *The Blackshirt* until 1934, when he became Mosley's legal advisor, defending BUF members in numerous civil and criminal cases.[32] In April 1937, the same month as Joyce founded the NSL, Lewis was declared bankrupt, and ceased working for the fascist movement.[33] He was divorced the next year, after which he disappears from the historical record.[34]

Inevitably, our knowledge of Woods' association with Joyce gives rise to a difficult and troubling question. To what degree was Woods himself drawn towards or involved with fascism at the time he was writing his Karelian memoir?

The evidence both for and against any fascist sympathies or affiliations is circumstantial. Regarding Woods' political values, we are already familiar with his battle-proven commitment to King and Country, his belief in discipline, virtue and fair play for the common man, his sense of personal grievance and vocal contempt for the inept, venal 'old gang' of party plutocrats, and his vision of a more honourable, honest and direct form of politics, in which all social classes and groups subordinated their sectarian interests to the common good. It will be remembered that in 1929 his valedictory words were a call to 'patriotism, principle and loyalty'. For Woods, the British empire was both a natural right and a duty higher even than the law (as his signature of the Ulster Covenant demonstrated). Yet the 'King of Karelia' understood that too often the practice of imperial power was degenerate and dishonourable. Woods' bitterness at the end of the North Russian campaign is palpable in his memoir as he describes the British abandonment of those they had recruited and used for their own ends 'to the "tender mercies" of their enemies'. 'One could not avoid the thought,' he wrote, echoing Churchill's sentiment cited earlier, 'that our ineffectual intervention was mainly responsible for their plight' (p. 293). None of these convictions or resentments, of course, make him a fascist, though many who shared his sentiments were drawn to the far right of politics.[35]

Indeed, Woods was in many respects of the 'type' who was attracted to far-right politics in this period. For one thing, 'fascism', as one historian has written, 'was the "soldier's socialism", the political form through which he could express the social idealism generated in the war and betrayed by the politicians'.[36] Among Mosley's followers were several prominent military men, such as Major-General J. F. C. Fuller, a brilliant tactical innovator in tank warfare and renowned historian, and Admiral Sir Barry Domvile, a former Director of Naval Intelligence, as well as many officers and soldiers, both serving and retired, of lower ranks. As well as fighting in the Great War, many had served in South Africa and other colonies, Russia during the intervention and Ireland during the civil war. Many, like Woods, had a clear sense of what, at least in principle, they believed elevated the 'White Man' above the 'black' native, and the Briton above all others – in racial, cultural and moral terms. In 1939, rumours circulated that Field Marshall Ironside, who had commanded the Archangel force in 1918–1919 and was appointed Chief of the Imperial General Staff at the outbreak of the Second Wold War (and was famously frank about his prejudices), was a clandestine BUF member.[37]

Woods himself was first and foremost a soldier, in his ethos, self-image and public persona. We know from the Karelian memoir that Woods met annually with other North Russian veterans at the Army and Navy Club (the 'Rag') during the 1930s (p. 296). He was also active in the British Legion. For William Joyce (who had himself once entertained military ambitions), as for Woods' Long Crendon neighbours, 'the Colonel' was a typical retired military man, dapper and upright, an excellent teller of 'good stories' about his campaign in Russia against the Reds and other foes.[38]

Fascism also held an appeal for 'displaced professional men' and 'unhappy imperial wanderers', who had, like Woods, been educated in a Buchanesque creed of British superiority, service and sacrifice, and who felt unvalued and alienated in post-war mass society. Some were listless, traumatised souls. Others were 'modern buccaneers' – loners, rebels and mavericks seeking fulfilment, or refuge, in the romance of imperial adventure (the officers volunteering for North Russia were dubbed 'Modern Buccaneers', as Woods recalls, 'by some bright lad in the War Office,' p. 150). For many, as one historian has written, 'long sojourns abroad also produced a highly unreal picture of England to add to more immediate grievances.'[39] Fascism met this need for fantasy in two ways, invoking, on the one hand, a future of technology, hygiene and health, and, on the other, a collectivist rural past, which many (such as W. E. D. Allen, or the historian Arthur Bryant) identified with the Elizabethan nation of the pre-bourgeois, pre-capitalist sixteenth century.[40]

The Tudor thatch, timber-frames and rolling farmlands of Buckinghamshire seem to have attracted more than their fair share of retired 'buccaneers', as well as armchair imperial adventurers, dreaming of just such a pastoral idyll. Many had the politics to match. Bryant had his country home at East Claydon, about twelve miles north of Long Crendon, where he regularly hosted leading fascists like Major Francis Yeats-Brown (formerly of the Indian Army, and author of the best-selling novel *Bengal Lancer*).[41] Michael Beaumont, a former Guardsman and Conservative MP for Aylesbury, a few miles to the east, declared to the House of Commons in 1934 that he was 'an avowed anti-Democrat and an avowed admirer of Fascism in other countries,' and asserted that there were a lot of 'respectable, reasonable and intelligent people' in the British fascist movement.[42]

The Conservative MP for Wycombe, just to the south, was Sir Alfred Knox, the Ulsterman who had fought with Admiral Kolchak in Siberia during the intervention, clearly enunciating at that time his hostility towards the 'Jew Commissary' and his contempt for the 'useless bourgeois'. During the 1930s, he demonstrated an equally zealous commitment to improving relations with Nazi Germany. To this end, Knox enrolled in the Anglo-German Fellowship, an organisation which also counted among its members General Ironside, Admiral Domvile and other prominent military men, as well as twenty-three other MPs, twenty-eight peers of the realm, and numerous industrialists, bishops and bankers.[43] Their enthusiasm for Hitler, of course, did not make them potential fifth columnists or even necessarily supporters of appeasement (though many were). Indeed, as has been noted, 'the majority of those British people who admired Nazi Germany were also highly patriotic; and these searchers after peace were often strongly militaristic as well.'[44]

One of the most active participants in the Fellowship (though he did not live in Buckinghamshire) was Lieutenant-Colonel Sir Thomas Cecil Russell Moore, an Anglo-Irishman (born 1886) who since 1925 had sat as Conservative MP for Ayr Burghs in Scotland. Before that, he had been attached to the Ministry of Home Affairs in Ulster for two years, and earlier had served on the General Headquarters Staff in southern Ireland.[45] Before that, Colonel T. C. R. Moore had served under Woods' command in Kem, as the Service Corps officer responsible for transport and supplies. In the Karelian memoir, Woods gratefully recalls that Moore 'did not allow his work to get the better of his unfailing sense of humour' (p. 279).

Unfortunately, Moore became more earnest after entering politics. Soon after his first visit to Nazi Germany in September 1933 he wrote: 'if I may judge from my personal knowledge of Herr Hitler, peace and justice are the keywords of his policy.'[46] The following year he declared that Mosley's fascists and the Conservatives had no 'fundamental difference of outlook' and were both motivated by 'loyalty to the throne and love of country'.[47] In 1936, Moore, together with Admiral Domvile and others, was among Hitler's guests of honour at the Nuremberg Rally. The following year Moore received a knighthood. For the rest of the decade he continued to sing Hitler's praises for bringing 'happiness, security and hope' to the German people, eliminating corruption and vice, investing in social progress and cultivating 'self-reliance, self-confidence and self-help'.[48] We know from the Karelian memoir that in 1938 Woods asked Moore to help him obtain a War Office pension for a Russian lady who had helped the British forces in Karelia and who was at that time living destitute in Paris (pp. 295–96).

Of course, the fact that Woods was in contact with Moore at this time does not imply he had any sympathy with the latter's political views. However, one octogenarian resident of Long Crendon recalls that William Joyce stayed with Woods at Well Cottage while the Colonel was 'secretary of an Anglo-German link group'.[49] If true, this would provide a more tangible link with Moore, who was a founding member of the Anglo-German Fellowship in September 1935.

However, the interviewee's reference is more likely to be to another organisation, called The Link, that Admiral Domvile established in July 1937. This organisation shared the Anglo-German Fellowship's aim of promoting a rapprochement between the two countries, but was less socially exclusive and, at leadership level, unambiguously aligned with the Nazi regime's ideology and aims.[50] During 1938, The Link grew rapidly, and by mid-1939 had enrolled over 4,300 members in its local branches, spread mainly around the London suburbs, the Midlands and the West Country. Northern Ireland had one association. These branches operated autonomously, arranging social events, film showings, tourist trips and exchanges, and other innocuous activities designed to foster, in Domvile's words, 'mutual sympathy and understanding between the peoples of Great Britain and Germany,' with only a leavening of overt political propagandising.[51] At local level, ordinary membership of the organisation did not necessarily imply raving anti-Semitism, pro-Nazi sentiment or subversive intent, though some branches, such as those in Belfast, West London and Central London, were more radical than others. Few of the officials and organisers in any branch could have been unaware of the leadership's views.

Indeed, many of the more active members of The Link also attended meetings of Joyce's NSL, and were associated with other far-right groups of the time, such as the Nordic League or the Right Club, the latter a highly clandestine group established in May 1939 by Scottish Conservative MP Captain Archibald Ramsay.[52] Joyce was involved in both these organisations. Another leading member of the Right Club was Anna Wolkoff, daughter of the last Imperial Russian Naval Attaché to London, who now ran the Russian Tea Room in South Kensington. In the late 1930s, these premises became the meeting place for many of London's anti-Semites and Nazi sympathisers (many of whom, including Joyce, lived in the immediate vicinity).[53] Alex Gambs, whom Woods employed in the late 1930s as a tutor for the IPS, associated socially with Wolkoff's émigré circle, though we have no evidence that he shared her political beliefs.[54] In November 1940, Wolkoff was imprisoned for ten years for breaching the Official Secrets Act. Among other things, she had transmitted classified information to her friend William Joyce, which he used in his early wartime broadcasts from Germany.[55]

We do not know whether Buckinghamshire boasted any local associations of The Link, or whether Woods was in any way affiliated to this organisation or other groups either here or elsewhere. Still, if our Long Crendon respondent's memory is precise with regard to both Joyce's visits to Well Cottage and the 'Anglo-German link group', then Woods maintained his association with Joyce until at least mid-1937 (when The Link was founded). If Woods was indeed active in pro-German circles in the second half of the decade *and* still associating with Joyce, whose pathological fanaticism became increasingly visible, even to his admirers, after his break with Mosley, it would be unlikely that Woods himself was not also entangled in far-right politics.

It is worth reiterating, however, that almost all this evidence is circumstantial. The remainder is speculative, and therefore does not constitute evidence at all. Oral history, especially, is unreliable and becomes more so as the time between the events recollected and the moment of recall increases. The Long Crendon resident cited above was only a boy in the 1930s. He remembers Woods as a man 'of medium height and very smart in a military fashion' (which is true) who won the Victoria Cross in the Great War (which is not). Untangling memory from hearsay is rarely possible, especially as Joyce seems now to have entered Long Crendon village folklore (otherwise populated by a disproportionate number of ghosts). Several long-term residents – many of whom do not recall Colonel Woods at all – report a rumour that Lord Haw-Haw lived in Well Cottage for a time. This we know to be incorrect.

Regardless of the veracity of any of this evidence, to impute fascist sympathies to a person on the basis solely of the society they kept, or where they lived, is nonsensical. In any case, we have good reason to doubt some of the material evidence we do have. In particular, it is highly improbable that Joyce and Woods were already 'old friends' by 1932, as the former claimed in several letters to Lewis. For one thing, the Colonel was twenty-six years Joyce's senior. He had been in London scarcely more than a year, and could not have known Joyce before 1921 in southern Ireland. They were also quite different personalities. Joyce was both a bookish intellectual and a violent thug.[56] Woods was decidedly neither.

Although we may glimpse affinities in some of their beliefs and values, their political creeds were poles apart in defining respects. Joyce was an hysterical bigot and arch-conspirator who advocated nothing less than anti-democratic revolution, dictatorship and race war. As an MP in the 1920s, Woods had consistently opposed extremism, sectarianism and discrimination on religious, political or national grounds. His robust individualism and inclusive sense of social responsibility implied disdain for any clandestine intrigue (witness his contempt for the inveterate White Russian conspirators in the Karelian memoir), for any would-be leader's claims to the unique truth, for adherence to any exclusive idea or organisation, and for any attempt by 'extremists' (as he had termed the temperance campaigners) to limit personal or collective liberties. He was conservative by instinct, hostile to revolutionary politics in any form.

In West Belfast in 1923, Woods had declared 'I am essentially a Democrat.' Fascists far less immoderate than Joyce rejected not merely the perceived abuse of democracy by plutocratic interests, but democracy itself as a dreary liberal charade, to be superseded by an authoritarian corporatist state. There is no reason to doubt Woods' commitment to the parliamentary system, however much he deprecated the politicians who populated it. Although of course it is possible that Woods' views changed after his double-defeat in Belfast in 1929, his earlier political trajectory gives no hint that he would be susceptible to extreme radicalisation; indeed it suggests the opposite.

Nor can Woods' invectives against the 'old gang' in his parliamentary campaigns, any more than his taste for torchlight processions, be taken as evidence of proto-fascism. This phrase, which originated in parliamentary disputes of the mid-seventeenth century, was common political parlance by the turn of the twentieth century, invoking youthful vitality and businesslike efficiency against conservative torpor.[57] Woods' repeated use of the expression points more to a lack of genuine intellectual originality and rhetorical inventiveness than to any particular political stance.

As suggested above, it is much more likely that Joyce first contacted Woods in late 1931, hoping for help in finding a job, and attached himself to the Colonel for only as long as he thought the latter might be useful to him. As one of Joyce's recent biographers has written, 'apart from a tiny coterie of individuals around him, Joyce went through associates at a rate of knots. He seems to have been the kind of individual who met people, used them, fell out with them and dropped them'.[58] Given Joyce's proclivities to both fantasy and self-aggrandisement, it is quite credible that he should boast to Lewis that the Colonel and he were 'old friends' to boost his own credentials in the eyes of his student. Lewis would probably have seen through the deceit as soon as he met both of them later in the year. The fact that Woods offered Lewis a full-time job in March 1933, a few months after the latter had begun to edit the BUF newspaper, suggests that Woods was not in close or regular contact with either of the younger men by this time.

This does not rule out the possibility that Joyce paid Woods one or more visits in Long Crendon later in the decade, perhaps en route between London and meetings in Oxford or Birmingham. Given Joyce's notoriety as a rabble-rouser even before the war, such a visit or short stay might have occasioned greater local interest and gossip than it really warranted, accounting for Lord Haw-Haw's special place in village memory.

The fact that many of Woods' 'type' and social milieu were attracted to fascism says nothing about his individual politics. Later in Woods' life he was reportedly 'scathing' in private conversation about Mosley's arrogant posturing.[59] Knowing what we do of Woods' character and values, it seems more credible that he criticised the fascist leader from a standpoint of moderation than of extremism. Most Conservatives, after all, disagreed with Beaumont, and believed the BUF to be repugnant, ridiculous or irrelevant. Distaste grew especially after mid-1934 when (partly under Joyce's influence) the rhetoric of the British fascists became more obsessively preoccupied with the Jews, a topic that at the time offended relatively few but enthused even fewer. We have already encountered Woods' dry and gently sardonic humour (evident also in the Karelian Diary) and may imagine he would have savoured novelist P. G. Wodehouse's character Roderick Spode, 8th Earl of Sidcup, the 'amateur dictator' and leader of the 'Black Shorts' ('By the time Spode formed his association, there were no shirts left'), with their salutation 'Heil, Spode!'[60] It is harder to imagine how Woods could have tolerated a 'pompous, conceited little creature' like William Joyce (as he was described in an MI5 report).[61]

Proto-fascist ideas did not always lead to fascism. Crozier's experience in Ireland, and his bitter subsequent struggles with British politicians and bureaucrats to defend his name and secure his pension, had led him to question the assumed benefits of modernity, culture and progress. 'Democracy,' Crozier wrote in 1932, 'if judged by the Black and Tan venture, failed after a million democrats had offered the supreme sacrifice for the salvation of England.'[62] His diagnosis of contemporary society and politics was that 'drastic diseases require drastic remedies.' We have already cited his call for a 'superman' with 'the Mussolini touch'.[63] Nevertheless, Crozier chose to follow the path of militant pacifism, becoming a leading patron of the Peace Pledge Union until his early death in August 1937. 'His fighting spirit,' wrote one of his obituarists, 'was so fundamental to his nature that it was translated – rather than transformed – into the sphere where he now sought to communicate his convictions of the futility of war even in self-defence.'[64]

Pacifism was the antithesis of the fascists' glorification of violence. In 1932, Crozier was among over three hundred people who volunteered their services to the League of Nations Union to place themselves unarmed between armies in a future war, in the belief that such an act would inspire the combatants to lay down weapons.[65] Just before his death, Crozier published a belligerently penitent memoir titled *The Men*

I Have Killed, which another obituarist declared 'best forgotten' and 'in the worst of taste' for its vivid portrayal of the drunken, unrestrained bestiality of men in battle.[66] It is interesting to speculate how Crozier would have responded to the threat of impending war two years later, when numerous Peace Pledge Union activists, including its chairman Stuart Morris, joined The Link, presumably unaware of the organisation's true nature and purpose.[67] It is clear that no straightforward equation can be drawn between, on the one hand, a person's background, experience, social identity or individual disposition and, on the other, their ethical values, political beliefs or party attachments.

Most significantly, we have found no extant evidence substantiating any connection between Woods and any fascist or radical organisation. If he played an active role in such a group it is likely that his name would have cropped up in one or another of the sources available to researchers and consulted for the present work.[68] Nor did enquiries to several specialist historians of British fascism turn up any references to either Philip Woods or Veronica Quested.[69]

Of course, the absence of contrary evidence cannot be used to prove that Woods was *not* involved in these circles.[70] But historians rarely have complete and definitive evidence, and so are forced to make reasoned judgements on the balance of probability. On this basis, we may conclude that Woods was not sympathetic to fascism or involved in any fascist organisation. Indeed, he most likely considered the shrill tenor of their arguments and the fanaticism of their stance to be repellent, and their wilder fantasies, prejudices and prescriptions to be preposterous, though he would have felt an affinity to a sub-set of their ideas and values.

In many ways, the complexities, ambiguities and contradictions inherent in Woods' political motivations serve, with no need for further elucidation, to epitomise the political choices facing middling British society at this time, torn between a weary disenchantment with the old and a hearty distrust of the new. Britain, as we know, rejected extreme political solutions. It is probable that Woods did the same.

Epilogue

Even if by 1939 Woods was disenchanted with the moribund politics of the time, and dismayed by the drift into war, this in no way overrode his patriotism. As soon as the Second World War broke out (just as Joyce was settling down in Berlin, and Domvile was – at least publicly – dissolving The Link), Woods rushed to re-enlist in the army. He was turned down because of his age.[1] At the start of September 1939, Woods was a few weeks short of fifty-nine, and had therefore already 'attained the age limit of liability to recall' four years earlier.[2]

One Long Crendon old-timer recalls that Woods 'was responsible for identifying William Joyce from his broadcasts.' There is no reason to doubt that Woods recognised the broadcaster (dubbed Lord Haw-Haw by a British humorist in mid-September) and reported this to the police. However, as Joyce's voice was particularly distinctive, and identified by numerous people, no inferences can be drawn from this concerning the intimacy or extent of their earlier acquaintance.[3]

Woods was now preoccupied, in any case, with more serious and pressing matters. In June 1940, the Colonel forwarded to General Ironside, now Commander-in-Chief of Home Forces (until his sudden removal in mid-July), a new scheme, designed by a former junior officer of the Karelian Regiment, for beacon communications designed to overcome the 'too serious defects in the defence of this country'.[4]

By the following year, Woods was working for the National Savings Movement in its East Riding division, moving north from Buckinghamshire first to the fishing port of Hull and later to the smaller and more attractive seaside town of Bridlington. The first National Savings campaign had been launched during the First World War to encourage people to invest in the war effort via special bond issues. At the end of 1939, a network of regional and local committees was established to coordinate fund-raising activities, fix targets and monitor progress. Chairs of these committees were usually retired officers or other dignitaries drawn from the local county: it is not known why Woods moved from Long Crendon to Yorkshire to take up this employment.

As well as promoting public parsimony, cash savings and investment in government loans (via defence bonds, war savings certificates, etc.), each year the National Savings Movement sponsored an intensive fund-raising week for a specific purpose, with poster campaigns, meetings and social events, such as concerts, church fêtes and tea-dances. In 1941, the East Riding National Savings Association and its sub-committees organised a 'War Weapons Week' and in 1942 a 'Warship Week'. The theme for 1943 was 'Wings for Victory' (in Bridlington, the local RAF band held a week of fund-raising concerts in June), and in 1944 it was 'Salute the Soldier'. It is likely that Woods was also involved in the 5th (East Riding) Battalion of the Home Guard.

During Woods' employment with the National Savings he acquired a large house and smaller flat in Bridlington, and sub-let Well Cottage to a family member. He remained in Yorkshire for a while after the end of the war, before returning briefly to Belfast and then to Long Crendon. In Northern Ireland, he started working again with his brother as a linen designer, specialising in high-quality 'damask' fabrics. Some time after the war, the family business was dissolved or sold. Back in England, Woods continued to carry out design commissions for Ulster linen firms as a freelancer, producing elaborate floral patterns for quilt covers, as well as beginning work on larger-scale tapestries as a hobby.

As Woods grew older and spent his days weaving, the British empire disintegrated. New nations across the world dreamed themselves into existence, often in ethnographic or cartographic configurations created by colonialism. After the Great War and Russian imperial collapse, the Karelians had failed in their campaign for national self-determination. Thirty years and another world war later, African and Asian populations drew inspiration, direction and strength from the same basic principles first articulated and given moral authority by Woodrow Wilson in 1919. This time the peoples prevailed. It was a new world of United Nations,

Cold War and nuclear weapons in which Britain played no major role. Within a few years, the name of the Ulster Volunteer Force would be revived in Northern Ireland by a paramilitary group committed to opposing the Irish Republican Army's struggle for a unified Ireland, and the province would be thrown into forty years of terrorism and civil conflict.

Philip James Woods died peacefully of a heart attack in Well Cottage, Long Crendon, on 12 September 1961, just before his eighty-first birthday.[5]

* * * *

Although Woods tried to publish the Karelian memoir during his lifetime, it is only now being brought to the public's attention. It is to be hoped that this work will stand as a testimony to a life that was in itself individual and remarkable, and at the same time emblematic of the experience of this lost generation of men – this is very much a story of men – whose late nineteenth century notions of idealism, heroism and honour faced the test of total war, imperial decline, social upheaval and political crisis. Some withstood the transition to the new century with dignity and forbearance, seeking to establish a humane new moral order to tame the chaos of modernity. Others succumbed to less noble impulses, sustaining and nurturing the rage, violence, destruction and turmoil that had already disfigured their own lives.

As historians, we have no way of knowing conclusively how Philip Woods responded to the challenges of the early twentieth century. The unanswered questions of his life, the lack of any definitive biographical resolution, do not really matter. They offer us – the historian, the reader, the contemporary commentator – room for reflection, for experiments in empathy and historical intuition. Woods was a man of his times, however singular and specific his personality and career. From present-day perspectives, we can make no simple judgements that are not anachronistic. We can only assess a person's actions in the past in the light of the dilemmas they faced and the choices available to them at the time, and speculate how we might respond to the new dilemmas and choices of our own age.

Part Two

Karelian Diary

Colonel Philip J. Woods

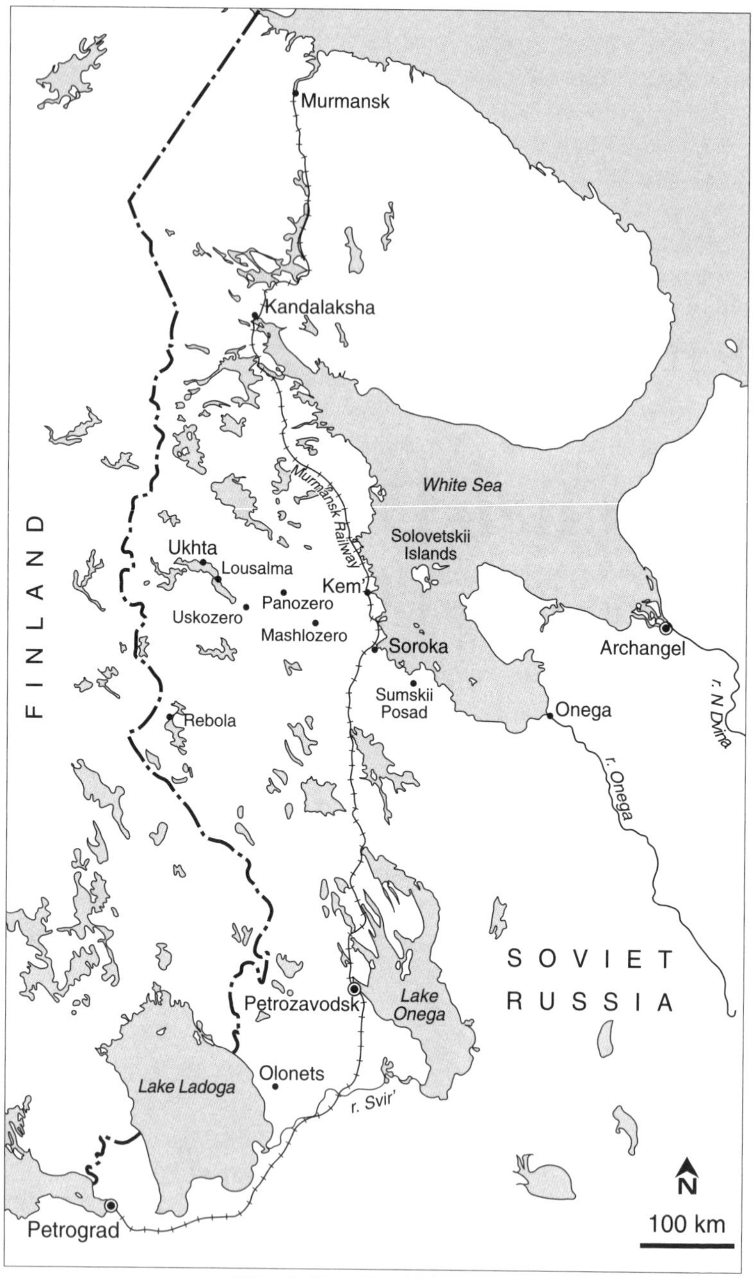

Map 2. Karelia, 1918–1919

Chapter Contents

Chapter 1: Arrival in Karelia
Recruitment – Rumours – "Modern Buccaneers" – Sea voyage to Murmansk – "The Woman of Death" – "Syren" – Arrival in Murmansk on Midsummer's Day – General Poole – Briefing on Mission – Murmansk Muslims – Train journey – Fellow passengers – Mosquitos– Major Burton – Arrival in Kem – Drake-Brockman.

Chapter 2: Formation of Regiment
Description of Kem – Royal Marines – First encounter with Karelians – Disarming the Bolshevik garrison – Resisting Spiridonoff – Allied military personnel – General Maynard – Creation of Slavo-Britannic Legion under Colonel Jocelyn – Karelians request aid to clear country of Finns and Germans – Beards – the Karelian Regiment – Gregori Leziff and Nicoli Petroff – Characterisation of the Karelians – Training – Serbs and Colonel Thornhill of Intelligence – Wine – Designing the Karelian Regimental insignia.

Chapter 3: The Royal Irish Karelians
Attitude of Karelian Regiment to Allies – Slavo-Britannic Legion – Sour cream – HMS *Nairana* – the "Irish Karelians" – Planning operations against Finns – Syphilitic Karelian officer – Embarking for August campaign – Flotilla – Description of Karelian landscape and nature – Karelian women – Shooting.

Chapter 4: The Ouchta Campaign

Summer 1918 – Tactics of the Karelian Regiment – Ground and smoke signals – Germans and Finns – Massacre at Uskozero – White Finnish propaganda – Barbarism at Lousalma – Lieut Kempuieff – Clearance operations towards the Finnish border – Advancing by river – Russian maps – Reaction of Karelian villagers to seaplane – Maynard's plans to withdraw Karelians to Kandalaksha – Woods remains as "King of Karelia" – Intelligence gathering in Finland – Major Burton, commander of Red Finnish Legion – Withdrawal plans cancelled – Bravery of Karelian women – Karelians practise hunters' techniques on captured Finn – Karelian refusal to take prisoners.

Chapter 5: Massacre at Voknavolok

Spreading disinformation – Assault on Ouchta – Escape of German officer – White Finn casualties – Massacre at Voknavolok – Heaton's wireless station at Uskozero – Migrating wildfowl – Description of Karelian houses – Rodents and cockroaches – Rivercraft – Exploits on waterfall – Return to Kem – Karelians' Widows and Orphans Fund.

Chapter 6: Visit to Solievetski

At Kem – Serbs – Russian New Murmansk Army – Russian intrigues against the Karelians and Allies – Deadly influenza – Karelian counter-intelligence – Mascherin – Suspected infiltration of Murmansk Army by Bolsheviks – Assassination attempts against Woods – Russian methods of interrogation – Organising winter supplies for Karelian population – Spring visit to Solievetski Monastery – the Archimandrite – Monastery Buildings and Gardens – Armoury and Treasury.

Chapter 7: Plots Against the Allies

Autumn – Sapper Kennedy – HQ of Karelian Regiment and District Command – Bolshevik agitation on railway at Saroka – General Zveginsiff and Engineer Sacharoff – White Russians conspire against Woods in Murmansk – Zveginsiff plots murder of Allies in Saroka – General Skobolcene of Russian Army – His hideous death – Friendly and unfriendly Russians – Essieff – Allied personnel.

Chapter 8: Winter in Kem, 1918

Winter 1918 – Aurora Borealis – Sounds of frost – Mickey and Meesha – Ahava's skiing – Russian hospitality and entertainments – Murder plot at fancy-dress ball – Threats of mutiny in Murmansk Army.

Chapter 9: Tour of Karelian Outposts
Funerals – Christmas in Kem Cathedral – Banquet – Tour of Karelian outposts – Sled-journey on Kem river – Storm at Panozero – Uskozero – Woods recalled to Kem – Blizzard – Epic journey – Maslozero – Naked girl – Russian conspiracy to disarm Karelians and seize Kem.

Chapter 10: Advice on Independence
Field Hospital – Brigadier-General Turner of the 237th Brigade – Reinforcements and new personnel – Karelian village headmen seek Woods' advice on national development – Visit of O. Tokoi, Red Finn leader – Lehtimäki – Murmansk orders Tokoi's arrest – Subterfuge – More Intrigues in Murmansk – Bear hunting – Knobs the Regimental bear cub – Murmansk Russians kidnap Mascherin – Arrival of General Yermoloff – Antagonism to Karelians – White Russians murder friendly Russian and spy on Karelian nationalists.

Chapter 11: White Russian Hostility
Brigadier-General G. D. Price takes over 237th Brigade – More Russian intrigue – Murmansk orders Karelians to be disarmed – Woods pre-empts Russian coup versus Allies in Kem – Reports of mutinies in Red Finnish Legion – Tokoi passed through Kem en route to Bolshevik lines – Arson attack on British officer in Kem theatre – Attitudes of White Russian officers to soldiers – Omar the Don Cossack takes revenge for fire.

Chapter 12: Spring Campaign
Major "P. J." Mackesy – Tour of inspection – *The Times* reports Karelian mutiny – Woods' protests – Allied reinforcements in Kem – Suspicious characters – Baron Tüsenhausen tries to incite Karelians to revolt – Capture – General Maynard and staff move to Kem – Preparations for Spring offensive to South.

Chapter 13: Petition to King George V
Delegation of Karelian village representative – Petition to King George V to take Karelia as Protectorate – British response – Visit of Foreign Office diplomat – Karelian letter to General Maynard – Karelian democracy – Request to attend Principo conference – Opposition to White

Russian government of North Russia – Karelian language question in district elections – Karelians meet General Yermoloff – Finnish spies.

Chapter 14: Reorganisation of Regiment
Dynamiting the river ice – General Price advance to south – Karelia Regiment in Kem reorganised – Formation of Olonetz 1st Battalion – Other Karelian units – British personnel – Major Filsell disastrously appointed to command Karelian Fighting Battalion – Karelians resign and desert en masse – Bolshevik agents in United State Navy agitate among Karelians – Admiral McCully – the Impossibly tall Lieut John Sullivan Long and his pet jackdaw – GHQ personnel in Kem.

Chapter 15: Onega Operations
Duck hunting and lethal cocktails – Death of the drunken jackdaw – Reports of Archangel mutinies – Low morale of Russian troops under General Price – Woods stationed in Sumski Posad – Description of village – Nearby syphilitic village – Ambush of advancing Bolsheviks – Telegraph communications – Bombardment of Onega.

Chapter 16: Evacuation
August 1919 – Order to evacuate North Russia – Woods' new horse – Fishing trip – the "Old Believers" of Sumski Posad – Peasant economy – Karelians resist order to disarm – Bolshevik withdrawal from Onega – Arrival of General Ironside – British snobbery – Accounting – Preparations for evacuation – Woods promises to return – Fears for remaining Russian friends and regrets abandonment of Karelians – Journey home – Effeim the Karelian servant – Fate of Russian friends – "Syren" reunions – Karelians drive Bolsheviks south to Petrozavodsk – Establishment of "Autonomous Republic" – 1938 – Kem convict settlement – Reports of fortification of Karelian border.

Chapter 1

Arrival in Karelia

"Will you volunteer for service out of uniform, and in any part of the globe to which you may be sent?"

This question was put to me and three other senior officers in a small back room of an empty house in Waterloo Place one spring morning in 1918. Coming as it did after six months' inactive but harassing command of a reserve battalion at home the enquiry appeared to be the answer to my numerous prayers to the War Office.

"You may have twenty-four hours to decide," said this gentleman.

One of us, a Brigadier, wanted to know all kinds of details; another said, very reluctantly, that he had a family dependent upon him; whilst the other Colonel and I remarked that we did not need twenty-four hours, being only concerned to find out when we could start. Our unquestioning attitude seemed to please. We were led into another and, if possible, smaller room where we were warned of much peril by land and sea, including the possibilities of assassination and imprisonment; but upon our remaining at least outwardly unmoved our last will and testament was made out for us and we were told to report at the Tower of London to be vetted, vaccinated and generally prepared for the sacrifice. I never saw my fellow victim again, and I suspected that he was

For further details concerning the characters and events mentioned in this memoir, please refer to Part One, Chapters 6 and 7.

denied the opportunity of more interesting service by the MO [Medical Officer] in the Tower.

On the following morning I reported at the Tower, was duly inoculated, vaccinated, and told to get tropical kit and second-hand mufti, and had a cell allotted to me; this arrangement, however, was modified and my parole accepted to remain within calling distance of a telephone at all hours of the day and night. Then ensued long days of waiting – hanging about clubs and hotels – afraid even to go to a theatre without making elaborate arrangements for receiving the impending telephone call. After ten days this state of anxiety was relieved when I received orders to report at King's Cross the next day at 5.30 a.m.

In the Station Hotel I found some thirty officers of all ages, ranks and regiments, amongst whom a persistent rumour circulated that Russia was to be our destination, but opinion was divided as to which particular port, the tropical kit being responsible for the choice of Vladivostock by one party, while various stores on the station platform labelled 'Newcastle' gave colour to the idea of the Baltic as the probable theatre of our future activities. The War Office Staff representative volunteered no information beyond instructing us to inform our friends and relatives that letters should be addressed to: A cypher name, c/o GPO [General Post Office], London.

After breakfast we entrained for Newcastle and there boarded the SS *Marseilles*, where we found that a machine-gun company of about two hundred men, a few RE [Royal Engineers] signallers and other details, and some fifty more officers, mainly of field rank and of every variety of service and regiment, were already aboard. It was not until the last gangway had been put ashore that we learned our destination – Murmansk, north Russia, the only open port in the Arctic Circle in winter – our information coming from the usual source, somebody's batman.

Our ship was not very large and only possessed limited accommodation, so that all the usual noisy, orderly confusion, arguments and vain seeking for better berths accompanied the departure of our band of "Modern Buccaneers", as we were dubbed by some bright lad in the War Office. We were vastly intrigued by the presence on board of several mysterious, bearded individuals in civilian clothes, who were variously rumoured to be the Tzar's ex-tutor, Trotsky, Stenko-Razin, Kerensky, Tolstoi, Rasputin and Bluebeard. However we discovered later that they were none of these celebrities, though we were somewhat consoled by the discovery that we were fellow passengers with the famous Lady

Regimental Commander of "The Women of Death". Her personal appearance was rather disappointing, not being particularly romantic, and the poor creature bore some traces of the recent lurid experience she had undergone at the hands of her own countrymen; I am sure she realised that she had our admiring sympathy.

For the first few days it was difficult to find any amusement to distract our attention from the excitement caused by six officers trying to shave simultaneously in a cabin with about three square feet of space and the involuntary gymnastics when dressing caused by the rough seas; but in comparison with the crews of the two destroyers which were escorting us our discomfort must have been the height of luxury. These two little ships had the worst of the weather. Viewed from our comparatively lofty decks the destroyers seemed to be engaged in a constant and violent effort to throw somersaults; they would leap out of the sea, showing more than half the length of their keels, then disappear again until nothing of them was visible but their stumpy masts and part of their funnels; now they would present a full view of their decks, every plank glistening and streaming, then the bilge would be presented and the upper works plunged into the huge seas. I felt pleased that I was not in the Senior Service.

There had unfortunately embarked with us a few microbes of the influenza epidemic which was so virulent in 1918, and these reduced our strength considerably, several valuable officers being seriously affected. The outbreak was very well controlled but the number of casualties resulting rendered the force (intended for operations at Murmansk under General Maynard) so depleted that he was compelled to ask for volunteers from the Archangel party, of which I was a member. Pleased with the outcome of my first volunteering I thought I might as well be consistent; thus the following day saw me a "Syren", and in possession of a passport setting forth the request and requisition of His Majesty's Principal Secretary of State for Foreign Affairs to allow William Thomas Peterson, a timber merchant, to pass without let or hindrance and afford him every protection and assistance of which he might stand in need.

We arrived at Murmansk on midsummer's day, and a more depressing place would have been difficult to find, viewed under the sombre light of the midnight sun. A wide bay of dull green water surrounded by low brown hills without any vegetation to relieve the eye, and a cluster of drab wooden huts or houses, occupied the middle distance. The old warship HMS *Glory* lay close in shore, while what the men promptly christened the "packet of Woodbines" – the old five-funnelled Russian battle-ship "ASKOLD" – lay farther out. Some fishing boats, unpainted and neglected, were tied up close to the dock, and numbers of small, derelict-seeming steam trawlers were moored in uneven rows. The town seemed to be abandoned by all but a few tough looking customers, mostly carrying rifles. A guard of two weird looking men, dressed in the usual blouse, top-boots and whiskers was posted at the iron gate of the entrance to the dock. These fellows appeared to obtain tremendous satisfaction from their job, which enabled them to scratch against the iron railing without obligation to the Duke of Argyll.

To General Poole, the GOC [General Officer Commanding], the time appeared opportune to explain the object of our presence in this part of the globe, and, at a conference held in the saloon, he informed us that we were there to create a diversion, by threatening Germany from the north and east, in order to prevent her troops in Russia and Finland from being withdrawn to reinforce the Armies in France.

This appeared to be a somewhat formidable task. and each of the audience felt that the War Office had, at last, recognised his own worth as that equal to a Division at least.

Several officers who knew the country gave us valuable hints as to our personal conduct. The MO, Major Fitzwilliam, in making one point, told us that the difference between British morals and those of the Russians, was that we had a high moral code, but did not live up to it: the Russians had low morals and did their best to maintain this standard.

There followed several days of inactivity for that part of the ship's company not responsible for the policy of the expedition, and a difficulty now became manifest, namely the determination of the lascar crew of the *Marseilles* to die. They said that they had been brought to hell. The sun never rose or set. Clearly this was purposely designed to prevent them from saying their prayers, without which they could not hope to gain eternal salvation. In vain the ship's officers prayed for them and to them, but little could be got out of them by either mental or physical appeal. I think some fourteen of the native crew attained their objective before this idea of an earthly Hades was finally abandoned; or perhaps the survivors were not of the same staunch conviction.

It was a great relief at last to receive orders to proceed down the line as far as we could go, with the town of Kem, about 350 versts distant as our ultimate goal; here we were to reinforce a company of Marines already there. Two other Colonels, Jocelyn, from the Territorials, and Keyes, from Intelligence, and I started off in uniform to the railway station; this was more in the nature of a 'halt', having neither platforms nor offices. Here our first contact with the Russian proletariat was not encouraging. A small compartment without cushions (this we subsequently discovered to be an advantage) was allotted to us by some sort of official, to whom scant respect was shown by his fellow-countrymen, as his decision was noisily challenged by as many Russian families as were able to get within shouting distance of him. One huge fellow, clad in the prevailing fashion of blouse, boots and hair, and accompanied by a stout and perspiring lady, several offspring, and the family bedding with its indigenous parasites, squeezed their way vociferously into the compartment despite our efforts to dissuade them. Colonel Keyes, however, after half an hour's oratory richly besprinkled with threats and language which we surmised was unfit for any lady's ears, managed to loosen the limpet-like attachment of our friends, and we pushed them out to join the throng on the ground, leaving behind them only a few souvenirs with which we could willingly have dispensed. After a tremendous amount of talk and shouting, and a series of violent arguments between the engine crew, the guard and the several station masters, we dashed off at the breakneck speed of about three miles per hour, gradually increasing to a reckless five or so, which almost derailed the engine and caused acute discomfort to the passengers. We had not proceeded far when apparently the water went off the boil and we stopped beside a large dump of cut wood, presumably intended for fuelling purposes. Here further argument ensued between guard, passengers and engine crew; indeed the interminable debate was resumed at every stop, and we finally came to the conclusion that they stopped the train every time a new aspect of the controversy occurred to any of the participants.

Approaching what should have been nightfall we drew into another 'station', this time with a hut for the housing of the telegraph instrument, and a large tank of hot water – the 'kepitoc'. The whole was enveloped in a cloud of mosquitos. The purpose of the hot water-tank soon became evident; men, women and children jumped from the still moving train with cans, kettles, jugs and all kinds of utensils – anything and everything in which tea could be made. The 'kepitoc' is the universal railway refreshment room of provincial Russia. The mosquitos I have not mentioned before, but they were in fact one of the most trying discomforts we had to contend with. The Arctic mosquito is a much larger and more savage insect than its African relative, and these stopping places were never cleaned, nor did any sanitary arrangements exist; hence the provincial Russian 'station' was an ideal breeding ground for these ferocious pests, while at the same time providing them with daily opportunities for fresh feeding on both passengers and refuse. The sound of their humming, or 'screaming', was very distinct, and it is no exaggeration to say that the clouds of mosquitos were so dense as to render it impossible to see the heads of one's fellow passengers standing no further distant than the length of a coach.

At Kandalaksha we lost one of our number. Major Burton, a young Canadian, alighted there to assist Colonel Marsh who commanded a small mixed force at this point. Marsh was hospitable and produced a whiskey and soda to cheer us on our way, but his news of 'blood and fire' from further south did nothing to raise our spirits. However, we thought that almost anything would be preferable to the mosquitos, upon which we had discovered retaliation to be both futile and exhausting. Marsh had the advantage of knowing the language and of being therefore able to address the railway officials in what appeared to us very satisfactory terms, mainly consisting of insults; though with my knowledge of Russian gained later I found the language totally inadequate to express annoyance in a straightforward manner, merely enabling one to cast reflexions upon the inability of the delinquent's ancestors to follow the path of moral rectitude – a method of invective far too indirect to be efficient! Colonel Marsh, however, seemed capable of putting some real substance into his conversation, and the malaise affecting the engine disappeared.

After a halt of three hours we had had sufficient rest at this station, and our train resumed its wearisome course through pine forests, swamp, more pines, birches, and more swamps – interminable miles there seemed to be of this scenery, punctuated with numerous and lengthy halts, sometimes for some specific reason but more often for none at all. Days without nights of this travelling, varying in detail only in respect of different lengths of halt and increasing bodily discomfort, such as the infrequent chances of a wash or a shave, the dust, the heat and the attentions of the small but lively denizens of our compartment, caused us to be positively pleased by the enthusiasm of some 'comrade' who tried a few pot shots at the train from the cover of the forest. There were no regrets when we eventually arrived at Kem, and were welcomed by Captain Drake-Brockman, of the Royal Marines. It will always be to the credit of a very gallant gentleman that he never by word or look betrayed his disappointment when he saw in two dirty and unshaven Colonels the only reinforcements he would be likely to have, Colonel Keyes having to go on south for service in another sphere.

Chapter 2

Formation of Regiment

Kem station we found to be important from the military point of view. It was situated on the north bank of the Kem river, which at this point is wide and swift. The railway was carried across the river on a strong and high wooden bridge of about 250 yards in length. There was also a branch line connecting the town with Popoff [Popov], a practicable port of considerable draught on the White Sea, on the north side of the river mouth five miles further east.

Towards Finland and the west, thick forest, swamp and tundra protected the railroad for many miles, the only alternative means of communication to the river being a dirt track, used by pedestrians, following its bank on the north side, and broken by several single plank bridges. The town was about two miles distant from the station, and consisted of a cathedral, a few shops, and quite a number of good sized houses arranged into about four streets, on the north bank of the river. Across the wooden bridge on an island there were barracks with accommodation for about 600 men, an ancient and dilapidated wooden church, and a three-storied theatre, also built of wood; indeed the only building in the whole place constructed of stone was the cathedral. Even the side walks consisted of planks laid lengthwise, three or four planks in width. The streets or roads were merely wide dirt tracks without any proper surface and these, when they were not knee deep in mud, were the source of clouds of blinding dust. The inhabitants, of whom there were about 3,500, were of very mixed origin and class, since Kem had been a penal settlement for political suspects in pre-war times, and was still the home of many who had not left with the first chance of release offered by the revolution. Perhaps they had come to regard Kem as a refuge.

Drake-Brockman and his company of Marines were living in goods trucks on the line at the station. His office and stores were in a dilapidated passenger coach, entirely devoid of glass, while the wash-house and latrines were in the forest that came down to the railway line on the north-west; these latter conveniences were an amusing novelty to the Russian soldiers, who did not appear to fraternise with the British but observed a sort of nervous armed neutrality which threatened at any moment to break out into open hostility. However, the Marines were prepared for any eventuality. We also learned that a "home made" armoured train (the armour consisting mainly of corrugated iron!) was being operated by a French Artillery section patrolling the line from the bridge which bore the Murmansk-Petrograd railway across the river to Kandalaksha in the north.

From the information at our disposal we gathered that we were in a very delicate position. Nobody seemed to know whether we were at war with the inhabitants or not; nor were the inhabitants themselves any better informed, and divided opinions on this point were emphasised by varying willingness or reluctance on the part of the railway officials to assist us. The engineer of the section, Argieff, was favourably disposed, and allotted a "teplushka", or goods truck, for the use of Jocelyn and myself, complete with brazier. For the rest we wisely relied upon the adequate 'scrounging' powers of the Marines, who had the British Tommy's genius for dispensing with languages in obtaining necessities well developed.

To complicate the already chaotic situation further, a deputation of bearded brigands now waited upon us and asked for our assistance to release them from the Bolsheviks, who were keeping 58 of their number in detention at the barracks in Kem. The reason for this, it appeared, was that these people, who were not Russians but Karelians, from the country lying to the west between Finland and the White Sea, then occupied by German-led Finns, would not bear arms or fight for the Bolsheviks. They begged for a dozen boxes of matches to burn every occupied village in Karelia. They were intensely in earnest, and we assured them that their request should be forwarded to Headquarters, as in fact it was.

To revert to the situation as between ourselves and the natives, some

The Old Cathedral of the Dormition (built 1717), Kem, January 1919

days of tension elapsed, each side watching the other and every movement being closely followed. Even our code wires from Murmansk were vetted, no doubt by the agents of our suspicious neighbours. At last the climax came, when we received orders from Headquarters to disarm the Russian garrison and put them on the other side of the river, across the bridge.

The performance of this order afforded considerable satisfaction and amusement to the Marines. Choosing a time when most of the Russians would be in their quarters, Drake-Brockman posted his men with excellent judgement and led a platoon into the barracks. One shot was fired by a Warrant Officer in order to emphasise the purpose of the visit, which was interpreted correctly and promptly. Showers of rifles with their permanently fixed bayonets fell from the windows, followed by belts and other equipment, producing the impression that the occupants were being taken to pieces! There were no casualties, though there very well might have been if the small Marine who carried out a sheaf of long Russian swords nearly as big as himself had stumbled.

When they learnt that they were not destined to be the objects of Marine target practice the prisoners seemed vastly relieved, and they quite cheerfully boarded the train which was to take them 16 miles or so down the line to be jettisoned. After they had arrived at their destination, however, messages bearing dire threats of revenge were brought back from the evacuated garrison Commander, Commissar Spiridonoff [Spiridonov]. He must have thought that we were endowed with as many lives as cats, for he promised to return with 6,000 men and slay us all, many times and in many different ways.

About ten days later a part, at least, of Spiridonoff's promise was observed. Reports came in from our Russian intelligence service that the Commissar, together with three trains and 3,000 troops, was advancing on Kem from the south, and would attack on the following day. After making the usual deduction (i.e. dividing by three) we arrived at an estimate of the threatened attack which, two days later, was found to be fairly accurate. The inhabitants of Kem were tremendously excited, some of them elated at the impending fate of the little British garrison, others – those who had something to lose – apprehensive at the prospect of invasion by Spiridonoff's rough diamonds. For ourselves, we were only a force about 200 strong, but our defence scheme had been well prepared, so that we were able to await the approach of the enemy without undue anxiety. Almost seven feet of efficient and humorous Sapper, Captain McKilligan, and his four men had mined the bridge; machine-guns covered every approach to it, and every available boat had been beached on our side and placed under guard; all cover had been burnt on the other side of the river, and range marks put out. The midnight sun insured us against the possibility of attack in the dark.

Meanwhile we received instructions from Headquarters at Murmansk to avoid bloodshed if possible, but to hold the position at all costs! To carry out these orders we arranged a small but influential reception committee, consisting of Corporal Fryer and two Lewis gun teams of the Royal Marines placed on either side of the railway line 200 yards south of the bridge, a plank across the line, a very nervous interpreter and myself, also very nervous, but fortified with a new tropical uniform and clean gloves. I think my tailor deserves his share of credit for the satisfactory results we achieved. At length the enemy appeared – Commissar Spiridonoff and some 800 men in one train, which approached us slowly and stopped at the sight of the plank across the line and my clean glove extended somewhat in the manner of a traffic pointsman. Heads protruded from every window, and there was an amazed silence. The interpreter asked the occupants of the first compartment the whereabouts of Spiridonoff. Some way down the train a few carriage doors opened, and I told the interpreter to order them closed at once, that they were on top of a mine, and that if they disobeyed we would blow them out of existence. I then gave the prearranged signal to Fryer, who opened up with a few bursts of fire on both sides of the train, carefully not hitting it. The Commissar, who was in the second carriage, was ordered out. He came up and wanted to talk, but I held out my hand for his revolvers (of which he had two enormous specimens, too heavy for any ordinary man) and told him to instruct his men to throw their rifles out of the windows. This they did, with the moral persuasion of a few more bursts from Fryer's guns to hasten them. The interpreter then entered the train to see that all arms were properly jettisoned, finding a few. While Fryer took care of the train Spiridonoff walked with me to the station to be interviewed, but he was so astonished at his position that he forgot to smoke the cigarette I had given him. After the Commissar had been very comprehensively examined by Major Rowlandson, a Staff Interpreter who had arrived for that purpose, he was escorted back to the train, which returned south with all its load of mischief, including their leader who was no doubt already turning over in his mind the possibilities of a future attempt in which he would not be so easily bluffed.

The British personnel in Kem station at this time consisted of Captain Drake-Brockman [with] two subalterns, Heaton and Norris, and his company of Marines; Captain McKilligan and four Sappers; Colonel Jocelyn and myself; our Allies were represented by Major Bataillard, a French intelligence officer, and the 'Armoured Train'. And now a few local Russians expressed a desire to take part in the defence, but nothing more tangible than interminable talk arose from this suggestion until the arrival of the C-in-C [Commander-in-Chief], General Maynard, on the 7th July. Upon the General's arrival a sort of levée was held on the station, where the local Mayor, Bailieff, and his councillors talked for several hours at the C-in-C, who then replied in about three minutes. The outcome of this conference was the formation of a body of local volunteers to be named the Slavo-Britannic Legion, and to be under the command of Colonel Jocelyn. No sooner had this been arranged than a party of about thirty wild looking men with shaggy bearskin hats, skin coats, and bristling with knives, axes and the inevitable whiskers, proceeded to hold forth at length to the General, who had the greatest difficulty in preserving a serious expression as he reviewed the weird array. There was some consultation between the

Chief and his Staff, upon the conclusion of which he called me into his carriage, and said:

"Woods, these fearsome looking fellows outside are Karelians. They want arms, a little food, and an officer to lead them. Their object is to clear the Finns, who are being led by German officers, out of their country. They won't take any oath of allegiance to the Allies, so that we should have to take them largely on trust. Would you take them on?"

I replied that I would.

"Well," said the General, "I think you could do something with them. But before you definitely decide I ought to warn you that the [White] Russian officers and the civilians here have no doubt that the Karelians will cut the throat of any foreign officer with them as soon as they get into their own country; all they want is the food and arms. Now what do you say?"

I answered that they seemed to me no worse than their neighbours and that my acceptance still held good; whereupon the General gave me his benediction and promised all possible help. He asked me what was the first thing to be done with them.

"Get their whiskers off to see what is underneath," I replied.

The General now introduced me to my new command, which collectively gazed at me with awe, but with a suggestion of hope in their eyes. Oddly enough, although a foreigner and a stranger to them, I felt that I had their confidence at once; no exchange of words was needed, and no difference of language prevented a thorough understanding between us. We were friends from the start.

With the aid of the interpreter I inspected the deputation. One boy, a youth of nineteen, was adorned with a marvellously luxuriant beard; I congratulated him upon the possession of this, but explained that in my country it would be taken as a sign of peace and surrender. He promptly agreed to its sacrifice. To get this motley crew into shape I was given the assistance of the interpreter, Lieutenant Heaton, Sergeant Walker, Corporal Fryer of the Marines, and two good Serbian NCOs. The men were to remain in the town barracks, where they lived with their families, but to draw rations and stores from the station. Our first task was to make them comfortable, and with this in view we had the barracks cleaned and allotted the women to their own quarters. Their position had not previously been defined, a lack of arrangement which, I gathered, had not been conducive to peaceful slumber for husbands and fathers.

The provision of transport was an urgent question, but by the lavish use of 'blarney' on the 'Zemstvoe' [*zemstvo*, the local council] this difficulty was partially overcome, and we found ourselves in due course the proud possessors of six ponies and so-called carts, these latter being crazy contraptions consisting of four wheels connected by three planks, and two shafts held apart by the usual wooden arch across the pony's neck.

When fifty outfits of khaki uniform arrived the opportunity arose to point out the enormity of whiskers and sundry growths of hair which still adhered to the faces of the more conservative warriors. This was the last appearance of hirsute decoration in the Karelian Regiment.

The next step was to provide arms. This was accomplished by collecting all the rifles and ammunition obligingly left behind by Spiridonoff and his men when they evacuated, and later we were fortunate enough to find on the railway two truck-loads of Russian rifles, ammunition, and four machine-guns complete.

The Regiment now numbered 65 able bodied men, a good nucleus, but far too insignificant in number to undertake the liberation of Karelia from an enemy whose strength was variously reported at 5,000 to 20,000 strong. After some consultation picket patrols were sent out, their duty being to watch the river and every forest track, to permit all travellers from Karelia to come in, but to prevent every person from leaving our area. Others were sent out as recruiting parties to various points in order to enlist as far as possible all Karelians working on the railway and at the port, as well as fishermen, hunters, lumber-jacks and farmers. The chief Karelians were invaluable in this work; Gregori Leziff [Grigorii Lezhev] was a natural orator, and Nicoli Petroff [Nikolai Petrov] a born soldier. What one of these excellent men could not accomplish by means of his peculiar gift the other achieved by his own method, so that it was not long before we had every Karelian of serviceable age and physical condition within the Regiment. In about a month we were 500 strong, the majority of splendid physique. and every man a marksman since the bulk of them were for the most part dependent upon their skill with a rifle for subsistence in a country where a cartridge was of great value and butcher's meat unknown. Every man of them had already served in the Imperial Russian army, and after a little drilling they became as smart on parade as any foreign troops in the ordinary course of events. Their discipline was excellent; no cases of insubordination or drunkenness occurred, and no complaints were lodged against them by the inhabitants of the town, and this despite the fact that they were cordially disliked by the Russian element, who never neglected an opportunity of warning me against them (it appeared that crucifixion at their hands was one of the mildest forms of death awaiting me!). But I never had cause then, or at any subsequent time, to distrust the genuiness or loyalty of the Karelians, who finally established a reputation for outstanding honesty which was recognised even by their enemies.

In temperament the Karelians were cheerful, alert, and quick to see the humour in any situation; they reminded me forcibly of Irish troops, who always seem to become more contented as conditions grow worse. As an illustration of this, I recall an occasion when a boat capsized in the Kem river tipping six fishermen into the water; the yells of laughter from their comrades on the bank were immediately echoed by the victims when they came to the surface. Instantly responsive to kindness, they could be intensely stupid and dour under coercion or bullying.

While the training and organisation of the Karelians was in progress some reinforcements arrived in Kem in the shape of two companies of Serbs, who had made their way up through Russia from the south, under Major Dukich. These men were fine big chaps, slow moving but hard to stop. Colonel Thornhill, an Intelligence Officer from the Archangel force, and the hero of many exciting adventures in Petrograd during the revolution, took a platoon of these Serbs across the Gulf of Onega to some small town which required attention, and he reported that they were brave to the point of recklessness, disdaining to take cover when advancing on any position in the face of rifle fire. They were successful in doing their job, but at the cost of unnecessary casualties for the reason mentioned.

Some large cases captured in this expedition and sent back to Kem in charge of one of Thornhill's intelligence men proved on inspection to contain wine. They were taken to the station and given into the custody of Drake-Brockman who, after finding guards for them for several days and having no instructions as to their disposal, asked me what he should do with them. Not averse to rendering assistance in this matter, I suggested that he send them down to my new quarters in the town, convenient to the barracks, where they would be safer and also save the Marines furnishing extra guards. This wine turned out to be extremely useful; it gave us great prestige in a town whose supply of wines and spirits was almost entirely exhausted, and the inhabitants of which were far from prohibitionist in outlook; moreover, money was not of much value as a purchasing medium. Judiciously used, the wine enlarged the Karelian transport by 400 per cent, as well as producing milk, bread, and a variety of other things which we did not know existed in the country. Drake-Brockman thanked me for taking the cases off his hands, and was most grateful for some bottles of sweet Russian champagne we sent him.

When General Maynard came down to inspect us we sent him a hamper containing some of these gaudily painted bottles of wine, some gold and some silver, with paintings on the labels of the various fruits from which they were made, and to this mark of goodwill he kindly reciprocated by sending us six bottles of Scotch whiskey. Had we anticipated this very satisfactory exchange we would have given him a packing-case of the wine! But I am sure that no thought of bargaining was in his mind; the General was always very hospitable, kind and thoughtful where his people were concerned, hence the remorse which has always haunted me since I learned, at a later date, that the consignment of wine had originally been meant for Headquarters! Thornhill called me a pirate and some other things equally unmerited, though he afterwards relented in his attitude. The General never uttered so much as a word of reproach, even when the subject was introduced in his own mess by me. I think he was relieved that he had not had to drink the stuff after I had described its resinous flavour. To heap coals of fire on my head he even sent me some more whiskey; however, heat in this form was not insupportable.

The appearance of the Karelian Regiment on parade, though good, always created a faint feeling of dissatisfaction. This was caused by the absence of any sort of regimental badge or insignia. Something had to be done about this, but the General Staff could not assist in a solution of the problem. Our new quarters in Kem were in a large three-storied wooden building, with the theatre on the ground floor and living rooms in the upper stories. The Sectional Engineer had occupied the second story until the Bolsheviks had shot him, and he had evidently had a nice taste in furnishings and entertainment. The salon contained a fine Bechstein grand piano, an HMV gramophone, a quantity of grand records, and a full-sized billiard table. For some reason the billiard table was the only article badly damaged by his successors, the cloth having been torn almost completely off the slate bed. Perhaps it was the colour of this cloth which suggested using it to advantage; anyhow a penknife and a piece of wood produced a printing block in the shape of a shamrock which, used in conjunction with one of our numerous ink-pads, enabled us to stamp the remnants of the green cloth, and have them cut up for cap badges. Following the custom in vogue at home, we gave a tea party to those Russian ladies of social instincts sufficiently charitable to forget their prejudices against the Karelians in their enthusiasm for the British. Each guest was requested to bring her scissors with her, and while two of the ladies provided variations of 'curate's delight' teacakes we provided the tea, and it only added to the novelty of the occasion if tin mugs had to do duty as china.

Our hospitality had the practical result of producing 500 neatly cut shamrocks. These were fastened to the men's caps by brass paper-fasteners, furnishing the last touch of uniformity. The men were immensely proud of their badges, which had the effect of improving the morale of the unit to a remarkable extent. The number of recruits continued to increase daily, but in the matter of badges Captain McKilligan came to the rescue when the billiard cloth was exhausted by producing beautifully made shamrocks, improvised by his ingenious sappers from old cartridge cases. Although these metal badges were provided with pin fasteners, the green cloth badges were always regarded as decorations of honour for the original volunteers.

The Karelian Regiment crossing the river at Kem, autumn 1918 (Cathedral of the Annunciation, built in 1904, in background).

Chapter 3

The Royal Irish Karelians

When General Maynard came down from Murmansk to inspect the Regiment at Kem he was somewhat disappointed to observe that drill was in the Russian method and language, but he quickly grasped the point that it had been found far more practicable for a few British officers to learn the Russian system, making slight modifications and improvement where necessary, than to teach 1,000 men, some illiterate, a new drill with – to them – foreign words of command. In other respects he was pleased with their discipline and appearance on parade. At the same time one could not help feeling that the General had a slight air of mistrust (a feeling no doubt implanted in his mind by his Russian advisers) which the Karelians immediately sensed and mentioned later. That they were accurate in their judgement was rather borne out when he insisted upon a personal guard of two Lewis gun teams of Marines for me. This was unfortunate, for although they always held him in the utmost respect they had no confidence in the quality of his friendship, and were even somewhat dubious when various concessions we obtained were, rightly, attributed by us to the Chief as their source. As an inevitable result they came to regard their own officers as their only true friends, an attitude which developed to such an extent that no order would be accepted or obeyed which did not emanate from the Karelian Headquarters, or contain confirmation by it, notwithstanding all efforts on our part to combat this tendency.

The Slavo-Britannic Legion had begun well under Colonel Jocelyn and shaped well, but he was sadly handicapped by the dearth of recruits, having a very restricted area upon which to draw; nor could he employ similar methods to ours in obtaining volunteers, the incentive in the case of his field being not quite so personally definite or urgent. In view of these factors 200 was a very creditable number, and the quality of the young men composing his Company was of a good standard. There was a certain amount of friendly rivalry between us, especially of the 'old soldier' variety where stores were concerned! But Colonel Jocelyn was a good sportsman as well as being a fine soldier. I cannot resist mentioning one little incident for my share in which I frankly confess I have no remorse. Jocelyn shared our Mess in the town. Here we had very little variation of 'Bully' or 'Maconachie' [tinned meat and vegetable stew], so that when we received occasional presents of butter, fresh bread or other delicacies we were very appreciative. In this instance a lady had sent a jar of cream, and upon its appearance at lunch Jocelyn, who occupied the most comfortable chair, said:

"Ah, here is some of this awful Russian cream! I know the stuff – as sour as vinegar. I won't have any; you can try it if you like."

I did, and found it beautifully fresh; but as Jocelyn obviously expected me to grimace I refrained from disappointing him and twisted my face into the appropriate expression of dismay. This caused him some amusement, and when I again offered him the cream, he replied:

"Not likely. Eat it all yourself."

This I proceeded to do, and his suspicions were aroused – almost too late. He tasted everything afterwards.

That we were not allowed to forget all British habits and amenities was largely due to Commander Cowan, his officers and men of HMS *Nairana*, originally an Australian line steamer, but now converted for use as a carrier of aircraft, then lying at Popoff, the port of Kem. Their hospitality was in the very best traditions of the Navy; as McKilligan remarked: "Go as you please, and come back when you can." The opportunity of having a bath in our own fashion, instead of the Russian steam bath, was very welcome, and none the less so on account of the spotless condition of the ship; here we were temporarily immune from attack by the bugs which infested the majority of buildings in North Russia. Roast beef served on white table linen was an event to us, accustomed as we were to the eternal bully-beef and canned rations usually taken on an ancient copy of *The Times* which had but lately been promoted from duty as covering for a biscuit tin. It was a great relief to be in the company of these cheery sailors and to hear their 'navy talk'; it afforded one a chance to readjust views and gain the right perspectives, a mental and physical refreshment.

Arrangements ware made with the pilots of HMS *Nairana*'s aircraft to reconnoitre and photograph the enemy strong points in Karelia, but only after a given date, as premature evidence of our interest in that country was not desirable. The machines were not of the latest types and their range was somewhat limited, but what was lacking in the craft was amply compensated by their pilots, who were big-hearted enough to undertake almost any duty to help us.

Because of its badge the Karelian Regiment was dubbed by the Commander-in-Chief "The Irish Karelians"; it was now placed on the pay roll of the British Army and received rations. By the end of July, 1918, we were ready to begin operations against the enemy.

During the period of training and organisation we had been preparing a plan of attack, maintaining a strict control of all traffic up-country and gradually gathering information as to the numbers and disposition of the enemy, who were reported to have their nearest post 16 versts up river. As the forest tracks were impracticable for troops we had been collecting all the boats within fifty miles, and when we had exhausted the supply we found that we had a flotilla of over 300 boats with 'yawl' cutaway bows and sterns in the fashion of the Norwegian 'prams', to facilitate landing on the river banks, and each capable of carrying twelve passengers or their equivalent in cargo.

At the outset of the campaign a difficult and unpleasant problem arose from the appointment of one of the Karelian officers. His presence with Headquarters was indispensable for very strong reasons of policy; he was an outstanding spirit, and the most enthusiastic patriot and politician of the Karelian people, holding great authority throughout the country; but he unfortunately suffered from a malignant form of the venereal disease prevalent in a country which had long been without medicine or medical services (the Karelians had not heard of any doctor being in their country for over fifty years!). The prospect of having to live in close contact with an infected person in billet and camp with the constant danger of contamination was not an enviable one for other members of the Headquarters Staff. Doctor H. Harrison, the well-known author of boys' books, who was attached to the Regimental Headquarters objected strenuously, as did Lieut Heaton of the Marines, nor did I view the situation with any degree of optimism, realising as I did that a report of such cases among the British officers would incur the displeasure of the War Office, who might also be sceptical regarding the source of such disability. However, I was of the opinion that our job had to be done whatever the difficulties. We had orders to carry out, and the performance of these orders must not depend upon any risk, no matter what the nature. The Doctor was won over to this view, and he exercised so much care with our utensils and equipment that none of our number was infected, nor did the Karelian officer ever realise that special precautions were being taken – a tribute to the Doctor's unfailing tact and ability, for which we shall always be grateful.

All arrangements were made for supplies and communications to be maintained, the base to be in charge of the highly efficient Drake-Brockman. At the time appointed the boats were loaded and crews told off to each, their places and duties thoroughly understood. The boats were rowed by women, a fact which added considerably to our strength. Healthy, capable and cheerful, these women were accustomed to doing rather more than their share of the work, and were quite at home in river craft, often rowing all day from seven o'clock in the morning until seven at night with only one rest of an hour's duration and against a current of 2½ to 3 knots. This they could and did maintain for days on end; and on landing it was their duty to cook the food on the camp fires so dextrously made by the men within a few minutes, wet or fine, with the aid of a small woodsman's axe such as most of them carried.

The advance and flank guards, scouts in the real sense of the word, set out on the 15th August, the evening before the start of the main column. Distributed in two boats, Headquarters consisted of Captain Harrison, RAMC [Royal Army Medical Corps], Lieut Heaton, Sgt Interpreter Lax, six Royal Marines, two Karelian officers and myself. The point of embarkation was about a mile above the river bridge, and no one present could ever forget the scene when the concentrated fleet of newly painted boats, covering a mile-long reach of the broad river from bank to bank, awaited the signal to move off. It was a warm summer's morning, and a cloudless sky was reflected in the crystal clear water which mirrored the vivid hues of the boats and their crews' costumes, broken only by the occasional dip of an oar and sometimes rippled by the light touch of a cat's paw breeze. Almost every craft – emerald green, blue, white or red – had its complement of four fresh-faced women rowers, each wearing the national costume of bright coloured skirt, low necked blouse embroidered in many colours, and a brightly tinted handkerchief tied round the head. They were all laughing, singing or calling out to friends and their voices, mingling with deeper toned commands and the noise of oars rattling in rowlocks, blended into a cheerful babel of sound, swelled by a multitude of echoes from the sombre forest of pines which lined the banks on either side. On the command to advance being given a thousand oars struck the water, churning it into foam, and soon small sails appeared, some made from flour sacks or patchwork material, being spread to catch the light air, while those less lavishly equipped hoisted small Christmas trees in their bows to lighten the work of the rowers. It was a novel and amazing picture of colour and animation, and one to remain indelibly in the memory.

Our progress up river was not uncomfortable as we had frequent opportunities of stretching our legs at the portages, of which there are nine between Kem and the lakes, varying from 100 yards to as much as 18 versts. Most of these could be negotiated by poling and towing lightened boats, but in two places there are waterfalls, round which we had of necessity to haul the boats overland. One part of a forest path we encountered during a portage led over a shaking swamp, where the ground sank several inches under one's weight, a curious sensation akin to walking on an air bed, a stick stuck into the ground at this point showed that the skin of the earth was only six inches thick. Here the grass was red, the undergrowth and bushes all crimson leafed, and even the tree trunks and foliage were red; these unusual conditions prevailed for a distance of about two versts before the country resumed its normal appearance. It was an eerie place, reminiscent of the stage setting for the demon in the pantomimes of childhood days.

Realising that we should have to sit facing our rowers for days and weeks, Gregori had made the view as easy as possible for us to endure; he had picked a crew of six of the prettiest girls in the country to 'man' the oars. These young women seemed rather afraid of us for a few days, until they discovered that they were in no danger of being shot or beaten, and that we had a genuine admiration for their strength and skill. Then they laughed and joked among themselves; then, too, I wished that I could understand their language, for more than once the two Karelian officers laughed but always refused to explain the joke. Nicoli said: "We do not want a boat full of red faces." They were always extremely modest, and up to their last day in the boat they always maintained complete respect for us, never speaking unless we addressed them, and then briefly. With our Marine servants and escort in the boat following, however, it was a different tale; Gregori had shrewdly chosen their crew with an eye to strength rather than beauty, so that they found more interest in regarding the banks than anything aboard their craft. But I must give every credit to these Marines; they always behaved as gentlemen, showing willingness to assist the Karelians, being eager to learn their ways, having full confidence in their new comrades and gaining theirs in return.

There was one slight backsliding from grace; Johnston, my red-haired batman, and a born comedian, pretending to assist a smiling cook to place a cauldron on the camp fire, put his arm round her waist. His head rang for hours with the playful box on the ears he received for his pains from the blushing lady. That was, I believe, the only amorous incident during the journey, and it was enjoyed by everyone but Johnston.

Day after day we rowed up the beautifully clear river between forest giants, their colour constantly changing with the light, the stern and gloomy atmosphere of the pines often relieved by tall, graceful silver birches for which Karelia is noted. There was nothing monotonous in our mode of travel, each new reach of the river having its own individuality in form and colour, as well as in the possibilities of action. We encountered an abundance of game – duck and all kinds of waterfowl, and in the forest capercalzie, blackgame and a variety of large partridge; there were also many squirrels and otters, and on one occasion we surprised a huge brown bear on the bank, and he in turn surprised us by the speed of his retreat. Once, rounding a sharp bend in the stream, we found ourselves close upon a wedge of wild duck. These birds did not betray any great alarm at our proximity and Heaton, laying aside his eternal novelette, said:

"There goes a fine dinner! Try a whack at them with your revolver, Sir."

There seemed to me to be far more chance of the birds being frightened than cooked; however, I took aim about six inches above the head of one duck about forty yards distant, and fired what proved to be the luckiest shot of my life, for not only was the duck decapitated but I won an entirely undeserved reputation as a deadly shot, which served me in good stead throughout my sojourn in Russia, adding to the respect with which I was already treated; for the story lost nothing in its recounting by the Karelians.

Chapter 4

The Ouchta Campaign

The outposts of the enemy had been accounted for by our advance guard, who had taken Padouzemskaia, at the foot of a waterfall; here we were able to form our first dump, while the Company operating on our left front simultaneously cleared Polovena. We found that the enemy had occupied every village to the west by small garrisons of any number from ten to eighty, and had constructed some blockhouses.

The methods employed by the Karelian Regiment in dealing with the enemy garrisons in occupied villages were almost uniform throughout, differing only in details usually dictated by geographical conditions or accident. It will be sufficient to give the customary scheme of operation in order that a clear understanding of the 'modus operandi' may be conveyed, and the whole series of attacks visualised up to the last stand and final expulsion of the invaders. To describe this it is necessary to emphasise the type of soldier employed on each side: on the one hand the Karelians were skilled hunters, woodsmen and trappers, capable of reading accurately the story conveyed by a few broken reeds on the river bank, a bent twig, or a bunch of grass floating in the water; trained in the Arctic Circle, where life is hard and the provision of food, clothing and shelter elemental necessities, they were tough and tenacious. They used smoke signals, and conveyed military reports by means of small twigs placed in some particular manner on or near the forest tracks [see diagrams on next page]. They took no prisoners, for these would require

Karelian code of signals and ground signs

By the arrangement of twigs or sticks placed on the ground near bends in the forest tracks, scouts were enabled to convey information as follows:

Smoke Signals

Caused by manipulating a blanket over a green-wood fire

1. Unlimited number of long puffs	Advance
2. Unlimited number of short puffs	Danger
3. One long puff	Remain where you are
4. Two long puffs	Help required
5. Three long puffs	Collect here
6. Four long puffs	All well

feeding, and giving valuable food to an enemy was not in accordance with their ethics. Moreover, the Karelians were fighting for their homes and their women-folk.

From the nature of enquiries made through our Foreign Office for missing members of the German-Finns engaged in Karelia it was not difficult to form an estimate of the quality of the troops opposing us. They appeared to have a number of German officers at their Headquarters at Ouchta [Ukhta], and some senior NCOs at different points throughout the country. The Finnish element consisted mainly of townsmen; trained soldiers but not skilled in woodcraft, they were average riflemen, but their machine-gunners were the most useful troops they had, holding every position to the limit of endurance. Their excellent qualities would have commanded more respect had they not used explosive bullets.

When it was decided to attack a certain village, natives of that village who were now members of the Regiment were called into consultation, and with their aid a map was made of the approaches, streets, houses, and available cover. Full information as to the numbers and disposition of the enemy was furnished by our scouts, so that with this and the local knowledge of our own men it was seldom difficult to draw up a plan of attack. Surprise was our best ally, and at this we always aimed, sending a force greatly superior in numbers to that of the enemy, watching exits, cutting off every line of retreat, and leaving no refugees to carry the news; these methods had the effect of keeping our casualty list at a remarkably low level.

In several instances variations of our original scheme of attack had to be adopted to meet altered circumstances. At Polovena, Gaikole, Panozero, Sopoyarka, Maslozero [Mashlozero], and Soposalma the operations varied merely in detail; but at Uskozero the action developed on different lines. This village sprawled for three versts along the river bank, and was divided by several small streams and creeks which rendered a surprise attack difficult to carry out with a limited number of troops. Late in the evening of the 27th August the Karelians entered the village from the forest and surrounded the enemy barracks, where they were surprised to find only ten men opposing them instead of the seventy expected. It appeared that a relief was in progress, forty men having recently left for Ouchta, and the remaining portion of the garrison being distributed over the village. The first shot, warning the Finns at the other end of the village, caused two of them to hasten up river for reinforcements. The Karelians disposed of some thirty of the enemy (all they could find), and started in pursuit of the party on the river. These men had turned back, and they encountered the Karelians in the forest about eight versts from the village. Here they were at a disadvantage, and after two hours fighting during which they lost some of their number, the enemy retreated to their boats at the top of the rapids about two versts up-stream. Here they were trapped and few of them contrived to reach cover on the opposite bank, the river taking its toll of wounded and non-swimmers.

On the following night a party of the enemy about 250 strong encountered our outpost at the south side of the rapids, driving it in. This eventuality had been foreseen, and strong support placed on both banks. The Karelians on the further bank worked round to the rear of the attacking force, while those on the south bank opposed them with machine-guns in front and worked gradually round their right flank, so that they were at length completely surrounded with the rapids as their only means of escape. The fighting was severe and many savage hand-to-hand struggles took place in the rapids, each combatant fighting to a finish. The Regiment captured three machine-guns with belts and ammunition, many automatic pistols, and a number of boats.

The "White Guard", as they [Finns] called themselves, had been led by a German officer, who perished near the river with many of his command. He had in his possession an interesting pamphlet printed in Karelia and entitled: "Why England wants Karelia". Subsequently we found that copies of this document had been distributed throughout the country, a fact no doubt largely responsible for certain proposals put forward by the Karelians at a later date. It was also not without effect on Bataillard, the French intelligence officer already mentioned, to whom it was sent at Kem.

The taking of Lousalma was a terrible example of the ruthlessness with which these people waged war. While it reflected great military credit upon the Karelian officer responsible for its success, the fighting did not exhibit the slightest trace of any recognition of humane principles in warfare, except perhaps if the view were taken that a quick end would be preferable to brief and extremely painful captivity, such as appeared to be the code on both sides. It is difficult for an onlooker who has not suffered the same experience to gauge the feelings towards the culprits of a soldier whose home may have been burned or womenfolk taken; nor is it possible to judge by the enlightened standards of Europe a people so far behind in social development, but it is also difficult to forget the slaughter at Lousalma, where the enemy were surrounded and driven on to a sandbank, on which they were butchered to a man, no quarter being asked or given.

Lieut Kempueiff, who led this attack, capturing two machine-guns and a quantity of explosive ammunition, was by nature a most kindly person off duty. I well remember his carrying the lame child of a neighbour many miles through the forest to have her attended by Doctor Harrison. At Ouchta he won the Military Cross, but was severely wounded, being badly shot in the stomach and taken unconscious down the river to a temporary hospital, which was in charge of a well-known maternity nurse. This lady was the first person Kempueiff recognised on regaining consciousness and, weak as he was, he could not resist asking her: "May I see the baby .... Is it a boy or a girl?" It was five or six days later before the Doctor was himself able to get down to attend to this patient, and when he arrived he was concerned about the gravity of the case, and gave the nurse detailed instructions as to treatment, diet and the like. Kempueiff listened with interest as these were interpreted for him, and then asked the Doctor: "Would it do me any harm to have a 'Maconachie'?" Harrison was not unnaturally horrified at this preposterous notion, and lectured the patient on the seriousness of being shot through the stomach and the folly of loading the inflamed organs with hard biscuit, vegetables and meat. After according him a patient hearing Kempueiff remarked: "I just wondered, because I have had two every day since I came." In two weeks the patient was walking, and in six he was back with his beloved guns. The Doctor always regarded him as a rather shabby trick on the medical profession.

As we moved up country recruits came in from every village for a hundred versts on either side; this was reported to GHQ by runner. All additions to our numbers were more than welcome, as the enemy in Karelia were supposed to outnumber us by four to one. Hence our amazement was great when we received an urgent relay post message to send down all recruits to build huts at Kola for the General! We knew that the General was doing everything possible to help us, so whence could this order emanate? We attributed it to a Staff Officer; but the pressing question remained, how to circumvent it? It would, of course, have been possible to drown the messenger and say that we had never received the message; however, he seemed a decent fellow, and at length we compromised by writing to Colonel Marsh, who had forwarded the order, that we could not read it, and would he repeat it? Meanwhile we knew that we could do quite a lot with the recruits before a reply arrived. At the same time a private message to Marsh, who was a very understanding person and good soldier enough to appreciate the issues, worked wonders, and he did his work at the other end so efficiently that we were eventually told to keep our recruits – to our great relief.

Our 'marches' were so arranged that we should arrive at the bottom of a rapid, and so at the beginning of a portage at meal times, and while the boats were being hauled or poled and the loads carried a few men would prepare fires, and the women have everything ready for them when they had finished their laborious work. This was always done in a surprisingly short time; each man being an expert at his job, there was no getting in each other's way and no slacking. Most of the portages were short, some being only about 200 yards, but two were about a mile long and a third was three miles; here the rapids were a wonderful sight, the foaming water rushing along at terrific speed and breaking up into spray against the larger rocks to form an iridescent veil of rainbow colours against the dark green of the forest background. At each portage we left some details as guards and a number of boats to facilitate the transport of stores. By this means much time and labour were saved, the required number of boats for the advancing troops being maintained at strength by those captured from the enemy, or placed at our disposal by the delighted inhabitants of the liberated villages; and our numerical strength increased daily.

Because of the necessity to extend operations on a wider front as we advanced, our progress slowed down considerably; we had also to keep pace with the companies employed on our flanks in dealing with village garrisons and outposts, combing the country for a distance of sixty miles on each side of our main line of advance. Incidentally, we found that the maps supplied to us by the Russian officials were so wildly inaccurate as to compel the conclusion that the surveyors had remained in Kem and plotted their surveys from gossip. In many instances towns were marked at as much as fifty miles from their actual site, while the courses of rivers were entirely imaginary efforts, possibly based on after-dinner information, and only occasionally approximating to fact by accident.

We could not afford to give the enemy the slightest opportunity of attacking our weakest point, the long line of communication and supply, hence our flanking companies were particularly vigilant. So zealous were they that on one occasion they captured a Red Finn scout of Major

Burton's; fortunately they brought him in alive, so that we were able to make contact with his column, which was advancing from Kandalaksha towards the Finnish frontier on our right flank, and distant about 75 versts. Meanwhile Burton's people had made a similar mistake encountering one of my couriers who was missing. This caused so much anxiety to General Maynard who had in consequence received no despatches from me for seven days, that he sent a sea-plane up the river in an endeavour to locate us.

The plane arrived after we had reached Lousalma, and in accordance with the code of signals we had arranged before leaving Kem we spread sheets in a field at the back of the village to mark our position. The excitement among the inhabitants was intense when the machine came droning out of the sky; but when it glided down on to the river and taxied up to the landing stage their agitation mounted to a frenzy. Many of the women came out into the road and knelt down, making the sign of the cross. I had never before had the experience of seeing an airman embarrassed until the moment when those two youngsters came ashore, to have their hands seized and kissed by the old women, who certainly imagined that they were messengers from heaven! The pilot and his observer passed off this reception remarkably well; I think the intense feeling shown by the villagers even imbued them with enthusiasm for the Karelians' cause.

We were about to move off from Lousalma when I had a most disturbing document delivered by Lieut Fryer. In order to reach me he had travelled at an average speed of over 40 versts per day, with relays of guides, over rivers and swamps, and by forest tracks for three days and nights – a remarkable exhibition of determination and stamina. This despatch contained a detailed account of the military situation of the whole Murmansk Force, and of the precarious position of the Karelians in particular [see Appendix A]. Giving his reasons, which were excellent in view of the alarming reports he had received concerning the number and intentions of the enemy, the General explained that according to GHQ Intelligence there were 70,000 Germans in Finland, and that a half of this number was threatening the Murmansk Force – by way of Karelia! The policy, therefore, was to withdraw all troops to the north almost at once, and abandon Kem and the railway south of Kandalaksha. The Karelians who could be persuaded to do so were to go to Kandalaksha; should they decline he could give us six months' supplies for 800 men, but could not guarantee winter clothing. The British staff of the Karelian Regiment was free to take any line of action it individually elected to follow, no pressure to be exercised by me to influence any one person's decision. All British officers were advised to join up at Kem before the end of September .... unless I wished to remain out as 'King of Karelia'. In any event, he would do everything possible to assist me.

This was a severe disappointment; moreover, it placed upon me the responsibility of either abandoning the whole country and people to the in no wise tender mercies of the enemy when he returned, or of pushing on and finishing what might possibly have been a two months' campaign in a fortnight. I was at all times anxious to carry out the wishes of the Chief, but I knew that it would be a hopeless task to attempt persuasion of the Karelians to leave the enemy in possession of their capital and abandon their wives, families and belongings to reprisals, the measure and manner of which it was not difficult to imagine; and this at the bidding of a Power to whom they did not technically owe allegiance. There was also the question of the officials, loyal Russians, and friends in Kem; no doubts could be entertained as to their fate when Spiridonoff and his Bolsheviks learned of their defenceless state. It seemed to me that if the policy favoured by Headquarters were adopted the good name of Britain would suffer, for the retirement would mean to the inhabitants simply betrayal. The matter was discussed with the Karelian officers, who agreed to carry out the General's instructions insofar as they were prepared to send from 400 to 600 unmarried men to Kandalaksha after we had conquered Karelia. Consequently I wrote to Colonel Marsh reporting the decision of the Karelians, together with my own – to stay with them until the job was completed.

In my communication to Colonel Marsh I also gave my opinion upon the proposed evacuation of Kem and its certain consequences, and suggested that this should be delayed until the latest possible moment, and further that the Karelians should be given the opportunity of supplying the required defence of that town. I added that the intelligence information received at GHQ was undoubtedly inspired, and that nothing approaching the numbers given existed except in the imagination of the enemy staff; that the Karelian intelligence reports did not in the slightest degree support the news and rumours from Sweden and elsewhere.

We had several good men, relatives of officers on the Karelian staff, who were collecting information for us in Finland and in whose veracity and loyalty we had the utmost confidence. Their latest reports gave our opponents as having about 3,000 troops in Karelia, with few reserves.

Some days later we had another visitor, Major Burton, who had travelled a hundred versts over the difficult country in order to consult with us about the abandonment of our little war. To say that he was indignant would convey but little of his feelings. During the war officers were sometimes wont to express themselves somewhat strongly when dealing with irritating incidents, but Burton easily outdistanced all previous efforts in this respect I had ever heard; he had an inventive turn of mind which fascinated the Marines and made the Doctor blush. From all this we gathered that he disapproved thoroughly of the new instructions. He stayed one night, leaving on the following day quite happy and reduced to the use of normal English again by the arrangements we made for future cooperation. Burton was a big man in every sense of the expression; brave, intelligent and cheerful, he was a most likeable personality. From that day we worked together in perfect harmony throughout the many difficulties which arose during our stay in Russia.

The Karelian Regiment was impressed with the urgent necessity of expelling the enemy in the shortest possible time, and we therefore took more risks than we should normally have done in carrying out our plans, thus losing some men who need not have been casualties in other circumstances. This race against time afforded in reality a new lease of life, and the satisfaction of everyone concerned was great when the orders to abandon Karelia and Kem were finally cancelled, and permission to carry on granted to Burton and myself. This made all the difference to our plans, as it would not now be necessary to guard our base at Kem against another enemy [the Bolsheviks] whilst still fighting the German-Finns in front. Occasionally enemy scouts contrived to get behind our main column, but they were accounted for either by the guards on the river or by the supply convoys.

One of these little scouting parties provided what might well be described in the popular press as an 'epic', an incident which acted as a great fillip to the morale of the Karelians. Two young members of our Womens' Auxilliaries in charge of one of the smaller supply boats had raced in front of the convoy in order to attend to some private and domestic matter of their own at the next village. Three Finnish scouts who had been lying in a boat concealed by the reeds and an overhanging tree watched the little craft approach up the farther side of the river. They waited until they judged the moment for action had arrived, and then pushed out into the stream, two of their number rowing and the third, balancing himself in the bows and gripping his rifle ready to fire, called upon the Karelian girls to halt. This order being ignored, the man with the rifle fired on them, but his position and the movement of the boats caused him to miss his target. Accordingly he fired several more rounds at a range of a little over 100 yards with no more serious result than the puncture of a biscuit tin. Then the Karelian girls appeared to waver and after a quick exchange of words turned their craft about and commenced to row towards the Finns. These warriors stopped rowing to watch the approach of their victims, one reciting to them meanwhile a list of the many punishments about to be meted out to them, and handling a German stick-bomb. The oncoming rowers, who appeared to be in a hurry to get it all over, pulled their hardest. When they had approached to about a boat's length the Finns yelled directions to the girls, cursing them for their clumsiness; but instead of following the directions they suddenly swerved, driving their boat with all their strength straight at the other and crashing it amidships. At the impact the man in the bow, who had laid down his rifle and was leaning over ready to grasp the gunwale of the other boat, lost his balance and shot headfirst overboard. The two rowers jumped to their feet, but a powerful and nicely aimed stab with an oar caused one to join his companion in the river, while the third received his quietus from the starboard oar which, swung at full momentum from the water, caught him in the neck. A few more thumps from the oars made little difference; the two men could not swim. They disappeared in the river, and their bodies were found later at the bottom of the rapids. The convoy guards got the first man and the boat. Ackolina and Sasha Nicolina were awarded the Military Medal, the first women to receive it, I think.

It was as well for these Karelian girls that they emerged so successfully from the encounter, for their fate in the event of capture hardly bears contemplation; no mercy was shown by either side, and many revolting cruelties were practised. As an illustration of the feeling between conqueror and conquered, we were marching along a forest track at a portage one day when I noticed something hanging from the lower limb of a pine tree, gently swaying to and fro in the breeze. It looked like a sack, old and tattered, with streamers hanging from it. Beside it was a frayed piece of rope. I asked Gregori, who was with me: "What is that, Gregori? Is it a scout's sign?"

"No," he replied, "the rope is what was left when we cut down Boris

Bogdanoff. The Finns had cut off his ears, fingers, toes and things before they hanged him. The other object is a Finn who was killed and his skin stuffed with leaves. He's there as a warning. The Karelians are good hunters and can take the skin off anything; but that is not a good sample; it was done in a hurry and has been there all the summer."

On another occasion I asked a Karelian officer: "Why do you carry that axe in your belt, Nicoli?"

"Oh well," came the ingenuous reply, "it's a good silent weapon for surprise parties, and always useful for abstracting information from the enemy – properly applied." He smiled, indicating the idea by placing the corner of the edge under his thumb nail.

Any remonstrance to these practices was regarded as weakness, hence I was able to make no more vigorous protest than to insist that they should cease while I was in the country. This was agreed to; but I strongly suspect that the agreement was taken to mean that I should hear of no barbarities. Certainly I saw none, and the few other exhibits of the taxidermist's art I came upon were old and weather-worn.

There was one point on which it was very difficult to reach an agreement. I wanted prisoners, in order to question them with a view to obtaining a more accurate estimate of the calibre of the opposing force; I knew their strength numerically, but their quality and experience in open fighting, knowledge of which was now more important to me, was difficult to obtain. If I asked for prisoners the answer was invariably: "I arrived too late to save any of them ..." or: "They were all killed in the first attack." General Maynard asked by every despatch for prisoners to be sent down, and it became increasingly difficult to make excuses for their non-appearance. At last I hit on an idea – to buy one. I offered a pound of tobacco for a prisoner, alive and uninjured. The Karelians thought I was insane. To offer real tobacco, and in such quantities, for a useless Finn who would have to be fed, and worse, be allowed to keep his own boots! (It was significant that almost every man in the Regiment was now wearing Finnish boots.) However, I got one prisoner by this means and, as I had no more tobacco with me, he was the only one. I had to send an escort with him down the river to Kem, not to prevent his escape, but to preserve his life – and his boots. He was a nice lad; he had been some sort of clerical worker and was quite out of his métier. He did not attempt to bluff or lie, and although his information was useless his attitude of complete defeat and his talk about Finland were encouraging to us.

Chapter 5

Massacre at Voknavalok

There was a difference of opinion between the Karelians and myself not regarding our objective, but the methods to be employed in attaining it. It was the common policy to clear the country of invaders, but while they wished to exterminate the Finns I desired to inflict a severe defeat upon them and chase them over the frontier. To this end a liberal supply of false information was spread about among the enemy by villagers straying into their lines, from which it could be gleaned that our strength was over 10,000 and that reinforcements were arriving as fast as they could travel. Colour was given to this story by the fact that we actually had taken villages as far apart as 60 versts almost simultaneously.

That our dissemination of false intelligence was quite as effective with them as theirs had been with our people at Murmansk is confirmed by the extraordinary ideas they conceived of our composition; a few weeks later complaints were made by the Finnish Government to the Foreign Office regarding the savage conduct of the Royal Irish Rifles at the taking of Robolskia [Rebola]. Another injustice to Ireland! This policy of exaggeration weakened the morale of an enemy already suffering from consecutive defeats; from the moment when the opposing forces first became aware of our presence in the country we had constantly allowed them to be aware of the fate met by their outlying garrisons and posts; and they were now further discouraged by a series of bombing raids carried out by aeroplane on Ouchta.

There were in Ouchta about 600 men entrenched, with plenty of stores and supplies. The place itself was a sort of miniature Gibraltar, built on cliffs sixty feet high, and facing west and south on to the great Ouchta Lake which at this point was eighteen versts wide; on the north it was protected for miles by a reputedly impassable swamp; while to the east two versts of bare fields without a leaf of cover, the harvest having just been completed, gave the plentiful machine-guns of the defenders every advantage. The officer commanding Ouchta was of field rank, and as far as we could learn had fortified the place very thoroughly; there were eight gun emplacements and as many machine-gun positions, sandbagged and wired, as were his firestepped trenches; these covered the lake front. More machine-guns and three trench mortars covered the stubble fields, while he had been content to place a few strands of wire across the swampy end of the town.

The seaplanes had carried out a reconnaissance at Ouchta during their raid, and they were therefore able to let us have some useful air photographs. We were informed that their visit had had a great effect upon the garrison, and that a further raid would be very effective if we could arrange our attack to coincide with it. This, however, looked like being a rather difficult feat to perform, since we had no telephone or wireless communication with the outside world, relying upon couriers who took six days down and nine or ten returning, and the 'planes' base was the *Nairana*, 200 versts away. The 'planes came to our assistance and bombed the enemy position with considerable effect, but owing to the conditions mentioned it was impossible to synchronise their raid and our attack, the launching of which under cover of darkness seemed to be the only alternative to a doubtful issue entailing certain and heavy losses. However, one of our scouts now volunteered the information that he knew of a track across the reputedly impassable swamp. This was welcome news, and was providentially the means of saving many Karelian lives.

The night of the 11th September was chosen for the assault. We waited until the last glimmer of light had faded from the western sky, and when it was very dark and still in the forest 600 men in single file crept out on to the treacherous marsh, all bright parts of their equipment covered. In complete silence they moved like shadows, no word being spoken even when the leaders found and cut the wire, at length reaching the cover of some outhouses where they lay upon the ground until the last man of the long file had arrived.

A quarter of a mile distant over broken ground partially covered with low bushes lay the town, with its lighted windows, and sounds of an accordion and voices were clearly audible as the whispered order for the advance was given. The Karelians began to move in open order across the rough ground; but they had not advanced more than half way when there came a shout and a shot from the right, a moment's silence, then more shouts and a fusillade followed by silence again. The enemy had an outpost group of nine men placed in a 'cover from view' shelter, and into this our men had walked. The enemy had no chance of survival, but they did succeed in warning the garrison by their rifle fire.

We subsequently learned that Major Kooczman, the German Commander, on hearing the sound of firing had hastily gathered together his German staff, much of his correspondence and such of the local funds as his predecessor had overlooked when he had fled to Finland two days previously with £6,000. With these he embarked in a motor-boat and, with ten boats in tow, fled to the westward; not, however, before destroying in the harbour and on the beach as many craft as possible in a short time by dropping bombs into them. While it prevented pursuit this strategy at the same time effectively cut off the retreat of the remainder of his garrison.

It was impossible to place a complete cordon round the town with the force available, but all points at which troops were known to be stationed were attended to. The main barracks were quickly captured, the enemy retreating and unwisely crowding into their drill hall. The result of this manoeuvre was reminiscent of a bombed dug-out in France; a machine-gun was placed at one window and another in the doorway, and bayonets awaited attempts at escape from the remaining windows. At other points opposition was quickly overcome, and the only living members of the garrison were those who had been fortunate enough to reach temporary safety in the forest, where they were hunted down and killed within the next few days. A few houses had to be burnt to drive out the enemy occupants. Some 150 White Finns were casualties, and an unknown number still in the forest or on the lake.

Correspondence captured showed that reinforcements had been asked for, without result; this contradicted the intelligence reports at Murmansk and confirmed our own views in the matter. Guns, trench mortars, machine-guns, ammunition, and quantities of supplies fell into our hands ... and, of course, the remaining boats. The capture of some enemy flags at Ouchta acted as a reminder that we lacked regimental colours, so in order to remedy this I wrote to my brother at home and ordered four flags to be made bearing the crest of the Regiment which was, it will be remembered, a green shamrock. To put the matter upon a more definite basis the field was coloured orange. This handsome flag was so much admired by the Karelians that it was eventually adopted as the national flag and when it was explained that the three leaves had a religious significance, representing Faith, Hope and Charity, it received the unstinted approval of the Church. St Patrick himself could not have criticised this interpretation of the message carried by the little plant from Slemish mountain. Our Standard flew from the flagstaff on the town hall of Ouchta, another from the barracks and wireless station of Uskozero, about ninety miles distant, the third at Kem barracks, and the other fluttered below the Union Jack on the mast of the Regimental Headquarters at Kem station.

The German staff and escort managed to reach the large village of Voknavolok about forty-five miles nearer the frontier, where they stayed awaiting reinforcements from Finland. At this place they were able to add about 200 to their number; but the delay of six days cost them dearly and their position became a death-trap, for the Karelians had time to surround them completely, and in greatly superior numbers. Against the wishes of the Karelians I wrote to the German commander offering him and his followers safe conduct to Finland, providing they walked out unarmed with four days' food supply. In this offer he evidently saw some trap and refused to surrender. It was a pity. On the 2nd October he tried to retreat to the frontier, but few of his men reached it. In one day's fighting alone he lost 214 killed, and the rout was carried on to the frontier.

Meanwhile I was compelled to leave Ouchta and travel post haste to Kem to take command of the troops at that town. However it was with an easy mind that I left, as I was now convinced that nothing could prevent a complete victory and the expulsion of the last invader from Karelian territory. A strong frontier guard was organised, and the protection of all strategic points adequately provided for. Heaton was left at Uskozero to superintend transport and supplies with a very efficient mule-pack wireless station. (The ingenuity displayed by the Karelians in erecting a 200 foot mast without gear was astonishing).

The absence of personal danger from enemy sources rather detracted from the excitement of the downstream journey, but this was in part compensated by the thrills attending shooting the rapids, and the greatly accelerated speed of the boats. The whole country had now changed its aspect and assumed autumnal tints. The wild birds were gathering for their migration south – swans, geese and duck. Rounding a bend in the river one did not find a few brace of duck swimming quietly out of the track of the boats; each new reach would be either deserted or else covered by hundreds of duck; indeed towards the end of the journey they were in flocks of thousands. The geese were more shy than usual, and were seldom seen on the river, preferring the lakes more remote from human routes. We tried to get a shot at some geese congregated on a large lake close to Panozero, but their sentries were wide awake and alarmed the flock, and in a moment the misty air was filled with the raucous honks of the birds and the flapping of thousands of wings as they rose in the darkness just before dawn. Before reaching Kem we saw the start of the final exodus, and a wonderful spectacle it presented.

The wild fowl which had been mustering all over Karelia for the flight south during the last two weeks, first, to use the military metaphor, in companies, then in battalions and brigades, had now amalgamated into vast armies, flying at varying heights as they climbed to reach the required altitude, and filling the air with the rushing sound of literally millions of wings. They covered the sky from horizon to horizon in ranks half a mile wide, extending the whole thirty versts of our view, neither end being visible. The depth of this mighty concourse was difficult to estimate; the swans and geese appeared to require greater height than the duck, flying at possibly 1,000 feet. The manoeuvring for position lasted about fifteen minutes; then, as if in answer to some invisible signal, every bird turned south in exact concert, the southern edge of this flying multitude marshalled into a definite line drawn by the leaders straight as an arrow across the sky, gradually shading off into the confusion of the stragglers hurrying into position. Gradually the sounds of them diminished and the sky lightened as the huge flock disappeared over the southern skyline, leaving a great silence and a sense of loss which prompted the reflexion that we should soon have to face the Arctic winter.

Only on one occasion, when the distance between villages was too great to accomplish in the day, had we to pitch our camp on the river bank. Here the mosquitos, awakened to a new lease of life by the warmth of the camp fires, welcomed our advent and we had in addition the undivided attention of the minute wood-midge, too small to be denied pleasure by any mosquito net. The Karelians said that these little pests could not see, but could only smell; they seemed to be all nose and very keen upon thrusting it into other people's business, as our swollen faces bore witness the next day.

The village billets were all similar in accommodation, being log-built houses of one story construction with a loft above for hay and implements, and having cellars beneath. One half of the house would be used for living rooms and the other as stables or cowbyres. An outside porch protected the door from the weather, the outer door being padded on the inside with blankets, skins or canvas. An inner door led from a tiny hall, where outer clothing is discarded, into the large square living-room with its scrubbed and spotlessly clean wood floor. On one side there would be two small windows; these were of double glass with all joints pasted up with paper or caulked with cotton wool. A quarter of the floor space was occupied by the great brick-built stove and oven, about five feet high, the top of which was the family sleeping place in the winter, and also in summer on days when there was no bread baking. In a corner would be the inevitable ikon, usually with its little red lamp of scented oil burning below. The log walls were bare except for an occasional coloured print from the Christmas number of some Finnish or Swedish journal; seldom were they Russian. The furniture consisted of a white scrubbed table, with two backless benches as the seating accommodation, and two supplementary Windsor type armchairs, disposed opposite corners of the room. The samovar would be ready boiling at any hour of the day or night. Ventilation is obtained by means of a three-inch pipe through the wall, the end being stopped when required by a round plug inside the house.

Every log-built Russian house has a peculiar smell, rather pleasant than otherwise, and reminiscent of that which one finds in the turf burning cottages in rural Ireland, suggesting leather, cigarettes, burning charcoal and bugs. The item in which the odours chiefly differ has a curiously scented musky aroma which can be immediately detected by the initiated. This little fellow thrives in the moss packing between the logs of which the buildings are constructed, and Russians are sensitive about their domestic pet, especially when he chooses to make his appearance at an inopportune moment. On one occasion, after dinner at a Russian house, I earned unpopularity by shooting a fine specimen with a small pocket pistol. I had thought it a pretty good shot to hit a sprinting target of that size at a range of four feet, but my host was lacking in appreciation. There is, however, another inhabitant of houses heated by the Russian stove system, the stove being his incubator and headquarters – the cockroach. Often measuring two inches from tip to tail, he cleans up all crumbs from the floor or elsewhere. He does not attack or bite human beings, but makes irritating noises, clicking and chirruping through the long and stifling nights. When disturbed in his night operations he develops astonishing speed in retreat, fairly clattering to cover. When his kind become too prolific the Russians leave the house for a few nights in the winter, allow the stove to go cold, and open all the doors and windows. The Arctic frost disposes of the trouble.

Egor, the broad faced, smiling steersman of our boat, was a noted riverman; he knew every rock, current and shallow for two hundred miles, and brought us safely down through all the rapids, including three miles of wild water below Panozero. To watch him at work was a lesson in navigation. Here he would swing hard on his steering oar, calling an order to the rowers (men this time), who responded on the instant, one side pulling and the other idle, or all rowing strongly to avoid some ugly submerged rock or undercurrent. Looking at the water alongside gave a curious impression of being stationary; a big wave would rise slowly beside the boat, in the fashion of a slow motion picture, threaten to fall upon us, and then gradually subside, to be replaced by another. A sense of movement could only be realised by glancing at the banks of the river or at an uncovered rock; these objects appeared to be flying past at tremendous speed, like the passing landscape viewed from an express train. The sensation was enjoyable, and not dissimilar to a gallop on a runaway horse in open country or a descent in a racing bobsleigh.

The waterfall at Paduzemskaia provided a certain amount of interest. In consequence of friendly disputes as to the possibility of negotiating this hazard in a boat two well-known rivermen undertook to make the attempt; this was not for monetary reward, but simply for honour and glory, and although they were offered money to do so they refused to carry any passengers. They first made a careful survey of the falls and traced the course of the main flood before it dispersed into broken water; then they boarded their boat, an elderly bearded man steering with an oar and a herculean Karelian sergeant rowing. We stood on the rocks at the top of the falls and looked down a cascade of fifty feet of roaring water which shot out a clear twenty feet from the broken bed with its own volume and velocity, with a curious oblique turn in direction, caused no doubt by the rock formation underneath, before it poured thundering into the deep pool below. In case of failure several boats had been stationed with ropes as near to the falls as was prudent to venture, though the chance of any person surviving the weight of water crashing down into the pool seemed remote. The little boat came on towards the edge of the falls, the steersman crouching in the stern staring intently ahead, the rower pulling gently. Then, as the bow began to tilt downwards, we heard above the roar of the water the shout of the steersman to his companion, who now began to pull madly with every ounce of his weight and strength. The bow turned slightly; then, when it reached the top of the curve, came completely out of the water, only about a third of the craft and the steering oar remaining in contact with the 'glassy glide'; finally it seemed to leave the water altogether before disappearing into the clouds of spray beneath. We thought they were surely lost, but after a nerve-racking interval the little craft emerged from the mists and smother of foam half swamped, its crew drenched but triumphant. Our Marines admired this feat more than anything they had seen in the country.

On our return to Kem I submitted to the War Office, through General Maynard, the case for the Karelian widows and orphans of soldiers killed in action, and asked what provision could be made for disabled men. The Karelians had not enlisted in the British Army nor taken any oath of allegiance, thus the circumstances were quite unprecedented in my experience. The War Office in turn asked for any suggestions I had to offer. I had had in mind a fur trading organisation to create a fund for our purposes, and this conception was approved by the War Office, Major P. J. Mackesy adding a valuable warning to be careful of accounts and so to avoid possible trouble in the future.

The fur trading, venture was a complete success. Hunters and trappers brought in some wonderful Arctic Red Fox, cross fox and a few silver fox skins. We paid from 10/- to 30/- for these and sold them to Allied Officers for sums ranging from £12 to £16 each! There were also a few lynx, martins and ermine skins, plenty of elk hides, and literally thousands of white Arctic hare skins. In spite of our fabulous profits the purchasers were pleased with their bargains when it was found that some officers on leave had been offered £35 for each fox skin and as much as £75 had been offered in London for one of our silver foxes.

The books were kept by an officer who, in his spare time between wars, was a professional accountant, so that on leaving Russia we were able to show the accounts in good order, with all pensions paid up for three months and a credit balance consisting of a very good 10 h.p. motor boat and £600 in cash. The War Office eventually allowed pensions for the Karelian widows and orphans and paid allowances to the disabled soldiers.

Chapter 6

Visit to Solievetski

We found upon arrival in Kem that many changes had taken place during our absence. Some kind of policy had been adopted, but its ultimate object was a mystery to those of us not in the confidence of the great, and it was quite evident that there were now currents and undercurrents in the political sea threatening to engulf purely military considerations and involve us in a maze of intrigue.

Captain Drake-Brockman was very pleased to be relieved of responsibility for the Kem district. There were now several non-British officers in the area who were sensitively senior to himself and who, in consequence, did little to smooth his difficulties. However, with the exercise of extraordinary tact and diplomacy he had managed to preserve at least some outward show of harmony among the heterogeneous units and varying interests now represented in the command. Another company of Serbs had arrived, with one or two high-spirited Subalterns whose ideas of amusement were often at variance with those generally accepted in the best 'trench circles', as we used to say in France. One of these young men, upon the objection of a mother to his over marked attentions to her daughter, had the old lady put out of her house, and posted a sentry to prevent her return! There was also a French howitzer battery, who were easy to deal with and most helpful. But a contingent of the [White Russian] New Murmansk Army was a different question. This force was officered by men who were distinctly anti-allied in their opinions as reported by the Intelligence, and obviously obstructionist in their actions. There was no friendship between the allies and these Russian officers, nor did our men fraternise with theirs; and those Russians, civilian or military, in the town who had been most friendly before the advent of the newcomer were with few exceptions afraid to offer us hospitality or to be seen in our company. Constant attempts were made by the administrators of this Murmansk Army to undermine our influence and authority with the Karelians, while at the same time reports were being made to General Maynard that the Karelians were simply awaiting an opportunity to rise and murder every Britisher in the country. These efforts were continued with increasing intensity until we evacuated the country, and they caused a certain amount of unnecessary friction between General Maynard's staff and ourselves. The influence of this propaganda with the staff in Murmansk was such that I think I myself eventually became the subject of suspicion, although it was never quite clear whether it was supposed that I should 'rise' with the Karelians and assist in the murder of my comrades, or simply annex Russia for my own use and fly the skull and crossbones over the Kremlin.

In addition to these embarrassments the troops were now attacked by an epidemic of influenza in the virulent form which swept Europe in 1918, taking a particularly heavy toll in England. Drake-Brockman's company of Marines suffered heavily, while it was a frequent occurrence to find a supply boat of the Karelians' hauled up on the river bank at a shelter hut with the entire crew of five lying dead inside. The Serbian company also lost many men.

The plotting of the Murmansk Russians compelled us in the interests of our own safety to organise and maintain a sort of counter-espionage system of our own. To this end we were fortunate in having the able and experienced help of an ex-Tzarist Police officer – Mascherin – who was now a Captain in the Murmansk Army, but stationed in Kem and distinctly pro-British in outlook. Mascherin had friends in the postal service, the telegraph office and the railways, so that he was in an excellent position to obtain 'inside information' by means of which he intercepted three attempts on my life. It may seen strange that such attempts should have been made by our Russian allies more especially as our ostensible objective was to assist them against the Bolsheviks from the south, and two possible explanations occurred to me: jealousy, or the infection of these Murmansk forces with the revolutionary virus. Perhaps it was a little of each, but in the main I inclined towards the latter solution, and I think this was the real underlying cause. It was significant that Russians in Murmansk had now abandoned the habit, instilled into them by their own officers as had formerly been the custom, of getting off the path when passing an officer, either Russian or British.

The first attempt was intercepted in ample time by Mascherin and his agents. Two men had been sent from Murmansk to Kem for the sole purpose of securing my early demise, but owing to the timely information of their errand at my disposal they were met at the station, questioned in the Russian manner, and assisted on their way to an amended but unknown destination. I was never told what became of them, but some months later a code message came to Kem from Murmansk enquiring their whereabouts; this was not addressed to me, but came to my notice through the usual channels. On thinking it over I was not very surprised to learn that they had not got back to Murmansk; Mascherin, in his peculiar position, could hardly have afforded to let them do so.

The Russian system of interrogation in such circumstances as these was, to say the least of it, rough and ready. The first step was to have the subject's outer clothing removed; then, standing before him and drawing the thongs of a knout slowly and suggestively through his fingers, Mascherin addressed pointed questions and required immediate answers. If the answers were not prompt and complete he gave the victim three fairly heavy cuts, and in normal cases this produced the desired information. In this particular instance the first of our visitors to be 'examined' was reluctant to talk, no doubt bearing in mind the consequences of divulging the names of his masters. His obstinate silence brought the knout seriously into play, and this, wielded by a man weighing seventeen stone and six feet three inches in height with the strength of exasperation behind each stroke, achieved what the preliminary warning had failed to produce. The names and all other necessary details were given. But the end of the 'examination' saw the victim unconscious and a bleeding mess.

The information thus gained was confirmed by the other prisoner in similar circumstances.

Mascherin was invaluable to us in his special capacity, and a good friend of the British personnel. I thought I knew him until I became aware of his method of interrogation, which caused me to realise the vast difference between the Russian outlook on such matters and our own. When I remonstrated with him he thought me insane, and I am by no means certain that he did not act contrary to my orders when occasion arose in the future.

The disappearance of these first two emissaries did not deter their masters from a further attempt, which took place some few months later. The men who were sent on this occasion were again intercepted, and I saw nothing of them beyond the reports of their bodies having been observed from time to time at various ice-holes in the river. A third abortive attempt of a like nature was made, but this time an attack of 'cold feet' on the part of the envoys prevented its development. Had these methods proved successful the Karelians would no doubt have been accused of my assassination.

The direct approach having proved unexpectedly difficult new methods were now tried to cause disruption between the Karelians and ourselves. A party of eight men was sent into Karelia from Polani Krug [Polyani Krug], a station close to our northern boundary, with orders to use every kind of propaganda against the British in order to obtain the withdrawal of the Karelians in Kem, and with the final object of seizing all stores up river. I imagine that the Karelian Regiment dealt with these men; they were never heard of again.

These distractions were merely incidents in a very busy time during which we were endeavouring to transport food into Karelia in sufficient quantities before the rivers became impassable. There was a hiatus of six weeks or more from the time when the rivers first became too frozen to be navigable and that when the ice was thick enough to bear the weight of loaded transport sleighs and horses. By this stage we had been able to convince the authorities that not only the enlisted men required food and clothing, but also the civilian population, who had been deprived of their cattle and grain by the enemy, and who would shortly be in a state of starvation without immediate assistance. Hence the work of organising supplies covered a widely scattered district, comprising in area about 20,000 square miles.

Some gossip occasionally reached my ears concerning an important monastery situated on Solievetski [Solovetskii] Island, which lay about thirty miles north-east from Popoff. I had heard that our naval authorities had destroyed a wireless station belonging to the monks, but as the island was not included in the Kem Command I was not greatly interested in its welfare.

One morning I was surprised to find three venerable holy men waiting at the office with a letter from the Archimandrite, or Archbishop of

Solievetski monastery, petitioning for protection during the winter months, when the ice on the White Sea would afford easy access for bands of armed bandits from the mainland. He stated that the monks had no material defence against violence and aggression and were quite untrained in the use of arms, although they possessed a complete battery of modern 12-pounder guns with ammunition and equipment, which had been presented to them by the Tzar; would we send a battalion of British soldiers, in the name of all that was holy! While regretting that the number of men requested was not available at the moment I said that we would do our best to meet the situation, but I gave it as my considered opinion that a battery of guns would act as a strong incentive for evilly disposed persons to attack the monastery with a view to seizing them and putting them to improper use; that the guns would therefore be much better in our care at Kem, while the monastery would gain greater security by their absence. I did not think it necessary to inform the emissary that the whole complement of Britishers in Kem at that time numbered about 250. The result of considerable negotiation between the Archimandrite and ourselves was that we despatched a platoon of the Slavo-Brittanic Legion, who were all Russians, to act as a guard during the dangerous months, and the Archimandrite was to ship the battery of 12-pounders to us in Kem. But my dreams of a Royal Irish Karelian Horse Artillery never materialised. General Ironside heard of the guns and put in a claim from Archangel for them before they were shipped, and the Archimandrite was sufficiently astute to play the Archangel claim against Kem's. I think he kept them himself in the end. The argument about these guns waxed so serious that General Ironside himself came from Archangel to Kem to 'talk the matter over'. He was irresistible for many reasons, but mainly on account of his personality, seniority of rank being omitted from consideration.

When the ice broke in the spring following I seized the opportunity of using the little steamer leaving Kem to relieve the guard on Solievetski to accept the often repeated invitation of the Archimandrite to visit him, and to thank him personally for the excellent treatment of his guard, as well as for many kind messages and some fine smoked salmon he had presented to our mess at frequent intervals. Dodging through the broken ice floes was slow work, and afforded ample time when we were within a few miles of the island to appreciate our objective. The land was low-lying and well cultivated, but with little timber; however, one's eye was attracted and held by the monastery itself which appeared to be many acres in extent and was surrounded by grey, loop-holed walls, grim and forbidding, supported at each angle by massive towers which were also loopholed to command the face of each 'curtain'. It was a veritable fortress town, curiously modified in appearance by scores of slender white minarets capped with bright green copper rising above the walls, the huge Byzantine dome of the chapel dominating the whole, and visible for miles at sea when the sunlight caught its golden shape.

Nearer approach revealed behind the well-built breakwater a fine harbour capable of accommodating four or five steamers of medium tonnage as well as the fleet of fishing smacks belonging to the monastery. A dry-dock and several loading cranes on the quay evidenced the handling of heavy transport.

After our steamer had been made fast to the quay by a gang of tonsured, brown-gowned lay brothers who all wore the Russian top boots in place of sandals we were welcomed by a group of priests in black gowns, and wearing the usual high black headdress tied with long, black veils. Mende (my interpreter) and I were conducted across a long drawbridge over the moat and through massive iron doors into a large stone hall, bare of all decoration or furniture; then through various stone passages into the presence of the Archimandrite himself.

He was standing in a bright, sunny room containing little furniture other than a spotlessly scrubbed white-wood table and a few wooden chairs; but one could only glean a hazy impression of the contents of any room where the Archimandrite of Solievetski was. He had a remarkable presence. A tall figure draped in the customary black gown and high headdress of his order, relieved only by a gold Russian cross suspended from his neck, he needed no insignia of rank to identify him as the leader and chief of a great and ancient organisation. I had never met any man of such extraordinary personal magnetism. A full black beard framed his dead-white face, and his large dark eyes, expressing kindliness and pleasure much more than any spoken word could convey, gave an impression of profound intelligence and understanding such as I had never seen in a human being. He radiated an atmosphere of absolute tranquillity.

I did not realise at this stage that he was able to read my mind like an open book, but I made this surprising discovery when it dawned upon me that he was constantly answering questions which I had thought but not uttered. It occurred to me that this faculty would reflect to my dis-

View of Solievetski (Solovetskii) monastery, spring 1919.

advantage in negotiations for guns – or any other attractive objects.

We enjoyed the hospitality of the Archimandrite's table in the form of beautifully cooked fish, new bread and milk, while our host had his one daily meal with us – a bowl of rennet. He gave us many interesting facts relating to the history of the monastery, which had been founded in the tenth or eleventh century and was the second in importance in the Russian Empire. Its full complement of monks, he told us, was about 1,200, but had now shrunk to less than half that number living in the establishment, although there were many lay brothers employed on the farms, in the fishing fleet, on the steamer, and in general trades and labour. It was obvious that a large permanent staff must be maintained to preserve the buildings alone in their perfect condition, and when it was considered that all the cloth used on the island was hand-woven and homespun, the leather cured and boots and sandals made, flour milled and baked, in addition to carpentry and work in the forge, a considerable number of men could be employed inside. The monks themselves had built their steamer and fishing fleet and had constructed the dry-dock, a deep-water harbour and a very effective breakwater. They had also built three huge four-storied blocks of dormitories, each capable of accommodating 700 pilgrims. The farms provided all the foodstuffs, and supported hundreds of fine Hereford cattle and many pedigree pigs, while the dairy was the largest and most modern and hygienic I had then seen.

The roads were better than those on the mainland, although they were not good compared with English highways; but they were submerged at frequent intervals when the wind blew strongly from the east, and the water was piled high on the low-lying coast. As we were being driven along the road to the home farm the monk chauffeur stopped the Ford and descended to chase a family of ptarmigan out of our path! The Archimandrite explained this extraordinary situation by mentioning that a strict law of the island forbade the killing of any living creature, hence it had been a bird sanctuary for hundreds of years. By the sides of the paths and amongst the flowers many wild seafowl were hatching out their eggs without paying the slightest attention to passers-by, and only exhibiting annoyance when a camera clicked within six feet of them. The only time the birds displayed signs of excitement was when a monk came down the path with scraps of fish for their refreshment, then the raucous cries of guillemots, cormorants and gulls were deafening, each sitting on its own nest trying to attract attention.

The gardens of the monastery were kept in a condition similar to those at Hampton Court and were stocked with plants and flowers one would not expect to face within the confines of the Arctic Circle. Paths wound past the picturesque white walls of the dormitories, schools, chapels and shrines, on which were painted twenty foot figures of golden-haloed saints decorating every available space, and with coloured wooden effigies in every niche offering support. High up on the walls of one large shrine there were some round, dark circles, covered with glass and having below them an inscription painted in bold lettering. These were proudly pointed out to me as the marks of cannon shot fired by an English fleet during the Crimean war; some ships, it appeared, had penetrated into the White Sea and attacked Solievetski. I apologised to the Archimandrite for this incivility, saying that it was before my time; he smilingly accepted my apology, adding that he was not in the monastery during the bombardment himself, but that he did take a pride in these little mementoes, and he pointed to a large pile of ancient cannon balls under a painted wooden canopy on carved pillars.

From the gardens one could better appreciate the beauty and elaborate decorations of the lofty towers with their cupolas, and the myriad windowed buildings, the wonderful old coloured glass windows of the chapel and the fine proportions of the great clock tower with its tremendous deep-toned bell, reputed to be audible in all parts of the island.

Leaving the open air and sunlight we were conducted into the central refectory through long, dimly lighted corridors with their stone floors worn smooth by sandalled feet through the years and their long galleries of sacred pictures and portraits of saints painted on the walls, sometimes with stone carvings elaborately framing them, and the indescribable atmosphere of incense and leather which pervaded the whole monastery. The refectory was a circular hall about 100 feet in diameter with a vaulted roof so low that I was astonished to find there were no central supporting columns, but that its immense weight rested on the outer walls alone. Here again paintings of religious subjects decorated the ceiling between each groin. Some of these works were much above average merit and, I was told, had been executed mainly in the 17th century, though many were much older than this. They had been restored at various times and all were cleaned at regular intervals, which accounted to some extent for the freshness of the colours. Long tables and plain wooden benches scrubbed to snowy whiteness occupied the centre space, the stone floor shone like polished marble through continual scrubbing and the bare feet of the brothers of this ancient order, for they discarded their footwear in this part of the monastery.

In a blaze of light on a shrine at the head of the line of tables shone a magnificent golden crucifix with wonderful effect. It was the sole object on eye level and caught attention to the exclusion of all else.

From the refectory we went to the armoury, which was situated in the defences, and on our way we walked through many corridors, passed some iron doors, and mounted stone stairways until we reached the gallery which was built through the centre of the outer walls. This gallery was about fourteen feet in width to allow the free passage of the defenders from place to place in the event of attack. The outer section of the wall was about twelve feet thick and loopholed at frequent intervals, while the closely mortised stones required little attention to maintain its perfect condition. Entered by a heavy iron door, the armoury was a large vaulted chamber, electrically lighted, in the lower part of one of the flanking towers near the gate, but unlike the refectory it had numerous columns supporting the roof. The contents were astonishing in their variety and number, forming a museum of outstanding interest. Ranged round the walls were racks containing every kind of weapon through every phase of development from long-bows and arrows to the 1914 machine-gun. Bills, battle-axes and maces, spears, pikes, lances, arquebuses, muskets, pistols, revolvers and automatics were arranged in chronological order from the left of the entrance, and every piece was in perfect condition, cleaned, oiled and ready for use. At intervals between the stands of arms were some fine specimens of armour, some of which were said to have been the property of crusaders. One suit in particular must have belonged to a 'Brass Hat' of the period, as it was most beautifully inlaid with gold in arabesque designs!

A curious evidence of the origin of the Russians lay in the distinctly eastern character of the earlier weapons, the curved blade and light grip on the swords and the delicate, almost effeminate decoration of the spears and lances. Some ancient catapults were very ingenious, and all the more interesting for the fact that one inspected them with the aid of electric light, and that they were close to a telephone. I was so much interested in these forefathers of artillery that the Archimandrite rather abruptly suggested a visit to the treasury. This sounded equally interesting and it began to appear exciting when we were joined by two huge monks who glided silently behind us. Our escort was explained by our host, who said it was a strict rule of the monastery that the treasury should not be opened unless in the presence of three of the chief priests, and there was only one key in existence which he always carried on his person.

An unexpected doorway led us into a labyrinth of passages and stairs until at last we faced a metal door about six feet high, two and a half feet wide, and three inches thick. This was painted green, no doubt for protection, as it was of solid gold. In this large, square chamber there were no windows but many electric lights, and I was given to understand that it had various safeguards of an ingenious kind which were very carefully not explained. The walls were draped with priceless old tapestries and gold embroidery, and many massive gold lamps, crucifixes and ikons hung from the supporting columns, as well as jewelled swords and other ornaments of a like nature. Some exquisitely painted miniatures of the Russian royal family, carved ivory ornaments, gold candlesticks and gold, ivory and shell ikons were in the glass cases round the walls and in the centre of the room; but a number of the cases were suspiciously empty, although the impressions of heavy objects remained on the velvet cushions under the glass, and the marks of other objects, differing in shape, appeared below those we were allowed to handle.

We had seen a wonderful and valuable collection of objets d'art, but that we had not seen the real treasury I was convinced. The absence of diamonds, emeralds and rubies was remarkable for the reason that these stones represented the popular form of gift to the Church in Russia from her wealthy members. However, it may have been a general policy to conceal their resources as a precautionary measure when entertaining strangers which prevented our seeing any of the splendid gifts reputed to have been showered upon the monastery by the late Tzar in 1913.

Finally I was taken into His Grace's private chapel, where he presented me with a fine ikon which he had blessed. Then he gazed at me for a few moments without speaking. I do not know whether he hypnotised me, but the result was as refreshing as a sound sleep would have been.

Aboard the steamer again and heading away from the harbour, I could not resist the wish to return to Solievetski again. But that wish will not be fulfilled. The little colony which took almost seven hundred years of labour to construct and organise, to which generations of artists had given of their best work in painting and carving, and to which kings, princes, noblemen and pilgrims had given freely of their wealth for the preservation of its welfare through the ages – this peaceful place where untold thousands of weary and despairing souls had found solace is now a Bolshevik penal settlement from which no prisoner returns alive.

Chapter 7

Plots Against the Allies

During the summer [of 1918] the railway authorities had under construction two new wooden buildings which were intended for use as railway offices on the Station; however, as an alternative to the old theatre in the town or a railway carriage we took them over to make Military Headquarters for the winter. Sapper Lieut Kennedy, a London actor and ex-officer of the world-famous 'Mounties', who had arrived in Kem as assistant, came to our aid with remarkable ingenuity in providing excellent interior plans and, most important, an electric lighting plant which made us independent of the railway and town supply, with all the untimely inconvenience that might imply on occasions. He had found an old disused steam-engine, and he also 'found' a dynamo some fifty miles away; he begged and borrowed wiring and fittings; and out of the contents of some obsolete goods wagons he produced material to panel the interior of the headquarters mess in Tudor style, but with indirect lighting reflectors contrived from ex-biscuit tins. The hand-painted lampshades on the dining-table lent quite a Mayfair effect which impressed all our visitors.

The new quarters were most convenient for the reason that we were easily accessible to travellers, and had a direct supervision over all trains arriving and departing. The houses, which were of single story construction, were built entirely of heavy dovetailed logs on piles. The ceilings were about fifteen feet high, and in the lofts between the ceilings and the high shingled roofs were some twelve inches of sand to retain heat and keep out cold. To each of these lofts there was an inspection door on the outside. The spaces between the piles were boarded in except at one end where a cellar door was placed. One house was occupied by Karelian Headquarters and the District Command Office and the other was being prepared for Colonel (now Brigadier-General) Marsh, who had promised to come down to Kem, though unfortunately he was prevented from doing so by ill health. General Marsh had a wide experience and knew the language and the people thoroughly; I had many useful tips from him as to the characteristics and habits of the Russians and methods of dealing with them, as the following instance will show. Under the Kem Command was Saroka [Soroka], a town on the White Sea some 35 versts down the railway line from Kem. Here there was a saw-mill with huge stocks of timber, and also the railway workshops for the section. We had a detachment of the [White] Russian army there under Colonel Krugliakov, who appeared to have a most uneasy post. The railway workers were difficult people to deal with being the constant target for Bolshevik propaganda and intrigue; and in addition there was living there a General Zveginsiff [Zveginstev] whose position in the field was not easy to define. He had a small staff of officers and no troops under his command but appeared to exercise some authority with the railway people. At last threatened strikes and stoppages in the workshops caused me to send two good intelligence men to investigate the origins of the trouble. Their reports were surprising, but were later confirmed by Captain Blennerhaaset who was in the War Office Intelligence Service. Briefly, these reports stated that General Zveginsiff was in communication with some person or persons in the enemy [Bolshevik] country, and that the head engineer, Sacharoff, was responsible for the propaganda and unrest; certainly some of his speeches as reported seemed to be quite warmly tinted. These items of information were duly communicated to Murmansk headquarters, and M. Sacharoff was placed under arrest by Colonel Krugliakov on my orders. Peace reigned once more in the workshops and timber yard, hence I was much surprised to receive the following telegram from General Marsh:

> "Following from GOC 'Syren'. To remedy the disorganisation of work in railway workshops at Saroka Sacharoff should be placed on parole and permitted to carry on his work at Saroka. He should be informed that this action is taken pending completion of enquiries into his case, etc. That no

reflection on the action taken by British Officers on his arrest is intended. It is solely for the expediency of the Railway service. Inconsiderate treatment afforded to Sacharoff on arrest and accommodation provided for him seem uncalled for and impolitic and should be enquired into. Report please to General Marsh."

I found it difficult to understand all the implications in this message, and wondered if Murmansk headquarters had been captured by the Bolsheviks. The reply telegram was no adequate expression of my feelings, and read:

"I am not aware nor is any person in Saroka aware of disorganisation of work there. Would you please forward any facts in your possession which would justify release of Sacharoff as I only possess the reverse at present. On arrest Sacharoff was placed by my orders in a separate compartment of a railway carriage lately occupied by British Officers and the best at my disposal. He has been living for some time in a private carriage belonging to a Railway official. His food is brought from the Officers' Mess. Am I to read your wire in clear as a reprimand?"

To this General Marsh replied:

"I only repeated 'Syren's' cipher telegram by mistake in clear. You are not to take it as a reprimand. Personally never heard of disorganisation of work, evidently reported direct to Murmansk through railway. Copy of my telegram to 'Syren' being sent you."

In his reply to Murmansk General Marsh repeated my telegram and added:

"Deprecate forming opinion on British officer's action before hearing his statement. I further deprecate the order for release of possibly dangerous prisoner without hearing reasons for his arrest by officer responsible for local security and respectfully request that Colonel Woods be given full discretion for the disposal of any person arrested by him."

This incident throws a strong light on the loyalty of General Marsh to his brother officers, and at the same time gives some inkling of the credulity and indiscretion of the new Chief of Staff [Lewin], who was acting on his own initiative whilst General Maynard was absent in England. This officer appeared to be surrounded by a somewhat anti-allied group of Russian officers, and was ready to give his trust and confidence to them too freely. His weakness in this respect sometimes caused a certain amount of friction, but had no bearing on any movement of importance as it was mainly confined to periods covering the absence of the GOC.

I had occasion to assert authority when a Russian Colonel with no credentials so far as I knew gave orders for the movement of troops in Kem district without reference to my or the Adjutant's Office. I countermanded these moves, and sent a polite letter to the officer concerned pointing out that I would be pleased to meet his wishes in any matter possible, but that as I was responsible for the district, orders for the movement of any or all troops in that command must be through my office. No reply was received to this, but about a fortnight later a Russian subaltern told a railway employee that "Colonel Woods had got a terrible reprimand from Murmansk headquarters that would put him in his place; in fact, he might be sent back to England."

I awaited confirmation of this garrison gossip with interest and some curiosity. In the course of a week I duly received the 'telling off' from Murmansk, couched in terms which betrayed a profound ignorance of the situation and circumstances on the part of the writer. I merely acknowledged receipt, but on our first personal interview afterwards he was good enough to make an ample apology. This was not broadcast.

The Russian General, Zveginsiff, at Saroka continued to be an enigma to many of us, and we were all interested in his curious conduct. One rumour had it that his wife was held by the Bolsheviks in Petrograd as hostage for his behaviour; this may have accounted for correspondence passing between the lines and several mysterious occurrences difficult of explanation. If he was not sympathetic to the Allies he was at least clever enough to conceal the fact where many other Russian officers were quite obvious. Some opinion of his attitude may perhaps be formed from an incident in which he was concerned.

One afternoon a resplendently dressed Russian lieutenant, gorgeous in all the paraphernalia of the General Staff, called at my Headquarters with an invitation from General Zveginsiff to a 'Praznik' to be hold in the cinema hall at Saroka. This magnificent messenger gave details of the entertainment to be provided; it was to commence at 2 p.m. with a banquet lasting until about 6 o'clock, then a film was to be shown, followed by a dance in the hall. 'His Excellency' hoped that all the British and Allied officers would be able to accept; a special train would be provided to convey the party to and from Saroka. It sounded most alluring to bully-beef and Maconachie fed guests! In fact, it sounded too good. The immaculate messenger was thanked and asked to convey my grateful acceptance, but I was not surprised at the curious little smile with which he received the commission as I had reports in my pocket from our intelligence which gave a slightly different programme of the proposed entertainment we were to enjoy.

Information had been gleaned from several sources, but the most complete details had been boastingly supplied by a Russian junior officer to his girl friend, whom he doubtless wished to impress with his importance and cleverness. This young lady happened to be one of the best members of our 'contre-espionage'. According to the information given the official programme coincided with the amended one up to 6.15 p.m. While the film was being shown and the cinema hall was in darkness our hosts and their friends were to leave their seats one or two at a time, giving natural excuses or none as the occasion required. Then the real enjoyment was to begin. From the space behind the screen a couple of already sighted machine-guns were to open fire through the curtain. At the two exits arrangements were made to give presents to those who escaped from the stalls. The only civilised part of the scheme was that we were to be well fed before being ushered into the next world.

We made our own plans according to our information and prepared a variation of the programs; but I am afraid one of our Allies must also have had a girl friend, because the day before we were to attend our own execution General Zveginsiff postponed the Praznik indefinitely "owing to the serious illness of his housekeeper!" Thus we had no definite proof of the General's complicity or innocence. He may have instigated the whole plan; he may have been a mere instrument; or he may have known nothing of the 'horse-play' proposed for his guests. It is to be hoped that the last conjecture was the true one.

I do not, however, desire to convey the impression that all the Russian officers we met had anti-allied convictions, or that they were by any means all prompted by a strange and misguided policy of self-interest and revenge. There were many who had the welfare of their country at heart, and who recognised that little could be accomplished without the aid of the Allies. Such a one was the newly appointed Commander-in-Chief of the Russian Army at Murmansk, General Victor Skobolcene [Skobeltsin]. This officer, with his Staff training and wide campaigning experience, had an unbiased knowledge of his own countrymen and the gift of seeing a situation as a whole. He asked me for a candid criticism of his command, and this I gave as fairly as possible solely from my own observations. He then told me that he could not see the slightest chance of success in this campaign as the "White" Russians were beaten before the start by intrigue, mistrust and absence of cohesion amongst the officers; but that one could only stick to duty even if it led to inevitable extinction. He always came to see me when he was in the Kem district, but each time I met him he appeared more worried and sad in contrast to the growing optimism he expressed. I think he had a premonition of a terrible end, and indeed the one he met must have exceeded in brutality anything he could have imagined. He was found in the neighbourhood of Kem crucified on a door. This was after we had left the district.

There were numerous Russian officers who cooperated with us whole-heartedly and whom we appreciated to the full. Our work was greatly facilitated by such men as Polebin, the captain of the port of Popoff, whose spontaneous kindness will be remembered by the officers and crews of our naval units when in that port, as also by the personnel of the RAMC, CCS [Casualty Clearing Station] and the French Howitzer Battery. He was a reliable friend to whom I personally owe many obligations; for example, the indefinite loan of a remarkable Arab mare, an animal a child could have ridden with a silk thread.

Polebin once gave me a fine Samoyede dog, but as the poor animal would not eat or leave his post by the window where he watched constantly for his master's return I was compelled to take the dog to his own home again to save his life.

Argieff, assistant Sectional Engineer on the railway, was an invaluable ally. He had a rare sense of humour and great courage, and frequently earned the bad feelings of his colleagues and seniors by his friendship with the British. There were others too, whose names are the only items I cannot remember, but whose cheerful assistance and unlimited hospitality will not be forgotten by me or, I venture to think, by any of those officers who served with me.

Essieff, the veterinary Colonel for the district, was in a category of his own. The quality of his friendship can perhaps best be illustrated by the "Ballymena Hymn": "Oh, what is there in it for me?" His pretty and attractive wife was an enthusiastic admirer of the British, and this caused him many pangs of unnecessary jealousy, at the same time detracting somewhat from the complete enjoyment of his company.

It was at Essieff's house in Kem town that various meetings of doubtful loyalty took place, and at one of these a newly arrived Russian Colonel foreshadowed events concerning the future of the Allies. It was evident from his statements that this officer was in a position to make authoritative assertions, as he had been in the confidence of the German Chief of Staff before leaving Berlin for England, although I do not suppose he had mentioned this fact to the British authorities whose hospitality, money, and free passage to Russia he had accepted. His report to the meeting of Russian officers was on these lines: The Allies would win this war; but the Germans had established caches of arms and munitions in Germany, Russia and elsewhere for future use. Every effort would be made to contrive differences and quarrels between Great Britain and America by propaganda and diplomatic methods. England would not fight again for France; therefore France would be attacked first, and after that the accursed English. Each could be conquered individually. Finally, this officer made a recommendation – which was approved and adopted by the meeting – that immediately the strength of the new Russian army numbered five bayonets to one of the British in North Russia the latter should be driven into the White Sea or exterminated.

I had every reason to believe that Essieff and his colleagues were in the confidence of our own Headquarters at Murmansk, and I feared to report this meeting in the absence of General Maynard on account of the inevitable revenge which would be taken upon my informant, hence I awaited an opportunity of making a private and verbal report to the General. Beyond this there was nothing to be done except to take all possible precautions to frustrate treachery without betraying my knowledge of what was afoot. The carrying out of these measures caused some slight friction, already referred to, between our temporary Chief of Staff and myself; but I dared not trust information of such importance to paper, and I also feared that the recipient might not fully understand the situation and consult some of his Russian advisers, a step which would have been the signal for the immediate assassination of our loyal friends.

At about this time all the healthy sanity of the British in Kem was augmented by a visit from Captain Philip Brocklehurst, of the 'Shiney Tenth' [10th Royal Hussars, 'The Shiners'], who came to buy horses for the Transport. Then came the well-known Captain 'Brocas' Burrows, a cavalry officer now engaged on intelligence work, who was able to supply the extra information required in classifying the various groups of Russians, making it quite clear that excessive optimism would be out of place; but his sense of humour helped us to keep the situation in its true perspective.

Commander Stenhouse, otherwise known to all as 'Stenny', came through Kem organising dog-transport over winter routes for Sir Ernest Shackleton. I was sorry to have missed Shackleton himself when he visited Kem, as I was then up-country; but I was later able to give him a detailed account of the resources and requirements of Karelia such as he needed with a view to future possibilities.

Captain Muir, another doctor, arrived to relieve Captain Harrison of part of the heavy work necessitated by primitive sanitary arrangements among a growing population. Lieutenant 'Nicky' Mende, a Russian-born Englishman who had gone over to England to join King Edward's Horse, was sent to Kem as interpreter, and proved a reliable, tactful and popular friend. He was followed by Captain Williams, a brother of the well-known author, Valentine Williams. This officer made an excellent Garrison Adjutant and we were sorry when he returned to England, as he had a thorough knowledge of the people with whom we had to deal and was most useful in suggestions for the benefit of the troops during the long winter which had just begun.

Chapter 8

Winter in Kem, 1918

The first snow had now come, followed by severe frost which finally rendered passage by river impossible; but we had completed all our arrangements so that the garrison and population in Karelia should be provided for until the ice became sufficiently strong to bear transport. The sun appeared only for a brief interval daily, low on the horizon, but the twilight lasted for a long time and when the sky was clear the brilliance of the stars was such as to render objects visible at about 200 yards, while on frosty nights the aurora provided sufficient illumination to double this visibility.

As precursor to a southerly wind the aurora assumed wonderful forms of light, from an exact reproduction of the active searchlights of a fleet of warships to the changing coloured stage lights of a Christmas pantomime, but instead of a restricted space the whole sky provided the transformation scene.

One evening before New Year there occurred an extraordinarily beautiful manifestation of the aurora, when the entire vault of the heavens became a vast glowing dome of light, streaming down from the zenith in glittering golden particles to the encircling dark horizon. The faintly gleaming reflections from the snow-bound earth did not diminish the majestic splendour of this awe-inspiring spectacle, which continued for several hours.

I thought that perhaps the Karelians would have some superstitious explanation for this electrical display; but when I questioned them the replies were merely that there would be a storm from the south. The Marines were more impressed. They were reduced to a significant silence, broken only by an occasional "Blimey!"

With the coming of winter I experienced another arctic phenomenon not met with in our latitudes. The "Snapping of Jack Frost's fingers" conveyed little meaning to me as a child; but in Northern Russia the children must have different descriptions of the vagaries of Jack Frost, the manipulation of whose joints could hardly produce such a volume of sound as greeted me one night in Kem! Some time after midnight, when the snow-covered country appeared to sparkle with diamonds and every object was visible for miles under the intense brilliance of an arctic full moon, I was walking to Kem from the station. Fifty degrees of frost had driven the inhabitants indoors, and created a silence so profound that the circulating blood sang in one's ears. Going through the old cemetery with its scores of wooden memorials, which lay in the most direct route, I was suddenly startled by a report like a pistol shot on my left. I took cover at once. But after a little thought and investigation I found to my great relief that the sound had been caused by the snapping and fall of a weather-worn wooden cross. I was amused at my momentary alarm when I remembered that no Russian would venture into the graveyard on such a night, or indeed on any night.

Arrived at the outskirts of the town, I had taken only a few steps on the board 'sidewalk' when a plank cracked under my weight. This seemed to be the signal for the commencement of a lively engagement. I stood still and waited anxiously to see the ancient wooden church fall to ruins, as seemed probable from the reports, bangs and smashes resounding from it. I heard the wooden bridge over the river apparently crash to destruction without visible movement. The theatre across the river appeared to harbour a score of invisible machine-guns all in action. Every house, roof and building in the town added its quota to the terrifying and almost deafening uproar.

I stood appalled in the shadow of a doorway, expecting to see all the inhabitants rush out of their houses; but none appeared to have heard, or if they did they had evidently become inured to the humours of nature, as there was no movement whatever.

In ten minutes or so the din died down into single reports, and then ceased entirely, leaving the bedevilled town to a silence more eerie than before.

The explanation of this curious occurrence given to me was simple, it being merely the effect of a heavy frost upon the moisture in the wooden structures, and at a point of development where any slight vibration would cause the result I had experienced.

Before Christmas of 1918 our first winter was well established, and the arctic conditions had now rendered the route over the frozen river suitable for communications and transport. Heaton, at Uskozero, appeared to be happy and content with his Karelian detachment and supply depot. His wireless station enabled him to receive news from many sources, and to send in daily requests for books and tobacco with his routine reports! The Garrison Company of the Regiment found guards on the station, the bridge and the railways; and as their scrupulous integrity became recognised they found travelling guards for all the supply wagons on the line. A Labour Company was stationed at Popoff, and in addition a number of skilled Karelians were employed in making wheels for wagons and 'dougas' – the high wooden arch above the draft animal's neck, used to maintain in position the shafts of sleighs and carts – of which there was a serious shortage in the north. These men also built the country sleighs, which were about nine feet in length, four feet wide, and about thirty inches high at the centre, with a canvas-covered hood over about a third of their length. In design they resembled clinker-built punts raised at the bow to protect the occupants from the hard caked snow flying from the horse's hoofs. Wooden runners were favoured in preference to iron, and as these were highly polished one horse could draw a very heavy load with ease over the frozen snow.

Gregori, the senior Karelian officer, detailed as driver for my lightly built sleigh a red-bearded giant who had a name as long as himself, but which we abbreviated for the sake of convenience to 'Mickey'. This appellation he accepted with the broad grin which appeared to be an inseparable part of his life. He brought with him a little bay horse which he introduced as Meesha, or "Little Mouse". Afterwards we found that this animal, only just over fourteen hands, was the fastest trotting pony in the country; he had the heart of a lion, and a journey of fifty versts was merely exercise for his incredibly speedy legs. It was a constant pleasure to ride behind him and listen to Mickey's conversation to his friend. I asked him one day what would happen if he were to use a whip or stick on Meesha. He stopped smiling, and his eyes grew wide as he shook his head and said solemnly: "The little one would die of a broken heart".

One item of the very comprehensive equipment supplied to the troops by the War Office was ski [*sic*], of the Swiss pattern, although the Karelians preferred to use their own, which were about sixteen inches longer and two inches less in width, with a toe-piece and ankle strap the only fastenings. We practised with these until we could remain perpendicular and travel with varying degrees of success, but we could never attain the proficiency of the Karelians who had been using ski since the early days of their infancy.

[Iivo] Ahava, an officer of the Scouts, occasionally gave exhibitions of remarkable skiing. He would drop down a 200 feet cliff by merely touching the ledges with the side of his ski, keeping perfect balance and without an appreciable pause, and in less time than it takes to describe he would be away like a swallow over the frozen river. At other times he would take out a fast reindeer, reputed to travel at a speed of forty miles an hour. This he harnessed by means of a trace, or light rope, fastened to its collar and then led under its body and secured to his own waist. The guide rein was tied to the base of the animal's antlers and held lightly in the driver's right hand, while in the left he carried a switch. At top speed he could control every movement – turn to the right or left, or come to a dead stop within a few feet, curbing with ease the wildest attempts on the part of the stag to escape.

No doubt Ahava had used the opportunities for skiing afforded by six months' snow out of the twelve in Karelia, where it was normal in any village to see children from four years of age flying down the hills with barrel staves or any odd pieces of flat wood strapped to their feet as improvised ski.

The severity of the climate and the absence of sunlight restricted our out-door activities and recreations to a few hours in each week, but the hospitable Russians offered frequent and varying entertainment. There was the interminable dinner, lasting from 3 p.m. until seven or eight o'clock, and usually consisting of 'zakooska', or hors d'oeuvres, of anything from twelve to forty varieties; soup, always excellent; fish in many guises; veal, also disguised; and other meats sometimes including boar and bearmeat. The service was mercifully leisurely and allowed time for much conversation and a cigarette between courses. Vodka was the aperitif and frequently the sole liquid refreshment where wines were difficult to obtain; however, being manufactured from pure alcohol and reduced to about 30 under proof, and used with discretion in a liqueur glass, its results were never embarrassing or conducive to any feeling other than good-fellowship.

Then there were new plays produced almost weekly by the postmaster of Kem town, and acted by himself and some of his enormous post-office staff; here apparently some thirty-five officials were required to deal with the half-dozen letters and a couple of telegrams which made up our normal weekly mail, and this afforded ample opportunity for rehearsal.

These plays were for the most part tragedies, with a vast amount of what we called 'wet' dialogue, because it consisted of so much weeping. The hero was invariably modelled on the lines of the morbid Prince of Denmark, but without action. The actors sat on wooden chairs or, in the case of the hero, on an upholstered armchair, and talked and talked and talked! The only change of scene was the relief of some actors by others, presumably when the former were exhausted. When the principal had a cold and was without a handkerchief the tragedy became intensified. Madness developed almost invariably with the progress of the plot, until at the end of about five hours the hero became really annoyed and killed, usually by poison, every other character in the play. Suicide of the hero was the traditional finale. After trying to maintain one position for so long on Windsor chairs we were in full accord with the author's ending, although in our opinion the play could usually have been improved by substituting the last act for the first.

A tactfully broached request for something in a rather lighter vein produced an amusing reflection on the habits of the English nobility. Our prolific playwright duly obliged with a comedy in which, as usual, he himself played the chief part, that of 'an English Lord'. He gave a highly original interpretation of this role. Throughout the whole play he reclined in a chair delivering brilliant aphorisms, meanwhile in a dignified manner picking his nose, examining closely the fruits of his labours, and then flicking the imaginary product nonchalantly on to the floor in the fashion of a snuff addict who has just taken a pinch from his box. The comedy was a riot.

The concerts were really enjoyable. There were a number of accomplished musicians, including several men with remarkably fine voices, and they were always willing to give their services for the benefit of any charitable object. Dances usually followed these musical evenings, and were invariably the complement of all entertainment. Dancing was a form of amusement immensely popular with all classes of the community, country dances being the most enthusiastically performed, sometimes with more energy than grace, but always with enjoyment to the performers.

It was hardly to be expected that these social affairs would remain innocent of intrigue, since they offered excellent opportunities for the advancement of our adversaries' schemes. A fancy-dress ball was chosen as the occasion for the employment of a quite ingenious plot to secure my removal from authority – if not further. The means employed was not new. It involved a beautiful and masked temptress who was to place me in a compromising position, in which I was to be 'discovered' by the lady's husband accompanied by at least two witnesses, one of whom was to be British. A brawl would then take place, followed by a report to the General Officer Commanding.

The scenery and properties were duly made ready for this drama: a small private room, furnished with a carpet, a settee, and a small table, on which were three bottles (two empty) and two glasses. The shaded lamp near the settee was fitted with a convenient switch, but two ceiling lights had a similar switch near the door; these the lady was to ensure would not be lighted when she led the sacrifice to the slaughter.

Timely information excited our interest, so we decided to attend. On the day of the ball Dr Muir, Lieut Mende, Lieut Smith, a machine-gunner who had arrived, Nicoli, Gregori and I held a committee of ways and means to make our own arrangements. The result of this was that we all wore exactly similar costumes, made up from brown dressing-gowns borrowed from the hospital, with our hooded windproof kit and snow glasses. This guise concealed our faces and hands. The slight difference in stature was adjusted as far as possible by the tallest wearing only slippers – also borrowed from the hospital – and the others slippers over their heeled shoes, the legs of the windproof suits being strapped under the feet.

When our hosts, who were also the plotters, saw six identically dressed figures enter the hall they were somewhat perplexed, and held hurried and obviously excited conferences which produced a surprising manoeuvre by one of their number, who insisted upon shaking hands very earnestly with each of us, clinging to our hands in the manner of a member of some brotherhood expecting a secret sign. It suddenly struck me that they were trying to identify me by the third finger of my right hand, which was permanently stiffened as the result of an accident on the football field. Only one of the Russians had known of this, and he was now putting his knowledge to practical use.

Soccer on the ice at Kem, 1919.

When it came to my turn my suspicions were confirmed, for my finger was deliberately searched for and tried. I was held fast by my now jubilant host while two of his friends approached, but I managed to keep them in front until my companions joined the group. However, they had succeeded in marking me, for as soon as the opportunity arose the Doctor whispered to me that the shape of a white hand had been put on my shoulder with either flour or powder. I told him to have Mende and Gregori join me immediately in the toilet. This they did, and while Mende kept the door fastened I changed dressing-gowns with Gregori, who now had his instructions. Mende and I thereupon ran the two miles back to our quarters and changed quickly.

We had not been reading very long when the telephone bell rang. It was our Russian hosts with a message for me. Mende told them that I was just going to bed, and suggested that the morning might be a more convenient time to talk business. Upon this they became excited and wanted to hear my voice, and I therefore asked them politely in what way I could be of service. They had evidently not had time to invent a plausible grievance so, after some hesitation, they said that they would like to see me at once. In half an hour an agitated gentleman was announced. His excuse was quite good. The story was that he had heard of a plot to shoot me at the ball, and he thought I was present, and meant to warn me; hence his anxiety to see me in the flesh and speak to me. His hands were shaking and he wiped the perspiration from his face frequently while speaking. I thanked him for his great concern and loyalty, gave him a drink, and sent him home.

The reports of the contretemps at the ball, received later from other members of the party, were amusing. All went well with the plot, as Nicoli had hastily impressed two Karelians similarly clad to make up the number of the 'hooded men' so that our absence was not noticed. Gregori in dumb show exhibited his admiration for the masked lady, and duly followed her into the trap. Here he immediately gave his full attention to the bottle so thoughtfully provided. When the great moment came the door was burst open by the infuriated husband accompanied by as many of his friends as the passage would accommodate, closely followed by the rest of our party. Gregori was holding the now by no means silent lady in his arms, to prevent her from leaving, as she intended when she discovered his identity. The husband rushed forward and struck Gregori, who promptly challenged him to a duel with revolvers there and then. The husband had quite an anxious time avoiding this development, as he had a wholesome respect for the Karelians' courage and readiness with firearms and little confidence in his own. The lady also had some bitter remarks to make, while his confederates openly and indiscreetly reproached him, thus making the plot public. Finally, in an endeavour to justify himself, he had telephoned me; but my presence at the other end of the wire was the last straw.

The old wooden theatre was the scene of many dramas besides those staged for entertainment, mainly because it was the centre of the social life of Kem, and therefore used as headquarters by various organisations in normal times. It was now a Karelian station, under the command of a newly recruited British officer, Major Harrison, who came to us from the West Yorks. He had had little time in which to acclimatise himself to the situation in North Russia, hence Gregori gave all the time he could afford to assist in the prevention of mischief.

Early one morning the telephone rang persistently in our quarters until Mende answered. It was Gregori speaking from the upper floor of the theatre. He urgently required my presence there, saying that a mutiny was threatened by soldiers of the New Murmansk Army.

While we dressed hurriedly Mickey brought the sleigh round to the door and we made a record trip to the town. It was one of the coldest nights I had up till then experienced, with seventy-three degrees of frost. Arrived at the theatre we found about fifty Russian soldiers in the yard at the back which was used as a transport depot; they were armed with rifles, those in the rear begging those in front to get out of the way, and all shouting together. We pushed our way through them until we reached a point near the centre of the disturbance, and climbed to the seat of an empty sleigh. Mende tried unavailingly to make himself heard, and it was necessary for me to use a similar tone to that employed in drilling a battalion before we could command attention. They were silent immediately. I began by calling them a lot of noisy children, and reproached them for getting me out of a warm bed on such a night; then I asked for one spokesman to come to the sleigh and tell me all about it. Now they were interested and, I think, a little amused at my accent. Finally, one of them started to make his way towards me when a young Russian subaltern ordered him to stand still, or he would fire. I ordered the subaltern to come forward, asked him his name and regiment, and informed him that he was under arrest.

The soldier then made his complaint. He said that he had been struck in the face with a stick by the officer who had spoken, and then threatened by his revolver. Turning to one of the four officer companions of the first I asked him if this was correct. Of course, he was unable to give a straight answer, yes or no, and as the men were getting restless again I told them to go back to their barracks, and that I would then enquire into the affair myself. They appeared satisfied with my promise, and went away quietly enough; but for a moment the situation was ugly when these five drunken young officers stood back to back surrounded by a crowd of infuriated men armed with the Russian rifles with their permanently fixed bayonets.

From Gregori's report it appeared that the arrested subaltern had ordered a soldier to stop dancing and relinquish his pretty partner to him; then, when the soldier looked angry, the officer had drawn his revolver and threatened to shoot. The man had gone away to barracks with his comrades and, arming themselves, they had come back to continue the argument. The subaltern was joined by his friends, who had also drawn their revolvers; and that was the position when our arrival had interrupted the proceedings.

I reported the affair to Colonel Baikoff and asked for a copy of the court martial proceedings on the subaltern, and I advised the Colonel as a matter of general policy to remove all the officers concerned to another district, or their lives would not be secure. This was done. I also advised tactful treatment of the men, but I am afraid that this advice was not taken. I kept my promise to the Russian soldiers and managed to have their scale of rations raised and supervised by our own staff; both actions were greatly appreciated.

Chapter 9

Tour of Karelian Outposts

The influenza epidemic was long in disappearing from Kem and Karelia, mainly owing to the apathy and natural fatalism of the inhabitants, and encouraged by the absence of ventilation in overheated and overcrowded habitations. The Karelians were especially vulnerable, and for many weeks we had two or three deaths daily among the troops in Kem.

The disposal of the dead in a fitting manner presented difficulties. Owing to the climatic conditions the ground was frozen as hard as iron to a depth of several feet, and this necessitated fires being made and maintained for many hours before it was possible to dig graves. The effect of these huge fires and the moving silhouettes and dancing shadows of their keepers was particularly weird amongst the black pines and painted wooden memorials in the cemetery.

Another obstacle was created by the serious shortage and growing expense of suitable wood for making coffins. The usual Russian shell was elaborately decorated and painted, and ordinary planking or rough unseasoned timber was considered quite inadequate for the purpose, as indicating a lack of proper respect for the dead. After conferring with Gregori and Nicoli we decided on a plan to overcome these conditions. We purchased a magnificent carved and painted casket, plentifully decorated with silver and gold leaf, which Gregori said "would be a pleasure for any Duke to be buried in." The difference between this coffin and any other was that it had a detachable bottom fitted so that after being lowered into the grave four cords could be pulled allowing the body, enclosed in a rough case, to remain, and the empty casket to be raised to the top. It was then kept in the cemetery, covered with a tarpaulin, until a decent interval had elapsed, taken back to the transport lines, and again made ready for the ceremonial occasion. The Karelians took a great pride in the new importance of their funerals, and the idea seemed to appeal as much to their sense of humour as to the economy in their make-up. Before authority was received from GHQ to meet the expenses of funerals from official funds the Karelians paid the charges from the proceeds of dances organised for the purpose.

In Kem the Christmas festival was made seasonable for the Britishers by the warm hospitality of the friendly inhabitants of the town, although one could not altogether avoid regarding the political calm as the possible prelude to another outbreak of trouble, and speculating as to its form.

I was anxious to witness a Christmas celebration of High Mass in the cathedral, but was warned by friends not to trust either the place or the occasion as guarantees of personal safety. Hence, dressed in a sheepskin-lined canvas greatcoat and fur head-dress such as was provided for all ranks, I made myself as inconspicuous as possible. I took no companions with me, so as not to attract attention and, arriving late, bought a taper and took up a position near the great door with my back to the wall, where I considered that the risk of unpleasantness was small. My position gave me excellent opportunities to observe my surroundings and the backs of a very large and mixed congregation – soldiers, peasants, women of all classes, some of whom were well dressed and possibly political refugees. Each person held a burning taper in his (or her) hand and everybody's attention was absorbed in front by three gorgeously robed priests and a Bishop, judging by his mitre, who were intoning the service at the magnificent altar. The walls were almost entirely occupied by numerous brilliantly illuminated shrines, with pictures of the various saints enclosed in gold and jewelled frames. Suspended from the lofty gilded ceiling, and dimly visible through the haze of the incense and thousands of burning candles, were five immense candelabra, throwing their mellow light down to meet the soft radiance which seemed to glow upwards from the mass of the congregation. The air was warm and heavy with the misty, aromatic perfume from the constantly swinging censers; but most impressive of all appeals to the senses was the singing of the concealed male choir. The resonant tones of the basses and the purity of the tenors and sopranos were quite equal to any opera at Covent Garden.

I was very glad that I had attended the service and was now considering leaving the cathedral when a movement at the altar caused me to hesitate. It was a procession, led by the bishop, and starting towards the door. The congregation fell back hastily to clear a passage for the host. In doing this a group of peasants in the rear crowded against me, acting effectively as a barrier to a hasty retreat. However, I was not conspicuous until one luxuriantly bearded member of the group pressed against me so closely that my taper set fire to his whiskers. They flared up instantly, and I had to clutch at the ruins in an endeavour to prevent injury to his eyes. Those within a short distance thought I had attacked the man until his roaring laugh and "Nitchy Vo! Nitchy Vo!" eased the situation. But the atmosphere had now taken on a new and less pleasing aroma.

I visited the cathedral subsequently on many occasions, mainly to hear the male voice music, but it was also the means of furnishing an important clue to the Russian character. I was told that once in Kem cathedral a pretended supplicant at one of the shrines in kissing the jewelled frame of the picture managed to bite a large ruby out of its setting!

There was an interesting religious custom observed in the Russian Church which could, on occasion, be quite delightful. Towards the end of the Easter Service the officiating priest announced to the congregation: "Christ has risen!" and the response was: "Truly Christ has risen." Then the priest came amongst the congregation repeating the words of the disciples at the sepulchre, receiving the response, and embracing the individual by saluting him or her on each cheek. The members of the congregation follow this by repeating the ceremony with their immediate neighbours in the Church, and afterwards in their own homes. The attractive part of the custom was that one was at liberty to select one's immediate neighbour or neighbours before the beginning of the service.

The week following Christmas was mainly devoted to the social amenities and exchange of visits terminating, so far as we were concerned in a dinner given by us to our Russian friends and allies on New Year's Eve. Our menu, the work of Lieut Kennedy, was impressive:

Hors d'oeuvres variés.

Soup .... Tomato.
Fish .... Boiled Salmon.

Entrée . . . . Boeuf a la Bonne Femme.
Roast . . . . Turkey.
Game.
Roast Beef.
Vegetables . . . . Potatoes.
Beans.
Riz au gratin.
Sweet . . . . Xmas pudding.
Savoury . . . . Angels on Horseback.
Pêche Melba.
Ices.
Café.
Fromage.

This menu [see p. 227] was perhaps the best part of the meal, but even so it was a triumph for our Marine cooks, who were really at their best when equipped with tin-openers. Fresh salmon was easy to obtain, and a species of wild turkey was purchased by two tins of Maconachie rations; but the 'Boeuf a la Bonne Femme' was a little imaginative camouflage for 'bully' fried!

The inactivity in military and political circles, combined with a spell of settled weather, afforded a favourable opportunity for a tour of inspection of the outposts in Karelia, and when we had made arrangements for all probable developments Mende and I, well wrapped in furs and blankets, set out in a mild 30 degrees of frost with Mickey and Meesha in the sleigh for the frontier. Our route lay mostly over the ice on the frozen Kem river, only leaving it where the road cut the bends. The country looked entirely unfamiliar under its heavy blanket of snow, and although it had appeared quiet during the summer it was now profoundly silent. All sounds of running water, roaring rapids and falls were stilled by the intense frost, which had formed ice many feet thick. It was only possible for us to judge when we were on the river by the wide path cut through the dark forest trees, as the snow covered both river and land under one level field of white.

The so-called road was a single track, charted by small trees fastened into the ice at intervals of about 100 yards, and packed hard by the runners of passing sleighs into a kind of causeway some six feet in depth. On each side of this path the loose snow was sometimes piled into drifts ten feet above the level of the lane; at other times it had blown away, leaving the highway as an embankment. When we met another sleigh we had to get off the road, which always meant a cold douche and a tremendous effort on the part of the little horse and ourselves to regain the track; it was the rule of the road that laden sleighs had the 'right of way' and as sleighs belonging to the peasantry travelling towards Kem were invariably loaded our luck was not on the comfortable side. However, these occasions were seldom more than twice daily, so we had but little cause to complain.

Mickey relieved the monotony of the journey by pointing out the breathing holes of foxes and other wild creatures. His keen eye seemed to be able to trace their runways under the snow, and once he stopped the sleigh to show us a hunt where a white hare was the quarry. All we could distinguish was a movement of some kind in the snow, but he described the course of the hunter and hunted as if it had been a bright light and a green background, instead of dim twilight and unbroken grey-white everywhere. His stories of ghosts and pixies were told in more effective surroundings than could be afforded by a warm English fireside. Mickey's immense bulk encased in a brawn canvas greatcoat, his beard, eyebrows and face covered in white rime as he held the reins loosely in huge blackened hands – for he never wore gloves in any circumstances; the little horse with his long coat covered in white and his sensitive ears pricking to every sound, many of which he alone heard in the black forest, a spray of fine snow coming from his nostrils where his breath froze at every exhalation; the oppressive silence broken only by the tinkle of the bell on the wooden 'douga' and the swish of the runners – this environment made an ideal setting for tales of snow-spirits and ghostly bears.

Our first halt was made at Paduzemskaia, in a house where I had passed the night during the summer and where sleep was broken by the roar of the falls. But now the rocks in the river bed were covered with solid ice so that not even the sound of a trickle of running water could be heard. The house had been 'frozen clean' of parasites, and the glowing stove in the corner of the spotless living-room and steaming samovar on the table made a welcome change from the sharp air of the road.

After looking over the quarters of our detachment and the stores we had a visit from the headman, who had some complaints of a not very convincing nature regarding civilian supplies and his own particular domestic affairs; but these were easily dealt with, and his usual smile was

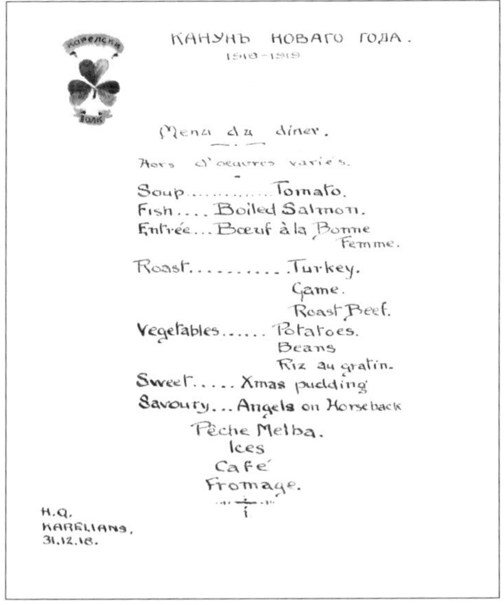
КАНУНЪ НОВАГО ГОДА.
1918 - 1919

Menu du diner.

Hors d'oeuvres variés.

Soup............Tomato.
Fish.... Boiled Salmon.
Entrée... Bœuf à la Bonne Femme.
Roast........... Turkey.
Game.
Roast Beef.
Vegetables...... Potatoes.
Beans
Riz au gratin.
Sweet..... Xmas pudding
Savoury... Angels on Horseback
Pêche Melba.
Ices
Café
Fromage.

H.Q.
KARELIANS,
31.12.18.

Lieut Kennedy's New Year's Eve menu, 1918 (the Russian writing on the envelope, above, may be colloquially translated as "We'll show the Finns!")

completely restored when we thanked him for his hospitality.

The next day was a repetition of the first, following the track over land, river and lake, except that we branched off the direct route to the frontier to visit an outpost at a village where eight men were stationed under Sergeant Bogdanoff, one of the original volunteers and a fine soldier. He gave us as a contribution to the Widows' Pension Fund a small collection of pearls which he had procured from oysters 'grabbed' from the bed of the river through holes out in the ice. They were not of particularly good colour or shape, but they evidenced excellent feeling on the part of the donor, and he was duly advised of their sale at a later date.

Mickey had been uneasy all the morning and urged the willing pony to greater speed than we had used on the previous day. When we asked the reason for this haste he pointed to several little whirlwinds rising on the snowfield, and said: "When the snow-devils walk they bring the storm on their tails. There will be a storm in four hours, and we have sixty versts to travel." How accurate his forecast was we realised as we caught the first distant gleam of light from Panozero. This was obliterated almost at once by a fury of swirling snow so thick that it was difficult to distinguish the form of our driver only three feet removed. Mickey simply dropped the reins on the horse's back and told him to carry on. "The horse knows best," he said; and his confidence was not misplaced for, dropping to a brisk walk, Meesha brought us into the village street in about ten minutes, and we were soon under cover with the usual glass of hot tea to thaw out our stiffened limbs.

Here we were storm-bound for sixteen hours, which allowed the little horse to obtain some rest and gave the small garrison a chance to show something of their remarkable control of skis. In this sport the children of the village were extremely expert, and were most amusing when playing a kind of 'tag' game, tumbles meaning little to their india rubber bodies. Wet feet caused no anxiety to their mothers, who simply removed the linen or cotton wrappings which every Karelian wears on his feet in place of woollen socks or stockings in winter or summer.

A clear sky and a brilliant moon promised good weather as we set out refreshed on our sixty mile drive to Uskozero, taking in two posts on our way, Sopovaraka and Soposalma, where we found everything in order. At the latter post the Corporal in charge told us that he had two new recruits for the Regiment. Taking us into a house near the men's quarters he introduced us to two fat babies – twin boys about a month old. He told us that one was named Fileep, after me, and the other

Nickolas, after Mende. This divided the honours without prejudice, but it cost me the last two half-crowns I had in English money, and set a fashion which became an increasingly heavy toll on my remaining personal possessions!

At Uskozero we found Heaton established in state with his wireless operators and Karelian henchmen. He had put on weight, and had obtained quite a reasonable mastery of the Karelian language. With pardonable pride he pointed out the 200 foot wireless mast erected outside his quarters, and described how it had been done without mechanical aid. Since this had been installed he had been able to receive news from home stations on his 'mule' set.

I spent most of the day going through his stores and checking up on issues. He had experienced some trouble with the distribution of the rum ration, as the local idea was to dispose of two weeks' supply at one sitting, which did not coincide with our intention and was not conducive to good discipline. We made arrangements for the disposal of his stock of rum in a spot easily accessible to him, so that small quantities could be issued gradually until it was exhausted; no farther supply would be sent up river to him except for his immediate staff or in emergency. A small supply was also left in the local hospital. Details of a new reindeer transport to augment his horse sleighs were also arranged to relieve his difficulties of distribution of supplies up country.

We gave Heaton a copy of our itinerary so that he could if necessary forward important messages by ski-runner.

Our next stop was at Lousalma, some forty versts distant, and, making good time, we arrived there at about midday. We had just had a talk with the NCO in charge when a ski-runner arrived roped to a fast horse and unrecognisable behind his coating of snow and rime. He had an urgent wireless message from Drake-Brockman at Kem, relayed by Heaton. It was in a private code of our own, and urged my immediate presence at Kem at any cost.

The seriousness of this message was obvious from the absence of any specific or detailed reason for its despatch, and it was evident that Drake-Brockman feared there might be a chance of some other station receiving and decoding it. There was nothing for it but to return in the shortest possible time, and by the most direct route; so telling Mickey to get ready we set off on our return journey with some apprehension, speculating on what we should find at the end of the trip.

We had consulted with Mickey about the necessity for a change of horses, and he had reluctantly agreed that 'the little one' could not do the whole distance without rest; so we had despatched another Karelian runner before we started to warn Heaton to have another horse ready for us on arrival and a hot meal prepared, also to arrange relays through Maslozero. Mickey insisted upon driving the whole way and leaving his beloved friend with one of his innumerable cousins in Uskozero until he was able to return for him. We did not press unduly as the little chap had already done a day's work and was beginning to show signs of fatigue; hence our messenger had arrived in time to allow Heaton to choose a good animal for our sleigh, and also to send messengers ahead to arrange for our reception at the next halts. I wirelessed Drake-Brockman simply accepting an invitation to the zoo, and warned Heaton to make no reference to me in messages or wireless reports; I also promised to let him know if there was any chance of a skirmish.

Within twenty minutes we were on the road again, this time behind a giant of a buckskin horse sixteen hands, very strong, and uncomfortably high-stepping for our low sleigh as we were constantly subjected to a bombardment of flying snowballs from his hoofs. But we did not complain as he moved well, the light sleigh being no more than ballast for his weight. It was only twenty versts to our first halt and Mickey kept the horse at his best pace, knowing that his work would soon be done and that there was no need to nurse him, hence we arrived at Sopovaraka in less than half-an-hour. We were off again in a few minutes, this time behind a hardy looking black mare Mickey seemed to know well and was pleased to drive.

Our next change of horses was over sixty versts further on and our driver handled this animal with admirable judgement, sometimes allowing her to drop to a fast walk. Fortunately, the country was mainly level, such inclines as there were being in our favour, so that our runners were an easy load.

On this part of the journey we were less fortunate. We had not got far on our way when the moon was obscured by storm clouds and a bitter wind began to lift the light snow into a stinging spray, and within a very few minutes we were battling through a full blizzard, the snow-laden wind making it difficult to breathe even behind the partial shelter of the sleigh's hood. The howling of the wind and the noise of the hard snow being hurled against us sounded like a stormy sea. It was impossible to see Mickey or indeed anything but the driving snow borne on a fierce blast which seemed to cut into one's lungs like a knife and chilled us to the heart. We knew only by an occasional rocking that we were moving, and all our blankets, skins, furs and felt boots were useless against the terrible cold which seemed to penetrate and freeze the blood. We had both reached the semiconscious stage of sleepiness when we were startled wide awake by our driver's voice yelling at us to bring our feet up. He roared that the blizzard was passing, and that this horse knew every inch of the way. He asked questions to make us talk, and so keep awake. We had almost given up hope of surviving the night when we noticed a perceptible dropping in the force of the gale; and within as short a time as it had arisen the wind died away. In the space of minutes the moon was shining brilliantly from a clear sky and deep silence, broken only at intervals by the crash of a falling branch torn from its parent tree by the weight of the snow, reigned again over this land of violent contrasts.

The temperature seemed to fall even lower than before, but at least it was now possible to breathe slowly and without pain through our woollen mouth-guards, from which we had frequently to shake the ice formed by our breath.

The last few versts of our journey lay through a dense forest of pines, whose shadows appeared as solid as themselves. No light showed to welcome us in distant Maslozero; the glittering roofs gave a false impression of distance, but promised warmth and security. As we approached the village we could discern no movement in the white streets, but as we drew abreast of the first house we were startled by a quiet voice close to the sleigh coming from a cloaked figure behind a bayonet, calling upon us to halt. Within a few moments we were taken to the school house by a burly sergeant, who explained that we had been expected three hours since and that he was on the point of sending out a search party to find us. We learned that it was now three o'clock in the morning, and that we had been travelling for over eighteen hours. We felt that it might have been years.

The relief from the storm and cold being almost unbearable, we were too exhausted to take much notice of our surroundings; but we had an impression of climbing clean wooden stairs and being told by a young woman draped in a blanket to wait while she got the samovar ready. In a dream-like state we realised that we were in a curious little school-room. By the yellow light of a single oil lamp we could distinguish a dozen little desks, some hanging maps and a blackboard. Soon the young woman returned, clad in a blouse and skirt and carrying the samovar which she placed on a small table. She suggested that we might like to remove our greatcoats in the next room, which was warmer, showing us to another door. This room was evidently used as her bedroom and living room; one corner was entirely occupied by a large four-poster, concealed by closely drawn red curtains. In another corner was built the great cooking and heating stove on the top of which we were to sleep, two feet from the ceiling. A whitewood table, two Windsor chairs and a handsome ikon in which perfumed oil was burning completed the furnishings.

We dropped into chairs and slowly began to divest ourselves of our outer wraps, belts and revolvers, allowing them to remain on the floor as they fell. We relaxed in the warmth of the room, unwilling to move an inch. Our chairs were placed facing the door, between the bed and the stove, with the ikon directly behind me. The airless silence of the house enveloped us like a thick garment; it was almost palpable, and started a singing in our ears.

After some time I thought I heard a sigh which came from nowhere, as I knew Mende had neither moved nor spoken. I dismissed the matter as imaginary; but shortly I heard it repeated and, looking closely at the bed, I though I saw a slight movement of the curtains. I silently indicated to Mende to watch the curtains, which then distinctly moved. We expected to see the family cat emerge, but what came into view startled us into complete wakefulness. The tall figure of a girl, entirely naked, her smiling face framed in a mass of long brown hair, advanced towards us with her hands outstretched in the most friendly fashion.

I quietly said to Mende: "Sit still; she's asleep." But a glance at her eyes made it obvious that she was wide awake, and also that she was quite unconscious of her unconventional appearance. She halted when she reached my straps and revolver and, picking up the holster, she began to hold a whispered conversation with someone invisible to me, who, judging from the girl's remarks, was leaning on the back of my chair. I could feel the hair rising on the back of my head, and after a few seconds I even imagined I could feel breathing on my neck.

The conversation, of which we could hear only one side, was evidently a discussion regarding our appearance, nationality, and equipment, and the reason for our presence. To all our visitor's questions we gathered from the comments we could hear that she was obtaining satisfactory replies.

This spell was at last broken by the hurried entrance of our hostess who rushed to the bed, seized a coloured quilt and, hastily covering the girl's form, hurried her out of the room. Presently she returned to collect more orthodox clothing for her charge, a constant flow of apologies accompanying each appearance, until she finally announced that 'chi' [tea] and bread were ready. She took this opportunity of explaining that our late visitor was a mental case whom she was nursing. She said that the girl was fourteen years of age and motherless, and that she had the gift of seeing invisible people with whom she habitually held conversations. Then, with a frightened look, she begged us to keep silent regarding the girl's behaviour, otherwise the authorities would remove her from the care of her friends and place her in an asylum. We promised to respect the woman's confidence. No useful purpose could be served by betraying it, and it would have been cruelty to report such a gentle creature as a dangerous lunatic. Also we could easily imagine what her treatment might be at the hands of officials such as those with whom we were already acquainted.

Refreshed with tea and bread, we removed our boots and climbed to the top of the stove, where we passed two hours of semi-suffocation before we were aroused by the arrival of Nicoli, who had come out from Kem to meet us and prepare us for developments in the town. After more tea and bread we felt ready for the road again, and under Nicoli's guidance we travelled by a circuitous route to avoid Paduzemskaia and the main track villages to escape any possible hostile observation.

Nicoli's information, fully confirmed later by Drake-Brockman, was to the effect that our Russian colleagues of the Murmansk Army had been informed by the headman of Paduzemskaia that I had left Kem on an extended tour of the frontier, and should therefore not return for several weeks. Accordingly they had evolved a plan to disarm the Karelians, on the pretext that the Regiment was about to mutiny, murder their officers, and seize Kem; also that I knew of this, having been warned, and had fled to Finland. The operation was to be put into practice on Sunday morning, when many of the Karelians would be attending their devotions.

The plotters had all the items of their programme 'cut and dried', but they had neglected to take into consideration our intelligence service and the wireless station at Uskozero; thus, when according to their calculations we should have been four or five days' journey distant, we were back in Kem on the Friday evening before the proposed 'coup'.

I was anxious to avoid any demonstration such as might alarm our friends and also indicate our source of information. Gregori and Nicoli were anxious to arrest the instigators and hang them at once. But although I thought this course would probably save considerable anxiety and perhaps, too, some more valuable lives in the future, I felt sure that this method would be frowned upon at GHQ whatever satisfaction it might have afforded the rank and file of the Murmansk Army. Much as it went against the grain, therefore, I could only pretend ignorance and carry out a routine relief of guards and posts; hence on Saturday morning two British officers were quartered at the Karelian barracks, and one British officer sent to take command at every post at the station and in the town. The Karelian guard on the railway bridge was strengthened by a Lewis gun team of Marines and headquarters guard was furnished with an additional machine-gun.

When I went out of my quarters on Saturday it was difficult to maintain an air of indifference. Almost every Russian official I met stared at me in such a manner as to make it quite obvious that I was an unexpected and unwelcome apparition. In their surprise they forgot their superficial politeness, and simply gaped. This I regarded an a genuine compliment. Needless to say, I made a mental note of those who exhibited chagrin as indicating at least a guilty knowledge of the conspiracy. Their plot was, perforce, temporarily abandoned and all remained quiet on Sunday; but we did not relax our vigilance or make any changes in the disposition of our men for some weeks.

Chapter 10

Advice on Independence

The troops in the Kem Command were constantly growing in number, and to reinforcements of RE, Ordnance and RASC [Royal Army Service Corps] was now added a complete field hospital, under Lieut Colonel Boswell. This was accommodated at Popoff with the howitzer battery of French artillery and a detachment of Karelians.

In arranging the hospital when he arrived Colonel Boswell was given the assistance of fatigue parties from the Karelian Regiment, and at intervals afterwards when occasion arose he would send a note to the Karelian officer in charge asking for a certain number of men to report to the hospital at a given time. This practice led one morning to a situation which caused much amusement to the whole Regiment.

A recently joined officer of the RAMC was taking morning sick parade at the hospital when a Karelian fatigue party presented themselves under a Karelian NCO The Doctor could not speak a word of their language, neither could the Karelians speak a word of English; but to them the word of a British officer must be obeyed in any circumstances. With due solemnity the doctor submitted each of the fourteen men to a thorough examination, as a result of which he sent five to bed in the hospital, dressed and bandaged four more for frostbite, which in the normal course of life they never noticed, and marked the remainder 'Medicine and Duty'. The NCO was given a strong dose of epsom salts and dismissed, chuckling, to lead the remnants of the grinning survivors back to barracks.

Colonel Boswell's orderly arrived shortly afterwards with a chit from the Adjutant asking if the Karelians had forgotten to send the fatigue party. The officer in charge of the Karelians went across to the hospital to obtain an explanation, and to inform the Adjutant that he was afraid to send any more men in case they were all put to bed. I do not know what the Colonel said.

In addition to the reinforcements mentioned Brigadier-General Turner now arrived in Kem, to command the 237th Brigade, replacing General Marsh, who had unfortunately returned to England in ill health. The Headquarters of this heterogeneous unit had previously been at Kandalaksha but Colonel Lewin, the Chief of Staff at Murmansk, thought that a senior officer on the spot would be an excellent antidote to the sense of superiority from which, in his opinion, I suffered. How far this view was the reflection of advice from his Russian friends was a matter for conjecture; all we were concerned with were the instructions given to the Brigadier by Colonel Lewin, which being translated meant "Woods must be sat upon!" This attitude was to be deprecated since it created an unnecessarily false and unfriendly atmosphere between General Turner and Karelian Headquarters, a feeling which was the more marked by reason of the fact that Brigade HQ and the General's quarters were in adjoining houses. However, when a week had elapsed without evidence of any attempt at suppression, and I had learned that General Turner was bored to tears with his own company, I called one afternoon and presented myself to my senior in his own quarters.

The General had evidently been given a curious impression of me, as his first ungracious greeting was: "Well, what do you want?" He glanced round hastily in such a manner as to suggest that he was about to reach for some weapon of defence!

He was quite surprised – and perhaps relieved – when I simply answered: "Tea, if you have any."

From that moment the feeling disappeared, and we became good friends. On further acquaintance I found that the strained relationship had been unwarranted. He had placed his own perfectly correct interpretation upon the instructions from Murmansk, and had never for a moment entertained the idea of putting them into practice or of interfering with the Karelians or the administration of district matters.

Colonel Steel, at the War Office in London, had early evinced a lively interest in the Karelian Regiment and was most helpful in sending various equipment to us direct. He was responsible for, among other things, the gift of some curiously shaped band instruments. He now sent us what we urgently needed – some British junior officers. He said he had vetted them all and was satisfied as to their quality. Twenty-eight were originally sent, but as they had to pass through Murmansk their number had been depleted by more than half by the time they filtered through to us, the larger fraction being detained for duty at GHQ However, we were more than pleased with those who arrived at Kem; every one of them had intelligence, pluck and initiative in plenty. Several of these young officers were later compelled to shoulder responsibilities of a nature equal to that of a Brigade Command, and they did not fail.

Supplementary to Colonel Steel's selection several junior officers of a battalion of the West Yorkshire Regiment which had arrived in the country volunteered and were seconded for duty with the Karelians. These were splendid fellows, and very keen on the regiment and its work.

We were now able to organise our establishment on better lines, with a British officer in command of each Company in Kem and two to assist Heaton up country. In the town Lieut W. E. Butler, late of the Manchester Regiment, and a repatriated prisoner of war from Germany, made a first class Adjutant for the Regiment. He was a valuable officer, possessing marked initiative and tact in dealing with the Karelians. Captain Gilling, late of the RGA [Royal Garrison Artillery], was appointed Garrison Adjutant, and Lieut Long, of the Coldstream Guards, was sent to take command at Saroka, a dangerous and difficult post which he filled with astonishing success considering his youth. Long was frequently faced with emergencies which had to be met and decisions which had to be taken on his own responsibility. Indeed the regiment and district were well served by all the new officers, every one of whom displayed the greatest interest and enthusiasm in his work.

Towards the end of January Gregori and Nicoli asked for an interview on private business, and that they might be allowed to bring three civilian friends from Karelia. When they arrived they brought with them the headman of Ouchta and the leaders of the two most important village groups further west. They asked permission to put their case to me as a private person and not in an official capacity and so to obtain my advice. They stated at once that they knew it was the British policy to leave Russia in the near future, and that they viewed with alarm the possibility of again being under Russian control. What, they asked, would I advise them to do, and what action would I myself contemplate if I were a native of Karelia?

I adopted the Irish method of answering one question by putting another, and my enquiry elicited the information that a national spirit was thoroughly aroused among the Karelians and that, much as they disliked the Finns, they hated and mistrusted the Russians, and had determined to become an independent nation if this were anyhow possible.

I sincerely sympathised with them in their predicament. Geographically they were most unfortunately placed. Russia was their neighbour in the north from Finland to a point beyond Kandalaksha to the White Sea, also in the east from the southern shore of the White Sea to a point near Petrograd in the south. Finland lay along their western frontier from north-west to south-east; thus Karelia was a long wedge-shaped territory with no outlet save at the White Sea.

To give advice on such a matter was a serious responsibility, and I asked for time to consider what in my opinion was their best course in all the circumstances. They agreed to wait; but in the meantime, they said, they would also like to consult an ex-Premier of Finland, who was now serving as a soldier with Major Burton, and they desired me to arrange that this man should be able to come to Kem for a few days. On the clear understanding that all conversations with this man should take place in the presence of my interpreter, and that no disloyalty to the Allies was contemplated I agreed to ask Major Burton to allow M. Tokoi to come as my guest to Kem.

A hint to Burton was quite enough, and the ex-Premier duly arrived at the Karelian headquarters, somewhat puzzled as to the reason for his invitation. He was a mild little man with an intelligent expression and grey eyes well set in a square, brown face, but with little to distinguish him from many other northerners I had met until he spoke; then his deep and resonant voice, capable of a great range of expression, indicated the practised orator. Thoughtfully, Burton had also sent an interpreter whose English was perfect to act as a check on the conversations. This man, Captain Lehtimäki was a fine looking specimen of manhood, but distinctly red in his political opinions; however, he gave me his word that he would not discuss politics in Kem outside the Mess, and this condition he scrupulously observed.

The Finnish politician's advice was entirely in keeping with his profession – it was given at great length and was quite non-committal; nevertheless, his conversation was interesting and his ideas of organisation sound. With a view to finding out anything that might in the future be useful to Gregori and Nicoli I drew M. Tokoi out as much as possible on the subject of the Finnish constitution. This was not at all difficult, as the constitution and its reforms were evidently a favourite subject with him; at the same time their discussion furnished us with much useful information regarding the practical working of a government.

M. Tokoi had been my guest for two days when I received a long telegram from GHQ Murmansk, informing me that a Finn named Tokoi had "escaped" from Kandalaksha and was supposed to be heading for Kem; would I arrest and hold him under a strong guard if he came into my district, as he was an extremely dangerous man.

This order placed me in an uncomfortable dilemma. To arrest one's guest seemed hardly the essence of hospitality; at the same time orders could not be ignored. I replied to Murmansk that the Finn was in my charge and that a report would follow. However, before my somewhat guarded report could have reached GHQ we received a further and more peremptory order to place the Finn in strict confinement immediately and wire compliance. Now, therefore, there was no other course but to obey. Accordingly, when the Doctor suddenly insisted upon examining M. Tokoi the latter was somewhat surprised; but his surprise grow to amazement when he was carried off to hospital suffering from appendicitis. No doubt he had been politically a sick man for some time, but this was probably the first occasion on which he had experienced diagnosis in advance of a physical malady. We duly reported by wire our compliance with the last order from Murmansk.

We visited the patient in hospital and sent him certain items of refreshment which were not prescribed on his diet sheet, while the hospital staff made him more comfortable than he had been for a long time. Two weeks later he left Kem to return to Kandalaksha without entertaining feelings other than those of gratitude for the hospitality he had received at our hands.

From Murmansk we heard little more of the matter, mainly, I presumed, because I had pointed out in my detailed report the great advantage of being present at any meetings between the Karelians and this 'dangerous' Finn and so being informed at first hand of all that passed. Such meetings would certainly have taken place otherwise without our knowledge or concurrence, and might conceivably have had different results. Some time later General Maynard remarked to me that I had been playing with fire; perhaps he was right, but I could not help thinking that we were all doing this although some of us were evidently not conscious of the fact.

Some six weeks after these events intelligence reports from official Russian sources began to come in giving lurid details regarding a meeting of Karelians which had been held in Kem to organise a massacre of all the British in North Russia. The plans for this 'coup' were set out in lengthy detail, a feat of imagination which would have earned my applause for the ingenuity of the authors but for its over close resemblance to the recent conspiracy which had caused my premature recall from Lousalma.

I gave the Karelians my advice as to their future action and asked them to consider it carefully before taking any course which might furnish material for propaganda to their enemies. This they promised to do. Our Company officers were in constant touch with their men and were able to confirm my own view that there was no unrest among them, nor even the slightest indication of discontent. Their time was quite fully occupied. Their new balalaika and mandolin band was a constant source of interest and amusement in the evenings, while during the day there was the furnishing of the various guards in the town and at the station, Lewis gun instruction, and ski drill.

Occasionally a few Karelians would organise a hunt, when news of a bear was brought in by a peasant or transport man. This was hardly 'hunting' in the English sense of the term; the bear had no chance whatever of escape. Usually the animal's den was located by some sharp-eyed observer, who had noticed a fine wisp of exhalation rising from a snowy bank, or some other likely spot. The place would be marked and reported to the nearest village. Then three or four men with guns and dogs would proceed to the scene of action, the men taking up positions at close range and loosing the dogs to arouse bruin. Wakened from his winter sleep, hungry and angry, the bear would rush out to punish his tormentors, and sometimes this rush occurred with such unexpected rapidity that one or two of the dogs got hurt; but the final result was invariably the same, and the hunters' bullets found their mark. A bear with two or three cubs would be especially dangerous to the dogs, and cases had been known where she had survived long enough to damage one of the hunters in defence of her young. The white-collared meat-eating were particularly dangerous. Not having any special use for the cubs, the hunters usually destroyed them with the mother.

We were presented with one of these orphan bear cubs, which must have been very young. It was a brown, shapeless bundle of fur, no larger than a Scottie dog. We brought him up with a baby's bottle for some weeks until he was able to take food from a dish. At first he was very shy, hiding in corners and crying piteously for his mother; but he soon made friends with a litter of mongrel pups, crossed sheepdog and retriever, with which we had also been presented in the course of nature by a homeless mother. The pups were about the same size as the little bear, but he could run faster and had a hundred cunning tricks for their undoing. He afforded us much amusement chasing or being chased by the little dogs – games in which he was always the winner. His greatest fault was his marked dishonesty; no amount of punishment could deter him from thieving jam or sugar wherever it might be, and the Karelian Mess servants had to keep a watchful eye on the table when it was prepared for a meal to protect it from raids which were planned with extraordinary cunning and carried out with speed, daring and skill.

In the course of two months he grew to a standing height of about three feet, and became too heavy-handed for the puppies, hence he was thrown more and more upon his own resources for amusement. His favourite pastime was to take up a strategic position behind the doors of the open gateway in the courtyard, concealed from view, where with one mischievous eye glued to the space between the gate and the post he could keep excellent observation on the road – and passing cattle. As the leading cow passed the gateway he would hurl himself out into the road at the heels of the animal, sending it careering in fright up the road with himself bounding like a brown ball in its wake. At the end of about a hundred yards he would abandon the chase and, exercising wonderful agility in escaping punishment from the irate drover, dodge off the road until an opportunity offered to return in safety to his ambush, where he would prepare for another sally.

Our tame bear furnished one particularly amusing incident. A Major Hart, of the Canadian Scottish, arrived in Kem one morning at about 5 o'clock with urgent despatches for me. These were brought to my room by an orderly, whom I told to rouse the Mess servants to get breakfast for the messenger and give him some of our magazines of ancient vintage to read while I dressed. After reading the despatches I proceeded leisurely to shave and dress, as there was no immediate cause for haste. In about

Knobs the Bear

three-quarters of an hour's time, therefore, I opened the door of the Mess room, and was astonished at the tableau presented.

Major Hart was in a chair, pressed back as close as possible to the wall. He was sitting rigidly still, his face blanched and his eyes fixed upon the brown figure of Knobs squatting on his haunches three feet distant in the middle of the table, among the dishes, with a tin of plum and apple clasped against his breast by one paw while licking the jam scooped from the tin off the other. The little brute eyed me warily, not moving until I stepped close to him with my hand raised to box his ears; then, like a brown streak, he darted under my arm and disappeared through the open door.

The expression on Major Hart's face was worth going a long way to see. For about a minute he was bereft of words, then, wiping the sweat from his head, he told me that while he had been taking his breakfast he had suddenly become aware that a bear was scrutinising him from the other side of the table! He had heard no sound of the animal's approach, and was afraid to call or move; he had therefore sat perfectly still for about twenty minutes, waiting for the bear to attack, while it occupied itself in finishing the jam, having already emptied the sugar-basin. I felt sorry for Hart, and refrained from pulling his leg. He was a good officer, who subsequently turned out most useful in command of the Karelian detachment at Polani Krug.

Some days after M. Tokoi had returned to his unit at Kandalaksha a determined effort was made by the hostile element in Russian circles to deprive us of the invaluable services of Mascherin. We had always feared that they must eventually become aware of his share in the disappearance of their gunmen, and now the tenacity of their attempts to remove him confirmed our worst fears. The first move in this direction took the form of an order from some Russian pundit at Archangel to proceed immediately and report for duty there. We knew as well as Mascherin himself what this meant, and the order was cancelled by me on the grounds that he was indispensable in Kem.

A few days later two NCOs and four men were sent to his quarters to arrest him on the faked charge of falsifying his books. We were in time to intercept this move by ordering the escort to bring their prisoner to Headquarters, together with all his books. A subaltern then came to our office and charged Mascherin with drawing pay and rations for two men more than his correct numbers. His books, which we examined in the presence of his accuser, proved this charge to be entirely groundless. I told Mascherin to demand an apology and the name of the original accuser; neither, of course, was ever forthcoming, and we had been fortunate indeed to secure his books before they were confiscated and altered to coincide with manufactured evidence.

Peace reigned for one day. Then we had a call from one of his men with the news that two officers had come to arrest him while he was in bed, and were now in his quarters waiting for him to get dressed. Hastily Mende and two Marines were despatched to 'arrest' Mascherin and bring him to Headquarters at once. Mende was just in time to take delivery of the prisoner from the hands of a very reluctant escort, and after a little argument induced the two young Russian officers to come in for refreshment. Despite the note furnished them to excuse their failure to their seniors they were very uncomfortable, and obviously fearful of their reception at Russian Headquarters. They stated that the charge against the prisoner was "failing to carry out an order, and not reporting to Archangel."

Our longheaded friend, the MO was again called into consultation, and the diagnosis in this case was so serious that Mascherin was ordered to hospital at once. We thought he would be safe enough there, but we were mistaken. On the fourth night of his residence in hospital he was knocked out in bed, gagged and bound, and spirited away in a sleigh, presumably covered with sacking and blankets.

For two days we could obtain no news of him, but on the third evening a platoon of the Murmansk Army arrived on the station from Kem town, bringing their baggage. Amongst the bundles of bedding, trussed up and covered as a bale, was poor Mascherin. We were powerless; we could not search the property of our allies. Nevertheless, I informed the officer in charge that, while I did not require an answer from him or any comment, I wanted news of Captain Mascherin when he reached Murmansk, where General Maynard would expect to see him to thank him for good work done. This at least had some effect, as we received a letter of farewell from Mascherin at Murmansk, in which he expressed his appreciation of our efforts to save his life, and concluded by mentioning that the British Staff at Murmansk had been very kind, but that he was being sent to Archangel as a prisoner, and that he knew from the companions selected to accompany him on the voyage that he could never hope to reach his destination alive.

This was sad reading and added nothing to the esteem in which we held our unscrupulous allies at Murmansk. It was now abundantly clear that they were prepared to stop at nothing in order to deprive us of any support they could destroy.

It was not long before we experienced another example of their methods. The officer commanding the training depot of the Murmansk Army at barracks situated between Kem and Saroka was a quiet, capable man, willing and anxious to help the Allies, always punctual with his indents for supplies, and invariably accurate in all his reports. Suddenly he was reprimanded from the Murmansk Army headquarters for not having more recruits, although obtaining them, was no part of his duty. Then unfounded complaints were received by him as to slackness of discipline shown by men under his command.

At first he told me that he thought he would soon be dismissed from his post; but I do not think he foresaw the actual method of his removal, which took place shortly after the receipt of the second reprimand.

One Yermoloff [Yermolov] had been appointed, presumably by the allies, as [Deputy] Governor General of North Russia, and in this capacity paid a visit to Kem. He arrived one morning with his staff in a special train with private coaches. As convention demanded I called upon him with Mende to interpret, and after being kept waiting the proper length of time to impress me with my own insignificance, was received somewhat brusquely by the Governor General and with obviously unfriendly looks from his staff officers, who glanced with great disdain at my field uniform. Undeterred by this reception I invited the General and one of his staff to dinner that evening at our Headquarters. Somewhat to my surprise he accepted, and duly arrived with a young ADC [Aide de Camp] promptly at the hour mentioned – a further surprise, as punctuality was not a custom usually observed in Russia.

He gave me the impression of being an honest man, but not a sufficiently strong one to control the disruptive forces with which he was surrounded. He was a stocky little man with a brown, earnest face and eyes capable of meeting one's own frankly. After congratulating the Karelians on the success of their little campaign in the autumn he said that there had been reports of mutiny and disloyalty in Kem district. This created the opening I was awaiting, and I gave him a frank statement of the exact position, the attitude of the Karelians towards Russia and the subversive attempts by some of his own officers to undermine the work of the Allies, not stopping at murder to attain their object. I also gave it as my considered opinion that the Karelians resembled the Irish in one respect – that they could be led, but never driven.

How much we gained by this open diplomacy can be gathered from the incident which took place on the following day. Our friend the Colonel in charge of the depot, was sent for by the Governor General and received with great kindness in the special coach. After being congratulated on his excellent work he was taken to the dining car and given a glass of wine before leaving. Within one minute he was lying dead beside the train.

We raised as much trouble as we could for his murderers by issuing orders to the doctor and the Marine Police for the exhumation of the body with a view to holding a post-mortem examination. This only had the effect of obtaining the required publicity and causing a certain amount of uneasiness to those concerned; the persistent efforts of the police to find the body only ceased when General Yermoloff personally issued an order to the effect that exhumation of the body must not take place. He left Kem without offering to return our hospitality.

I am afraid that every British officer in Kem who knew the facts of this affair lost any degree of sympathy he might previously have entertained for the Russian cause. Indeed, in Mess I was obliged to assume a deafness from which I have never suffered in order to avoid having to comment upon suggestions of suitable reprisals in the interests of justice.

The Governor General next turned his attention to the Karelian situation. Here his efforts did not meet with much success. A number of spies were sent up into the country to obtain the names of political leaders, no doubt with the intention of having them all executed at an early date. Gregori, now a Major, informed me very soon of the presence of these men and their object, and asked for instructions regarding them. He was told that we had no knowledge of the issue to any person or persons of permits to travel in the area, and that no specific instructions could therefore be given. Nicoli applied for and was granted two weeks' leave. From this he returned with a vast fund of information regarding the personnel at Murmansk; we did not ask him any questions as to the source of this fresh information, or how it was obtained.

Chapter 11

White Russian Hostility

There now arrived in Kem a squadron of the RAF, under a very young commander and even more youthful officers. Their machines arrived in sections and at intervals by rail, so that they had a good deal of time on their hands. This afforded plenty of opportunity for getting into mischief, and caused us considerable anxiety, mainly because they soon became the quarry for every enemy agent, male and female, in the country. The leakage of information entailed, though no doubt unintentional and due to the irresponsibility of extreme youth, nevertheless became so serious that we were compelled to edit all orders issued to British units so that they could not divulge any item of tactical importance. On occasion we even made use of this medium to circulate information we desired the enemy to receive.

One of the most popular guests in their Mess was a Russian who visited them frequently under the pretext of exchanging languages. He had explained to them that he knew no English, and they saw no reason to think otherwise; we, however. were aware that he had been living for seven years in Liverpool before the war. His activities were carefully noted and most of his correspondence intercepted by our Intelligence.

Brigadier-General Turner was feeling the strain of the climate and was merely worried by recital of the intrigues and plots with which we were surrounded, and I did not therefore cause him more inconvenience than was necessary in this respect. Nevertheless, he asked for relief which was granted, Brigadier-General G. D. Price arriving to take over command of the 237th Brigade. Unfortunately he had received instructions similar to those given to his predecessor, namely "to sit upon Woods". He endeavoured to follow out these instructions with zest until such time as he discovered their absurdity.

I shall always remember with amusement my first interview with General Price. This took place in the sitting-room at the Brigade quarters. General Turner was standing with his back to the wall, his smiling, cheery face full of anticipation for the battle to come. General Price was pacing up and down the room with his hands clasped behind his back, a look of grim determination on his face, his monocle firmly fixed and his chin stuck out at its most uncompromising angle. His first greeting was:

"You're Woods? Sit down, and I'll tell you the situation here as I know it."

Without answer from me he then proceeded for some twenty minutes to give me a resume of the Murmansk version of the military and political situation in Kem District and Karelia.

I did not interrupt or make any comment until he had finished; then, in reply to his barked: "Is that correct?", I merely said: "No, Sir."

General Turner was highly amused, while General Price was furious, demanding angrily what I meant. I asked leave to give my version of the political situation as I knew it to be, and General Turner in his role of referee thought this would be fair. So I gave General Price a short history of events since we had occupied Kem, making three main points of difference from his recital: first, the loyalty and honesty of the Karelians; second, the treachery of a group of the Russian officers; and third, the misplaced confidence of GHQ in the last mentioned clique.

It was obvious that General Price believed what I had told him; his rather aggressive attitude relaxed, to be replaced by one much more natural to him; and it was not long before we were able to discuss affairs quite amicably. Later we became on quite friendly terms, only occasionally interrupted when he would remember that I had to be suppressed; then there were slight differences. These usually took the form of trying to outwit each other. When he won he was pleased, and when he was not successful he was always sportsman enough to take defeat in good spirit. My own respect and liking for General Price was shared by every officer in the Command, and his advice was very useful in dealing with some of the problems with which we were frequently confronted.

Early in his command of the Brigade attempts were made by the unfriendly Russian party to make use of the General as a tool for their own purposes. He had not been long installed when General Zveginsiff came from Saroka to call upon him. But if they had been given to understand that he would be malleable in their hands they were soon to find that they were misinformed. Complaints were made to him about my 'high-handed treatment' of certain Russian officers; but those who lodged them always came out from the Brigadier's quarters with much less confidence and swagger than they took in with them. They soon left him in peace.

Sometimes I would ask his advice regarding methods of countering some move on the part of our hostile friends, when he would say:

"Don't tell me anything about it. I do not want to know anything about how you bury them."

Failure to enlist the sympathy of the Brigadier on the spot spurred the intriguers to a fresh and more successful attempt at misleading GHQ Murmansk. One morning I received an imperative order from the Chief of Staff to disarm the Karelians, beginning immediately with the troops stationed at Kem station and town; Brigadier-General Price simultaneously received orders from the same source to see that the order issued to me was carried out, and to have a Marine guard posted at Brigade HQ

I gave the Brigadier the reports of our intelligence service, and from these it was clear that a further plot was being engineered to get the Karelians disarmed and then attack the British, leaving none alive to contradict subsequent statements. As usual the Karelians were to be blamed, and it would have been said that they had rebelled and, with arms previously concealed, murdered us all.

General Price was seriously and not unnaturally perturbed by the situation, so I asked him to have no official cognisance of any action on my part beyond what he could not avoid seeing. To this he agreed, with the sole stipulation that I must hand in to Ordnance the six Lewis guns in possession of the Karelians at the station. This I promised to do.

I then saw Captain Smith in his Ordnance stores situated in two railway wagons on a siding and made arrangements with him for the handing in of the Lewis guns and rifles. The Karelians were ordered to parade with these at the stores, and told that Ordnance wished to check as a matter of routine the number of arms held by them. We handed in the guns at one side of the wagon and then marched round to the other side, where we drew eight Lewis guns with the necessary ammunition drums and twenty-four rifles, all on my indent. I duly handed the Ordnance officer's receipt for six Lewis guns with eighteen drums of ammunition and twenty-four rifles and bayonets to the Brigadier. Nicoli and Gregori were the only two Karelians who ever knew the meaning of this manoeuvre.

We had to move quickly to prevent our intentions from becoming known and to make our dispositions without embarrassing the Brigadier with guilty knowledge; hence it was necessary to clear the station of all possible observers before we posted four Lewis gun teams in the attic above Brigade HQ, which they entered through the outside door at the end of the building. These commanded the approaches from the south, east and west, and also covered Karelian HQ in the next house on three sides. In the attic of our own HQ we posted two Lewis gun teams and four crack snipers. The two houses made excellent block-houses, proof against rifle or machine-gun fire, as the sides of the attics where the roofs met the floors had been sand-bagged soon after we took possession of the buildings.

Two Maxims and their teams were placed in the rocks at the back of the station, and a screen of scouts posted to command every approach to the railway bridge or the station itself in the event of a surprise attack being attempted from the town via the river. As an extra precaution a Company of Karelians was posted under the bridge, and in addition the Brigadier had the Marines posted at various strategic positions near the railway; so that any hostile attempt on our quarters would meet with a warm reception. The Marines and the Karelians always worked together in perfect harmony, and there was no danger of mistakes.

When all lights in the railway offices were extinguished long before the usual time, and the telephone line to Kem town became dead, we expected some manifestation. But although we waited two hours more all remained quiet – almost too quiet. At last, a little after midnight, General Price and I went out to have a look round the station. There was no sign of movement anywhere, but I think he was a little disturbed when we were challenged several times in Russian. However, he was satisfied that no antagonistic intention lurked behind Nicoli's cheery "Good morning, gentlemen", spoken from an apparently empty railway wagon.

We learned from Nicoli that he had had the plotters in Kem under observation all the evening; that at about ten o'clock their men were ready to march on the station; but that after they had been joined by two men, who arrived in a great hurry, they had held an excited conference and then dismissed their followers. He told us that they were still being watched and that we should be aware within a few minutes of any significant move they might make. He added that it was quite safe to go to bed, and that he would awaken us in good time should anything develop.

Unfortunately nothing did develop. In spite of our hasty precautions some of their spies on the railway had reported that the Karelians were not disarmed as they had hoped and expected.

General Price did not know then or, so far as I am aware, at any time what measures had been taken to prevent our wholesale massacre, or that I had deliberately disobeyed in spirit for the first time in my life a direct order from superior authority.

Reporting to GHQ I stated that it was impossible to carry out the order to disarm the Karelians; that partial disarmament would have been dangerous, causing the risk of rebellion among even the most loyal troops; and again pointed out where real treachery was to be found.

I was backed up by the Brigadier, who reported on the steadiness and loyalty of the Karelians notwithstanding frequent attempts by the Murmansk coterie to associate them with minor disturbances and various alleged mutinies in Burton's Finnish Legion. Certainly this unit appeared to be restless; and their discontent had not been diminished by the arrest of their leaders and periodical disarmament of the men. I do not pretend to know how far this method of dealing with the Legion was justified; but I know that Burton had a most difficult position to maintain, and that only his personal popularity with the men added to the exercise of considerable tact on the part of General Maynard when he returned to his command prevented the development of a very ugly situation.

Eventually a group of the leaders from the Finnish Legion, including Lehtimäki and Tokoi were expelled from North Russia. In accordance with this decision they were entrained for the Soviet frontier, and orders from Murmansk warned us that no communication must be allowed between the Karelians and the Finns when the latter passed through Kem station, where the train halted for an hour. Burton sent a wire asking us to meet the train and wish Tokoi good luck; he liked the man despite his political colour, and was sorry to lose him. In order to carry out the instructions from GHQ without making it obvious to the Karelians that they were suspected of being prone to 'red' contamination, the Finns were met at the station by Mende and Drake-Brockman, who brought them direct to our mess. Here they were given a meal and entertained until the train left. We parted on amicable terms and at the same time had succeeded in carrying out orders.

The two upper floors, the stables and the courtyard of the theatre in Kem were being used as Headquarters for the transport section of the Garrison Company, and Major Harrison, late of the West Yorks, who commanded this company had his offices and lived in a flat on the second floor above the auditorium, while the top floor was occupied by servants and transport men with their wives. The public part of the theatre consisted of a stage, several dressing-rooms and a level-floored hall capable of accommodating about five hundred people. This was more commonly used on Saturday and Sunday evenings for dancing than for theatrical performances, the dances being organised by various bodies and usually open to all who could pay ten kopecks at the door. But it was noticeable that the Karelians, though extremely fond of dancing, did not attend dances organised by the Russians, but instead kept a watchful eye on the proceedings.

At about two o'clock one Sunday morning Major Harrison was awakened by a light in his face. Jumping out of bed, he opened his bedroom door to investigate, but was driven back by smoke and flames cutting him off from the stairs. He had just time to break his double windows, fling some hastily seized clothes to the ground, and follow them himself thirty feet to the snow beneath. He and two transport men were able to get the horses out, but nobody could have saved the people on the top floor. Two men, three women and several children were burned to death.

The whole building was constructed of well seasoned wood and the flames travelled at an amazing speed all round the walls, so that the interior quickly became a roaring furnace, making a vast torch to light up the whole town and countryside. Being late in the town that night I was early on the scene. So far as I could judge there was not the remotest chance of saving anything, nor could all the fire brigades in Russia have prevented the total destruction of the building. But it was clearly imperative to take some steps to localise the blaze and, hastily collecting some soldiers, both Russian and Karelian, who had appeared, I sent them to arouse the inhabitants and to see that two or three men armed with wet sacks were placed on the roofs of adjoining houses to beat out the sparks which were showering over the town.

The heat was intense. Pieces of burning wood two feet long shot up into the air, borne by the flames to a height of a hundred feet and, falling, were a source of danger to surrounding buildings and onlookers alike. It was patently impossible to get at the fire-buckets in the theatre – indeed no living person could venture within a radius of forty yards of the fire – and in any case the river was frozen to a depth of six feet at its nearest point, with only one small space kept open for domestic purposes. The transport men produced a few buckets but their efforts were entirely ineffective.

When the fire was at its height the Russian Commandant, Colonel Baikoff, excitedly rushed up to a small group of newly arrived soldiers of the Murmansk Army and, addressing them as dogs, ordered them to get buckets and form a chain from the river. One man saluted and asked where the buckets could be found and if they should get implements to break the ice on the river. The reply was astonishing. Baikoff drew his revolver and placed it against the man's chest, threatening to shoot when he had counted three. Putting my hand on the Colonel's arm I asked him if he would help me to have all the roofs in the town manned, explaining that his house and the Murmansk Army barracks were in danger. He spun round with his revolver pointed at me for a moment until he recognised who was addressing him; then he said that he had given these men an order and he was going to shoot the mutinous vermin at once. The men looked anything but submissive under this sort of discipline, and in order to avoid bloodshed I quickly took hold of his arm and wrenched the revolver out of his hand. Whether he liked or not the responsibility for maintaining order in the district was mine.

This scene created a painful impression and I reported the whole incident to Murmansk.

There was some speculation as to the origin of the fire, and it was popularly supposed that a dropped cigarette end had caused the outbreak. Whether this was the solution or not we were embarrassed by the loss of comfortable and convenient transport quarters as well as a certain amount of paper money, books and stores. Major Harrison lost all his personal property, but at least saved his life. He had one further stroke of good fortune; when he jumped from his window he landed in a snowdrift which broke his fall and prevented his suffering serious injury.

For some time we could not ascertain whether Omar, the Don Cossack caretaker of the theatre, had survived the fire, but he was eventually found sitting on the river bank, weeping bitterly. This was a sur-

Omar the Cossack with Capt Gilling

prise as he was a stolid creature whom we had thought incapable of any display of emotion. Omar was a Tzarist relic; he had been personal servant to the Chief Engineer of the railway section, who had formerly occupied Harrison's flat, and when his master had answered a summons to Petrograd on business – from which he had never returned – had been left in charge. Nobody had interfered with him, and how he lived and fed himself was a mystery but he was always ready to defend his master's property, if necessary with his life. He was about forty years of age, six feet four inches in gaunt height, all bone and muscle, never speaking unless addressed and then replying in monosyllables. He had the art of moving silently. He always wore the Cossack uniform, and in his top-boots and high-necked Kasakeen coat with silver bandolier and silver-studded belt from which hung a razor-edged sword he was a sinister figure with whom none desired to be intimate. He had only one friend, a large black and white cat whose summer relaxation was to sit on a stone in the river, the icy water almost up to its neck, fishing for fry and sticklebacks.

It was natural that he should dislike the Bolsheviks who had torn the cloth of his master's billiard-table. Fortunately he approved of the British, and with a little tactful appeal to his pride we enlisted a most useful member in our intelligence service once he was convinced that his information would be safeguarded from leakage.

Two days after the fire he told me he had discovered that a couple of soldiers of the Murmansk Army had intentionally set fire to the theatre. Asked if he could obtain sufficient proof to warrant their arrest he said that of course there would be no proof, because a dozen witnesses would be ready to swear that the men were miles away. He added that no arrests would be necessary, but that he could deal with them himself. He did.

I could not help thinking that Omar's wonderfully balanced blade, so keen that he would often cut a floating feather in two with it for our amusement, was a merciful end for the incendiaries. They would have received very different treatment at the hands of the relatives of those who perished in the fire.

Chapter 12

Spring Campaign

General Price had by now developed a lively interest in the political manoeuvres of our Russian neighbours in Kem, in pursuance of which he lit upon an idea for the discovery of our channels of information. The outcome of this trend of thought was a rather diffident suggestion that one of us should sacrifice rank and honour to the extent of making friends with some of the ladies of the town in order, as he abruptly expressed it, "....to get a line on these ******s who want to do us in."

I agreed with the General that it would be most useful, and asked when he would like to begin. I further volunteered to get some addresses, assuring him that he could rely entirely upon my discretion! It cost me a large whiskey and soda to restore the friendly tone of the conversation. Eventually I gave him, without mentioning individuals, a general idea of the organisation Drake-Brockman had built up, and he later met and thanked our chief agent for the splendid work done, regretting that for obvious reasons no public recognition was possible.

Early in March, presumably with the idea of brightening our dull existence in Kem, GHQ sent Major P. J. Mackesy, GSO2 [2nd General Staff Officer], on a visit of Inspection of Karelia and the Karelian Regiment. Fortunately "P. J." held very human views on life and turned out to be possessed of an unusual sense of humour.

Major Mackesy duly set out upon his tour to inspect the frontier guard. Gregori, informed of the proposal and asked to assist in facilitating the Major's journey, wished to know if we approved of this trip (a question not unnaturally prompted by the attitude of GHQ towards the Karelians). In point of fact most of the men, nearly all of whom had agricultural holdings, had been granted leave to make their preparations for the spring grain sowing, the frontier being perfectly safe owing to the thawing condition of the snow and rivers, which would obtain during the following month or six weeks and thus render any sort of military operations out of the question. Assured that we had no objection to Major Mackesy's trip Gregori threw himself wholeheartedly into the preparations. The first point that occurred to him was that if the Major were to derive any satisfaction from this outing he must have something to inspect. Accordingly he organised a mobile platoon to travel from post to post after inspection, Mackesy's driver regulating the speed en route between posts to adjust the time factor.

But Gregori had underrated the Staff's powers of observation, for on his return to Kem Major Mackesy informed me that we were being deceived, and that at several posts in the forest he had inspected the same men as he had seen at the first! That he learned little of the political situation in the district was not surprising; the Karelians were by now thoroughly well aware of the suspicious attitude of GHQ Murmansk towards them and therefore regarded emissaries from this source as antagonistic from the outset; and no people could be more densely stupid than these northerners when put upon their guard. Hence I fear his opinion was formed in somewhat unfavourable circumstances. But in spite of a divergence of views on certain matters of policy we were sorry when he returned to Murmansk.

One afternoon Gregori came to the office with a cutting from *The Times*, which someone had translated for him. The item of news as reported had disturbed him intensely. Having read the paragraph of Russian news I sent the following telegram to Murmansk:

> "The 'Times' of the 25th April published a report as emanating from you that Finns and Karelians attempted to mutiny. I beg most respectfully to protest against the accuracy of this statement where it affects Karelians and respectfully suggest that it should be contradicted without delay. It was proved on the occasion reported that no more loyal troops exist in Russia. You would right an injustice and prevent considerable harm being done by correcting this report." Woods.

The reply did not allay the indignation of any of us. It read:

> "Quite understand your feelings. I feel exactly the same with regard to many reports I read. but it is quite impossible to get some home people to see matters in this area in right light."
>
> General Maynard.

In order if possible to secure definite action we tried again with the following protest:

> "As the report published was official from the WO. I assume that the WO and public believe my command to be out of hand and disloyal. I most respectfully ask that this report be contradicted at home officially and publicly to rectify a grave injustice to myself, my officers and the Regiment. You are the only person who can do this to my satisfaction. Apologies for communicating but know you will understand special circumstances."
>
> Woods.

This produced much better results and brought an official message as follows:

> 237th Brigade.
>
> "Please inform Colonel Woods in reply to his Number W8 that I have read report in question and agree that it gives wrong impression. I have accordingly cabled War Office asking for publication of statement to effect that Karelian Regt remained absolutely loyal through period of unrest and disregarded all Bolshevik attempts to stir up mutiny or disloyalty. He can inform Regiment of this and add that I never had any doubts regarding loyalty of Regt to him and myself. The only danger was that agitators might induce the more ignorant to join in some foolish enterprise which they might not consider disloyal to me but which might have compelled me to take action. The Regt however by its staunchness in time of trouble has now shown that even this danger does not exist and I rely on its loyalty as fully as does Colonel Woods."
>
> General Maynard.

Thus ended satisfactorily an incident which might have had serious consequences to the whole expedition. We were grateful for the prompt action of the General and for the tone of his message to the Regiment; this cancelled the effect produced by the crass stupidity of the person responsible for the report to the War Office and at the same time added to the General's own reputation for justness.

Kem was now rapidly becoming crowded with troops of the Allies. A battalion of Italians under the command of Colonel Sifola, French Infantry under Colonel Bégou and details of our own came to reinforce those already stationed there. Major Samuelson came from Murmansk to supervise food supplies and, unofficially, to keep everybody pleased. In addition to these legitimate arrivals there was an influx of Russian officers, the majority of whom said they were colonels and were of such ages that while some appeared to have been commissioned in the cradle others must have been instructors in the use of the bow and arrow. Their duties were not defined, but they were attached to the Murmansk Army. There were also a few civilians who may or may not have been Russians and who appeared to be possessed of ample funds for the purchase of supplies in the town. The Intelligence service had little sleep or leisure checking up as far as possible on these itinerants. The usual report was that Archangel had been their last port of call.

One of these was a Baron Tüsenhausen who said he was a Russian but whose manners and bearing were more in accordance with the nationality suggested by his name. Officially he had no connection with the Murmansk Army, and was willing and indeed anxious to be on friendly terms with us. In particular he courted the regard of the Karelians. He never brought his wife to call and never invited any of the Staff back to his house; but as we had no intention of telling him anything we were always 'at home' to him. His lack of hospitality, not at all in the Russian tradition, was a further cause of suspicion. The attitude of the Karelians towards the Baron was both amusing and illuminating. Whenever he addressed them they became so blank and stupid that it was obvious to us that they thoroughly distrusted him. After a few weeks of ineffectual friendship with us he finally threw in his lot with the Murmansk Army.

Gregori reported some of the questions the Baron had asked him. They were all on familiar aspects of the situation: "Why did the Karelians serve such awful fools as the British?", "Why not be a man and command his own people?" and so on. Finally he had offered his services to the Karelians if they would get rid of the British staff. All this made it difficult to be cordial to the Baron, and we were not altogether sorry when he transferred his favours elsewhere; nevertheless we managed to keep a certain amount of supervision on his actions, which were not those of an innocent person.

Shortly after the abandonment of his fruitless task among the Karelians Baron Tüsenhausen applied for a permit to go on a hunting trip into Karelia. This was granted with the proviso that he should not go further west than Panozero, a restriction which would have placed hundreds of square miles at his disposal for hunting purposes. But he did not appear satisfied that any limitation should be put to his complete freedom of movement, his plea being that all the best game was to be found near the frontier. We pointed out that as he was a newcomer and unfamiliar with the country he might find any shooting near the frontier misunderstood, and further that elk was to be found in large numbers east of the railway line, between Kem and Saroka. Eventually he expressed himself as satisfied with the territory we had mapped out for him. Nicoli was informed of the 'hunting trip' and given instructions to meet the case.

The nature of the reports on Tüsenhausen's movements was not unexpected. He had travelled from village to village, questioning the inhabitants on political subjects and their attitude towards the British. Angered at the information he gathered or disappointed at the lack of satisfactory results, he abruptly attempted a dash towards the frontier. This was anticipated, so that when he made a detour to avoid Panozero he and his servant were halted by a patrol which had been awaiting him and now asked for his permit.

While the leader of the patrol was reading the pass the Baron attempted to reach his revolver, but was persuaded to desist from physical resistance by the presentation of a bayonet point to his throat. This, however, did not prevent him from exercising his vocal powers upon the soldiers, and in his arguments against interference he employed every means from abuse and bullying to bribes. But it was all of no avail; he was disarmed and brought back to Kem under escort.

Nicoli was instructed to have him released when he reached the first town guard post, and restore his revolver and rifle. Upon regaining his liberty the Baron promptly came round to our office to protest against the 'high-handed' action of the Karelians and demanded that the men who had arrested him be shot! We assured him that they would receive the treatment they deserved, adding that it might be dangerous to shoot them at the moment. He took all this quite literally and even was

'The White House', Kem, 1919

encouraged to bring out the hackneyed story of a widespread plot to murder us all, this time with the variation that we were to be destroyed "in our beds".

Questioned as to what sport he had met with he was vague regarding the extent of his bag. We did not press the question but pretended to be quite interested in two fine fox skins he had with him. We politely refrained from commenting on the fact that they were cured, also that we knew where he had bought them and the price he had paid.

There were rumours of an advance to the south by the allied forces, under General Price, in the spring when the snow and ice had melted, and preparations for this move now occupied much of our time and ingenuity; accommodation had to be found for the troops, while stores and all the usual details of transport had to be arranged. At the same time we had to seek new Headquarters for the Karelian Regiment and the District Office, as General Maynard and his Staff were moving to Kem and our very comfortable house had been judged suitable for their occupation. We accepted eviction philosophically when we were fortunate enough to find a large, three-storied house in the town. This building near the cathedral was named 'The White House' and stood alone in its own gardens, isolated from other buildings by a small river crossed by a wooden bridge. The absence of sounds of shunting engines at night was a welcome change.

Amongst the various transport animals arriving in Kem were some South American mules – fine animals averaging sixteen hands, they occasioned excited comment in the town, such hybrids never having been seen before in this part of the world. Mickey thought them a joke, and their ears and tails caused him endless amazement. He was still more surprised to find that they were not intended to be eaten. His way of putting it was "No Maconachie?" When one of the mules showed its paces by trying the traditional hand-balancing act he danced and shouted with excitement; but he would not go too near these "half-devils". The mules were not a success; they never became accustomed to vehicles nor did they thrive in the climate.

Chapter 13

Petition to King George V

Towards the end of February, to our great satisfaction, we were able finally to refute all the warnings we had received over a period of months regarding the alleged intention of the Karelians to mutiny.

A deputation of twenty headmen representing all the Karelian towns and villages called at our offices led by one Teitove [G. Titov], a woollen manufacturer from Petrograd, who had with great difficulty returned to his native district especially for the purpose. These men were obviously not of the peasant class from which our soldiers were mainly drawn, but were educated people including university tutors, engineers, business men, and even a few who had returned from Australia and America.

They wished to present to His Majesty King George V a petition praying to be taken under the protection of the British flag. After long and careful consideration they had now summarised the reasons for their decision, and these were set forth in a document of which the following is the very literal translation made at the time:

> To Colonel Woods, of the British Service,
> Commanding the Karelian Voluntary Regiment.
>
> For representation of the following request to
> HIS MAJESTY THE KING OF GREAT BRITAIN

In the name of all the Karelian Population, and as the result of many meetings and discussions, we have the great honour to forward to YOUR MAJESTY, the following:

Before our Home Country was invaded by the White Guard Finns Karelia was for several centuries under the Rule of Russia.
The Revolution which has expired has not given anything at all to alleviate the situation. We expected much to come from this source.

After that, the Border of Karelia was forced and invaded by White Guards (Finns and Bolsheviks), with the idea to rob Karelia and put us under Finland. Then we went to the Commander of British Forces in Murmansk and received rifles and ammunition, and with our little force drove out the enemy who were a great many times stronger than we were.

Karelia on its own is a very small country, being bordered on the West by Finnland [*sic*] on the South by River Svere [Svir], on the East by Onega Lake and River and White Sea and on the North the Arctic Ocean.

Karelia is thickly wooded and has many lakes and rivers in which there are many large rapids and waterfalls, and also a lot of various valuable minerals.

It is centuries that Karelia has been under Russian Rule and slavery. Russia having all the power over Karelia was holding her in darkness, preventing any education and sucking all the goods out of us and Karelia never had any benefit from them. To live together with Russia, we cannot, and point blank refuse to do so. With Finnland [*sic*], which in a very low way attempted to govern our Home-land, after having robbed our villages, taking away our last penny, to be friends is an impossibility.

We, the Population of Karelia, wish to thank HIS MAJESTY from the very bottom of our hearts for the aid he has given us in driving the White Guard Finns out of our beloved Country. We all desire, from the bottom of our hearts for the British Government to take us under their protection, giving us the right to govern Karelia as we desire. Delegates from all parts of Karelia wish to visit England and to let

Britain know the History of Karelia and how the Country is at present.

> We do beseech the British to take Karelia as a British Protectorate, as every Power is tearing Karelia to pieces.
>
> This petition is laid down very much curtailed but we would like to lay before you all our requests once more, with all particulars, providing and certifying our requests with the signatures of the People in Karelia, which we would like to present to YOUR MAJESTY if YOUR MAJESTY would grant.
>
> We, the undersigned, have been selected by the Delegates of Karelia*

I agreed to forward the Karelians' petition by official channels, and sent it to Brigadier-General Price as the next senior officer. He, like myself, had no experience in such matters; however, the document was duly forwarded to General Maynard with a covering note, and the GOC despatched it to London.

Unfortunately some inkling of the existence of this petition and its despatch to London had leaked out in Kem. Attempts were made to

* Woods has transcribed this letter from the original English translation. He also retained the Russian version of the letter in his private papers, which reveals some inaccuracies in the translation. According to the Russian document, the signatures were as follows (the first three names are handwritten, the remaining eleven are typed). The reference to Aleksandrovskii county [*uezd*] is to the formal pre-revolutionary name of the Murmansk administritive area (i.e. the Kola peninsula, north of Karelia).

Major	P. Lezhev
	G. Lezhev
	S. Peterson

From the localities [*volosti*] of Kem' and Aleksandrovskii districts [*uezdy*] occupied by the Finnish Legion Captain Ivo Akhava [Ivo Ahava]

Representatives from the localities of Kem' district

Kondokskaya district	[Name unreadable]
Maslozerskaya district	Mikhail Pakhtev'
Tungudskaya district	A. Evtyufin'
	N. Godeev'
Ukhtinskaya district	Aleksei Popov'
Yushkozerskaya district	G. Titov'
Pogosskaya district	G. Popov'
	F. Nikiforov'
Voknavolotskaya district	Fedor Pertuev'
	Kiril' Bogdanov'

ascertain the exact terms from both Mende and myself, but we said we did not know what the Karelians wanted as we never read communications addressed to other people, and suggested that they should ask Gregori who would probably tell them all they required to know. This suggestion was not acted upon.

Another person who did not take a very favourable view of the situation was Major Battaillard, the French Intelligence officer; this was most noticeable in the sudden change in his attitude towards us, which altered from good-natured banter to one of frigid politeness.

In the course of a few days General Maynard travelled down to Kem from Murmansk, to inform us that the scheme was impracticable and would not be accepted by the British Government. In support of this contention he propounded several cogent arguments; nevertheless I thought that an interest in Murmansk, the only open port in the Arctic during the winter months, might possibly outweigh the geographic difficulties, more especially as it was increasingly plain that the Murmansk Army unaided could not hope to succeed against the Bolsheviks, and also that Karelia would make a useful buffer state in the north. Incidentally a workable gold-mine close to the railway in southern Karelia, deposits of gold, silver and lead, and hundreds of square miles of virgin forest with plenty of water power seemed to offer attractions from the commercial point of view.

Shortly afterwards a well-known diplomat [Lindley], representing the Foreign Office, came out from England to deal with the Karelian petition. Warned in advance of the time of his arrival at Kem, I went to meet him on the station. A tall, slim figure, clean-shaven and with hair greying at the temples, he came across the railway lines smiling and with outstretched hand. His first greeting was:

"Well, Colonel Woods, is this another Irish leg-pull?"

I hastily disclaimed responsibility; but I do not think he was entirely convinced by my denial. However, he informed me that the Government had carefully considered all aspects of the position and reluctantly come to the conclusion that it was impossible to accept Karelia as a British protectorate. He mentioned that the presentation of the petition had occasioned much annoyance to some of our allies, by whom I was blamed as the instigator of "the British plot to seize Karelia".

He asked me to inform the Karelians of the Government's decision. I objected to this for two reasons: firstly, I maintained that he was better fitted to sugar the pill, and that as the spokesman of the Government a formal reply from him would be expected to the Karelian's formal application; and secondly, I had no wish to witness the disappointment which I know the British decision would inflict on them. Hence I did not attend the meeting which was convened to receive the Government envoy and hear his message.

I cannot pretend that my own disappointment was not almost as keen as that of the Karelians'; also, I feared that this refusal to accept the Karelian offer might affect their loyalty to the Allies in future operations. But the palliative must have been well used, for the Karelians never altered in their friendly attitude towards us, nor did their respect for British authority abate in the slightest degree. Nevertheless it was obvious that they were bitterly disappointed.

Their antipathy to Russian control must have been deep seated, and every possible avenue seemed to be explored by their leaders to obtain some kind of independence. Hence I was much surprised some few weeks later to receive the following document from their leaders for transmission to the British authorities. It was couched in different language and bore many more signatures than the first document I had received. It was translated from Finnish into Russian and then into English. The clear translation for this is as follows:–

> To, General Officer Commanding in Chief the Allied Forces, Murmansk.
>
> Sir,
> We, the undersigned members of the representative Committee elected by the Karelian People, beg to be allowed to submit for your consideration the results of our discussion of the letter received from you in answer to the petition which we addressed to General Officer Commanding 237th Brigade.
>
> We regret that the tenour [*sic*] of your answer is not such as to foster a properly contented state of mind in the Karelian People. The contents of the letter hardly appear to be founded upon principles either of democracy or of the autonomy of individual races; although the Allied Governments have solemnly declared that these principles are the basis of their present policy. To one it would almost seem, who was unacquainted with the writer of the letter, that he was not fully

cognisant of the intense patriotism of the Karelians and of their ardent desire for freedom.

> In view of the general tone of the letter, we deem it expedient more explicitly to express our point of view, and we have the honour to request that you will be kind enough to reconsider the following points:–
>
> (1) The committee of which we are members has been selected at a meeting of representative delegates from the villages of the whole country, and has been given full power to conduct all the affairs of the Karelian People, for the conduct of which affairs it has been made responsible.
>
> (2) As far as this committee can gather from the Press, the Allied Governments invited to the projected Conference on the island of Principo not only representatives of the various recognised Governments (in Russia) but also delegates from such political and national groups as had at that time no political individuality. For this reason the committee wished to appoint a representative of the Karelian Nation to attend the proposed conference.
>
> (3) In March of last year, when an understanding was reached between Leaders of the Allied Forces and the Murmansk Soviet, by which the Allied Forces were to occupy the country in order to stem the flowing tide of Russia's national foes, the Karelians were asked by the Soviet whether they would agree to this step being taken. The Karelians assented to this proposal, and, at the same time, an arrangement was made by which the Murmansk Soviet should retain the authority which it held at that time. But when, at a later date, the temporary Government was formed and a deputy-governor appointed, it was done without consulting either the Karelian People (as if the Karelian People were incapable of assisting in these two operations) or the Allies. In our opinion it was essential that, as the Karelian People was not consulted, the Murmansk Soviet should have consulted the Leaders of the Allied Forces.
>
> (4) The proposals made by the Allied Governments for the conference at Principo dispel every doubt as to the readiness of the Allies to

recognise the feasibility of a meeting with the Russian Soviet Government. The Karelian Committee trust that, in these circumstances there was nothing very ridiculous in their hope that they, too, might be permitted to send representatives to that conference.

(5) In your letter the statement is made that the contemporary elections for the District Councils in the Kem area give the inhabitants an opportunity to choose such representatives as they really wish to act for them. We imagine that this statement which has no foundation upon solid fact, was made because you have been misinformed as to the true nature of these elections; for their organisation was not such as to ensure that the future District Councils could be considered to be fairly elected and really to reflect the opinion and desires of the electorate, as it should do. The Official advertisement of the elections implied, though it did not actually state, that the business in these District Councils would be transacted in Russian and not, as it should be, in Karelian. The Karelians have repeatedly asked to have all notices in connection with the elections printed in Karelian, but without success. For this reason those Karelians who neither speak nor understand Russian cannot possibly acquire all the information necessary for their full participation in the elections. We ask, Sir, how such a method of election, in which we are thus prevented from taking our just part, can be expected to express the will of the whole electorate? It follows that as these District Councils are chosen by one section of the electorate only, it has at heart the welfare of that section alone. Assuming that it is desired to establish a District Council which will fairly and equably represent the electorate, it is surely imperative that all the inhabitants of twenty years and over, and all the volunteers who have served in the army, be not only accorded the right to vote but also afforded every facility for the exercise of this right. To ensure this, it is necessary that all the notices in connection with the election be printed in the language of the people, that is Karelian; and that the same language be used in the debates of the District Councils. We should like to add that, in view of the fact that practically the entire population of the country speaks only Karelian, these demands are not exaggerated.

In conclusion, we have the honour to point out that we have never asked nor expected the Allies to concern themselves with the internal affairs of Karelia, so long as we are left free from external interference. While Karelia rejoices in this happy condition, it lies with us, the members of the representative Committee, to guide the Karelian People and to safeguard their interests to the utmost of our ability. Previously the Government of the Tsar, and of those to whom he delegated his authority, absolutely prevented the least attempt at the development of Karelian nationality, education and agricultural business. Our dearest wish is that the Allies will not support the old regime in preventing Karelia from seizing this opportunity of setting her house in order,

Kem 25/3/19.

It was signed by elected representatives, whose names, for obvious reasons, cannot be published.*

I was not in sympathy with the action taken at the time, and I have seen no reason to alter my opinion since. The action taken by the authorities on receipt of this document created a very dangerous situation, considering the tempers of those most nearly concerned. The GOC informed General Yermoloff of this correspondence, and proposed that he should interview this representative Committee himself.

The Karelian chief headmen were summoned to meet the Russian Governor-General one morning, in his private train at Kem station. Care was taken that none of them carried arms. General Yermoloff received them in state, allowing them all to stand to attention whilst he addressed them. No doubt this reception reminded them of pre-war days, when the Russian official took to himself the authority of an archangel and did little to promote a friendly atmosphere. After listening to a severe reprimand for their mutinous behaviour in expressing themselves at all they were asked to state their grievances, if any. Their ambitions must have been very frankly stated, for the meeting ended in great heat on the part of the Governor-General and a grim stony coldness on

* The signatories of this letter, according to the original typewritten English translation in the Woods' papers were: "Members of the Representative Committee, Alexanor Maskevitch, Simon Epiphanoff, Peter Lejeff, Ivan Ahava, Ivan Gavriloff". Again, some of these names have been inaccurately rendered in translation. The members of the Karelian National Committee were in fact Iivo Ahava (from Ukhta district), Egor Lesonen (Voknavalok), Aleksander Maskievich (Rugozero), Semen Epifanov (Rugozero), and Ivan Gavrilov (Kesten'ga). Major Grigorii Lezhev and Captain Peter Lezhev of the Karelian Regiment were given a special mandate by the February Assembly to participate in the National Committee. See O.V. Itkonen, *Muurmannin soumalainen legioona: varustettu kartalla ja sarjalla liitekuvia* (Helsinki: Kansanvalta, 1927), p. 90.

the part of the Karelians. It did nothing to shake their convictions when they were told that they were mutinous swine, dogs of no pedigree and that the whole breed would be shot, and what caused them most uneasiness, that the British officers would be replaced by Russian. This last threat disturbed them so much that it was found necessary to drop a hint to the Governor-General that he was under the protection of the British, and that those wearing the uniform were therefore responsible for his safety while in Kem.

A Committee of the headmen appealed to me for guidance as to their future policy. But, much as I sympathised with them, I could not advise upon their political aspect of the situation without compromising General Maynard's intentions; hence I told them to wait until the position became a little more clear, and suggested that in the meantime they should organise their system of local and national representation to include the use of the ballot-box. I advocated the formation of a National Savings Bank and a trading society on cooperative lines, this being suitable in a country where there were no class distinctions; the few private traders could be employed as managers or senior executives in the venture. These schemes appealed to their thrifty instincts, and they agreed that by organising both the people and the resources of the country they would be in a much stronger position to deal with events.

We had evidence that Karelia's political situation was interesting to other countries when two Finnish officers were brought in by a Karelian patrol which had picked them up near our southern frontier. When challenged, these Finns said that they were envoys from their Government to the British commander; but they had no papers to prove their story, and we sent them to Murmansk.

Shortly after this a Finnish girl, about twenty and dressed in men's clothing, was arrested up-country and escorted to Kem. As a result of cross-examination we found that she was a well-known prostitute from Helsingfors, chosen and sent by the Finnish authorities to ascertain the exact situation in Karelia and to "make friends with the British Commander of the Karelians, who would not shoot her as a spy". This girl had travelled hundreds of miles alone through a hostile country, mostly on foot and in arctic weather, carrying her food in a rucksack – a terrible ordeal. Her papers were so arranged as to show that she was a financial defaulter and ostensibly a fugitive from judgement of the Finnish courts, but taken with her own story under examination they were not convincing. After a few days close arrest she was conducted back to the border, and, under a white flag, handed over to a Finnish outpost with the advice not to repeat her adventure on pain of death.

Chapter 14

Reorganisation of Regiment

At the first sign of approaching spring the railway engineers began to dynamite the ice on the river at numerous points above the bridge in order to minimise the danger to its structure when the thaw proper set in. It was not long before we saw how necessary these precautions were. When the cracking became extensive massive slabs of ice were driven over the broken edge on to the surface of the fixed ice, piling up into great blocks forty feet above the level of the river and over the banks, threatening momentarily to overwhelm the bridge.

It was an anxious and strenuous time for the engineers. After a full day's work they had frequently to carry on far into the night by the light of flares, clambering perilously over the loose and treacherous undulations to place their explosives where they could be most effectively used. Several of these men were badly injured owing to subsidence of the packs upon which they were engaged in preparing positions for charges.

Despite all their efforts the ice accumulated above the bridge until the topmost blocks came over the parapet on to the permanent way. The pressure must have been terrific, and the total destruction of the bridge seemed inevitable; but by almost superhuman efforts on the part of the Russian engineers, aided by our own Sappers, the danger was at length averted. One of the engineers lost his life when the mass suddenly gave way, crushing him against a pier. The roar of the released ice blocks could be heard for miles, and it was many days before the sound of collisions between the floes and rumblings over the rapids diminished in volume. After an interval of a week the noise was resumed when the ice floating down the river from the great lakes reached Kem, its advent heralded by a sharp fall in temperature which continued for about a fortnight. On some of the floating ice were fragments of the winter road, which could be identified by the small trees and poles used as guideposts still erect on their surfaces.

On one of these miniature icebergs a small and terrified dog had been marooned, and it was with considerable difficulty and risk that he was rescued by some of the Karelians who, carrying long poles were extraordinarily skilful in the use they made of the swiftly moving pieces as stepping-stones to reach their objective, selecting with unerring judgement those capable of bearing their weight.

Before the ice had broken on the river the inhabitants of Kem had sawn blocks from the virgin ice clear of the paths and sleigh roads to fill their cellars, which acted as excellent refrigerators during the summer heat. Even in the hottest weather at the end of the summer the ground was never thawed out to a depth of more than five or six feet, so that the ice kept well below ground.

The intensive propaganda employed by the Russians in Murmansk against the Karelians was all too fruitful in results with General Maynard; but notwithstanding the dislike for the Karelians and all their works which it engendered in the minds of the GOC and his Staff the services of the regiment were indispensable to the Allies, who were now acquiring extended lines of communication incident on General Price's advance to the south. But Headquarters' suspicion of the Karelians was no greater than the mistrust they [the Karelians] entertained towards both the Russians and the Allied Command; so that I was compelled to report to General Maynard that the complete unit was averse to any move from the Kem river so long as the Murmansk Army were in the neighbourhood, fearing as they did an attempt on the part of the Russians to occupy Karelia in the absence of its fighting men.

The men of the Regiment were always well informed regarding the attitude not only of the Russian Staff, but also of each individual member of the Allied Staff at Murmansk. Thus when General Maynard issued orders for the reorganisation of the Regiment these had to be explained and my own personal guarantee given for the General's good faith in dividing the unit into the new formations.

They also viewed with grave suspicion the appointment of a Russian officer, who had been ordered to report to the Karelian regiment for duty, in an endeavour to begin upon a system of replacement of British by Russian officers. It was mainly due to the tact and unusually alert understanding of Count Bennigsen that he was at first tolerated and later respected by the Karelians for his gallantry, human understanding and gift of leadership with the Olonetz [Olonets] or 1st Battalion.

The Regiment was reconstituted to provide, in addition to the Olonetz Battalion,

(a) A mobile fighting battalion, to consist mainly of young men and new recruits;
(b) Pioneers;
(c) Garrison guards;
(d) Frontier guards; and
(e) A labour battalion.

These units were officered as follows:

Major H. S. Filsell	Cmdg 1st Service Battalion
Capt E. C. Lance	Adjutant, 1st Service Battalion
Capt F. Smith	Transport Officer & QM
Capt J. B. Noel	Company Commander
Capt L. J. Graham-Toler	Company Commander
Capt F. L. Allan	Platoon Commander
Lieut F. W. Hill	Interpreter
Lieut D. Drew	MG & LG Officer
Lieut S. Forbes	Platoon Commander (acting Company Commander)
Lieut A. Pryer	Platoon Commander (Assistant Adjutant)
Lieut J. Leadbeater	Platoon Commander
Capt J. R. Harmer	Frontier Guard
Lieut J. Thompson	Frontier Guard
Capt E. H. Heaton	Garrison Guard*

* *Author's note: Although officially appointed to command of the Garrison Guard, Heaton was detained up-country until nearly the end of the campaign, and this unit was in charge of Lieut J. S. Long.*

Lieut E. D. Mackay	Garrison Guard

Major W. H. Harrison	Labour Batn
Lieut W. M. Robertson	Labour Batn
Major E. Rait-Kerr	Pioneer Company
Capt Stranack	Pioneer Company
Lieut J. Mills	River Transport
Lieut W. Butler	Regimental Adjutant
Lieut R. S. Robinson	Records
Lieut N. E. Mende	Interpreter
Lieut W. Little	Adjt Labour Batn
Lieut A. C. Thatcher	RQM

The Olonetz Battalion had been doing excellent reconnaissance work under Major Drake-Brockman, and had successfully carried out attacks on White Finn villages and garrisons in south-west Karelia. But the new "fighting battalion" was inaugurated in circumstances highly unfavourable to recruiting potentialities, and I was aware that a selected number of young men whose presence we could well have spared in the event of trouble had been ordered to "volunteer". The majority of the men, including the best soldiers and scouts, either joined other units or drifted away to their homes to harrow and prepare their farms for crops (owing to the shortness of the summer, ploughing and sowing were done in the autumn, and when the snow disappeared the young shoots were already through the ground); but each man retained his arms.

These adverse conditions were discouraging enough; but the last chance of achievement was finally dissipated when GHQ, with what can only be described as complete lack of judgement, sent a most unsuitable officer from Murmansk to command this battalion [i.e. Karelian Volunteer Battalion].

Major Filsell was in many respects an excellent officer, and one with whom I should have been pleased to serve in an English regiment; but ten years service in the King's African Rifles from which he had only recently arrived did not fit him to command these men of the Arctic. The history of the Regiment and a résumé of events since the arrival of the Allies in North Russia were given him so that he might be able to orient himself mentally to his new command; he had Captain Fryer as Adjutant, and Nicoli, Gregori and Lieut Forbes, of the Grenadiers, were appointed company commanders; but with all these provisions for smooth administration he never understood his men.

Filsell did not know a single word of the language, and it was therefore to be regretted that he was impatient with the Serbian interpreter, and seemed unable to realise the futility of trying to train men for ceremonial parades when they would be needed for very different work immediately, or to appreciate that it was the goodwill of the Karelian leaders alone which prevented the entire battalion from disappearing.

In these circumstances friction was to be expected. But it was not long before the lack of harmony became so serious that Nicoli and Gregori resigned, while Fryer applied for a transfer. Some fifty men deserted, being unable to resign, and those who remained did so only because they had no homes to go to. They were regarded and spoken of by their CO as "niggers" – a word they recognised – and he refused to have the Karelian officers in his Mess, while Fryer was ostracised because he had been a ranker.

The men were made to wear ammunition boots, which hurt their feet, and do PT drills and parades more frequently than Kitchener's Army during the days of intensive training. Musketry instruction they understood and liked; but these hard-bitten foresters, fishermen and timber men could not understand the necessity for 'physical jerks' or the ill-concealed contempt in which they were held by their commanding officer. Altogether it was not a matter of great surprise to me that desertions occurred frequently, and that the sick parade became the chief event in the day's routine.

To add to the difficulties of preparing this battalion for active service the barracks were visited by two Bolshevik agents, who appeared in the guise of United States seamen, from the crew of Admiral McCully's flagship, which had put into Kem port. One of these men, who was able to speak Russian, had informed the Karelian soldiers that the regimental badge was the insignia of slavery; that the Irish soldiers had all risen and murdered their officers; and that this example had been followed by thousands of their English and Scots comrades. They were exhorted in the light of this information to tear their cap-badges from their uniform and trample on them.

These "Americans" made presents to the Karelians of chocolate, cigarettes and a case of whiskey. Three of the more foolish became sufficiently intoxicated to destroy their caps, for which they were exceedingly sorry after they had been dealt with by the Regimental Police in a typical and suitable manner.

I reported the matter to GHQ, and, with Major Meiklejohn of the Intelligence and two Karelian soldiers, went to interview Admiral

McCully at Popoff. The US Flagship was one of "Ford's Fleet", built for use and entirely devoid of luxurious furnishings. Bare pipes, valves and screw-taps all over the steel decks and bulkheads gave the ship a most workmanlike appearance. The Admiral received us very courteously, and expressed himself as being shocked to learn that any member of his crew could be guilty of treason against the British. At our request a full muster of the ship's crew was mustered and paraded for identification.

The composition of this ship's company was a surprise to me and differed greatly from that of a US destroyer in which I had once been a guest. It was made up of many different nationalities: Japanese, Chinese, Portuguese, Spaniards, Negroes, Mexicans, Swedes, Hindus, Malays, Polynesians and many whose origin was, to us, obscure. The two Karelian soldiers were unable to identify any of the men before us; but after a good deal of enquiry it was found that two men were absent in the sick-bay, or elsewhere. It was ascertained that one of these was a Pole who had lived in Glasgow for some years. I requested Admiral McCully to hand this man over to us, but he refused, promising, however, to deal with the fellow himself.

We advised the Admiral that we always had a warm welcome for friends, but that Kem would be out of bounds for members of his ship's company other than officers or men bearing passes signed by the Admiral himself. He quite understood the necessity for these measures and agreed to restrict the crew's liberty accordingly.

I have often admired the ingenuity of sailors, but it occurred to me that even this must have been strained when orders had to be conveyed without confusion to a body of men of which about forty per cent did not understand the English language. We asked the Admiral how he overcame this difficulty, but he assured us that nothing could be more simple!

We never learned what action was taken by the Admiral in the case of the two Bolshevik agents, but I personally hoped that the abstraction of a case of whiskey from his stores would add zest to their punishment.

As mentioned in the list of officers now holding commissions in the Karelian Regiment (see above) the Garrison Company was commanded by Lieut John Sullivan Long, who invariably received his full baptismal names by virtue of his own stature and slimness. He was so tall that it would have seemed incongruous to call him by his short surname. Long had to remarkable extent the entertaining gift of being able to train wild animals and birds. At the beginning of spring, he climbed the steeple of the cathedral in Kem to secure a young jackdaw from the parental nest. He kept this fledgling in his room, feeding it and nursing it until it was old enough to fly, by which time he had taught it to eat from his lips, come to call, and from its perch on his shoulder whistle "Pop goes the weasel"; it could also give a creditable imitation of a piccolo solo from a gramophone record.

When Long rode on his rounds visiting the various posts Jack always accompanied him. Sometimes he left his master's shoulder to chase an insect or another bird, but he would always return again regardless of all distraction or noise. Often when Long was in HQ Mess we would notice that Jack was absent, and when we enquired as to his whereabouts the answer would be: "Oh, he's just visiting his friends." The meal finished, Long would put his head out of the window and give a peculiar whistle; then, out of a group of noisy relations in the cathedral belfry, Jack would come skimming down and glide down through the window to alight on his master's plate or his shoulder.

The establishment of GHQ with all its impedimenta and personnel at Kem station was a welcome event which added much to the social life of the place. Hospitality and willing cooperation replaced the long-distance paper battle in which we had been sporadically engaged hitherto. True, the usual enquiries regarding the number of cases of 'plum and apple' in stock continued; but the replies now could be, and were, couched in language suitable to the occasion and involving less risk of a court martial to the interrogated when delivered personally to the sender.

Colonel T. C. R. Moore, the officer responsible for transport and supplies to the civilians and troops of all nations comprising our force, did not allow his work to get the better of his unfailing sense of humour. I shall always remember with gratitude his help and patience in dealing with ever changing numbers and inadequate transport.

A few minutes' personal conversation with Colonel Schuster, too, produced better results than could have been achieved by reams of irritating correspondence.

Major Mackesy, familiarly known to his many friends as "P. J.", was no stranger to us, having visited us in March, and out of his abundant sense of humour and efficiency was able to give valuable advice and assistance in solving the many problems which arose almost daily out of the reorganisation of the Karelians.

Major Grove, Major Steel, Lieut Rogerson, and indeed every, member of the Staff proved the best of comrades in circumstances which brought out the true qualities of each individual taking part in the operations. The only surprise I experienced was to find in General Maynard the most vociferous 'dummy' at bridge I had ever encountered!

When the ice had cleared sufficiently another useful – and cheerful – addition was made to the British personnel in Kem by the arrival of HMS *Attentive*, a light cruiser under the command of Captain Altham, which had been at Kem port during part of the previous summer. On this occasion her stay was brief, and she was succeeded by our old friends on HMS *Nairana*, with her seaplanes.

Chapter 15

Onega Operations

The Karelians had raised sufficient funds by the sale of furs and the manufacture of cart-wheels to purchase an almost derelict 30 h.p. motor-boat. This was intended to tow laden boats on the lower reaches of the river. The thirty-five foot hull was in good condition, but this could not have been said for the German engine which had not received attention or care for some considerable time. However, the chief engineer from the *Nairana* and the mechanics kindly undertook the reconditioning of the motor for us. Many of the parts had to be replaced and tested before these experts pronounced themselves satisfied with the engine's performance. But when it was finally passed as serviceable we hired the boat on Sundays for trips on the river and round the small islands near the estuary, where there was some rough shooting.

On these occasions the boat's crew were two naval ratings, and the guests usually Commander Johnston and a few brother officers, the chief engineer, and the pilot from the *Nairana*. These officers frequently provided the liquid part of the day's rations, and they inaugurated a competition regarding the concoction of the most fearsome – if not always the most palatable – cocktail. (If my memory does not betray me, Butler, the Regimental Adjutant, was the winner). But this was not the first story of mixed drinks to have a fatal ending.

One Sunday, when Lieut John Sullivan Long and his friend Jack were guests aboard the *Korelski*, the jackdaw insisted upon visiting each person seated in the cockpit and taking a sip from his glass. After a few rounds he retired to his master's shoulder and fell asleep, but was soon roused by the buzzing of a large yellow insect which was flying about in the cockpit of the launch. He shook his feathers and gave chase. The fly eluded him and made for the shore, with Jack in pursuit. They followed a zigzag course close to the surface of the river – too close, for poor Jack touched with the tips of his wings in the choppy water, and before we could put about and reach him he was drowned. Long did not speak, but he carried the little body home with him.

In the spring and early summer our advance to the south under General Price (or Uncle Dudley, as he was now affectionately known to his friends) was progressing well against considerable difficulties, not all of which were created by the action of the enemy.

From the Archangel front, on the eastern side of the White Sea, came news of hard fighting and mutinies. A Bolshevik force was attacking from the south, led by a woman known as Bloody Rosa*. This lady made a practice of dealing with prisoners herself, mutilating them unspeakably before they were put to death, and her devilish habits had made her name feared throughout the whole of North Russia.

A Russian battalion under British command had mutinied at Onega and murdered every officer with the exception of Colonel Andrews, who had been taken as a prisoner to Moscow (this officer was released by Lenin after some months' imprisonment and returned to England. In about 1923 he was killed in a garage jointly owned by the late Brigadier-General F. P. Crozier and himself).

These items of news had a disturbing effect upon the men of the Murmansk Army creating additional anxiety for those responsible for the operations. The undermining of the morale in the Russian troops under General Price's command would have been an easy enough task at any time, and recent developments at Archangel deprived them of any desire for fighting they may previously have felt. Although they had not as yet reached the stage of mutiny they were dour and silent, with no evidence of the relatively high spirits exhibited by our troops in France even when wet, dirty and exhausted.

General Price has since told me that his successes in the south were almost entirely due to the handful of Britishers, the Canadians, and the Karelian Olonetz battalion which never let him down.

* Rosa Zemliachka (Zalkind) (1876-1947), Political Commissar of the Bolshevik Thirteenth Army, later a prominent member of Stalin's regime.

Onega, being in the hands of a strong Bolshevik force, constituted a serious threat to General Price's communications, as the railway was a mere ninety miles distant with little or no opposition to overcome en route. A direct road to Saroka along the southern shore of the White Sea through Sumski [Sumskii] Posad would have permitted a mobile force to move swiftly and attack the railway, which was particularly vulnerable by reason of its many wooden bridges. Hence I was pleased to receive orders from the GOC early in July to proceed to Sumski Posad, which was a large village on the Suma river, with instructions to organise the inhabitants with a view to holding the road from Onega against any advance of the Bolsheviks towards the west. He could not afford to give me any troops from Kem, but as a result of some persuasion I was allowed to take a platoon of Serbians, and managed to 'wangle' a section of howitzers, under Captain Luck. I had with me Lieut Mende as interpreter and Gregori, who had volunteered to come. We also appropriated two Lewis gun teams from the Karelian Garrison Guard, so that altogether we felt quite optimistic.

Our land forces were later augmented by two high-powered submarine chasers, each carrying a three-pounder and a machine-gun. These were to cooperate with us inshore on the White Sea; but unfortunately they were never both in commission at once owing partly to recurrent engine trouble and partly to their enormous fuel consumption. They had two 45 h.p. engines each, and we were fortunate to have one of them working on one engine when required.

Sumski Posad was a picturesque village of the usual timber houses, built on each side of the river and connected by two bridges, one across some rapids at the top end and the other opposite the church at the north. The west bank rose steeply from the river and on its crest the church tower commanded a view for many miles in three directions over the flat countryside, which was cleared of forest growth and appeared to be extensively cultivated. To the east, however, the woods were only cut back to a distance of about a mile, and it was from this direction therefore that we might expect unpleasantness.

When the usual precautions had been taken we commenced a house to house canvass, but our chances of finding likely recruits were not bright in a district which had already been combed by Colonel Krugliakoff for his 'Partizans' and conscripted by the Murmansk Army. We did however, succeed in impressing some really hefty women and one man whom Luck said we had "rifled the graveyard to find".

Nevertheless our efforts in this direction enabled us to fill in the enquiry wired from GHQ – "What is your strength of recruits?" – by replying truthfully: "One old man has flocked to the Standard."

I asked Gregori to send for some of the old members of the Karelian regiment now in their homes, and within a few days twenty-five cheerful and hardy men had appeared, ready and keen to begin on another campaign.

In our efforts to raise recruits Mende and I had travelled up the river to a small village where we had heard that there were some men still living. This we found to be the case; and it was not long before we discovered the reason for their exemption by our precessors. Every man, woman and child in the entire village of 400 inhabitants – and there were many children amongst them – was infected with syphilis, for the most part in advanced stages. The appearance of most of the inhabitants was too horrible to describe; indeed, so repulsive were these poor wretches to look on that Mende and I were actually sick, and missed several meals before we could rid ourselves of the nausea induced by the revolting sight.

Gregori afterwards told us that there had never been any medical service in this part of the country, in which even the priests did not seem to be interested. He said that it was a vicious circle; that incest had been responsible for the disease, and that now the disease was perforce responsible for the incest.

Our scouts had done their work well and cleared the country up to a point in the Onega road where a natural position afforded remarkable advantages. The track lay for some miles between swamp on one side and the sea on the other; it passed through two large outcrops of rock overgrown with shrubs and small trees, which gave excellent cover for our Lewis guns and riflemen. Scouts reported the approach of an enemy force which they estimated at 500, including cavalry. Making suitable arrangements, therefore, with Lt Commander Johnston, who had succeeded in coaxing the engines of his chaser into action, we waited patiently for the attackers to appear.

It was surprising that any person pretending to be a leader of men could be so reckless or careless as the commander of the Bolshevik force which advanced along the Onega road. He had neither scouts nor advance guard, but came on slowly along the seven foot road with about thirty mounted men in front and a rabble of infantry immediately at their heels.

Sending the agreed signal to Johnston from the rear of the seaward hill we waited, holding our fire with difficulty, until the mounted men were about thirty yards distant from the ambush. Then the Lewis guns on either side opened fire, supported by riflemen – and women – who could not miss at such a range.

The result was chaotic. Those of the mounted men who had escaped the first burst of fire turned their horses back into the infantry, trampling the wounded and knocking down the living. Riderless horses added to the confusion by stampeding through the fugitives, who threw down their arms and ran for their lives. There was no way of escape open to them but the long road without a vestige of cover down which they had come, and as they ran Johnston's 3-pounder dropped shell after shell on their line of retreat with deadly effect. Having already taken the ranges of this particular spot he was able to fire very accurately.

It would have been an easy matter to have wiped out every man of the entire enemy force; but I saw a greater advantage in allowing some to escape, so that the story of the debacle might discourage further attempts on the part of the Bolsheviks to attack the railway. Knowing well the Russian peasant's propensity for exaggeration I judged that the effect of this repulse would be great – a surmise which was borne out by reports from our intelligence.

In order to enhance the impression created by this defeat I sent a telegram from Nuchta [Nukhta] over the Government wire to the headman of Luginovski, a village some thirty miles distant, ordering him to prepare accommodation for two British infantry battalions, a squadron of cavalry, two batteries of artillery, a machine-gun company and supply wagons, requiring billets for 95 officers and a suitable camping ground with horse lines conveniently situated. Under the telegraph system operative in Russia at this time a wire sent from one station to another was simultaneously received by every instrument on the entire section, thus my message from Luginovski would be transmitted to Onega, Archangel and elsewhere. Evidently there was no limit to the sphere of reception of this message, which may even have astonished Lenin in Moscow, for some Allied officer whose name was unknown to me and whose strong points were neither discretion nor imagination wired from another outlandish post asking General Maynard where he had obtained the troops referred to!

I hoped that this enquiry would not be accurately interpreted in Onega, and I do not think it was, as the Bolsheviks withdrew all their men on the west of the town, and our scouts encountered only small disconnected parties afterwards.

Having garrisoned the Serbians in Nuchta and placed observation posts in every village up to Onega itself, with a relay service of runners from the most advanced scouts, I considered that we had carried out our instructions, and that further action could not be taken without reinforcements. Our 'chasers' would be of little assistance in an attack on Onega itself, although Johnston was enthusiastically inclined to make the attempt. However, two small monitors [gun boats] approached Onega and indulged in some target practice, during which the enemy took cover in the neighbouring forest, returning to the town when the monitors had steamed away.

The inhabitants' respite was brief. Shortly afterwards Captain Wharton arrived off Onega with a monitor of larger tonnage and, from a long range, dropped a few 15" shells into the town. The rumbling roar of their passage through the air resembled that of an express train crossing a viaduct, and the explosions shook the ground for miles, levelling many houses. An immense crater in front of the church caused that edifice to assume a crazy angle after the fashion of the tower of Pisa.

These bombardments had a demoralising effect upon the population and it was not until several hours after the shape of the monitor had disappeared from the horizon that the people emerged again from hiding. They stood in awe-stricken groups discussing the damage, with little evidence of contemplating immediate reprisals; but as we had no troops available to take advantage of their obvious disorganisation we were compelled to allow this opportunity to pass, merely keeping close observation. But the effect of this preliminary barrage afforded an excellent pointer for future operations.

Chapter 16

Evacuation

Early in August the situation was complicated by the receipt of peremptory orders for the complete evacuation of North Russia by the Allies. This meant that I must make my headquarters in Sumski Posad so as to be in closer touch with Kem and the hundred and one administrative arrangements in the District Command and for the Karelians.

Butler, at Kem, must have had little sleep or rest during this period. Fortunately he was reliable and possessed excellent judgement, taking much of the burden from my shoulders.

Strenuous, too, as this time must have been for GHQ at Murmansk, they seemed unexpectedly to be seized with a spirit of levity, which evinced itself in various ways. One such instance was the despatch to me of an animal which arrived in response to my urgent request for a horse. I had hitherto been using one of Luck's gunner horses; but the new charger was a veritable freak. It had the highest and longest withers I have ever seen on any animal outside the giraffe pen at Regent's Park, a very short and sloping back, with no space for a saddle, ending in a bony rump adorned with a tail about the size of a toy terrier's. This creature of seventeen hands was almost as indecent at the other extremity, having a large fiddle head indifferently supported by a long yew neck. It was wonderfully ribbed and had feet resembling natural snow-shoes. Also, we suspected that the horse was mentally deficient, as it had an insatiable appetite for newspapers and old clothing!

For a time all my remonstrances to GHQ were ignored, although I eventually drew attention to the fact that mounting this animal was a feat which could only be performed from an upstairs window, and suggested that a step-ladder should have been included with the saddlery. We also indented for six feet of hemp rope from which to manufacture a false switch for attachment to its tail as a concession to normal modesty.

My repeated protests to GHQ at last received attention. I received a registered parcel containing Mackesy's compliments and a fresh lemon! The former delighted the horse, while the latter was used in an appropriate manner.

To the disappointment of the inhabitants of Sumski Posad and the surrounding country this equine comedian was concealed in the gunners' lines, and I still availed myself of Luck's charity for a mount, alternating this method of transport with a Ford 1-ton lorry where the dirt roads permitted its use. But these tracks at their best invariably required the services of the spade and pickaxe which were part of the Ford's equipment to extricate us from huge potholes and soft places.

The best road in the district followed the bank of the river Suma for some miles, and it was this one we used when Major Mackesy again visited us on a tour of inspection. On this occasion he brought with him a beautiful and expensive fishing rod and a grand collection of flies, with a view to trying his skill on the salmon.

We found a likely-looking pool, and nearby a rotting punt which was capable of remaining afloat with two passengers for about twelve minutes before sinking. Mackesy set up his tackle and started fishing.

We knew that there were plenty of fish in the pool, for we could see them moving; but they were singularly unenterprising fish, and refused to be tempted by any of the varied and attractive patterns presented by the fisherman. After three fruitless hours' casting Mackesy's patience was exhausted, though his language gathered in strength with each helpful suggestion offered by his audience. Eventually he retired, wet and discouraged.

We cheered him a little and aroused his curiosity by suggesting the use of a Mills [grenade], fished dry (we always carried a few of these in the toolbox of the Ford in case of emergency), but when he realised how we proposed to get results from the water he was horrified. However, although to his credit it must be said that he was entirely out of sympathy with our poaching methods, he was not too much of a purist to refuse his share of the resulting catch.

On our way back Mackesy was not too pleased to see small children snatching fish with ridiculous ease by means of a wire hook.

The people of Sumski Posad employed communal salmon-traps made of withes and cunningly built at the bottom of some rapids near the upper bridge. The fish were cleaned and smoked in huts erected on piles, which lined the river banks and lent an almost Venetian touch to the village.

My billet was in a pretty little cottage belonging to members of the 'Old Religion', the exact tenets of which I could never thoroughly grasp. For some time I was not aware that I had been causing much unhappiness to my hosts by my almost unconscious habit of whistling in the mornings. Now this, according to their belief, was the music of the Devil, and it was therefore the outward and visible sign of my being possessed, body and soul. The family ikons were covered with cloths and the lamps beneath them extinguished. Finally, the local priest visited the house in my absence and went through all the ceremonies of exorcising evil spirits.

Clearly something was seriously amiss, but I had no idea what. Accordingly I asked Gregori, and when he enlightened me as to the cause of their tribulation I refrained from making noises at variance with my host's religious scruples. Hence the priest achieved a success which must have exceeded even his most sanguine expectations.

There appeared to be some superstition regarding whistling all over Russia. Russian soldiers never indulged in this method of enlivening a march; instead they sang, with an appointed soloist and an organised chorus.

Sumski Posad was a pleasant station, affording many advantages. Here we were able to get fresh vegetables, butter, cream, eggs and, from a nearby convent, white raspberries – luxuries which with little exception we had not enjoyed since leaving England. The district had been a prosperous peasant community, each small-holder with his farm within a short distance of the main village as was the case throughout all northern Russia, where isolated farmhouses were rare. In clean and substantially built dwellings, well stocked and furnished, the people were comfortable and contented. Kindly and hospitable, they were strong adherents to the 'Old Religion', as was made evident by the number of wooden crucifixes at prominent places in the neighbourhood, differing from the orthodox in that they had double wooden cross-bars fixed to the base, and coloured cloths fastened to them, notably on special feast days.

Administrative difficulties attending the disposal of stores and the attempted replacement of British personnel by Russian in the Karelian battalions were numerous, and were not simplified by the distances between Headquarters and the various units involved. Heaton, at Uskozero, had many problems, chief of these being the provision of extra river transport; the Karelians were strongly against any concentration of boats in the neighbourhood of Kem, anticipating trouble with the Russians there in the conviction that the latter would attempt to seize all boats as soon as the Allies evacuated the district. This impasse necessitated a hurried journey to Kem by sea in Johnston's chaser, which on this occasion performed in an exemplary manner, allowing me sufficient time at my destination to settle the question of transport, deal with several other urgent matters, and return to Sumski Posad before midnight of the same day.

The reluctance of the Karelians to lend their boats was symptomatic of their state of mind since the reorganisation of the Regiment. They were now quiet and watchful, assuming a serious demeanour quite at variance with the smiling cheerfulness of other days. I did not know if they were aware of General Maynard's proposal to disarm them, a wish he had already expressed to me and had no doubt discussed with certain members of his own Staff; but in any case I could only view the plan with apprehension, and when consulted I gave it as my opinion that it would take six months in time and a British Infantry Division in strength to achieve even partial success in such a project. At the same time I reminded the General of the nature of the country and the character of its people. Greatly to my relief the scheme was abandoned; but whether or not the Karelians had precise knowledge of the General's intentions regarding their proposed disarmament I knew that they were very sensible of his attitude towards them and consequently suspicious of any orders from this source affecting themselves. Hence all such orders had now to be explained by me, and a sort of personal guarantee of their good faith given in order to ensure obedience – a state of affairs I did not consider it desirable to bring to the notice of GHQ, since no advantage was to be gained by further aggravating the mutual lack of confidence.

There was no doubt in my mind at the time, nor is there now, that had the Karelians been completely antagonised our withdrawal from

North Russia would have been rendered appreciably more difficult.

I was fortunate in being able to retain the full confidence of the Karelians, and those who were serving with us now on the Onega road were splendid fellows, keen and reliable. Moreover their reports were always intelligent and prompt. From these it became evident that the morale of the Bolshevik troops in Onega had reached a low ebb, and that any demonstration from our side would probably meet with but little resistance; on the other hand, an abortive attack with the few available men we had at the moment would have had the effect of restoring their self-confidence and stiffening their resistance in the future. Hence we were glad to learn that reinforcements were being sent to us for the purpose of clearing the town. However, before this development took place the Bolsheviks themselves evacuated Onega, but not before setting fire to many of the principal buildings and taking away with them as much plunder as possible. Only a small party was left on the southern outskirts of the town, more for purposes of observation than as a rear guard.

On the following day General Ironside's troops from the Archangel Force marched in and occupied Onega without resistance. Now therefore, our objective was achieved and our period of active usefulness in the area ended, the only duty devolving upon us being the maintenance of intelligence posts at Nuchta and Sumski Posad. In early September these were handed over to a Russian force detached from General Price's command in the south, and leaving Mende to settle the small domestic details in Sumski Posad I returned to the railway at Saroka by road.

In the station I found a train filled with British troops returning to Murmansk. Making my way to a compartment with complete and unbroken window-panes, I climbed to the door (Saroka, like all other railway stations in the North, was devoid of platforms) and bid a cheerful "good afternoon" to a scowling Major and an immaculate Captain, who informed me that the compartment was reserved for officers! This reminded me that my 'working kit' was somewhat the worse for wear. However, I extracted some amusement from the situation by asking in broken English their permission to remain. This was ungraciously refused, whereupon I advised them to go and seek another compartment where they would enjoy complete privacy in which to discuss the glory they had won. This was in the nature of a 'blow below the belt' according to reports of 'mistakes' recently made by this unit – mistakes which had been responsible for their early withdrawal. It was not well received. After swallowing some obstruction in his throat the Major asked me if I held a commission; but my reply, although it did not enlighten him on this point, seemed to add fuel to his irritation, so that our conversation ended in a muttered wish for a highly uncomfortable future for me.

Drawing into Kem I thought I had kept up the joke long enough and I invited them to join me in a drink. Unfortunately this was not adequate for the establishment of friendly relations, and I was not altogether sorry that our relatively short journey together was coming to an end.

In Kem a few busy weeks followed clearing up all the outstanding administrative matters relating to the District accounts, which were rendered all the more complicated by frequent changes and fluctuations in the currency. Some units were paid in the "British" roubles, which had been introduced to replace the Russian equivalent, while others were paid in the old rouble which gradually depreciated in value until it became practically worthless. Captain Gilling, however, had carefully kept his books up to date despite the confusion, so that there was no great difficulty in closing them.

Butler, assisted by Robinson, had dealt with the soldiers' pay of the Karelian Regiment and its various detachments very creditably. These two officers had also kept the accounts of the Widows' and Orphans' Fund which, when handed over to the Karelians, showed a credit balance of about £600 and a serviceable motor haulage boat, together with considerable stores and equipment.

A further attempt was now made to persuade the Karelians to hand in their machine-guns and ammunition; but this, I fear, met with little success as all portable arms seemed mysteriously to have disappeared up-country under various pretexts, and on investigation it was found that the only available weapons in Kem were some old French rifles for which there was no ammunition in the country!

Those Russians of the civilian population in Kem who had been friendly towards the Allies viewed with dismay the prospect of our evacuation which they regarded as foreshadowing their early death at the hands of the Bolsheviks, who would inevitably occupy the district after our departure. In all too many cases these gloomy forebodings proved accurate. Some hope was raised by a rumour that they were to be evacuated at the same time and given asylum in England; but when this was officially contradicted they were reduced to a despairing and fatalistic acceptance of their fate.

There was little enough that could be done for these unhappy loyalists. The only action I could take personally to help them at all was privately and unofficially to enlist the sympathy of the chief Karelians on behalf of those Russians who had been our staunch friends in the past, in order to facilitate their passage through Karelia to Finland when the situation became such that their escape from Russia was imperative. The Karelians promised to do everything in their power to carry out my wishes.

They were very anxious to secure my promise to return to Karelia as soon as I could obtain my release from British service. They made a most flattering offer for myself and any ten junior British officers I desired to have with me any time. I was touched by this confidence and loyal attitude to myself, which I regarded as a favourable comment on my leadership. They were quite aware that I would not have the support of the British Government. It would not have been difficult to secure the requisite number of British subalterns, as all those who had served with the Karelian regiment or had come in contact with them, were anxious to remain in the country, despite the fact that there had been no leave during their service in North Russia, and that a return home would be entirely problematical. Usually a few words to these volunteers, pointing out the duty to their own country, was sufficient to dissuade them from immediate headlong action. But with Lieutenant Kennedy it was more serious, and I was compelled to use all my powers of persuasion and argument before I could turn him from his intention to throw in his lot there and then with the Karelians. I knew that he was well fitted to combat the hardships and rigours of a life in the sub-Arctic climate, as he had been an officer or the Royal North West Mounted Police, but I pointed out that until our return to Karelia (if ever possible) he would be alone and cut off from all communications. Eventually he accepted my advice, and I assured him I would not return without him.

It was a very unsatisfactory ending to an undertaking which had developed from its original intention to prevent the German Forces in the Northlands from reinforcing their armies on the Western Front, into a campaign against Bolshevism for which we were not organised or prepared in any way. When definite operation orders for the evacuation of Kem and Karelia were received, the pleasure we would have experienced at the prospect of seeing home in the near future, was marred by contemplation of the fate in store for our Russian friends, whom we were abandoning to the "tender mercies" of their enemies. One could not avoid the thought that our ineffectual intervention was mainly responsible for their plight.

With all our stores, equipment and accounts in order, and all Regimental British officers and personnel recalled to Kem we were ready to embark when the troop ship arrived at Popoff. The Karelian staff came to the dock to speed us on our way, and it was only upon the promise to return as soon as possible that I was able to refuse the valuable parting gifts from my loyal comrades. Many of our Russian friends from Kem also came to wish us Godspeed, but numerous others feared to draw the attention of enemy spies by being present: how immediate and real was their danger I did not realise at the time. The only cheerful passengers were a few Russian refugees and some British privates. We, who had been in close contact with our friends ashore realised that we were saying goodbye to those who were condemned to die. The last we saw of them was a mass of waving hats, dominated by the tall, black figure of Omar, the Cossack, waving his sword.

We called at Murmansk, where we embarked General Lord Rawlinson, General Sir Charles Maynard, who came aboard very ill, Brigadier General Price and their respective staffs and various details. While waiting at Murmansk I endeavoured to buy one of Shackleton's Canadian huskies. He was a perfect Irish Terrier in every way and point, except in size. He stood as high as the largest wolfhound, but his owner would not part with him.

Our journey home was made in an ex-German liner, surrendered to the Allies and now named the *Leviathan*, I believe. Before handing over this ship the Germans had damaged the sea-valves and otherwise done useful work amongst the engines which necessitated frequent halts to effect repairs and remove sand from the pistons. All this added to our dissatisfaction at the termination of an unfinished task, preventing us from enjoying the feeling of freedom from responsibility usually experienced by the "returning warrior". The absence of a Naval escort was the first and most significant proof that the war was indeed over and our work finished.

I brought to England with me as a servant a very intelligent Karelian youth, well known to the British personnel of the Regiment for his wit and his knowledge of the English language. After we had arrived in Ireland and I had installed the lad in my home for two days, the cook left suddenly and the maids said they would not sleep under the same roof with a young savage! Enquiry proved that this boy had shown his dagger to the women and had dramatically demonstrated how he had cut the throats of innumerable Germans and others who had incurred his displeasure. Admonition was quite useless, promises of good behaviour were not kept and when a second collection of maids had threatened to leave I induced my brother to accept him as a house-boy. His conduct was exemplary for four days, but the exhibition in the kitchen of a photograph, taken by Mende, of some Karelian boys pretending to behead one of their number, with Effeim as the executioner, proved too much for the domestic staff. Throwing dexterity with a hatchet and the exercise of an inventive imagination wrote finis to his service in Ireland. He was then placed with some Russian friends in Richmond, Surrey, where within a few days he won great credit and received the thanks of the police for his bravery in stopping a runaway horse in the crowded streets of that town. The true story of this exploit was that Effeim saw a riderless horse galloping down the road towards him, and acting upon the belief that "finding is keeping" made a very plucky and successful effort to capture the prize. He was very disappointed to be disillusioned by the owner – a policeman! However, the public attention he had earned gained for him employment with a local dentist, where, no doubt he was happy in his suggestive surroundings. He remained there for some years, until he eventually returned to Russia.

Events took me out of England within a period of two weeks, to serve in the Lithuanian army, and it was in Kovno that I had the first news from my friends in North Russia. Argieff, late Sectional Engineer of the Murmansk railway, wrote from a concentration camp in Finland giving me the names of those who had escaped the debacle consequent to our evacuation of Kem: Col Essieff and his family, Madame Elena Fiersof and several others, who had rendered us splendid service. Fortunately I was in touch with the British military attaché in Helsingfors [Helsinki] who was able to secure the release of our friends and assist them to reach France. My absence abroad prevented me from keeping in touch with these homeless people, but recently I have seen Madame Fiersof who is now domiciled in Paris, where she receives a pension of sixty francs per month from the French government for her services to the Allies during the North Russian operations. The story of her adventures would be too harrowing for polite ears, but the bald patches on her head where her hair had been torn out, and the black scar on her mouth where she had been struck by the butt of a rifle almost twenty years before, still evidence the treatment she received at the hands of four of her countrymen

– while we were embarking on the troopship a few miles distant. She was rescued naked, senseless and bleeding by a party of Royal Engineers who had been left behind to "clear up" in Kem. In 1938 Lt Col Sir Thomas Moore, MP, at my request, endeavoured to obtain some small grant or pension for her from the War Office, but unfortunately we were unsuccessful as there is no such financial provision for such cases.

Pesycof [Peskov], another useful member of our intelligence, reached London with his mother and sisters, where he owned and drove a taxi until he died recently. The Governor-General Yermoloff was killed by the Bolsheviks in Murmansk, and General Skobolscene is reported to be the proprietor of a garage in Paris.

The surviving Officers of the "Syren" force foregather from all parts of the world to hold their annual reunion at the "Rag" [Army and Navy Club], and Count Bennigsen is always our honoured guest. Invariably there are some absentees on these occasions, but one in particular frequently claims my thoughts. Kennedy, the one time leading member of Miss Sybil Thorndyke's company, disappeared from London in 1925, leaving no trace of his destination with any of his family or friends. This silence on his part has been maintained up to the present. I wonder if it is possible that he found he could not wait for me, and so went back to work with Nicoli and Gregori in Karelia,

The Regiment we had raised acquitted themselves well in a campaign against the Bolsheviks in Murmansk, driving them down the railway to below Petrozavodsk, clear of Karelia. They then made peace with the Soviet and obtained the Status of an "Autonomous Republic", but I doubt if this condition satisfies their conception of independence. Of the individual leaders I have heard nothing since saying "good-bye" on the quayside at Popoff.

Kem, is now the headquarters of a convict settlement where nightmare conditions are said to prevail; while the island and wonderful old monastery of Solievetski have been converted for the temporary use of condemned prisoners, and provides accommodation for those sentenced to life imprisonment. No prisoner ever returns from the island.

Karelia has been mentioned recently in press reports from Russia, with regard to vast fortifications which are said to be under construction along the entire length of the Finnish-Karelian frontier. This appears to me to be somewhat unnecessary, as the results obtained would scarcely compensate the cost of the labour and material. The greater part of this border is swamp, river and trackless forest.

Chronology of events in 'Karelian Diary'

1917	
23 December	Allied Supreme War Council agrees to support anti-Bolshevik troops in Russia.
1918	
15 March	Bolsheviks sign Peace Treaty with Germans at Brest-Litovsk.
16 March	General Alfred Knox submits memorandum 'The Delay in the East' recommending despatch of five thousand Allied troops to Archangel.
3 April	General von der Goltz lands with German troops in Finland.
24 May	Britain reinforces contingent of 160 Royal Marines at Murmansk landed in March with 370 troops under command of Major-General F. C. Poole.
3 June	Allied Supreme War Council approves despatch of larger 'Syren' force under command of Major-General C. M. Maynard to Murmansk. Poole then to transfer his troops to Archangelsk, retaining overall command of Allied Forces in North Russia.
18 June	Departure of British forces from Newcastle on board *City of Marseilles*.
23 June	Arrival of British forces in Murmansk.
27 June–3 July	Maynard establishes Allied control along Murmansk

	railway with troops at Kandalaksha and Kem (under Major L. A. Drake-Brockman). Bolsheviks under Commissar Spiridonov withdraw southwards.
3 July	Woods departs from Murmansk on armoured train. Arrives Kem.
6 July	Allies sign agreement with Murmansk Soviet to supply region south to Kem. The Soviet to retain control of administration and Russian military units.
7 July	Maynard visits Kem, instructs Woods to recruit and lead Karelian troops.
1 August	Poole lands in Arkhangelsk. White Russian Provisional Government created to govern Northern Region, including Arkhangelsk, Murmansk and Karelia.
9 August	Maynard returns to Kem, reviews Woods' new Karelian troops.
15 August	Woods departs from Kem with three columns of Karelian Regiment to counter German-led White Finnish incursions across border.
28 August	Woods' forces take Uskozero.
30 August	Karelian troops fighting at Panozero. Woods learns that two thousand White Finns counter-attacking from south-west.
11 September	Woods reports from Ukhta: 'The enemy suffered a severe defeat ending in a complete and disorderly rout.' Karelian forces to returns to Kem.
22 September	Karelian forces surround remaining White Finns on island near Voknavolok.
7 October	After dissolution of Murmansk Soviet, regional administration transferred to Deputy-Governor M. Yermolov, subordinated to Governor-General in Arkhangelsk.
13 October	Woods reports that 214 White Finns killed after attempting to break out of Voknavolok siege. 'There are no White Finns now in Karelia in the area under my command.' End of campaign.
16 October	Poole leaves North Russia, replaced in Arkhangelsk by Brigadier-General Edmund Ironside.
5 November	Maynard's Murmansk forces, including 237th

	Infantry Brigade (under Brig-Gen F. G. Marsh, to which Woods' Karelian Regiment subordinated), made independent of Ironside's command at Arkhangelsk.
11 November	German armistice with Allies ends war in west.
4 December	Marsh invalided home. Woods assumes command of 237th Brigade for a few days until arrival of Brig-Gen M. N. Turner (CC 236th Brigade). In early January, Brig-Gen G. D. Price takes command of 237th Brigade.
1919	
12 January	Turner meets Woods and Drake-Brockman to agree winter disposition of Karelian troops. Maynard deploys 4th Karelian (Olonets) Battalion under Drake-Brockman in south of region versus Bolsheviks.
21 January	Woods forwards to Price Karelians' first petition to 'His Majesty the King of Great Britain' requesting self-determination under British protection.
7 February	Maynard reviews Karelian Regiment in Kem, issues military decorations. Discusses with Price and Woods preparations for transfer of Karelian Regiment to White Russians, leading to appointment of first Russian officer, Count Bennigsen, to 4th Karelian (Olonets) Battalion. Then meets Red Finnish leaders Oskari Tokoi and Verner Lehtimäki.
14 February	White Russian Deputy Governor-General of Northern Region V. V. Yermolov sends damning report on Karelian Regiment and Woods to Governor-General E. K. Miller at Archangelsk.
16–18 February	Meeting of Karelian representatives in Kem, organised by Grigorii Lezhev and Iivo Ahava. Resolved on elections to Karelian Constituent Assembly, representation at Paris Peace Conference, and establishing interim National Committee. Price read out telegram from Maynard and delivered his own address rejecting any demands for Karelian self-determination.
18 February	Colonel Lewin, Maynard's 1st General Staff Officer, meets with Yermolov and Colonel Kostandi, Chief of

	Military Department of the Murmansk Region, agreed to limit Karelian range of operations, restrict new recruitment, replace British officers with Russians, and merge 4th Karelian (Olonets) Battalion with Slavo-British Legion detachments in southern Karelia to form a mixed Karelian-Russian Olonets Regiment under Lieut-Col L. G. Moore
18 February	Allied forces capture Segezha from Bolsheviks in central southern Karelia.
4 March	British War Cabinet in London discusses withdrawal of North Russian forces during summer. Schedule for evacuation agreed later in month.
5 March	Fearing insubordination, Price demands Karelian Regiment surrender Lewis guns and ammunition. Woods circumvents order.
11 March	Maynard meets with Yermolov in Kem after receiving Karelians' second petition for British support. Interviews Karelian leaders, dismisses their requests, but resists Russian calls to undertake punitive measures.
31 March	Having received reports of possible revolts on 10 April led by Bolshevik sympathisers in Murmansk, Finnish Legion and Karelian Regiment, Maynard takes preventative measures. Subsequently, White Russians arrest and expel large numbers of suspected Finnish and Karelian Bolshevik agitators from Allied-held territory.
6 April	Woods transmits message to Maynard asking 'Syren' to acknowledge the Karelians' continuing loyalty.
8 April	Report implicating Karelians in a mutiny published in The Times
9 April	Further report in *The Times* on 'Royal Irish Karelians'.
12 April	Woods detains Iivo Ahava in Kem after receiving White Russian complaints about him. Despatches Ahava to rejoin Finnish Legion, but Karelian officer is reportedly murdered by Serbs on orders of White Russians.
29 April	After Woods protests to Maynard regarding 8 April report in *The Times*, the newspaper publishes a War

	Office statement under heading 'Staunch Karelian Allies'.
26 April	Maynard learns that White Finnish volunteers advancing against Bolsheviks at Olonets and Petrozavodsk.
April-May	Allied forces, including Olonets Regiment, push south from Segezha towards Lake Onega.
11 May	Olonets Regiment successfully engage Bolsheviks at Karelska Maselga. Death of Major L. A. Drake-Brockman. On same day, Woods formally takes over command of Kem District.
18 May	Allied forces capture Povonets on Lake Onega.
20 May	Order issued to dissolve unified Karelian Regiment, forming separate Volunteer Battalion, Pioneer Company, Frontier Guard, Garrison Guard Company and unarmed Labour Battalion. Woods retains overall command of new units and is promoted to full rank of Colonel.
21 May	Allied forces capture Medvezh'egorsk.
6 June	Arrival of General Skobeltsin in Kem to take command of Russian Murmansk Army.
8 June	Karelian soldiers in Kem refuse to obey orders after conflict with RAF officers. Woods temporarily defuses tensions.
19 June	Woods and other Allied officers visit United States flagship in Popoff bay to interview Admiral McCully about alleged anti-British agitation among Karelians by American sailors.
30 June	Dissolution and re-organisation of Karelian Regiment as above takes place.
2 July	Against background of continuing desertions and indiscipline among Karelian troops, Woods sends letter to Col H. S. Filsell, CO of Volunteer Battalion, admonishing him and his officers to treat Karelians as 'White-Men'.
5 July	Maynard and Russian General Marushevskii address Karelian forces in Kem, warning them to cease insubordination or face consequences.
11 July	Karelian Volunteer Battalion departs Kem for

	Povonets to prepare for operations against Bolsheviks in southern Karelia.
18 July	Woods complains to Major Grove of 237th Brigade HQ that Filsell 'persists in treating the Karelians as black men' and recommends his replacement. Brig-Gen Price does not accept Filsell's offer to resign battalion command.
19 July	Maynard inspects Filsell's Karelian Volunteer Battalion and Colonel Krugliakov's partisan regiment at Povonets.
20 July	Mutiny of 5th Russian Infantry Regiment under Colonel Andrews in Onega section of Archangelsk.
21 July	Karelian representatives meet at Ukhta, ratify February resolution on self-determination and elections. Under increasing Finnish influence, National Committee reformed as Provisional Government of Archangelsk Karelia.
24 July	Maynard despatches Woods from Kem to Sumskii Posad to organise local partisan forces in territory between Onega and Soroka, maintaining land communications between Allied Murmansk and Arkhangelsk commands.
5 August	As a result of continuing desertions, Maynard's HQ reports that the 'Karelian Pioneer Battalion has ceased to exist'.
13 September	Filsell's Karelian Volunteer Battalion ('nearly all raw recruits') launches successful operations in southern Karelia.
1-27 September	Evacuation of Archangel.
14 September	Final push south on Murmansk front to consolidate line at river Suna north of Petrozavodsk. On same day, Maynard's HQ issues order disbanding Karelian Volunteer Battalion by end of month, transferring all troops to Russian Army under Skobeltsin's command.
19 September	Maynard's HQ issues order for Woods to hand over command of Soroka district to Russian Army and return to Kem.
22 Sept–12 Oct	Evacuation of Murmansk.

Appendices

(Source: P. J. Woods collection, Imperial War Museum Department of Documents, Box 78/24/1. Reproduced with permission.)

A.

Letter from General C. M. Maynard to Colonel P. J. Woods, 29 August 1918 (typed), with appended note from Brigadier-General F. G. Marsh to Col Woods, 31 August 1918 (handwritten).

Murmansk
29th August, 1918

Dear Woods,

From your letter of 23rd August you evidently are not yet aware of the broad military situation, so I'll tell it to you roughly. It was this situation which caused me to instruct Col Marsh to order your withdrawal to KEM at the end of September. I cannot impress it too strongly on you and all Officers out here that neither the FINN nor the BOLSHEVIK is our chief enemy. To me it is not a great matter whether you clear KARELIA of White Finns or not. Your expedition is exceedingly useful, as it guards a certain extent of the western flank, gives your men experience, and enables you to get recruits. But I want such recruits to fight the <u>GERMANS</u>, who are the only people we need worry about very much. At the present moment there are 70,000 Germans in Finland, of whom some 35,000 are in the northern half. Of the latter, about 12,000 to 15,000 are directly threatening KANDALAKSHA and may commence their attack on the railway at any time. You see therefore your position. If the railway is cut north of KEM before the winter sets in there will at any rate be a chance of getting away the Kem garrison by sea, and, even if the railway is not cut, and we are not attacked at KEM, I have no intention of leaving any garrison at Kem after the beginning of October. What will you and your force do then, if you don't get back to Kem by the end of September? When we leave Kem the Bolshevik will almost certainly move up there, so the chances of your fellows being able to get away by sea from Kem may be impaired by the fact of your having to fight for your port of embarkation. Still there may be a chance of getting away by sea up to the beginning of December; after that there will be practically none, as we cannot risk a ship getting frozen up in the White Sea. Remember too that unless I get your Karelians I'm bound to give up KANDALAKSHA also, so that you will have no troops of ours nearer you than 30 miles south of Murmansk, unless by any chance Burton's Finns get their toes in like your fellows, and refuse to fight anywhere except in the neighbourhood SW of Kandalaksha. However they won't do this if I can help it, for it is essential to my plans that they should come up north.

Now of course you and your men could do very useful work by staying out as free-lances in Karelia, if you have got them well enough in hand to induce them to attack the German right flank, if the Germans advance from the west towards Kandalaksha, or to damage the railway and worry their lines of communication from the south, if the Germans and Bolsheviks endeavour to move up the railway. But how would you manage for supplies and accommodation in the winter? Colonel Marsh could arrange to send to Kem for you sufficient supplies for say 800 men for 6 months, but could you possibly manage to get this amount moved from Kem to your part of the world? Also, if you did manage it, what guarantee could you give me that these supplies would not fall into the hands of the Germans, Finns or Bolsheviks, to all of whom supplies are of far more value than recruits. Also what about your winter clothing? It has'nt [*sic*] even arrived from England yet, and may not come for weeks. Thus, unless you come up the line the probabilities are you will never get it at all, for its [sic] any odds against my being able to get it down to Kem before the end of September. You see there are other things to think of besides the feelings of your Karelians.

I cannot help feeling that you might be able to persuade them to go to Kandalaksha if you pointed out that:–

(A) They will be free to operate from there into their own country.
(B) They will be kept together as an entire Unit.
(C) That only in this way can they get the warm clothing which is coming out for them, and be assured of food supplies in the winter.
(D) That only thus shall I be able to supply them with machine guns which will be of any use in winter.
(E) That there is accommodation for them at Kandalaksha to which they can return after their expeditions to free their own country.
(F) That it is not only the Finn they must regard as their enemy for it is known for a certainty that German troops are preparing to invade Karelia. And they cannot hope to compete successfully against the Germans unless they have a proper base, with supplies and ammunition, such as Kandalaksha would afford.

As regards (B) I would do away with the detachment I have proposed to have at the bridge over the NIVA SE of IMANDRA lake, as, if they were at Kandalaksha and were driven out, they could get back towards MURMANSK by getting to the east side of the NIVA over the sea ice, or cross the NIVA much higher up towards the NW where it expands into a lake which would freeze over. Now I don't want to endanger your life, or the life of any Britisher with you, therefore I wont [*sic*] tell you to <u>order</u> your men to Kem by the end of September and then move to Kandalaksha under compulsion. Put the above considerations before them, and make any appeal you can to their patriotism, pointing out how much it is to their advantage in the long run. If they decline to leave their country, (but not before) say that you will leave them their rifles and ammunition and get as much food up to them as you can, but that you cannot do more. Then see if you can get any volunteers to accompany you back to KEM with a view to carrying out my wishes.
If they decide that they will not leave their present neighbourhood,

then I am not going to order you or any of your Officers or other Britishers to remain with them, and if any of you care to do so, it must be with your eyes clearly open. I would get Colonel Marsh to send to Kem supplies for one month of 800 men, and additional ammunition if you want it. I would also send winter clothing if it comes in time. But even if you got all you wanted of above, you must remember that you will be absolutely cut off from the remainder of my force for about 8 months, and perhaps altogether unless you manage to work your way down on foot to MURMANSK, for the railway to a practical certainty will be cut.

Colonel Marsh, under whose orders you are at present, has seen this, and will forward it (together with any instructions of his own) by an Officer to whom the whole situation will have been explained. You must send this or some other Officer back to Col Marsh as soon as you can, with a letter giving your decision, and full details as to your requirements, according to whatever course you decide upon. This must be done quickly, especially if any Britishers decide to remain out. I do not want you to bring pressure to bear on any Britisher to remain with your crowd, if they decline to fall in with my wishes. In fact I consider if they decide to take their own line, it would be wiser for all Britishers to join up at KEM by 30th. September, unless you are prepared for an exceedingly rough winter as a sort of King of Karelia. I will uphold you whichever line you take, but there must be no compromise as regards dates, as I cannot forego cutting the railway should the necessity arise, or be hampered by the necessity of bringing the Karelians away by sea after I have abandoned KEM, which will probably be early in October.

If you leave your crowd behind, impress on them the necessity of worrying as much as they can any German troops who may try to reach the railway through Karelia, especially in the northern part near Kandalaksha. Tell them too that any man who reaches here with any information of German movements will be well rewarded. Do not think I dont [sic] sympathize with your position. I do most heartily, but I have to take a broader outlook than you have to. Deal direct with Colonel Marsh about all this. He is here with me now, and knows the whole situation. If you can persuade your fellows to go to Kandalaksha, you will have done the best day's work of your life. Best of luck to you whatever course you are compelled to follow.

Yours sincerely,
C. M. Maynard

ACC 2
Kandalaksha 31st Aug.

Dear Woods

I have carried this with me, arriving here today, and passing it at once to OC Kem* to read and to pass to you by the officer who presents it. Please acknowledge its receipt by telegraph from Kem referring to it as ACC 2

I'm afraid it seems hard to you to be asked to abandon the force you have organized, but that is the only alternative if they refuse to come north and join our defensive force outside Kola.

But this was the only reason for our moving south at all, viz: to collect and organize the local inhabitants.

I await your decision: Is your force coming back to Kem by 30th September or not? I have to adapt other plans to your decision.

It is not going to be an easy or a pleasant job for me either, but the longer it is put off, the less feasible it becomes.

Yours sincerely
F. G. Marsh.

* The Commanding Officer in Kem was Major Drake-Brockman [ed.]

B.

Transcript of address by Brigadier-General Price to assembly of Karelian representatives at HQ of Karelian Regiment, Kem, 17 February 1919, including telegram to Karelians from General Maynard (typewritten, in Russian, with numerous handwritten corrections and amendments)*

Gentlemen,
His Excellency General PRICE, Commander of 237th Allied Brigade, has ordered me to read to you the following telegram that has been received from the Chief Commander of the Allied Forces in Murmansk.

Telegram

The Allied Command does not support any proposals for separation from Russia.

The dependence of the Karelians on Russia is absolutely essential in the interests of both.

The Allied Command will concern itself with the welfare of the Karelians, as it has previously done, but only if they acknowledge that they are part of Russia.

His Excellency General PRICE has also ordered me to make the following announcement:

"I am sure that the representatives of Karelia will agree with me that as yet the time has not yet arrived to speak of independence. The objective which brought the Allies here, and in pursuit of which the Karelians have lent such strong and loyal assistance, is the eradication and annihilation of the Bolsheviks. You all know what Bolshevism is – it is the destruction and theft of all possessions; your money will be taken away, not one home will be safe; and even your wives and

* Maynard's telegram and Price's proclamataion were of course written in English, then translated into Russian for delivery to the Karelian delegates. The document reproduced here is the editor's re-translation from the Russian text preserved in Woods' private papers, and therefore may differ in phrasing from the English originals, which have not been located in the UK or Russian archives.

daughters will be forced under a recent decree to become the common property of everyone. Therefore until the Bolsheviks and their sympathizers are destroyed there cannot be order, peace or security for any people among whom they live. You will be told that Bolshevism exists in England, France, Italy, and America. It is a lie. It is true that there are Bolsheviks in Germany who want to bring the anarchy and devastation that exists in Russia to their own country, but the German people know what Bolshevism is, especially those who work on the land and want peace and tranquillity, and so are now fighting against Bolshevism and have almost defeated it there. That is why it is the duty of all the Allies – English, French, Italians, Russians and Karelians, to battle this evil here in Russia as well, following the example of our former enemies, until Russia is cleansed and freed and can rebuild its great state that is now helpless because of the criminal undertakings of the Bolsheviks.

Only once this is accomplished will the time be right to convene a great assembly of the representatives of all the peoples who are under Russia's power and those peoples who have helped Russia in its time of unhappiness will be able to present their requests for local self-administration elected by themselves. By this I mean that the population of this region will take charge of its own internal affairs – while such matters as post and railways should remain under the jurisdiction of the central authorities.

At the same time, the Allied Command will continue in future, as it has in the past, to look after the welfare of Karelia. As soon as the region is sufficiently pacified and freed from bolshevik influence, we shall direct all our energies to providing food, clothing and agricultural tools, and everything necessary for the Karelians to be able to develop their region and its productive forces, and in this way secure a hitherto unknown prosperity.

The government of the New Russia will be a power elected by all the peoples which together form its wide empire. Therefore it is the duty of all Karelians to direct their energies towards pleasing this Russian government which will, of course, include their own representatives, and to which authority they will submit their petition on local self-administration.

I therefore ask you, the representatives of Karelia, to return home and explain to your compatriots that the peace, prosperity, and happiness of Karelia are only possible through close union with the fractured and devastated Russia of our times, and through the restoration of a great, unified and free Russia in the future. The dawn of this rebirth is already approaching ..."

C.

Letter from Col P. J. Woods, Officer Commanding Karelian Regiment, to Lieut-Col H. S. Filsell, CO 1st Service Battalion, Karelian Regiment, Kem, 2 July 1919 (typed, unsigned)

TO: CO 1st Service Btn Karelian Regiment

I wish to draw the attention of your officers to the following points:–
(I). The Battalion under your command having been cleared of all doubtful cases and unwilling soldiers, is in my opinion, now composed of the best fighting materials in the world. Some of your younger officers may consider that they know all about Karelians, but I assure you that they have not even begun to get any idea of their courage, ability, and natural fighting qualities. No doubt there will be a few cheap sarcastic smiles, or remarks, re. this, when they mentally review the little experience they have had – but I have seen the Karelians fight – I know what they can do, and if treated as 'White-Men' will act as such, better than many other men who have had a better chance.

(2) The Karelian 'Cadet' has been placed during the last month in an extremely difficult position. He has been treated as a 'Native' by the British officers, and by the Karelian soldiers as a suspicious person. These officers are ready and willing to respond to every act of kindness shewn and the man who can speak the language is the man who can back you up or let you down, when the necessity arises. The Karelians Cadet is a White-man and are loyal – in spite of past treatment – and a lot depends upon that loyalty, which again boils down to the manner in which you treat them; therefore, the making or marring of a fine fighting unit depends upon your realising what you now have the honour to command, and upon your forgetting narrow and absurd prejudices.
(3). I wish to emphasise that the men you now have the honour to com-

mand, have resisted the propaganda of their relations and 'friends'. They have held out against the temptation of their women, they have left their families at the bidding of a Foreigner – because they want to fight the Bolshevik – not because they are compelled to, Finland has been feeding their families for nothing – to keep them out of the Regiment. Still they came in. Considering that they had so many agitators working against them unchecked, I consider that the Battalion is composed of the best men one could desire to command.

(4). If there is any officer who has the idea that when the first shot is fired the men will bolt, I want him to come back here at once. I can find him employment with some other Unit where his confidence would remain unshaken. There are many officers here who would only be too pleased to relieve any officer in the Service Battalion.

(5). Nicoli Rogief is with the Service Battalion by his own request. He was the leader of the Karelian Regiment during the operations against the German-led White-Finns last Summer. He was recommended by me for the DSO. He led his two companies (500 men) in five engagements with extraordinary brilliancy and success. He knows more about Forest Fighting than any Britisher in Russia. – He also knows more about leading Karelians in a fight. He is letter perfect in the Russian Drill Book, therefore if you neglect to avail yourselves of his experience and ability, and still persist in treating him as an ignorant native – why you are wanting a little in brains yourselves.

Officer Commanding Karelian Regiment

D.

Address by Major-General C. M. Maynard, Commander-in-Chief of Allied Forces, Murmansk, to Karelian Volunteer Battalion and Karelian Pioneer Company, Kem, 5 July 1919 (typed transcript).

Men of the Karelian Volunteer Battalion and of the Karelian Pioneer Company:–

The time for plain speaking has arrived and I am going to speak to you very plainly indeed. What I am going to say does not of course refer in any way to your British Officers but only to you Karelians.

To begin with then I want you to understand once and for all that I have no intention whatever of allowing the indiscipline which you have shown lately to continue. I have had more than enough of your non-sense and it has got to stop. The method I shall take to stop it depends on yourselves as I will explain later.

I have know for a long time that agitators have been at work amongst you with the object of making you disloyal both to your own Country and to the Allies. I also know that many off you have been such ignorant fools as to believe these agitators, and have been persuaded to forget everything done for you both by myself and by Colonel WOODS during the past year. You do not seem to realize that for months past you have been for little or no use as Soldiers to me or to anyone else, yet you were paid and fed just as if you were real soldiers instead of useless shams. That could not go on for ever; for why should you be paid and clothed when you were doing practically nothing for your country or for the Allies at a time when every man fit to be called a man should have been doing his share to help his Country and the Government which has given him law and order, money and food. I therefore gave you a chance of doing useful work. I formed a new Battalion, a new Pioneer company and other units which you were told you could join if you so wished. You were not compelled to join any of them and the conditions of service were explained fully to you. You who are here now on parade joined the Battalion and the Pioneer Company of your own free will yet no sooner had you joined than you began to give trouble. You appeared to think that you could go when you liked and come when you liked and do what you liked. There were many cases of insubordination and some of desertion and the whole time you were disloyal enough to listen to propaganda directed against the Allies who were doing everything for you. Both Colonel Woods and myself put up with this for some time because we hoped you would come to your senses, but the number of cowards amongst you who have deserted and the number of cases of insubordination amongst you makes it necessary for me to show you clearly that I am not going to be fooled by you any longer. Do you think that as Commander-in-Chief, of the Allied Forces which now include thousands of Russians, I am going to continue worrying myself about a handful of Karelians many of whom are disloyal and the greater part of whom are showing themselves less fit to be soldiers than their women folk. Why, you are the laughing stock of the Russian Troops now at the front and quite rightly so. They say that you want to shelter behind them, that you care for nothing except filling your bellies and obtaining your pay and that you have not the courage to stir a hand to do anything for your Country. Not only do the Russian troops at the front say this but all the Allies and all the Russia Civilians say the same and they are perfectly right to say it. As regards those who have deserted already, they have deserted while on active service. They knew quite well what they were doing and if caught they cannot be surprised if they are made to pay the full penalty – which is death. Their names will be given to the Russian authorities so that it is not at all likely that they will able to escape detection and trial at some future date, if not now.

I want to give you men one last chance, so that you will not meet the same fate as is lying in wait for those who have deserted and I do this chiefly for the sake of Colonel Woods who has worked heart and soul on your behalf for a year, and who is bitterly disappointed at your conduct.

I therefore tell you now that every man amongst you who wishes to go can do so at once. But he must understand clearly that he goes under the following conditions:–

1. He gives up his arms and his uniform
2. He ceases to draw pay and rations both for himself and his dependents.
3. His name will be given to the Russian Authorities and he becomes liable at once to mobilisation in the Russian Army.

4. He will not draw food through the local ZEMSTVO. Arrangements have already been made to ensure this; for why should the local authorities feed a man who thinks only of himself and is not willing to do anything for his country.
5. Under no circumstances will he be allowed to rejoin.

I will even go further and allow any man who wishes to withdraw from the fighting units now on parade to join the Labour Battalion instead. This gives a chance for the more faint-hearted of you to continue to draw honest pay and food. Those of you in the Volunteer Battalion who are still willing to prove that you are men will be sent very shortly to a station further to the South. You will not be placed in the front line yet, because I do not consider that you are yet sufficiently well disciplined and trained, but you will draw the extra pay drawn by men in the front area and you will meet inhabitants who can speak with first hand knowledge of the atrocities committed on men, women and Children by the Bolsheviks whom the fools who have been agitating amongst you endeavour to paint to you as true patriots.

You now have your free choice. You must make your decision within the next 24 hours and any man who wishes to leave the Volunteer Battalion or the Pioneer Company under the conditions I have already stated must inform Colonel Woods before this time tomorrow. After that I can allow no further change of mind.

Those who stay on will be treated by me as they always have been treated fairly and squarely so long as they do their duty. If they fail, in their duty or show any signs of insubordination they will be dealt with without hesitation, for I will not allow any more conduct similar to that of the past few weeks. If they care to transfer to the Labour Battalion they can do so. Those who are too frightened to run any risk of fighting may wish to do this. They can go altogether from any Karelian Unit, but in this case they will be mobilized in the Russian Army if they belong to one of the classes already mobilized. If they do not belong to any such class they will cease to draw pay and food from any source and will run the risk of starvation as they deserve. You have heard, and this is my final decision brought about by your own foolish and criminal conduct.

I have done much for you and have decorated many of you for services in the field but you have done everything possible to shake my confidence in you as loyal soldiers. You have shown yourselves utterly devoid of gratitude, and you will have to prove your merit before I can again regard you as Soldiers in any way worthy of my trust or worthy to have British Officers in Command of you.

I have written out this speech in order that it may be impossible for you to say later that I have said anything different to what I have said. To make this doubly sure, I have had copies taken to post up in your Barrack rooms. Everything now depends on what you yourself decide. I want no unwilling soldiers who are the laughing stock of everyone in the district.

Your decision must be made now and it must be final.

C. M. Maynard. Major General.

Notes

Chapter 1 The Royal Irish Rifles: Thiepval Wood, July 1916

1 For the official regimental history of the battle, see Charles Graves, *The Royal Ulster Rifles*, Vol. 3, [1919–1948] (Mexborough, Yorks: Royal Ulster Rifles Regimental Committee, 1950), pp. 309–17. For a more recent account, see Tom Johnstone, *Orange, Green and Khaki: the Story of the Irish Regiments in the Great War, 1914–18* (Dublin: Gill and Macmillan, 1992). Among the best general histories of the Somme are Peter Hart, *The Somme* (London: Cassell, 1996) and Martin Middlebrook, *First Day on the Somme: 1 July 1916* (London: Penguin, 2006).

2 F.P. Crozier, *A Brass Hat in No-Man's Land* (London: Jonathan Cape, 1930), p. 101.

3 Keith Jeffery, *Ireland and the Great War* (Cambridge: Cambridge University Press, 2000), p. 56. The Battle of the Boyne took place at Drogheda, about forty miles north of Dublin, on 1 July 1690 (by the Julian calendar). It is nowadays commemorated by Ulster Unionists on 12 July according to the Gregorian (new style) calendar. For personal testimonies of the 36th (Ulster) Division's engagement on the Somme, see Crozier, *A Brass Hat*; Philip Orr, *The Road to the Somme: Men of the Ulster Division Tell their Story* (Belfast: Blackstaff Press, 1987); Myles Dungan, *Irish Voices from the Great War* (Blackrock: Irish Academic Press, 1995).

4 Crozier had led his men so gallantly that it was later decided to take no disciplinary action against him. See Dungan, *Irish Voices*, pp. 105–06.

5 These and subsequent communications are cited from the First World War papers of Colonel Philip James Woods, in the Imperial War Museum Department of Documents (hereafter IWM), Box 78/24/1; and from the 9th Battalion, RIR, War Diary, in The National Archives (TNA): Public Record Office (PRO) War Office (WO) 95/2503.

6 Message reproduced in Crozier, *A Brass Hat*, facing p. 110. Underlining in original.

7 Testimony of W. E. Collins, cited in Timothy Bowman, *The Irish Regiments in the Great War. Discipline and Morale* (Manchester: Manchester University Press, 2003), p. 126. Other accounts suggest that up to seventy survived.

8 Crozier, *A Brass Hat*, pp. 109–10; Orr, *The Road to the Somme*, pp. 181–83; Bowman, *The Irish Regiments*, p. 125.

9 Woods Papers, IWM 78/24/1.

10 Quoted in Jeffery, *Ireland and the Great War*, p. 58.

11 Photographs of many of these murals are reproduced in the web-site, with an extensive historical text based on Orr, *The Road to the Somme*, compiled by the South Belfast Friends of the Somme Association, at http://www.belfastsomme.com

Chapter 2 The Lad from Sandy Row: Family and Childhood

1 Jonathan Bardon, *A History of Ulster* (Belfast: Blackstaff Press, 1992), p. 515.
2 James I in praise of one of his Scots Ulster overlords, cited in ibid., p. 122.
3 Ibid., pp. 139–42.
4 Ibid., p. 180.
5 This paragraph, and later genealogical information, is based on interviews and correspondence with Mr Edwin Woods, County Cork (great-grandson of Philip Woods' uncle Jeremiah); on freeholders' records available on-line from the Public Record Office of Northern Ireland (http://www.proni.gov.uk), on *Burke's Peerage* and on Christopher Brennen's family history available at http://www.dankat.com/brennen/chap2.htm (accessed 29 June 2006).
6 J. Dubourdieu, *Statistical Survey of County Down* (Dublin: 1802), quoted in Peter Gibbon, *The Origins of Ulster Unionism. The Formation of Popular Protestant Politics and Ideology in Nineteenth-Century Ireland* (Manchester: Manchester University Press, 1975), p. 25.
7 A. T. Q. Stewart, *The Ulster Crisis* (London: Faber and Faber, 1967), p. 43.
8 Harry Ludlum, *A Biography of Dracula. The Life Story of Bram Stoker* (London: W. Foulsham & Co. Ltd., 1962), p. 13. See also Barbara Belford, *Bram Stoker. A Biography of the Author of Dracula* (London: Weidenfeld & Nicolson, 1996), p. 29.
9 Bardon, *A History of Ulster*, p. 326.
10 Quoted in Gibbon, *The Origins of Ulster Unionism*, p. 72..
11 On Sandy Row and Shankill in these years, and the changing socio-economic character of rioting, see Gibbon, *The Origins of Ulster Unionism*, pp. 67–86.
12 Philip Woods' birth certificate is among his personal papers.
13 Information from the Clwyd-Powys Archaeological Trust web-site at http://www.cpat.org.uk/ (accessed 19 August 2006).
14 Jones, Maldwyn A., '"The Impecunious Millionaire": The Career of Sir John Puleston, MP,' *Transactions of the Honourable Society of Cymmrodorion*, No. 4, 1997, pp. 28–47.
15 See *The Belfast and Province of Ulster Directory of 1892* (Belfast, 1892), p. 719.
16 See the *Belfast Directory*, 1895, p. 730; 1896, p. 760; 1897, pp. 512, 911.
17 According to Woods' own *Who's Who* entries. Curiously, the School Album does not list either Robert or Philip Woods as having studied at 'Inst'. (it is not certain that these lists are complete). See John H. Robb, Joseph R. Fisher, *Book of the Royal Belfast Academical Institution* (Belfast: M'Caw, Stevenson & Orr, 1913).
18 See John Jamieson, *The History of the Royal Belfast Academical Institution, 1810–1960* (Belfast: William Mullan & Sons, 1959), pp. 204–205.
19 On Inst. sporting activities in the late nineteenth century, see ibid., pp. 104–08, 122–29.
20 Samuel Smiles, *Self-Help: With Illustrations of Character and Conduct* (Boston: Ticknor and Fields, 1866), pp. 335–36.
21 Robert Woods makes his first independent appearance in the *Belfast Directory* of 1898. His address is recorded as Killowen House, Farnham Road, Bangor, p. 1094. The coincidence of this with his father's disappearance from the directory might simply suggest that the latter retired and moved with his wife to Bangor at this time to live with his eldest son.
22 From the School Album, in Robb and Fisher, *Book of the Royal Belfast Academical Institution*.
23 Information on Robert Woods' connection with the White Star Line from the family.
24 The chronology of this period is based on Wood's *Who's Who* entries, 1918–1921. From 1923, when Woods became an MP in Northern Ireland, he revised his autobiography to omit mention of his four years' employment between finishing the Belfast School of Art and leaving for South Africa, perhaps because it would permit the reader to calculate that the subject had left school at sixteen, and not attended any higher educational establishment.

Chapter 3 In Defence of Empire: South Africa with Baden-Powell, 1901–1903

1 Entry for Col Philip James Woods, *Who's Who* (London: Black, 1918), p. 2610.
2 Keith Terrance Surridge, *Managing the South African War, 1899–1902. Politicians v. Generals* (London: The Royal Historical Society, Boydell Press, 1998), pp. 104–09.
3 Letter from Milner to Chamberlain, 28 October 1900, in *The Milner Papers. South Africa, 1899–1905*, ed. Cecil Headlam (London: Cassell, 1933), Vol. II, p. 168.
4 Surridge, *Managing the South African War*, p. 127.
5 Letter from Milner to General N. G. Lyttelton, 18 November 1902, in *The Milner Papers* Vol. II, p. 396.
6 This paragraph and the next draws on Lord Baden-Powell of Gilwell, *Lessons from the 'Varsity of Life* (London: C. A. Pearson, 1933), Chapter VIII.
7 Quoted in Albert Grundlingh, '"Protectors and friends of the people"? The South African Constabulary in the Transvaal and Orange River Colony, 1900–08,' in *Policing the Empire: Government, Authority and Control, 1830–1941*, eds. D. M. Anderson and D. Killingray (Manchester: Manchester University Press, 1991), pp. 168–82, here p. 169.
8 John Buchan, *Prester John* (London: Penguin, 1983), p. 198.

Chapter 4 No Surrender! Linen, Gun-Running and the Ulster Volunteer Force, 1904–1914

1 Woods' entry, *Who's Who* (1918), p. 2610.
2 *Belfast Directory*, 1907, p. 1134.
3 The marriage was announced in the *Belfast News-Letter*, 10 August 1907, p. 1.
4 *Belfast News-Letter*, 20 April 1923.
5 Both started in 1903, see the School Album, in Robb and Fisher, *Book of the Royal Belfast Academical Institution*.
6 See Patrick Buckland (ed.), *Irish Unionism, 1885–1923. A Documentary History* (Belfast, HMSO, 1973), pp. 204–05.
7 Ulster Unionist politics had first crystallised under the leadership of wealthy landowning interests, who suffered economic and social decline, and a corresponding loss of political influence, in the latter part of the nineteenth century. See Alvin Jackson, *Colonel Edward Saunderson: Land and Loyalty in Victorian Ireland* (Clarendon Press, Oxford, 1995). On Unionist political organisation at this time, see also Buckland (ed.), *Irish Unionism, 1885–1923*, pp. 99-101.
8 Thomas MacKnight, *Ulster As It Is: or, twenty-eight years' experience as an Irish editor* (London: Macmillan, 1896), Vol. II, pp. 152–3.
9 Buckland (ed.), *Irish Unionism, 1885–1923*, pp. 59–60, 72, 84 and passim.
10 Alvin Jackson, *Home Rule: An Irish History, 1800–2000* (Oxford: OUP, 2004).
11 Roy Hattersley, *The Edwardians: Biography of the Edwardian Age* (London: Abacus, 2006), pp. 187–88.
12 See Patricia Jalland, *The Liberals and Ireland: the Ulster question in British politics to 1914* (Brighton: Harvester Press, 1980); Alvin Jackson, *The Ulster Party: Irish Unionists in the House of Commons, 1884–1911* (Oxford: Clarendon Press, 1989). For those interested in exploring this topic further, a fascinating set of contemporary statements of British support for the Unionist position can be found in the volume *Against Home Rule: the case for the Union by Arthur J. Balfour; J. Austen Chamberlain ... (et al.) with an introduction by Sir Edward Carson and preface by A. Bonar Law, MP*. S. Rosenbaum (ed), (London and New York: Frederick Warne & Company Ltd., 1912), which is available on-line at http://www.ucc.ie/celt/online/E900031.html (accessed 19 August 2006).
13 Stewart, *The Ulster Crisis*, p. 37.
14 'Ulster, 1912', in *The Works of Rudyard Kipling* (London: Wordsworth, 1994), pp. 232–33.

15 For a short but readable recent biography, see Alvin Jackson, *Sir Edward Carson* (Dublin: Historical Association of Ireland, Dundalgan Press, 1993). See also Geoffrey Lewis, *Carson, The Man Who Divided Ireland* (London: Hambledon, 2005).
16 See Patrick Buckland, *James Craig: Lord Craigavon* (Dublin: Gill and Macmillan, 1980).
17 The Covenant can be searched online via the web-site of the Public Record Office of Northern Ireland, at http://www.proni.gov.uk/ulstercovenant/index.html (accessed 12 June 2006).
18 F. P. Crozier, *Impressions and Recollections* (London: Werner Laurie, 1930), p. 63.
19 Ibid., pp. 83–84.
20 In fact, Crozier was forced to resign his regular commission in 1907, and his commission in the reserves two years later, both times for dishonouring cheques (a result of his heavy drinking). In 1909, his commanding officer opined that Crozier 'is totally unfit to hold HM's commission, and has [...] brought discredit on the Service and appears only too likely to bring more discredit in future.' See Crozier's War Office file in TNA: PRO WO 374/16987. He overcame his alcoholism during his stay in Canada, see Crozier, *Impressions and Recollections*, pp. 136–41.
21 Crozier, *Ireland for Ever*, pp. 34–35.
22 Stewart, *The Ulster Crisis*, p. 99.
23 From *Newtownards Chronicle*, 31 October 1914, quoted in Orr, *The Road to the Somme*, p. 54.

Chapter 5 The Shankill Boys: France, 1915–1918

1 Crozier, *A Brass Hat*, p. 54.
2 Timothy Bowman has recently shown that, contrary to accepted tradition, there was no wholesale transfer of UVF units into the 36th (Ulster) Division, and in the Belfast battalions only a minority of officers had in fact served in the UVF, see 'The Ulster Volunteer Force and the Formation of the 36th (Ulster) Division,' *Irish Historical Studies*, Vol. 32, No. 128 (Nov. 2001).
3 Crozier, *Impressions and Recollections*, pp. 156–59.
4 Crozier, *A Brass Hat*, p. 37.
5 The judgement on Crozier was made by Second Lieutenant Stewart-Moore in later memoirs, quoted in Bowman, *The Irish Regiments*, p. 30.
6 Crozier, *A Brass Hat*, p. 54; *Impressions and Recollections*, p. 161.
7 Crozier, *A Brass Hat*, p. 61.
8 Bowman, *The Irish Regiments*, pp. 113, 116–17.
9 Crozier, *Impressions and Recollections*, pp. 163–64.
10 Ibid., p. 169.
11 Crozier, *A Brass Hat*, p. 96.
12 See 9th Battalion RIR War Diary, TNA: PRO WO 95/2503.
13 *The Times*, 27 October 1916, p. 6.
14 This and subsequent details from Crozier, *Impressions and Recollections*, pp. 178–79.
15 The promotion was published in *The Times*, 22 March 1917, p. 6.
16 See Ian Passingham, *Pillars of Fire: The Battle of Messines Ridge, June 1917* (Thrupp: Sutton Publishing, 1998).
17 Crozier, *Impressions and Recollections*, pp. 179.
18 Crozier, *A Brass Hat*, pp. 163–64. The standard history of the battle is Leon Wolff, *In Flanders Fields* (New York: Viking, 1958, repr. London: Penguin, 2001)
19 As of summer 2006, Philip Woods' own military records are still held by the Ministry of Defence (no inference may be drawn from this fact regarding their content), and unavailable for the present research. It is possible that they might cast further light on his service history.

Chapter 6 King of Karelia (1): Intervention in North Russia, 1918

1 For overviews of the contentious and 'mythic' nature of Karelian history, see Hannes Sihvo, 'Karelia: history, ideals, identity. Karelian history from the Finnish viewpoint,' in *Karelia and St Petersburg. From Lakeland Interior to European Metropolis*, eds. Eira Varis and Sisko Porter (Joensuu: Joensuu University Press, 1996), pp. 11–25; Hannes Sihvo, 'Karelia: Battlefield, Bridge, Myth,' in *Finland: People, Nation, State*, eds. Max Engman, David Kirby (London: Hurst, 1989), pp. 57–72; and Max Engman, 'Karelians between East and West,' in *Ethnicity and Nation-building in the Nordic World*, ed. Sven Tägil (London: Hurst, 1995), pp. 217–245. Finnish speakers should consult Heikki Kirkinen, Pekka Nevalainen, Hannes Sihvo, *Karjalan Kansan Historia* (Porvoo; Werner Söderström Osakeyhtiö, 1994). For the religious identities of eastern and western Karelia, see John H. Lind, 'The Legacy of the Russo-Swedish Peace Treaty of 1323: Confessional Conflicts in the Border Region,' in *The Dividing Line. Borders and National Peripheries*, eds. Lars-Folke Landgren and Maunu Häyrynen (Helsinki: Renvall Institute, 1996), pp. 233–40. For the origin and development of the Karelian language, see Paul M. Austin, 'Soviet Karelian: the Language that Failed,' *Slavic Review*, Vol. 51, No. 1(1992), pp. 16–35.

2 For the population, see Nikolai Ozeretskovskii, *Puteshestvie po ozeram' Ladozhskomu i Onezhskomu* (St. Petersburg: Imperatorskaia Akademia Nauk, 1792), pp. 191–92.

3 K. Bergshtresserom' (ed.), *Opyt' opisaniia Olonetskoi gubernii* (St. Petersburg, 1838), pp. 16, 92.

4 V. P. Semenov, *Rossiia. Pol'noe geograficheskoe opisanie. Tom 3. Ozernaia oblast'* (St. Petersburg: A. F. Devriena, 1900), pp. 106–07.

5 See Roy Robson, *Solovki: The Story of Russia Told through Its Most Remarkable Islands* (New Haven, CT: Yale University Press, 2004).

6 For the tale of one English explorer, see Giles Fletcher, *Of the Russe Commonwealth*, reprinted in *Russia at the Close of the Sixteenth Century*, ed. E. H. Bond (London: Hakluyt Society, 1856).

7 See Robert O. Crummey, *The Old Believers and the World of Antichrist: the Vyg Community and the Russian State, 1694–1855* (University of Wisconsin Press: Madison, 1970).

8 Theodor Homén, *East Carelia and Kola Lapmark, described by Finnish Scientists and Philologists* (London: Longman, 1921), p. 178; I. P. Pokrovskaia, 'Naselenie dorevoliutsionnoi Karelii po materialam peripisi 1897 g.,' in *Voprosy istorii Evropeiskogo Severa: mezhvuzovskii nauchnyi sbornik*, ed. I. I. Kiaiviariainen (Petrozavodsk: PGU, 1974), p. 94. These figures are, of course, all contentious.

9 For an engaging history of Finland in the context of its 'frontier' location, see Anatole G. Mazour, *Finland Between East and West* (Westport, Conn.: Greenwood Press, 1956).

10 Extracts from M. A. Castrén's travel account were translated into Russian in *Etnograficheskii sbornik*, Vyp. IV (St. Petersburg: Imperatorskoe Russkoe Geograficheskoe Obshchestvo, 1858), pp. 251–62. For the *Kalevala* history, see Michael Branch's introduction to W.F. Kirby (trans.), *Kalevala* (London: Athlone, 1985); Keith Bosley, *The Kalevala* (Oxford: OUP, 1989), 'Introduction.'

11 For the role of Karelia in Finnish cultural nationalism, see Hannes Sihvo, 'Karelia: history, ideals, identity'; Sihvo, *Karjalan kuva. Karelianismin taustaa ja vaiheita autonomian aikana* (Helsinki: Helsinki Yliopisto, 1973); Mauno Jääskeläinen, *Die ostkarelische Frage. Die Entstehung eines nationalen Expansionsprogramms und die Versuche zu seiner Verwirklichung in der Aussenpolitik Finnlands in den Jahren 1918–1920* (Helsinki: Finnish Historical Society, 1965) pp. 18–40. For Karelia in Finnish folklore, see William A. Wilson, *Folklore and Nationalism in Modern Finland* (Bloomington, Ind.: Indiana University Press, 1976), esp. pp. 141–42, 148–55. On Sibelius and Karelia, see Willam A. Wilson, 'Sibelius, the Kalevala, and Karelianism,' in *The Sibelius Companion*, ed. Glenda Dawn Goss (Westport, Conn.: Greenwood Press, 1996), pp. 43–60; and Erik Tawaststjerna, *Sibelius, Volume 1, 1865–1905* (London: Faber & Faber, 1976), pp. 96–123, 145–49. On painters Akseli Gallen-Kallela (most famous for his *Kalevala* pictures) and Pekka Halonen, see Kirk Varnedoe (ed.), *Northern Light. Realism and Symbolism in Scandinavian Painting, 1880–1910* (New York: The Brooklyn Museum, 1982), pp. 108–21. On the development of Finnish 'territoriality', see Anssi Paasi, *Territories, Boundaries and Consciousness. The Changing Geographies of the Finnish-Russian Border* (Chichester: John Wiley and Sons, 1996).

12 Examples of the Finnish nationalist account of Karelia include: Homén, *East Carelia and Kola*

Lapmark; W. van der Vlugt (ed.), *Oost-Karelië / La Carélie Orientale* (Helsinki, 1923); *East Karelia. A Survey of the Country and Its Population and a Review of the Karelian Question* (Helsinki: Academic Carelia League, 1934). Finland's World War II alliance with Nazi Germany produced more ambitious visions of Finland's 'living space', see Väinö Auer, Eino Jutikkala, *Finnlands Lebensraum. Das Geographische und Geschichtliche Finnland* (Berlin: Alfred Metzner Verlag, 1941); Constantin von Stamati, *Die Kola-Halbinsel und Ostkarelien* (Berlin: Selbstverlag der Publikationsstelle, 1941).

13 See Stacy Churchill, 'The East Karelian Autonomy Question in Finnish-Soviet Relations, 1917–1922,' PhD thesis submitted to the University of London, 1967, pp. 39–79, published in Finnish only as *Itä-Karjalan kohtalo, 1917–1922: Itä-Karjalan itsehallintokysymys Suomen ja Neuvosto-Venäjän välisissä suhteissa, 1917–1922* (Porvoo: Werner Söderström, 1970).

14 Marina Vitukhnovskaia, 'Cultural and Political Reaction in Russian Karelia in 1906–1907. State Power, the Orthodox Church, and the 'Black Hundreds' against Karelian Nationalism,' *Jahrbücher für Geschichte Osteuropas*, Vol., 48, 2001, pp. 27–28.

15 See E. Iu. Dubrovskaia, 'Protivoborstvo panfinizma i russkogo velikoderzhaviia v Karelii,' in *Voprosy istorii Evropeiskogo Severa*, ed. M. I. Shumilov (Petrozavodsk: Izd. PGU, 1991), pp. 55–62; Vitukhnovskaia, 'Cultural and Political Reaction in Russian Karelia in 1906–1907.'

16 Quoted from pamphlet *Novyia dannyia k panfinskoi i liuteranskoi propagande v' Belomorskoi i Olonetskoi Karelii* (1907), p. 1.

17 *Pravoslavnaia Kareliia. Ocherk'* (Petrograd, 1914), p. 85.

18 V. I. Lenin, *Polnoe Sobranie Sochinenii*, Vol. 3, p. 596.

19 A recent readable volume on the British intervention is Clifford Kinvig, *Churchill's Crusade: The British Invasion of Russia 1918–1920* (London: Hambledon Continuum, 2006). The best diplomatic history to date is still Richard H. Ullman, *Anglo-Soviet relations, 1917–1921*, 3 vols. (Princeton: Princeton University Press, 1961–72). For military detail, using some Soviet materials and engaging first-person testimonies by Allied officers, see Christopher Dobson and John Miller, *The Day We Almost Bombed Moscow* (London: Hodder and Stoughton, 1986). For other works, see notes below.

20 C. M. Maynard, *The Murmansk Venture* (London: Hodder and Stoughton, 1928), p. vii.

21 Major-General Sir Alfred Knox, *With the Russian Army, 1914–1917, being chiefly extracts from the diary of a military attaché* (London : Hutchinson & Co, 1921), Vol. II, pp. 509–11.

22 Cited in John Swettenham, *Allied Intervention in Russia, 1918–1919, and the part played by Canada* (London: George Allen & Unwin, 1967), pp. 39–40.

23 Anthony F. Upton, *The Finnish Revolution, 1917–1918* (University of Minnesota Press: Minneapolis, 1980).

24 For Ahava, see O.V. Itkonen, *Muurmannin suomalainen legioona: varustettu kartalla ja sarjalla liitekuvia* (Helsinki: Kansanvalta, 1927), pp. 125–29.

25 For a detailed study of German interests and actions in Karelia in 1918–1919, see Jääskeläinen, *Die ostkarelische Frage*, pp. 141–49.

26 On the construction of the railway and of the Murmansk port, see Alfred Knox, *With the Russian Army*, Vol. II, pp. 509–11; Reinhard Nachtigal, *Die Murmanbahn: die Verkehrsanbindung eines kriegswichtigen Hafens und das Arbeitspotential der Kriegsgefangenen (1915 bis 1918)* (Grunbach: Greiner, 2001).

27 See Richard H. Ullman, *Anglo-Soviet Relations, 1917–1921*, Vol. 1, *Intervention and the War* (Princeton: Princeton University Presss, 1961), p. 109.

28 On the Murmansk Soviet, see Ullman, *Intervention and the War*, pp. 114–119; and Robert Jackson, *At War with the Bolsheviks. The Allied Intervention into Russia, 1917–20* (London: Tom Stacey, 1972), pp. 34–37. On Zveginstev and Veselago, see Michael Kettle, *Russia and the Allies 1917–1920,* Vol. II, *The Road to Intervention, March-November 1918* (London: Routledge, 1988), p. 231.

29 Maynard, *The Murmansk Venture*, pp. 38–39.

30 Ullman, *Intervention and the War*, p. 179.

31 On the Czech Lgion, see J.F.N. Bradley, *The Czechoslovak Legion in Russia, 1914–1920* (Boulder, New York: Columbia University Press, 1991).

32 'Short History of Events in Russia from November 1917, to February 1919,' War Office report, 28 February 1919, reproduced in *British Documents on Foreign Affairs: Reports and Papers from the Foreign*

Office Confidential Print, Part II, Series A, ed. D. Cameron Watt (hereafter *Confidential Print*), Vol. I, p. 438.

33 Maynard, *The Murmansk Venture*, p. 29.

34 Botchkareva was a Siberian peasant woman, born 1889, who had followed her husband into the Russian imperial army in 1916, and remained fighting after his death. General Edmund Ironside, in command of the Archangel force from October 1918, cites a White Russian 'Order of the Day' of 27 December 1918, ordering Botchkareva out of uniform, on the grounds that 'the summoning of women for military duties, which are not appropriate for their sex, would be a heavy reproach and a disgraceful stain on the whole population of the northern region.' In Edmund Ironside, *Archangel, 1918–1919* (London: Constable, 1953), pp. 76–78. See also Maria Botchkareva's memoir, *Yashka: my Life as Peasant, Officer and Exile* (London: Constable & Co., 1919).

35 For other accounts, see Dobson and Miller, *The Day We Almost Bombed Moscow*, pp. 49–50.

36 P. Kandaouroff, 'Le Chemin de Fer de Mourmansk,' *Revue de Génie Militaire*, Vol. 60, 1927, p. 262.

37 See George F. Kennan, *Soviet-American Relations, 1917–1920*, Vol. II, *The Decision to Intervene* (London: Faber & Faber, 1958), pp. 21–26.

38 Cited in Dobson and Miller, *The Day We Almost Bombed Moscow*, pp. 59–60.

39 For Tokoi's political career to date, see Upton, *The Finnish Revolution, 1917–1918*. For the May agreement, see Itkonen, *Muurmannin suomalainen legioona*, p. 47.

40 See Churchill, 'The East Karelian Autonomy Question,' pp. 183–90. The Red Finns will not be discussed in detail here except where relevant for understanding Karelian events. In Finnish, see Jukka Nevakivi, *Muurmannin legioona. Suomalaiset ja liittoutuneiden interventio Pohjois-Venajalle 1918–1919* (Helsinki: Tammi, 1970).

41 Maynard, *The Murmansk Venture*, pp. 30–31; Maynard's report to Poole, 9 September 1918, enclosed in Maynard's despatch to Winston Churchill, 1 March 1919, in TNA: PRO WO 32/5698.

42 Three of these officials were subsequently killed in controversial circumstances, see Dobson and Miller, *The Day We Almost Bombed Moscow*, p. 56. For Soviet historians, this was the start of 'mass terror against local officials loyal to the Soviet authorities', c.f. V. V. Tarasov, *Bor'ba s interventami na severe Rossii (1918–1920 gg.)* (Gosudarstvennyi izdatel'stvo politicheskoi literatury, Moscow, 1958), p.81. For Spiridonov's own account of these events, see pp. 82–3.

43 Maynard, *The Murmansk Venture*, pp. 49–50; Maynard's report to Poole, 9 September 1918, in TNA: PRO WO 32/5698.

44 See War Diary, North Russia (Syren Force), Kem Operations, TNA: PRO WO 95/5426.

45 See also telegram from Brig-Gen Poole, Murmansk, to Director of Military Intelligence, War Office, 25 June 1918, in TNA: PRO WO 33/962, No. 25.

46 Woods reports this as 7 July. Maynard relates these events in his memoir, but dates them after the Allied occupation of Soroka in mid-July, *The Murmansk Venture*, pp. 64–65.

47 Cited in Ullman, *Intervention and the War*, pp. 184–85.

48 War Diary, North Russia (Syren Force), General Staff (hereafter War Diary, General Staff), TNA: PRO WO 95/5424.

49 For Reilly's role, see Kettle, *The Road to Intervention*, p. 331.

50 Telegrams from Drake-Brockman to Marsh, 21 and 23 August, Kem Telegram Log, Woods Papers, IWM 78/24/1.

51 Field Message Book, Woods Papers, IWM 78/24/1.

52 Telegram from Maynard to Director of Military Intelligence, 29 October 1918, in TNA: PRO WO 33/962, No. 502.

53 Telegram in Woods Papers, IWM 78/24/1.

54 13 September, Field Message Book, Woods Papers, IWM 78/24/1.

55 18 September, in op. cit.

56 3 October, in op. cit. For the 'flu epidemic, see telegram of 24 September, Kem Telegram Log.

57 27 September, Field Message Book, Woods Papers, IWM 78/24/1.

58 13 October, in op. cit.

59 Telegram from Krugliakov to Marsh, 21 October, Telegram Log, Woods Papers, IWM 78/24/1.

60 Despatch in TNA: PRO WO 32/5698.

61 Maynard, *The Murmansk Venture*, pp. 94, 96
62 Medical Officer's Report, 5 June 1919, in Woods Papers, IWM 78/24/1.
63 24 October, Telegram Log, Woods Papers, IWM 78/24/1. The Defence of the Realm Act, passed on 8 August 1914, gave the government executive powers to suspend freedom of speech and assembly, imprison without trial and to requisition resources for the war effort.
64 Shackleton joined Maynard's staff on 15 November, advising on winter clothing and footwear and the use of skis and dog sleds (which were not successful, as the huskies had a tendency to attack passing reindeer. See 'Memorandum', in War Diary, General Staff, TNA: PRO WO 95/5424; Swettenham, *Allied Intervention in Russia*, pp. 189–90.
65 See Maynard, *The Murmansk Venture*, pp. 101–103.
66 Letter in Woods Papers, IWM 78/24/1.
67 Crawford left a diary of his adventures, see Dobson and Miller, *The Day We Almost Bombed Moscow*, pp. 60, 116 and passim.
68 Letter dated 11 September, Woods Papers, IWM 78/24/1.
69 Secret Brigade Order ACC3, signed F.G. Marsh, 11 Sept. 1918, in Woods Papers, IWM 78/24/1.
70 'Distribution of Units in 237th Brigade, December 1919,' in TNA: PRO WO 106/1149.

Chapter 7 **King of Karelia (2): Nationalist Dreams and Imperialist Realities, 1919**

1 Swettenham, *Allied Intervention in Russia*, p. 54.
2 For the White Russian government, see Ullman, *Intervention and the War*, pp. 254–55.
3 See Maynard, *The Murmansk Venture*, p. 38. The Soviets denounced Zvegintsev as a 'traitor', see Tarasov, *Bor'ba s interventami na severe Rossii*, p. 61.
4 These operations are described in detail in Maynard, *The Murmansk Venture*.
5 On Ironside, see Ullman, *Intervention and the War*, p. 256; Dobson and Miller, *The Day We Almost Bombed Moscow*, pp. 137–39; William Soutar, *With Ironside in North Russia*, London, 1940. See also Ironside, *Archangel, 1918–1919*.
6 27 September 1918, War Diary, General Staff, TNA: PRO WO 95/5424.
7 4, 8 December 1918 and 7 January 1919, War Diary, Brigade HQ, 237th Brigade, TNA: PRO WO 95/5427.
8 Cited in Michael Kettle, *Russia and the Allies 1917–1920*, Vol. III, *Churchill and the Archangel Fiasco, November 1918 – July 1919* (London: Routledge, 1992), p. 490.
9 Maynard, *The Murmansk Venture*, pp. 261–62.
10 See 'Report on North Russia,' by Sir Henry Wilson, 1 Dec 1919, to Secretary of State for War Winston Churchill, in *Confidential Print*, Vol. I, p. 427.
11 See Richard H. Ullman, *Anglo-Soviet Relations, 1917–1921*, Vol. II, *Britain and the Russian Civil War* (Princeton: Princeton University Presss, 1968), p. 198. See also the evacuation schedules in *Confidential Print*, Vol. I, pp. 468–70.
12 For discussion of the withdrawal, see Winston Churchill, *The World Crisis*, Vol. V, *The Aftermath* (London: T. Butterworth, 1929), pp. 252–4.
13 Maynard, *The Murmansk Venture*, p. 112.
14 Casualties from Wilson's 'Report on North Russia,' *Confidential Print*, Vol. I, p. 428.
15 Churchill, 'The East Karelian Autonomy Question,' pp. 108–13.
16 Ibid., pp. 122–25, 137–52.
17 For the Allies and White Russians' attitudes towards the East Karelian question in international diplomacy, see Jääskeläinen, *Die ostkarelische Frage*, pp. 152–68, 205–13.
18 Telegram from Maynard to Director of Military Intelligence, 5 November 1918, in TNA: PRO WO 33/962, No. 536. Ahava's transfer is discussed by Churchill, 'The East Karelian Autonomy Question,' p. 205, citing the memoirs of two Red Finns, Oskari Tokoi and O.V. Itkomen.
19 Telegram from Maynard to Director of Military Intelligence, 17 February 1919, in TNA: PRO WO 33/966, No. 1155.

20 Woods letter to Price, 21 January 1919, Woods Papers, IWM 78/24/1. A typescript in Russian, with three original signatures (two legible), and an English translation, are also in this folder.

21 7 February 1919, War Diary, General Staff, TNA: PRO WO 95/5424. Maynard characterised Bennigsen as a 'capable and gallant soldier' in *The Murmansk Venture*, p. 183.

22 8 February 1919, War Diary, General Staff, TNA: PRO WO 95/5424.

23 See TNA: PRO FO 175/1/889, pp. 1–2.

24 Ibid., pp. 2–3.

25 Ibid., p. 3.

26 Ibid., pp. 4–5.

27 17 and 18 February 1919, War Diary, General Staff, TNA: PRO WO 95/5424. Col Kostandi, Chief of the Military Department of the Murmansk Region, was also present at the 18 February meeting. See also Bennigsen's letter to Woods, 27 Feb 1938, in Woods Papers, IWM 78/24/1.

28 Maynard had interviewed Tokoi and Lehtimäki in Kem on 7 February, see War Diary, General Staff, TNA: PRO WO 95/5424.

29 On the assembly, see E. Iu. Dubrovskaia, 'Iz istorii podgotovki Ukhtinskogo s'ezda predstavitelei Karel'skikh volostei,' in *Voprosy istorii Evropeiskogo Severa*, eds. A. I. Afanas'eva and M. A. Mishenev (Petrozavodsk; Petrozavodsk State University, 1998), pp. 65–67; Jääskeläinen, *Die ostkarelische Frage*, p. 198; Churchill, 'The East Karelian Autonomy Question,' pp. 212–15. For the Soviet interpretation of this 'counter-revolutionary' congress of Karelians 'kulaks', see Tarasov, *Bor'ba s interventami na severe Rossii*, pp. 86, 215–16. The minutes of the meetings are reproduced in the memoirs of Red Finnish legionnaire O.V. Itkonen, *Muurmannin suomalainen legioona*, pp. 87–90; and are also in the Ingman collection, file B3:1, Finnish National Archives.

30 Resolution reproduced in D. G. Kirby (ed.), *Finland and Russia, 1808–1920. From Autonomy to Independence. A Selection of Documents* (London: Macmillan, 1975), pp. 248–49.

31 Itkonen, *Muurmannin suomalainen legioona*, p. 90.

32 5 March 1919, War Diary, Brigade HQ, 237 Brigade, TNA: PRO WO 95/5427.

33 Undated letter to 'Panozero men', in Woods Papers, IWM 78/24/1.

34 Ignat'ev's memoirs reprinted in V.I. Goldin, *Belyi Sever. 1918–1920 gg.. Memuary i dokumenty. Vypusk 1* (Argus: Arkhangel'sk, 1993), p. 155.

35 See V.V. Marushevskii, 'God na Severe, avgust 1918 g.–avgust 1919 g', *Beloe Delo*, Vols. 1–3, 1926–27, published in the Soviet Union in 1930, here reproduced in Goldin, *Belyi Sever*, pp. 170–341.

36 Goldin, *Belyi Sever*, pp. 188–89.

37 F. Lambert, British Supply Controller, Murmansk, 'Narrative of Supply Mission, June 1918 to approx. late March 1919' (undated), TNA: PRO FO 175/7, Para. 44.

38 Letter of 5 April 1919, TNA: PRO FO 175/1/1108.

39 Letter from Lindley to Curzon, 5 March 1919, TNA: PRO FO 175/7/885, p. 6.

40 O. Tokoi, *Maanpakolaisen muistelmia* (Helsinki: Tammi, 1959), p. 289.

41 17 March 1919, War Diary, General Staff, (Appendix), TNA: PRO WO 95/5424; and Maynard's telegram to War Office, 30 March 1919, TNA: PRO WO 33/966, No. 1461.

42 Maynard, *The Murmansk Venture*, pp. 182–83.

43 Telegram, Drake-Brockman, in Rugozero, to Woods, at Kem, 25 March 1919, in Woods Papers, IWM 78/24/1. Underlining in original.

44 30 March 1919, War Diary, HQ 236th Infantry Brigade, TNA PRO WO 95/5426; telegram, Maynard to War Office, 31 March 1919, TNA: PRO WO 33/966, No. 1474. See also Maynard, *The Murmansk Venture*, pp. 207–215.

45 Maynard, *The Murmansk Venture*, p. 251.

46 See Maynard's telegram to the Foreign Office of 31 March, in TNA: PRO FO 175/1/1057; and his 'Report on Intended Bolshevik Disturbances, April 1st – 15th 1919,' Appendix to April, War Diary, Brigade HQ, 237th Brigade, TNA: PRO PRO WO 95/5427.

47 Cited in Kettle, *Churchill and the Archangel Fiasco*, p. 314.

48 This version is described in Itkonen, *Muurmannin suomalainen legioona*, p. 99, also cited in Churchill, 'The East Karelian Autonomy Question,' pp. 220–21.

49 On 6 April, Woods wired Maynard requesting Syren formally acknowledge the Karelians'

absolute loyalty against '<u>all foes</u>', in Woods Papers, IWM 78/24/1.

50 Materials on this dispute in Woods Papers, IWM 78/24/1; see also 12 April 1919, War Diary, General Staff, TNA: PRO WO 95/5424.

51 Itkonen, *Muurmannin Suomalainen Legiona*, p. 91, cited in Churchill, 'The East Karelian Autonomy Question,' p. 222.

52 Maynard to War Office, 26 April 1919, TNA: PRO WO 33/966, No. 1700.

53 See Maynard, *The Murmansk Venture*, p. 228; letter of Bennigsen to Woods, 27 Feb 1938, in Woods Papers, IWM 78/24/1.

54 Syren Orders No. 22 and No. 24, Appendices A and F, May 1919, War Diary, General Staff, TNA: PRO WO 95/5424.

55 Syren Order No. 31, Appendix M, May 1919, War Diary, General Staff, TNA: PRO WO 95/5424; also telegram from Maynard to War Office, 22 May 1919, TNA: PRO WO 33/966/1960.

56 Maynard, *The Murmansk Venture*, pp. 256–57.

57 8 June 1919, War Diary, General Staff, TNA: PRO WO 95/5424.

58 Confidential Circular, 10 June 1919, Woods Papers, IWM 78/24/1.

59 On McCully, see Charles J. Weeks, *An American Naval Diplomat in Revolutionary Russia. The Life and Times of Vice-Admiral Newton A. McCully, 1867–1951* (Annapolis, Maryland: Naval Institute Press, 1993).

60 19 June 1919, War Diary, General Staff, TNA: PRO WO 95/5424.

61 Telegram, Woods Papers, IWM 78/24/1.

62 Woods to CO 1st Service Bt., Karelian Regiment, 2 July 1919, in Woods Papers, IWM 78/24/1.

63 Marushevskii's speech is in Appendix A to July War Diary, General Staff, TNA: PRO WO 95/5424. Marushevskii alludes to this event in his memoir, reproduced in Goldin, *Belyi Sever*, p. 321.

64 Woods Papers, IWM 78/24/1.

65 Maynard, *The Murmansk Venture*, p. 260.

66 War Diary, Brigade HQ, 237th Brigade, TNA: PRO WO 95/5427.

67 17–18 July 1919, War Diary, General Staff, TNA: PRO WO 95/5424.

68 Op. cit..

69 24 and 25 July 1919, in op. cit.

70 Report from Brig-Gen G.D. Price, C-in-C 237th Inf. Brig., to Syren HQ. (undated, late Sept), in 237th Inf. Brigade, Operation reports, TNA: PRO WO 95/5427.

71 Maynard, *The Murmansk Venture*, pp. 290–91.

72 28 July, War Diary, General Staff, TNA: PRO WO 95/5424.

73 Appendix to September, in op. cit.

74 See, for example, the long petition submitted to the British embassy in Stockholm on in January 1919 by Karelian émigrés in Helsinki asking to be able to present their case directly to Murmansk HQ to 'correct the wrong impression and false reports about the Karelians,' in TNA: PRO FO 608/187/223-32; and the Foreign Office report on the Karelian question, dated October 1919, in ibid., 235–42.

75 The following is based largely on Churchill, 'The East Karelian Autonomy Question'; Dubrovskaia, 'Iz istorii podgotovki Ukhtinskogo s'ezda'; Mazour, *Finland between East and West*, pp. 62–71; Jääskeläinen, *Die ostkarelische Frage*, pp. 205–72.

76 For the Red Finns' 'revolutionary nationalism' in relation to Marxist and nationalist conceptions of space and territory, see Nick Baron, 'Nature, Nationalism and Revolutionary Regionalism: Constructing Soviet Karelia, 1920–1923,' *Journal of Historical Geography*, Vol. 33, No. 3 (2007), pp. 565–95. On Edvard Gylling's concept of a 'Greater Red Finland', see Markku Kangaspuro, 'Nationalities Policy and Power in Soviet Karelia in the 1920s and 1930s,' in *Communism National and International*, eds. Tauno Saarela and Kimmo Rentola (Helskini: Finnish Historical Society, 1998). Kangaspuro has also written the standard work on Red Finnish nationalities policy in Soviet Karelia, *Neuvosto-Karjalan taistelu itsehallinnosta: nationalismi ja suomalaiset punaiset Neuvostoliiton vallankäytossä 1920–1939* (Helsinki: Suomalaisen Kirjallisuuden Seura, 2000), with English summary.

77 See Nick Baron, 'Conflict and Complicity: The Expansion of the Karelian Gulag, 1923–1933,'

Cahiers du monde russe, Vol. 42, Nos. 2–4 (2001), pp. 615–48; and 'Production and Terror: The Operation of the Karelian Gulag, 1933–1939,' *Cahiers du monde russe*, Vol. 43, No. 1 (2002), pp. 139–80.

78 On Karelian economic and demographic development, see Nick Baron, *Soviet Karelia. Politics, Planning and Terror in Stalin's Russia, 1920–1939* (London: Routledge, 2007).

79 See Austin, 'Soviet Karelian: the Language that Failed' (cited in Chapter Six, n. 1 above).

Chapter 8 Baltic Interlude: Lithuania, 1919–1920

1 Martin Petter, '"Temporary Gentlemen" in the 'Aftermath of the Great War: Rank, Status and the Ex-Officer Problem,' *Historical Journal*, Vol. 37, No. 1 (1994), pp. 127–52.

2 See Philip Ollerenshaw, 'Textile Business in Europe During the First World War: The Linen Industry, 1914–18,' *Business History*, Vol. 41, No. l (1999), pp. 63–87.

3 See Olavi Hovi, *The Baltic Area in British Policy, 1918–1921* (Helsinki: Finnish Historical Society, 1980); Alfred Senn, *The Emergence of Modern Lithuania* (New York: Columbia University Press, 1959).

4 Crozier, *Impressions and Recollections*, pp. 241–42. The British consistently refused to send official aid, see TNA: PRO Foreign Office (FO) 608/187/92 and *passim*.

5 Crozier retired from the British army on 31 July 1919 with permission to retain the honorary rank of Brigadier-General, see TNA: PRO WO 374/16997; *Impressions and Recollections*, pp. 240–41.

6 For Crozier's appointment to the Lithuanian army, see letter from Lithuanian Plenipotentiary Delegate in London to the Foreign Office, 22 September 1919, in TNA: PRO WO 374/16997.

7 Crozier, *Impressions and Recollections*, p. 246.

8 On the German volunteers, see Robert G.L. Waite, *Vanguards of Nazism: The Free-Corps Movement in Postwar Germany, 1918–1923* (Harvard University Press: Cambridge, Mass., 1952).

9 *The Times*, 9 September 1919, p. 9.

10 See letter from General A.J. Turner, Head of British Military Mission in Baltic States, to CIGS, 11 February 1920, reproduced in *Confidential Print*, Vol. 2, p. 256.

11 *The Times*, 9 December 1919, p. 13.

12 *Confidential Print*, Vol. 2, p. 256.

13 Crozier, *Impressions and Recollections*, p. 246.

14 Letter from Col R.B. Ward to Earl Curzon, 12 Feb 1920, in *Confidential Print*, Vol. 2, p. 140.

15 Op. cit..

16 *The Times*, 28 Februrary 1920, p. 15.

17 Crozier, *Impressions and Recollections*, p. 247.

18 Woods' papers include a letter addressed to him in Kovno, dated 31 April 1920, in IWM 78/24/1. A letter from Colonel Ward to Earl Curzon. 3 March 1920, proposes to use Russian-speaking officers from the British army as instructors in the Baltic, partly to countermand growing French influence in the region, in *Confidential Print*, Vol. 2, p. 264.

19 For example, see his letters to *The Times*, 12 March 1920, p. 12; 13 May, p. 12; 26 May, p. 8.

20 Reported in *The Times*, 26 April 1920, p. 13.

Chapter 9 Belfast's Fighting Colonel: Northern Irish Politics and Parliament, 1921–1929

1 Works which offer engaging surveys of Ulster's history in the 1920s include: Michael Farrell's 'anti-imperialist and socialist' treatment, *Northern Ireland: the Orange State* (London: Pluto Press, 1976); Patrick Buckland, *Irish Unionism*, Vol. 2. *Ulster Unionism and the Origins of Northern Ireland, 1886–1922* (Dublin: Gill and Macmillan; New York: Barnes and Noble Books, 1973); Buckland, *A History of Northern Ireland* (New York: Holmes & Meier, 1981); Thomas Hennessey, *A History of Northern Ireland, 1920–1996* (London: Palgrave, 2000).

2 Quoted from the *Westminster Gazette*, 2 September 1920, by D. G. Boyce, 'British Conservative Opinion, the Ulster Question and the Partition of Ireland, 1919–21,' in *Irish Historical Studies*, Vol. 17, No. 65 (1970), pp. 89–112.

3 Buckland, *Irish Unionism, Vol. 2.*, pp. 158–68; Sir Arthur Hezlet, *The B Specials. A History of the Ulster Special Constabulary* (London: Tom Stacey, 1972).

4 See Buckland, *Irish Unionism, Vol. 2*, pp. 113–28.

5 Buckland, *Irish Unionism, Vol. 2*, p. 132. See also Patrick Buckland, *The Factory of Grievances. Devolved Government in Northern Ireland, 1921–39* (Dublin: Gill and Macmillan; New York: Barnes and Noble Books), pp. 2–4; R.J. Lawrence, *The Government of Northern Ireland. Public Finance and Public Services, 1921–1964* (Oxford: Clarendon Press, 1965), pp. 19–29.

6 See Buckland, *Irish Unionism, 1885–1923*, pp. 402–26; Buckland, *Irish Unionism, Vol. 2*, pp. 135–43.

7 Crozier's own memoir of this sorry episode can be found in his *Ireland for Ever* (London: Jonathan Cape, 1932). See also Richard Bennett, *The Black and Tans* (London: Times Mirror, 1970), pp. 63–64, 146–49 and *passim*.

8 See *The Times*, 23 February 1921, p. 10; 24 February 1921, p. 11; Crozier's private correspondence with the War Office, in TNA: PRO WO 374/16997; Crozier, *Ireland for Ever*.

9 Crozier, *Impressions and Recollections*, pp. 293–94.

10 Ibid., pp. 294, 320. Italics in the original.

11 For accounts of the violence and destruction in Ulster during 1921–22, see Buckland, *Irish Unionism, Vol. 2*, pp. 168–174; Farrell, *Northern Ireland*, pp. 39–65; Bryan A. Follis, *A State Under Siege. The Establishment of Northern Ireland, 1920–1925* (Oxford: Clarendon Press, 1995), pp. 83–115.

12 Brief biography in John F. Harbinson, *The Ulster Unionist Party, 1882–1973. Its Development and Organisation* (Belfast: Blackstaff Press, 1973), p. 193.

13 Follis, *A State Under Siege*, p. 99.

14 Bardon, *A History of Ulster*, pp. 516–17.

15 I have thoroughly checked the complete lists of Auxiliary recruits, to be found in TNA:PRO HO 184/50–53. For analysis of these files, and a brief history of the division, see A.D. Harvey, 'Who were the Auxiliaries?' *The Historical Journal*, Vol. 35, No. 3 (1992), pp. 665–69.

16 Reported in the *Belfast News-Letter*, 28 April 1923, p. 5. Woods refers to his application to the Temperance League in a parliamentary debate on licensing, 18 May 1923, in *Parliamentary Debates: Official Report (Northern Ireland, House of Commons)*, Vol. 3 (HMSO: Belfast, 1923), p. 999.

17 For social conditions and policy, see R.J. Lawrence, *The Government of Northern Ireland. Public Finance and Public Services, 1921–1964* (Oxford: Clarendon Press, 1965). Brief discussion of social policies in longer-term perspective may also be found in Derek Birrell and Alan Murie, *Policy and Government in Northern Ireland. Lessons of Devolution* (Dublin: Gill and Macmillan, 1980).

18 Patrick Buckland, 'A Protestant State. Unionists in government, 1921–1939,' in *Defenders of the Union. A survey of British and Irish unionism since 1801*, eds. D. George Boyce and Alan O'Day (London: Routledge, 2001), p. 218.

19 *Belfast News-Letter*, 15 March 1923, p. 8.

20 Op cit..

21 Buckland, *Irish Unionism*, 1885–1923, p. 427

22 *Belfast News-Letter*, 1 March 1923, p. 4.

23 Ibid., 24 April 1923, p. 8.

24 Ibid., 26 April 1923, p. 8.

25 Ibid., 27 April 1923, p. 5. Woods' reference is to the Ulster Tower, opened by Sir James Craig and other Northern Irish dignitaries in November 1921 to commemorate the sacrifice of the 36th (Ulster) Division in the Great War. To the present day, this memorial has played a central role in the politicisation of public memory of the battle.

26 *Belfast News-Letter*, 24 April 1923, p. 8.

27 Ibid., 26 April 1923, p. 8.

28 Ibid., 15 March 1923, p. 8; 7 April, p. 10; 1 May, pp. 7, 8.

29 Ibid., 21 March 1923, p. 6; 19 April, p. 7; 21 April, pp. 6, 8; 26 April, p. 8; 2 May, p. 8.

30 Ibid., 1 May 1923, p. 8.

31 Robert Woods, reported in ibid., 26 April 1923, p. 8.
32 Reported in ibid., 3 May 1923, p. 5.
33 Ibid., 4 May 1923, p. 7.
34 Buckland, *The Factory of Grievances*, p. 26.
35 *Parliamentary Debates, Vol. 3* (1923), p. 999.
36 Ibid., p. 1864.
37 Debate on Prime Minister's Address, 10 March 1925, *Parliamentary Debates, Vol. 5* (1925), pp. 28–29. See also Woods' statements on 21 April 1925, in *Parliamentary Debates, Vol. 5*, pp. 145–46; and to the second parliament on 7 March 1929, in *Parliamentary Debates, Vol. 10*, p. 633.
38 See Buckland, *The Factory of Grievances*, pp. 222–36.
39 Ibid., pp. 999–101, 1131–32.
40 *Belfast News-Letters*, 31 March 1925, p. 6.
41 Ibid., 2 April 1925, p. 8.
42 Ibid., 31 March 1925, p. 8.
43 Ibid., 27 March 1925, p. 6.
44 Ibid., 27 March 1925, p. 8.
45 Woods' statement of 21 April 1925, in *Parliamentary Debates, Vol. 6* (1925), p. 145.
46 For full electoral data and analysis, see James Knight and Nicolas Baxter-Moore, *Northern Ireland. The Elections of the Twenties* (London: Arthur McDougall Foundation, 1972).
47 See *The Times*, 7 April 1925, p. 14.
48 Buckland makes this point in *The Factory of Grievance*, pp. 30–31. See also Follis, *A State Under Siege*, p. 176; Harbinson, *The Ulster Unionist Party*, pp. 211–14.
49 For example, Woods' speech of 16 April 1925, in *Parliamentary Debates, Vol. 6* (1925), pp. 86–87.
50 See *Parliamentary Debates, Vol.* 7 (1926) and *Vol. 8* (1927).
51 *Belfast News-Letter*, 20 May 1929, p. 13.
52 Debate on Prime Minister's Address, 11 March 1926, in *Parliamentary Debates, Vol.*7 (1926), pp. 128–29.
53 Debate on Voting and Redistribution Bill, 7 March 1929, in *Parliamentary Debates, Vol.10* (1929), p. 633.
54 Robert Woods, reported in *Belfast News-Letter*, 14 May 1929, p. 9; 15 May, pp. 14, 15.
55 *Belfast News-Letter*, 29 May 1929, p. 14.
56 David Officer, 'In Search of Order, Permanence and Stability: Building Stormont, 1921–32,' in *Unionism in Modern Ireland. New Perspectives on Politics and Culture*, eds. Richard English and Graham Walker (London: Macmillan, 1996), p. 141.
57 *The Times*, 27 May 1929, p. 8.
58 *Belfast News-Letter*, 25 May 1929, p. 5.
59 *Belfast News-Letter*, 27 May 1929, p. 10; 28 May, p. 11; 29 May, p. 14; 30 May, p. 11.
60 *Belfast News-Letter*, 27 May 1929, p. 10.
61 *The Times House of Commons* (London: Times Publishing Co., 1929), p. 136.
62 *Belfast News-Letter.*, 1 June 1929, p. 7.

Chapter 10 New Beginnings: London and Lord Haw-Haw, 1930–1939

1 The first mention of his membership is in *Who's Who* (1926), p. 3174.
2 *The Times*, 17 February 1928, p. 17.
3 Reported in Woods' divorce, *The Times*, 12 December 1933, p. 4.
4 Op. cit.. Florence Woods' barrister was Mr Clifford Mortimer, father of the writer John Mortimer and subject of the latter's play *A Voyage Around my Father* (1969).
5 Information from the family, and from the Buckingham constituency electoral register (with thanks to Long Crendon historian Eric Sewell for the latter details).
6 For engaging general histories of this period, see A.J.P. Taylor, *English History, 1914–1945* (Oxford:

Oxford University Press, 2001); Piers Brendon, *The Dark Valley: a Panorama of the 1930s* (London: Pimlico, 2001), esp. 175–202.

7 As recorded by British diplomat, politician and author Harold Nicolson, cited in Robert Skidelsky, *Oswald Mosley* (London: Macmillan, 1975), p. 224.

8 Ibid., p. 206.

9 Ibid., pp. 66, 93, 226.

10 See ibid., pp. 244, 301, 330 and 342. Allen later fell out with Mosley, and left politics to pursue business and research into Georgian art and history. Mosley believed that Allen was reporting to MI5, see D.S. Lewis, *Illusions of Grandeur. Mosley, fascism and British society, 1931–81* (Manchester: Manchester University Press, 1987), p. 82.

11 *The Times*, 8 July 1931, p. 1.

12 The first use of the new phrasing in *The Times*, 25 Oct 1932, p. 3.

13 Woods' work on the Karelian memoir can be dated both from his private papers (which include letters received in 1938 from former Karelian comrades, such as Fryer and Bennigsen, evidently written in reply to his own requests for information) and internal textual evidence. For example he writes: 'In 1938 Lt. Col. Sir Thomas Moore MP, at my request, endeavoured to obtain some small grant or pension for [a mutual acquaintance] from the War Office, but unfortunately we were unsuccessful' [pp. 294–95]. Woods' use of the simple past tense indicates that he wrote this final section of the text later than 1938. His reference to 'recent' press reports that the Soviets were constructing fortifications on the Finnish-Karelian border also dates it after late 1938 (see, e.g. *The Times*' reports of a new Soviet 'Maginot Line,' 25 August 1938, p. 9). It is also notable that Woods does not mention the Soviet-Finnish War (the 'Winter War'), which the USSR launched across the Karelian border in December 1939. This suggests that he completed his first draft before this date.

14 For the first IPS letterhead, see the University of Sheffield Library, Special Collections, Joyce Manuscripts, 166/2/x (i) and (ii). The later IPS letterhead in possession of the family.

15 Information on Desbrow's LSE degree from *The Times*, July 31 1936, p. 16.. See also his obituary in *The Times*, 30 November 1973, p. 20.

16 For Alexander E. Gambs, see e.g. *The Times*, 12 October 1923, p. 1; 13 January 1928; p. 10.

17 Typescript of Joyce's statement reproduced in Peter Martland, *Lord Haw Haw. The English Voice of Nazi Germany* (London: The National Archives, 2003), p. 199.

18 See Francis Selwyn, *Hitler's Englishman: the Crime of Lord Haw-Haw* (London: Penguin, 1993).

19 Quotations from Joyce's reference from the principal of Battersea Polytechnic, cited in Mary Kenny, *Germany Calling. A Personal Biography of William Joyce, 'Lord Haw-Haw'* (Dublin: New Island, 2003), p. 85.

20 Kenny, *Germany Calling*, p. 87.

21 See the IPS's letter to C. C. Lewis, 18 February 1932, in Joyce Mss. 166/2/xi (i); Kenny, *Germany Calling*, p. 89.

22 Exercise III, 'Speeches,' Joyce Mss. 166/2/i, pp. 1, 9ob.

23 Exercise V, 'Current Topics,' Joyce Mss. 166/2/i, pp. 9-9ob; undated letter, 166/1/v, pp. 1–3.

24 Letter of 5 April 1932, Joyce Mss. 166/1/i, pp. 1–5.

25 Letter of 11 May 1932, Joyce Mss. 166/1/ii, p. 2.

26 Letter of 11 May 1932, Joyce Mss. 166/1/ii, p. 2; undated letter, 166/1/v, p. 3.

27 Metropolitan Police Special Branch report, 24 March 1937, TNA: PRO HO 144/21063, p. 233.

28 Kenny, *Germany Calling*, pp. 108–27.

29 For Lewis' lecture to Royal Institute of International Affairs, see Joyce Mss. 166/2/xii; lecture to Royal Asiatic Society, in *The Times*, 26 January 1933, p. 15; for editorship of *The Blackshirt*, see *The Times*, 15 November 1934, p. 4.

30 Notes to Joyce Mss. at www.shef.ac.uk/library/special/joyce.html (accessed 15 June 2006).

31 Woods' letter to Lewis, 27 March 1933, Joyce Mss. 166/2/xi (ii).

32 For Lewis' defence of former Labour MP and Joyce devotee John Beckett, see *The Times*, 27 August 1934, p. 7. For his defence of five fascists charged in the aftermath of the 'Battle of Cable Street,' see *The Times*, 6 October 1936; p. 4.

33 For Lewis' bankruptcy, see *The Times*, 28 March 1941, p. 10.

34 *The Times*, 1 February 1938, p. 5.

35 See Stephen Cullen, 'The Development of the Ideas and Policy of the British Union of Fascists, 1932–40,' *Journal of Contemporary History*, Vol. 22, No. 1 (1987), pp. 115–36; Richard Thurlow, *Fascism in Britain. From Oswald Mosley's Blackshirts to the National Front* (London: I.B. Tauris, 1998); Richard Griffiths, *Fellow Travellers of the Right. British Enthusiasts for Nazi Germany, 1933–39* (Oxford: OUP, 1983); Roger Griffin, *Fascism: A Reader* (Oxford: OUP, 1995);

36 Skidelsky, *Oswald Mosley*, pp. 319.

37 University of Sheffield Library, Special Collections, British Union Collection, 7/Wise (i) and (ii).

38 Joyce to Lewis, marginal annotations to typescript, in Joyce Mss. 166/2/iii. Woods private papers include a set of cards listing 'keywords' relating to his Karelian adventure, which he presumably used for giving lectures on the subject.

39 Skidelsky, *Oswald Mosley*, pp. 318–320.

40 W.E.D. Allen (under the pseudonym James Drennan), *BUF: Oswald Mosley and British Fascism* (London: John Murray, 1934). On Bryant, see Andrew Roberts, *Eminent Churchillians* (London: Phoenix, 1995), pp. 287–322.

41 Roberts, *Eminent Churchillians*, p. 293; Griffiths, *Fellow Travellers*, pp. 17–18 and *passim*.

42 Lewis, *Illusions of Grandeur*, p. 146; Griffiths, *Fellow Travellers*, p. 54.

43 See *The Times*, 3 December 1937, p. 18. Griffiths, *Fellow Travellers*, pp. 182–86; Simon Haxey, *Tory MP* (London: Victor Gollancz, 1939), pp. 194–237.

44 Richard Griffiths, *Patriotism Perverted. Captain Ramsay, the Right Club and British Anti-Semitism, 1939–40* (London: Constable, 1998), p. 69.

45 *The Times House of Commons* (1931), pp. 110–11; *Who's Who* (1931).

46 Cited in Griffiths, *Fellow Travellers*, p. 157.

47 Cited in Haxey, *Tory MP* p. 235.

48 Cited in Griffiths, *Fellow Travellers*, p. 158.

49 I am grateful to Eric Sewell for conducting interviews in Long Crendon on my behalf.

50 On Domvile and 'The Link,' see Griffiths, *Fellow Travellers*, pp. 179–82, 307–17; Griffiths, *Patriotism Perverted*, pp. 39–42; Simon Haxey, *Tory MP*, 203–7; and Domvile's autobiography, *From Admiral to Cabin Boy* (London: Boswell, 1947), pp. 64–78

51 See Domvile's letter to *The Times*, 8 August 1939, p. 7.

52 On the Nordic League, see Griffiths, *Patriotism Perverted*, pp. 45–47. On Ramsay, see ibid., p. 77–127 and *passim*.

53 Ibid., pp. 248–49.

54 *The Times* lists numerous Russian émigré social functions in the late 1920s and 1930s, especially funerals, attended by both the Gambs and Wolkoffs.

55 Ibid., pp. 258–72; Bryan Clough, *State Secrets: The Kent-Wolkoff Affair* (Hove, East Sussex: Hideaway Publications, 2005).

56 See the MI5 report on Joyce, written by Agent 'M' (Charles Henry Maxwell Knight), dated 21 September 1934, judging that his 'mental balance was not equal to his intellectual capacity,' in Martland, *Lord Haw Haw*, pp. 120–23.

57 I am grateful to Chris Wrigley for pointing me to late 19th and early 20th century uses of the term.

58 Peter Martland, personal correspondence with the author, 24 July 2006.

59 Information from the family.

60 Spode first appears in *The Code of the Woosters* (1937).

61 Cited from 'M''s MI5 report, in Martland, *Lord Haw Haw*, pp. 120–23

62 Crozier, *Ireland for Ever*, p. 205.

63 Crozier, *Impressions and Recollections*, pp. 320–21.

64 *The Times*, 4 September 1937, p. 12. For his indefatigable struggle against the War Office, which his widow continued after his death, see TNA: PRO WO 374/16997.

65 Michael Pugh, 'Pacifism and Politics in Britain, 1931–1935,' *The Historical Journal*, Vol. 23, No. 3 (1980), pp. 643–44.

66 *The Times*, 1 September 1937, p. 14.

67 Griffiths, *Patriotism Perverted*, pp. 57–58, 180–81 and *passim*.

68 Materials searched include BUF publications *The Blackshirt*, *Action*, *Fascist Quarterly*, and *British*

Union Quarterly; The Link's journal *The Anglo-German Review*; other far-right rags such as *The New Pioneer*, *The Patriot*, and *The Britisher*; plus Home Office, Metropolitan Police and Intelligence files preserved in the National Archives which include extensive lists of people attending meetings or otherwise associated with the BUF, NSL, Nordic League, etc., esp. TNA: PRO HO series 45, 144.

69 I am grateful to Julie Gottlieb, Richard Thurlow and Peter Martland for responding to my enquiries.

70 There is always further research which could be undertaken, e.g. Woods military records (still held by the Ministry of Defence); further oral and manuscript testimonies of the 9th Battalion's action on Somme (see, e.g., Dungan, *Irish Voices*, p. 213); Domvile's diaries for The Link's local associations and activists (National Maritime Museum, Greenwich); or one of the Long Crendon district newspapers (e.g. *The Thame Gazette*).

Epilogue

1 Information from family.

2 For Woods' retirement from the officers' reserve, see *The Times*, 25 September 1935, p. 6.

3 For the 'guessing-game' regarding Lord Haw-Haw's identification, see Kenny, *Germany Calling*, pp. 144–47. The British authorities only officially identified Joyce as the broadcaster in April 1941. For the naming, see Jonah Barrington (pseudo. of Cyril Carr Dalmaine), *Lord Haw-Haw of Zeesen: being a complete and revealing biography of Germany's No. I English radio announcer, together with some hitherto unpublished details of his love life with Winnie the Whopper, his marriage to Lady Haw-Haw, and his associations with Mopey the Baby, Auntie Gush, and Mr Smarmy* (London: Hutchinson, 1939).

4 The scheme had been devised and sent to Woods by Captain W.E. Butler who had been Woods' regimental adjutant in Karelia, see Woods Papers, IWM 78/24/1. For Ironside's brief tenure of the Home Forces command (27 May to 19 July 1940), see *The Ironside Diaries, 1937–1940* (London: Constable, 1962), pp. 339–87.

5 Death certificate, as well as fabric samples, in the possession of his family.

Index

Page numbers from Part One are in roman, Part Two in italics.